"In *Beyond Eureka!* Marylene reminds us that innovation (and innovators) never operate in a vacuum. By better understanding her concept of 'innovation kairos,' anyone, from venture capitalist to inventor, can improve their chances of bringing change successfully to the world."

—Chris Yeh, general partner, Blitzscaling Ventures,
and co-author of *Blitzscaling*

"A profoundly original thinker, Marylene offers unique and deep insights on the why, how, who, and where of innovation in *Beyond Eureka!* Not just in start-ups, but in labs and companies. Not just in tech, but in every facet of industries. It blows up myths and provides guideposts for the effective enablement of future innovation."

—Sramana Mitra, founder and CEO,
One Million by One Million (1Mby1M)

BEYOND EUREKA!

BEYOND
EUREKA!

THE
ROCKY
ROADS TO
INNOVATING

MARYLENE DELBOURG-DELPHIS

FOREWORD BY GUY KAWASAKI

Georgetown University Press / Washington, DC

Library of Congress Cataloging-in-Publication Data

Names: Delbourg-Delphis, Marylène, author. | Kawasaki, Guy, 1954– writer of foreword.
Title: Beyond eureka! : the rocky roads to innovating / Marylene Delbourg-Delphis ;
foreword by Guy Kawasaki.
Identifiers: LCCN 2023018228 (print) | LCCN 2023018229 (ebook) |
ISBN 9781647124229 (hardcover) | ISBN 9781647124236 (ebook)
Subjects: LCSH: Creative ability in business. | Technological innovations.
Classification: LCC HD53 .D446 2024 (print) | LCC HD53 (ebook) |
DDC 650.1—dc23/eng/20230424
LC record available at https://lccn.loc.gov/2023018228
LC ebook record available at https://lccn.loc.gov/2023018229

© This paper meets the requirements of ANSI/NISO Z39.48-1992 (Permanence of Paper).
25 24   9 8 7 6 5 4 3 2 First printing
Printed in the United States of America
Cover design by Amanda Hudson, Faceout Studio
Interior design by Paul Hotvedt

Contents

Expanded Contents

Acknowledgments

One rarely writes a book completely alone. . . .

To start, I'd like to thank my daughter, Sophie Delphis, for reading over my manuscript and for her suggestions. I am truly blessed that she never stopped being interested in the world of business and more specifically of innovation even as she became an opera singer. Many thanks to Dan Farber for his extraordinary guidance, his sharp questions, and invaluable recommendations. Thank you to Joanna Hoffman and Alain Rossmann, stars of innovation in Silicon Valley, for whom technological evolution is part of a whole, the social and cultural world in which we live. Alain also introduced me to the champion of "remarkable people": Guy Kawasaki, then Chief Evangelist of the Macintosh, who became the co-founder of my first American company. Since then, Guy has always been a dedicated friend.

Many thanks to the countless colleagues, employees, students, and clients who have inspired me. They embody the fact that creative energy is rank-, race-, and gender-agnostic, and that great organizations are breeding grounds where ideas can germinate, then be tested and acted out. They evidence the power of teamwork to fortify each and everybody's grit and perseverance in innovative journeys, during the course of which we regularly discover that what we don't know challenges what we believe we can control. How often we feel jolted in a cacophonic present that doesn't necessarily expect us, and where nothing is won forever!

I am also immensely indebted to the reviewers and Faculty Board of Georgetown University Press. They read the text from different, yet complementary, perspectives, and their feedback has allowed me to further elaborate on my own thought process and sharpen my focus. I am grateful to all of them, as well as to Hilary Claggett, for believing in the perspective of this book, for their help and their trust.

Foreword

Did you know that most venture capitalists assume that entrepreneurs can build the product that they are pitching? This is true whether the product is a software application, social media platform, cure for cancer, or single-drop-of-blood diagnostics.

The primary question in their mind is, "How big is the market for this product?" and not, "Can they really make it?" Ridiculous, I know, but I was once a venture capitalist, so I was as guilty of this as anyone.

The underlying tension is the conflict between two philosophies: "ideas are hard, implementation is easy" versus "ideas are easy, implementation is hard." The older, and hopefully the wiser, I get, the more I am in the "ideas easy, implementation hard" camp.

This issue is the crux of *Beyond Eureka!* One must stop conflating innovation and entrepreneurship. They are not the same thing, and they represent completely different challenges and opportunities.

There are dozens of books about how to start a company—I've written one too. But there are few about the nitty-gritty of taking an idea and making it a reality. The path is rocky, difficult, and treacherous, and it can use up your funding and even get you imprisoned.

There is no better book to get you beyond your Eureka! moment than Marylene's. It is a deeply analytical and all-encompassing summary of the history of implementing innovation. It is loaded with stories and lessons that you will not read about in other books.

And honestly, I would be surprised if you don't conclude that ideas are hard and implementation is hard too. If both were easy, more people would be successful. Now go forth and be remarkable.

Guy Kawasaki, Chief Evangelist of Canva,
Host of *Remarkable People* podcast

Introduction

I have not failed. I've just found 10,000 ways that won't work.
—Thomas Edison

"There must be a better way." It's the impulse of inventors and innovators throughout history who have wanted to improve on what they see or use. The same Albert Einstein who established the theory of relativity filed for a slew of patents for a home refrigerator in 1926 with his friend Leó Szilárd, who later developed the concept of nuclear chain reaction.

Einstein had just read a terrible news story: an entire family in Berlin had died because of the toxic gasses that had leaked from the pump of their refrigerator. Both appalled and interested, Einstein and Szilárd came up with new methods to design and manage cooling mechanisms. Yet their initiative collapsed. Einstein was already an internationally recognized genius. Szilárd, albeit younger, was known as an outstanding physicist. The two associates were not dreamy scientists. They knew what they were doing. So why did they fail?

They worked hard to carry out their project, just as all innovators with ambitious goals do. After several iterations, an alliance with a manufacturer that experienced financial difficulties, the sale of one of their patent applications to Electrolux in Stockholm, and a partnership with the Citogel company in Hamburg to produce an immersion cooler that worked well but was dependent on a then-unreliable German water system, Einstein and Szilárd designed an electromagnetic pump that Allgemeine Elektricitäts-Gesellschaft (A.E.G.) agreed to develop in 1928. In 1931 the pump was mounted in the cabinet of a General Electric refrigerator with a potassium-sodium alloy as its liquid metal and pentane as a refrigerant, and it went into continuous operation at the A.E.G. Research Institute.

1

Some issues (like noise) still plagued the device, but Einstein and Szilárd had solved so many hair-raising problems already that there was no reason to think they wouldn't be able to succeed, all the more so as they were surrounded by a competent team.[1]

So, what happened? It's hard to pinpoint the exact reasons for their failure. As is common when a need is identified, Einstein and Szilárd were not the only ones working on addressing it. Had competitors taken hold of the space? No. Was Einstein and Szilárd's solution too difficult to implement? The latter is a possibility, as, in the meantime, Charles Kettering's team at General Motors had adopted a different approach with a gas trademarked as "Freon" whose patent they issued to Frigidaire, a company owned by General Motors. In 1930 General Motors and DuPont had formed Kinetic Chemicals to produce the gas—deemed to be safe at the time.[2]

Could Einstein and Szilárd, supported by A.E.G., still have competed? In theory, yes, because A.E.G. was the largest electrical manufacturing company in Germany and one of the heavyweights in the world. In practice, however, no. Szilárd had tried to interest a few US and British organizations. But who wants to partner with companies of an economically and politically shattered country?

The Einstein-Szilárd initiative fizzled out when A.E.G. eliminated projects deemed nonessential in a depressed environment where people were not clamoring for fridges in droves. Then, in 1933, Einstein and Szilárd, both Jewish, had to flee Germany. The story doesn't quite end there, though. This early mechanism turned out to be a first step in Szilárd's approach to cooling nuclear reactors. The duo was also effective at convincing President Roosevelt to start the Manhattan Project to produce nuclear weapons destined to outpace Nazi efforts already under way.

The innovation graveyard is filled with flops. One of Bill Gates's favorite books is a classic on this theme: *Business Adventures: Twelve Classic Tales from the World of Wall Street* by John Brooks; originally published in 1969, it tells the story of multiple failures.[3] Depending on the source, between 70 percent and 95 percent of all new products don't pan out, and these statistics don't even include millions of nonstarters like a 1928

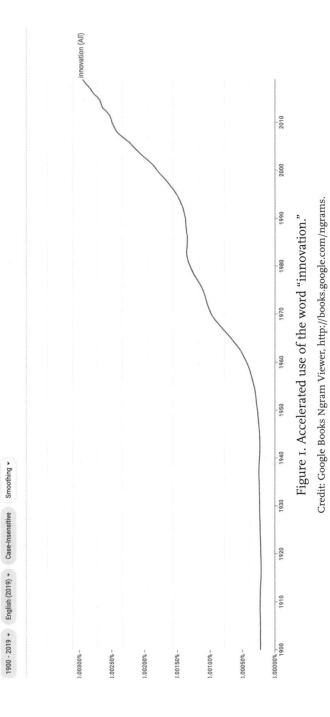

Figure 1. Accelerated use of the word "innovation."

Credit: Google Books Ngram Viewer, http://books.google.com/ngrams.

watch-case phonograph or Hugo Gernsback's 1963 television goggles.[4] "What were they thinking?" we might sometimes wonder.

For fame or for shame, the innovation game is hard. But we go for it. It's a must for existing companies to survive, and for new entrepreneurs it's an irresistible call. In our homes, we are inspired by dozens of innovations whispering in our ears, "Why not me?" Your KitchenAid dishwasher is the umpteenth version of an appliance Josephine Cochrane introduced at the 1893 Chicago World's Fair. Your Melitta coffee filter makes you think of Melitta Bentz, who founded her company in 1908 in Germany. Your Dyson bagless cyclonic vacuum cleaner is evidence of the rewards afforded to those who never stop trying. When I take a picture of a child, I often think of Philippe Kahn, who created the first camera phone in 1997 so he could immediately send a picture of his newborn daughter. Our environment is populated by human beings who made it what it is.

We live around things that were once budding innovations, and we have come to expect a steady stream of them to satisfy our appetite for new things. The popularity over the past decades of the word "innovation" has grown massively, as is clear from Google NGram, which charts the yearly count of words or phrases based on its word-search database containing several billion words (see figure 1).[5]

WHAT CAN BE SEEN AS AN "INNOVATION"?

In this book, I will apply the word "innovation" to the implementation of something new, as implied by the Latin etymology of the word (*novus*). An important factor here is *implementation*, meaning that an innovation is developed for *and* commercialized in a marketplace and is perceived as such by that marketplace. This innovation can be a product, a service, a process, or a business model, or a combination thereof.

This base definition of innovation doesn't say anything about its size. It can be small, large, or anything in between. It can require gigantic investments as well as minimal ones, as outlined in *Jugaad Innovation*.[6] It can even be relative. For example, drilling water wells would not be an innovation in Minnesota but might be in parts of Africa. Also, for something to be considered an innovation, not everything has to be new. Between the first mass-produced velocipede in the early 1860s and the chain- and derailleur-free bicycle Driven produced by CeramicSpeed at the end of the 2010s, you'll find countless intermediate innovations.

Business models and processes can be innovations unto themselves and unrelated to product innovation. For example, John Rockefeller didn't invent oil refining, but he ended up owning 90 percent of the US market thanks to a series of novel (and often wild) monopoly-building methods centralizing Standard Oil holdings. Lawsuits forced the breakup of the company and did so through yet another type of innovation, a legislative one embodied in the extension of the Sherman Antitrust Act of 1890, which was originally used to control unions. Of course, you can have product innovations associated with business models. The iPhone is a product innovation coupled with a new business model, notably the App Store. Or, a business strategy can cast an old business model in a new light. The idea of building Apple Stores was counterintuitive in 2001, a time when everybody predicted that e-commerce would decimate everything brick and mortar, but it was a creative way for a technology brand to build customer loyalty.

Business model and business process innovations can be attached to new products and services as well as older ones. Sometimes, process innovation can require product innovation. This was the case for products with interchangeable parts. A novel production process was promoted in the eighteenth century by a French artillery officer, Jean-Baptiste Vaquette de Gribeauval, to standardize the manufacturing of muskets. It was successfully carried out by Honoré Blanc, who demonstrated the principle on muskets with interchangeable locks to Thomas Jefferson, then the American ambassador to France. Jefferson understood that this process would not only free the United States from European vendors but also accelerate production of military equipment and other goods. He was unable to persuade Blanc to emigrate, but after returning to the United States Jefferson worked to fund the development of a similar system with George Washington's blessing. In 1798 the US government contracted Eli Whitney, often considered as the inventor of a machine that separated cotton fibers from their seeds (the "cotton gin"), for the production of twelve thousand muskets. At about the same time, Eli Terry developed, with no government funding, a milling machine to produce interchangeable parts and was close to introducing his mass-produced clocks.

The need for part interchangeability spurred several innovations in the nineteenth century. First, the process itself precipitated the invention of thousands of new machines and tools to make interchangeability applicable at scale. Second, combined with mechanization, it changed labor. Because it powered a division of labor between manufacturing, assembly, and repair tasks, the need for skilled workers was reduced. This development had the double effect of eliminating many artisanal skills and allowing for faster training of workers in a predominantly rural economy. Finally, interchangeability and mechanization led to the design of assembly lines that spread everywhere, from meatpacking to mining to car production.

Interchangeable parts advanced hardware and social innovations (for better and for worse) and became a foundational component of additional business innovations, such as "planned obsolescence." This idea is attached to Alfred Sloan, who had become the president of General Motors (GM) in 1923 (although he spoke of "dynamic obsolescence").

In the mid-1920s, car manufacturers were starting to fear market saturation. In order to sustain sales, Sloan established the idea of regular annual changes in the car industry, a concept applied by the bicycle industry when sales had stalled earlier in the century. This beginning of the "model year" practice, whose goal was to emphasize car ownership as a status symbol, ultimately led to "dynamic obsolescence." Ford wasn't too keen on this game plan until he saw GM surpassing his sales in 1931—also the year the first university-based executive education program started at MIT under Sloan's sponsorship. The principle of dynamic or planned obsolescence was diversely appreciated, lauded by some and vilified by others as systemic waste-making. The fact is, though, that planned obsolescence requires coming up with something new, big or small, all the time.

Business process innovation can have long-lasting consequences. In the early 1980s, the term "outsourcing" started to be used when a company was contracting work outside the organization, and by extension to a foreign supplier—which made the word overlap with an older term, "offshoring." This approach is often associated with the 1990s' enormous increase of outsourcing activities in manufacturing. I learned about the principles in the fashion industry. As a young journalist, I wondered why Pierre Cardin was both admired and getting the cold shoulder. So, I asked the president of the French Couture association about his ambivalent perception of Cardin. I expected to hear some spicy gossip, but instead he whispered in my ear: "He produces his shirts in China." A few years before, in 1979, Cardin had made headlines for presenting his couture collection in the Communist country, but France was now disapproving of the fact that Cardin was extending his reach beyond wealthy patrons to new customers via lower prices thanks to a new production process.

Cardin wasn't only opening a new market in a country where Westerners thought there was none; he was training and building that market as well as leveraging its resources and talent.[7] He ended up being the most influential designer in China. A lot has changed since his ingress there, notably the Chinese entry into European fashion. Quite a few items that you see as "Made in Italy" today are produced in Italy by immigrant Chinese workers controlled by Chinese industrialists.[8] We can think of this as a reverse outsourcing of sorts. Business process innovation can have far more wide-ranging effects than many product innovations and create an impact that goes far beyond what their initiators intended.

It's possible to innovate in countless ways. So . . . how are you going to turn your own Eureka! moment into reality?[9]

STARTING ON THE ROCKY PATHS OF YOUR INNOVATION JOURNEY

First, I assume that you are familiar with a number of excellent books that explain how to pitch, start, manage, and scale a company. They are must-reads whether you are a founder or employed in an established company. That said, the knowledge you get from those books is no guarantee of success. Despite the abundance of books over the last forty years, few new ventures survive. We may surmise that the ones that did were aided by this literature, but this assumption may not even be fully verified. While the number of firms created today is much higher than in 1900 for multiple reasons (including population increase; socioeconomic, societal, and geopolitical changes; access to capital; and knowledge distribution channels), it's not clear, all things otherwise equal, that survival ratios are higher today than in 1900. This point about the survival ratio of the new firms, though, is not an indictment of the way how-to knowledge was communicated in 1900, nor of modern books on entrepreneurship. These books provide the basics and can help reduce risks of failure caused by sheer ignorance, even though you must also remain aware that it's always difficult to build a business, as emphasized by great books such as Noam Wasserman's *The Founder's Dilemmas* or Ben Horowitz's *The Hard Thing about Hard Things*.[10]

And if you want to really innovate, it's even trickier. Like others advising entrepreneurs, I tell them to solve a problem customers are willing to pay for. But what if people aren't really aware of the problem you believe you have identified? When we innovate, we have to contemplate and speculate on a potential market more than on a preexisting one, a need more than a demand, or a possible interest more than actual expectations. As we move beyond the joy of having a great idea, our Eureka! moment, we soon realize that we have entered a realm of uncertainty. Not only do guidebooks about entrepreneurship fail to meaningfully increase success ratios, but also by often implicitly assuming that entrepreneurship and innovation are interchangeable notions, they rarely elaborate on why trying to innovate can be so challenging. There is a difference between starting yet another neighborhood pizzeria and becoming a pizzaiolo who develops a cult following.

ADDRESSING INNOVATIVE ENTREPRENEURSHIP CALLS FOR A DIFFERENT PERSPECTIVE

Executives and company founders must broaden their knowledge of how innovations have happened over the decades as well as develop critical thinking capabilities to accurately evaluate the intricacies of the environment they want to have an impact on or correctly read the meaning of any snag they might encounter. They must be ready to not only "think again"—to rethink their opinions and generally accepted ideas—but, even more important, to think "thick," to realize that complexity can't always be distilled into simple takeaways and that important questions rarely get definitive answers.[11] For that, they need to have a grasp on the various layers that make up the environment they are entering and master the linguistic and ideological framework for articulating their journey.

A few professors of entrepreneurship describe applying a pragmatic, creative approach in the face of uncertainty as the "effectuation" dimension of entrepreneurship. One of them is Saras Sarasvathy, the author of *Effectuation: Elements of Entrepreneurial Expertise.*[12] Based on her interviews with entrepreneurs, she discusses the dynamics of the effectual process, that is, how they develop an adaptability that enables them to leverage circumstances as they occur. Effectual entrepreneurs focus on what they can do, without worrying too much about what they ought to do. Effectuation is about exploiting contingencies, something that is especially critical when you innovate. Chapter 2, which I dedicate to the early history of Kodak, illustrates this approach and shows how versatility and agility help to deal with the unforeseen.

As they become "effectual," entrepreneurs are led to dampen the power of common mottoes such as "be a visionary," "disrupt if you don't want to be disrupted," "shift paradigms," "fail fast," or "think big." They'll have multiple reasons to wonder to what extent innovation is about breaking things, realize that shifting paradigms might lead nowhere and that the "next big thing" might just be a shiny object, or that deterring competitors is unlikely if they are the first on the market. In short, they'll revisit prêt-à-porter mantras, and understand why many of them are not absolute but rather historically defined notions such as the idea of "disruption," which I will extensively discuss in chapter 3. Even more important, they'll need to dissect the meaning of seemingly simple words like "time," "opportunity," and "customer."

The founders of Webvan, a famous flop during the dot.com era, were not unintelligent. They simply forgot that "timing" is a multispeed construct and raced ahead of where the market was. Entrepreneurs often court "early adopters" only to find out that this first wave of customers isn't as relevant as originally believed.

As familiar as "adoption curves" are, these may not be relative to only one product created by one company but to multiple products created by multiple organizations. For example, when the iPhone came out, it could directly address the "early majority" built by the antecedent parade of personal digital assistant devices (PDAs).

More often than not, the idea of "competitive analysis" addresses the tip of an iceberg and overlooks the much larger landscape of an assortment of products, services, processes, and frameworks that pile up over time and constitute what I call an "innovation stack," which can mix components from categories that we initially see are separate. For example, a marketer who wants to venture into virtual reality had better be familiar with habits forged by the gaming industry over the past twenty years as well as the legacy financial constraints attached to distributing interactive apps through the Apple App or Google Play store.

Guidebooks provide the knowledge we need to begin. This book aims to address the continuous restarting and recontextualizing that innovation requires beyond an initial "spark," how to persist amid the uncertainties, mysteries, and doubt in an innovation bubble. It explains why we frequently experience the limits to our own agency.

WE ARE ALSO PAWNS ON A WIDER CHESSBOARD THAT CAN ESCAPE OUR IMMEDIATE GRASP

Guidebooks bolster our individual sense of power, but innovators are part of a collective dynamic that only a few books describe. Among those that do, I'd mention Tony Fadell's *Build: An Unorthodox Guide to Making Things Worth Making*, in which he recounts his path from General Magic to Nest via Apple.[13] It shows that innovations that we see as seminal events on a timeline result from much longer gestation happening within genealogies of knowledge into which entrepreneurs must find their way.

Innovating requires a deep understanding of where we might sit in the innovation stack before we start.

As we move on, we also see that the stack is dynamically altered by other entrepreneurs exploring the same territory as well as social or economic circumstances. But the makeup and making of the innovation stack (even the concept itself) are regularly understated or even overlooked, and yet any innovation is relative to previous innovations and part of a history of artifacts, itself part of a history of people. This realization may curb the scope of an individual innovator's grand dream of "changing the world" to a more incremental accomplishment, but the latter can still be extremely meaningful. As a result, when we discuss entrepreneurship through the innovation lens, the dichotomy between success and failure may be somewhat blurred. As you'll see, the vast majority of PDA companies failed—and yet they produced innovations that were critical building blocks of the smartphone industry. So, while standard guides focus on the individualist aspect of entrepreneurship, this book also emphasizes the collective dynamics into which we are thrown when we innovate, including the (often) mind-boggling complexity of the world in which we're trying to innovate.

So what should you expect? This book doesn't offer a set of recipes, even though I offer a few recommendations here and there. You don't need yet another inventory of silver bullets or step-by-step techniques to become a master of the metaverse, find the panacea for glioblastoma, reimagine your existing business, or revise your entire positioning using artificial intelligence. If there were unequivocal methods for creating triumphant realizations, everybody would know them by now. As innovators, you can't hope that any given innovation model will provide you with a code to access the holy grail. You can't hope that analyzing the success of any given innovation will give you more than parsimonious clues about its replicability. You have to accept that more often than not, predictability is nothing more than a simplistic retrospective rationalization. So, the best course of action for you is to embrace the arduousness of the innovation journey you're embarking on or have already started. You have to think "thick" if you don't want to feel helpless when you encounter a situation that disturbs your thought patterns.

My purpose is to help you build additional intellectual muscles and develop the pragmatic creativity that will enable you to revisit beliefs and postulates that unbeknownst to you may constrain your thought processes, and place under a different light examples of entrepreneurial innovation that have petrified into decontextualized role models.

It's useful to critically analyze the knowledge we believe we have, for despite the flash of genius that we associate with our Eureka! moment, an idea is not an instance of spontaneous combustion. Much like a lightning strike, innovation is the result of a complex system that seems to come from nothing or dissipate for no apparent reason when we don't have the tools to interpret the larger picture. As innovators, we are part of a historical process that doesn't unfold linearly but provides us with a large repository of stories that highlight how both innovators and their intended customers are products of their time. That's why New York citizens in the early twentieth century didn't see bikes, let alone electric bikes, as a possible way to address the pollution caused by horse manure. That's why creating and producing a new detergent doesn't happen with a snap of the fingers (and why so many costly marketing campaigns also fail). Awareness of older or recent history is also what enables us to interpret data and statistics more accurately.

We all know the consequences of ignoring factual contextualization and history in the political world. Why should things be different in the innovation-driven entrepreneurship sphere? Innovation is a branch of what Herbert Simon called "the sciences of the artificial."[14] So, similarly to how a physics student must be familiar with how Newton's three laws of motion came about in order to get a physics degree, innovators must understand that Edison was not simply being oratorical when he said, "I have not failed. I've just found 10,000 ways that won't work." What Edison did was to explore and test dozens of potential ideas through an intense immersion within the cultural, socioeconomic, and temporal environment that was his. Great innovators enshrine a profound cultural richness within their innovations (knowingly or unknowingly) and remind us how much of an interdisciplinary field innovation is.

HOW TO USE THIS BOOK

I've chosen to structure this book around the analysis of twelve common questions. This selection results from conversations with the dozens of aspiring innovators in organizations of all sizes that I have advised in the course of my career and my own experience as a serial CEO in the technology industry. The questions are simple, but you'll find that they often congeal around a collection of questionable assumptions and inferences drawn from inaccurately reported or oversimplified examples. Addressing them rarely leads to perfect answers but will also make you realize why the world is hackable in multiple ways. There are multiple roads to innovating, multiple facets to innovation, and maybe not as many fixed sets of dos and don'ts as you might think.

1. Are you an inventor or an innovator?
The word "inventor" is used far more than the word "innovator" and is often the term chosen to describe heroes such as Edison or Steve Jobs. However, as we reflect on the innovation process and its outcome, it's useful to keep in mind an operational distinction between "invention" and "innovation" even though they can be intertwined, especially in technology-based domains. Inventors and innovators have two different roles and perspectives. Inventors focus on their area of expertise and advance that domain without necessarily thinking of commercial applications. Innovators start from a market that reflects the spirit of the time, and their mission is to create a business by offering products capable of attracting customers. Think of them as great stage directors. Can inventors also become businesspeople? Sure. But don't try to evade the inventor-innovator difference by saying that you are an entrepreneur. In fact, the word "entrepreneur" was created to establish a distinction between what an inventor does and what the person who markets a product

does, regardless of whether or not it contains an invention. For clarity purposes, let me indicate that I may use "innovator" and "entrepreneur" interchangeably (although not all entrepreneurs are innovators) and that under the term "inventor" I will also include scientists and researchers.

2. What is a typical innovation journey?

More often than not, it's like a roller coaster with more angst than amusement. I chose to discuss the story of the first two decades of Kodak, which illustrates how its founder, George Eastman, moved through difficult paths fraught with obstacles. This has been the fate of most innovators throughout history, and it's no different today. They don't jump curves. They move through treacherous terrains in a nonlinear fashion. Eastman's journey shows that supporting one's "big picture" idea requires factoring in an entanglement of human and technical hazards demanding sustained attention and that executing on strong strategies can depend on many tactical moves. What makes innovators survive is a pragmatic creativity that enables them to change course when necessary and an uncanny ability to navigate foggy environments. While it's true that they have to envision the future, they have to be more than the "visionaries" portrayed in often-hagiographic success stories: They must "see," that is, widen their aperture and sharpen their vision. The well-known demise of Kodak will not be addressed in this chapter: it happened some fifty years after George Eastman's death.

3. Do you need to be disruptive?

Clayton Christensen's books shaped the disruptive innovation lexicon, opposing it to sustaining innovation. His approach came in the wake of the golden age of studies started in the 1960s aimed at conceptualizing and classifying innovations based on a variety of macroeconomic or company-level criteria. Christensen was not the first to discuss the idea that some innovations can disrupt existing domains and types of competencies by making them obsolete, but he created a huge footprint that positioned the disruptive lexicon into marketing mottoes. Yet how do you know when your innovation is disruptive? Can a quest for disruption valuably influence your journey? This is unclear. Do you develop an Apple watch because you want to disrupt the Swiss watch industry or because you want to create something special for your audience? My point is that the disruption framework sometimes relies on debatable assumptions and might mislead innovators in both startups and large companies more than guide them.

4. When is the right time?
This question is part of the well-known adage that you have to be at the right place at the right time. Sure, but what does "time" encompass here? When we want to innovate, we step into the timeline of the space we want to impact. As entrepreneurs, we hope to become part of its acceleration. We operate at a high velocity often directed by our desire to outpace competitors. However, the pace at which our ideas evolve may not be synched with our potential customers' consumption pace. So what do we do? Innovators are tasked with the difficult problem of coming back down to earth, meeting their customers' tempo, and trying to accelerate it. Successful innovators that we see as being "forward thinking" may not be so because they achieve the impossible task of seeing ahead into the future. Forward thinking is, in actuality, deeply understanding the present and from that viewpoint having a better view into the future. That concept is something I will illustrate using the history of search engines as a case study and further develop in chapter 5 with the notion of innovation kairos.

5. What is a window of opportunity?
Electric bicycles appeared at the same time as regular ones. Why did it take one hundred years for them to become popular? How is it that, although contemporaneous and also "bicycles" themselves, e-bikes didn't benefit from the same "window of opportunity"? It's important to realize that for innovations to take hold, you have to assess if and how the overall environment you operate in is ready to take them in. If that environment is ready, you're exploiting existing expectations by delivering what some researchers called a "market pull innovation," and you may not really innovate. If you believe that you're more of an agent of change,

you're dealing with a "push innovation." But, then, what makes you think that people will adopt your ideas? What you see here is that both the notions of "window" and "opportunity" can be perplexing. If the window is a wide aperture through which anybody can enter, how will you break away from the pack? If it's only a lucarne, how will you know that there is a wide potential out there? And what is "opportunity"? By definition, it's an occasion or situation that makes it possible to do something. Sure, but what are the components of that "situation" at any given time? That's what I will call "innovation kairos." I define it as an entangled environment of ideological, societal, cultural, political, economic, and human layers constantly mutating in parallel at their own speeds, and in which an innovation will either remain unheeded or, oppositely, break through those layers to then drift into the mores and potentially shift existing paradigms.

6. Can competing innovations coexist?
The energy harbored within the innovation kairos at the end of the 1970s and early 1980s allowed for the emergence of a large number of personal computer companies. Many died for various reasons that didn't always have much to do with the nature of the innovation they were offering. What I focus on here is how between the end of the 1970s and the end of the 1990s, Apple (before the iPod era) thrived, nearly died, and ultimately survived for the same reasons it almost disappeared. So what were the innovation kairos components embraced by Apple that made the company go through this roller coaster? And how is it that another company, Microsoft, which would also become a heavyweight, succeeded within the same innovation kairos with a completely different approach? That's when we discover that revolutionary or evolutionary perspectives are not necessarily incompatible and may not be necessarily reflective of a higher or lower innovative intensity per se. The innovation kairos allows for the coexistence of competing innovations and reminds us that innovation is not a zero-sum game.

7. Why is standing out challenging?
Why can it be so hard for innovators to stand out long enough to earn a more visible place in the memories of most historians? Innovations

can happen in dormant spaces, but they more commonly evolve in bus-tling spaces with so much activity that they have the potential to power the emergence of many new ideas that eventually split into multiple di-rections. Innovators step in with the conviction that they'll be able to leave their mark, but they are often engulfed by the flames they stir up. The case study of the history of PDAs shows how the iPhone recombined multiple innovations that all had their raison d'être under one overarch-ing concept that reset the paces of several layers in the innovation kairos.

8. Can David thrive in Goliath's world?
While innovators in startups are flooded with pep talks that make them feel like special underdogs, they have to know what they are up against, namely, established companies. Before you assume that companies are shorter lived because of the accelerating gale of allegedly disruptive tech-nologies, take a reality test: the average age of the companies listed on the S&P 500 Index and Fortune 500 is close to seventy. These companies make up a significant part of the innovation kairos and hold huge insti-tutional clout. They exist within a complex texture of customers, implicit or explicit balances of power with their competitors and "coopetitors," alliances, professional organizations, and lobbies. In other words, the eco-system to which they belong grants them a tentacular might. If some go through rough times, they can also resurface thanks to various business mechanisms (acquisition, diversification, merger, etc.) or rekindle the innovation spirit that made them exist in the first place. They compete with each other more than with the Davids, against which the odds are stacked anyway. This is a challenging landscape for startups, but what characterizes innovation isn't simply the fact that it's something new. It's something that you have to market in a world that doesn't expect you.

9. Where is the right place?
The innovation kairos is a broad and complex expanse with a lot of win-dows opening on a lot of opportunities. So from where can we discern the best opportunities for innovation? In other words, what's the right place to operate from? In reality, there are many of them. The "geogra-phy of genius" is composed of multiple places, often called "business

clusters," which, for a variable period of time, coalesce dominant trends of the kairos in particular domains. They are both observatories and scale models of the innovation kairos that help entrepreneurs and large companies alike navigate the environment in which they're operating as well as identify areas ripe for change, key drivers, and new industry directions. However, selecting one country or city doesn't preclude you from continuing to check what's going on around the world and the multiplication of geographical hubs in "startup nations." As a result, in a world where innovation is widely distributed, choosing a cluster or even an incubator isn't always easy. Your selection could vary depending on many aspects of the stage and state of your business as well as your goals down the road.

10. Do you need to be connected to succeed?

Thomas Edison and Steve Jobs may belong to different eras, but they share a cultural ethos and connective tissue transmitted through people. One of Edison's early employees, Arthur Kennelly, became a professor of electrical engineering at Harvard and MIT, and Vannevar Bush was his doctoral student. Then Frederick (Fred) Terman was Bush's doctoral student at MIT—the same Terman who started to build what was to become Silicon Valley—and he had David Packard and William Hewlett among his students. When Steve Jobs was twelve, he cold-called Bill Hewlett to request leftover electronic parts to build a frequency counter. Hewlett not only gave him what he wanted but also offered him an internship that summer. Meanwhile, two other Terman students were Russell and Sigurd Varian. Among the early employees of their company, there was a bookkeeper, Clara Jobs, Steve Jobs's mother. Despite the individualistic mythologies that geniuses can just walk in and show their magic, the history of innovations displays a different story. Genealogies of people canvas the innovation kairos and mark the educational and financial routes that drive innovations: circles, organizations, companies, laboratories, and educational institutions transmit knowledge and know-how.

11. Are women and minorities unwelcome?
The very same intertwined networks that structure the innovation kairos explain why women and minorities have been quasi-excluded from the history of innovations. Recoding the traditional genealogies of knowledge won't happen overnight, as is clear from a detailed analysis of the representation of women and minorities at the top echelons of some of the mechanisms that activate the innovation kairos and ensure the perpetuation of its logic, that is, universities, labs, companies, and venture capital. Innovation (and writing about it) may remain a predominantly male thing for a while. There are exceptions to the rule, but exceptions can only change rules at a very slow pace. Yet they do. By increasingly slipping through the cracks of a system that was designed to treat them as consumers, women and minorities as innovation producers may do more than offer product or process innovations and create interstitial transformations forcing societal innovation, at least in some countries.

12. How can organizations remain innovative?
Behind every innovation, successful or not, there are people. There are people with an idea we'll either adore or discard; people who implement this idea brilliantly or awkwardly; people who are able, unable, or unwilling to test the viability of ideas; people who tweak or refractor existing ideas; people who support and finance ideas or, in contrast, people who mismanage, sabotage, or steal others' work. Innovation, regardless of the angle you take, is all about these people, whether they operate in their homes or behind the walls of the organizations that employ them. It's not companies, as entities, that innovate. It's the people they employ who do. So, when you hear about companies having problems innovating because of their corporate structure, translate the problem. Who in companies restricts and obstructs novel ideas, and why, given that most CEOs tell you that innovation is key to the future growth of their organization? Companies don't fail because they're not disruptive enough or because they've been disrupted. They fail because the people who manage them don't want to admit that creativity is rank agnostic or don't realize that

people working deep down in the trenches also participate in the innovation process.

Only a larger conceptual and historical context can give us a sense of the stagecraft that governs the innovation scenography we want to step into. This wider backdrop allows us to better factor in how innovation takes place on a stage that at any given time combines microhistories, viewpoints, idioms, and value systems that can't be synopsized through simple constructs, rules, or archetypes. It enables us to come to grips with the fact that while believing we are designing the future, we are only coming up with a "next" iteration of something in a multivariate and crowded present. It makes us more prone to accept that our nonuniqueness can be a blessing more than a curse and that many people we may not even see as innovators are actually part of the innovation world.

I dedicate this book to entrepreneurs as well as managers and employees in larger companies with a growth mindset. Overly neat, prescriptive instructions beget nice performers with a fixed mindset but not innovators. When, instead, we're challenged to "seize opportunities" with an innovator's ethos, we prospect our surroundings as a treasure trove from which to build. It's continuous and reflective learning that enables us to conceptualize something new and gives us the free-spirited strength to deliver on our belief that "there must be a better way." Sometimes we come up with magic, sometimes we don't . . . but regardless of the size of the dent we're able to put in the universe—to paraphrase Steve Jobs's expression—and even if we fail, we may still meaningfully contribute to the world.

1

Are You an Inventor or an Innovator?

Creativity is intelligence having fun.
—Albert Einstein

Behind innovations, there are people. We should always call them "innovators," but we don't. We often say "inventor" or "entrepreneur" instead. Why? This chapter details important linguistic legacies and explains why a lack of precision in business talk may obscure an important fact—that inventors and innovators look at the world from different perspectives and have different goals—and why these distinctions shouldn't be blurred away by the pervasive use of the word "entrepreneur."

A SHORT HISTORY OF WORDS

Until the first Industrial Revolution, businesspeople were referred to with terms describing their activity (merchant, financier, manufacturer, etc.) or their specific craft (cabinetmaker, carpenter, etc.). The early nineteenth century extended this vocabulary with appellations that appeared in the eighteenth century, notably, "businessman," "industrialist," and "entrepreneur," for practical reasons: A new generation of political economists discussing the new capitalist economy needed to delineate the role of its various protagonists. They more specifically focused on the people inventing new products or processes, on the one hand, and the people whose mission it was to finance and introduce products to the market, on the other. While the word "'inventor" had been commonly used since the early sixteenth century to characterize the former, labeling the latter was not so obvious.

The word "innovator" existed, but, along with the word "innovation," it reeked of a bad rap. As recounted by Benoît Godin, "from the sixteenth to the eighteenth century, the word innovation was rarely used in isolation. It was always used in conjunction with adjectives (e.g.: 'dangerous', 'violent', 'pernicious', 'zealous', 'unscriptural', 'schismatic'). Pejorative associations also abounded: 'ignorance and innovation', 'superstition and innovation', 'usurpation and innovation', 'revolution and innovation.'"[1] It's only in the nineteenth century that the word "innovation" won acclaim, but the word "innovator" didn't gain traction. It's the term "entrepreneur" that took off, mostly thanks to Jean-Baptiste Say's *Traité d'économie politique* in 1803.

"Entrepreneur" had been previously used by the French-Irish economist Richard Cantillon (1680–1734). He had defined entrepreneurs as the goods and transaction agents in the economy value chain and the risk takers willing to bear with uncertainty: "The farmer is an entrepreneur who promises to pay the property owner, for his farm or land, a fixed sum of money . . . without having the certitude about the advantage he will draw from this enterprise."[2]

Cantillon was largely forgotten in the early nineteenth century, but Say had the wherewithal to spark acceptance for this word, making use of his thought leadership and business background. His father was in the silk trade in Lyon and had sent two of his sons to complete their education in England, where Say landed a job with two sugar merchants. Later, one of his brothers, Louis, took over a sugar refinery in Nantes (France) that was using a method for industrial production of sugar from beets invented by Jean-Baptiste Quéruel.[3] In 1815, however, the company switched to sugarcane. The success of the business was no longer tied to beets but to the optimization of the refinery process regardless of the raw material.[4]

The dawn of a new era led Say to emphasize not only the risk taken by entrepreneurs but also how their mission differed from what inventors/scientists do: "One man studies the laws and conduct of nature; that is to say, the philosopher, or man of science, of whose knowledge another avails himself to create useful products."[5] For Say, entrepreneurs are the ones who artfully execute to put products on a market. "In our days," he wrote, "the enormous wealth of Britain is less owing to her own advances in scientific acquirements . . than to the wonderful practical skill of her adventurers at the useful application of knowledge, and the superiority of her workmen in rapid and masterly execution." In other words, "once the system of nature is discovered, the production resulting from the discovery is no longer the product of the inventor's industry. The man who first discovered the property of fire to soften metals, was not the actual creator of the utility this process adds to smelted ore. That utility results from the physical action of fire, in concurrence, it is true, with the labour and capital of those who employ the process."[6]

Say's writings became extremely popular, and "entrepreneur" was embraced internationally. Over a century later, after distinguishing invention and innovation, Joseph Schumpeter also stated, "The individuals who carry [innovations] out we call Entrepreneurs."[7] It's only in the second part of the twentieth century that the term "innovator" started to take off but without ever catching up with the term "inventor." Within the same time frame, however, "entrepreneur" became so fashionable that it distanced both "innovator" and "inventor" as is clear from the Google NGram in figure 2.

In his 1985 book, *Innovation and Entrepreneurship, Practice and Principles*, Peter Drucker used "entrepreneur" and "innovator" interchangeably.[8] Today, "inventor" remains more popular than "innovator," although many prominent names we see as great inventors were, strictly speaking, much greater innovators. The case of Alexander Graham Bell comes to mind. He was an inventor, yes, but not of the whole telephone. As noted by Derek Thompson, "the problem that Bell solved was to turn electrical signals into sounds. But this was such an obvious extension of the telegraph that there were many people working on it. Philip Reis had already designed a sound transmitter in 1860, and Hermann von Helmholtz had already built a receiver."[9] Thompson cites Mark Lemley, who emphasized

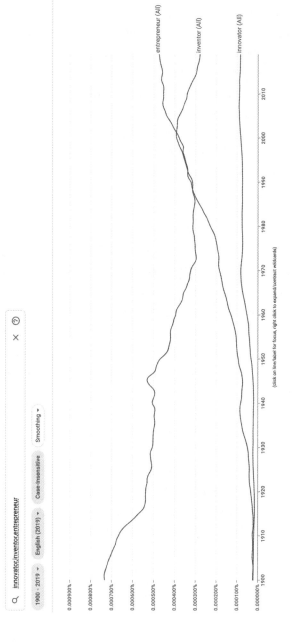

Figure 2. Comparing the popularity of the terms "innovator," "inventor," and "entrepreneur."

Credit: Google Books Ngram Viewer, http://books.google.com/ngrams.

that "Bell's iconic status owes as much to his victories in court and in the marketplace as at the lab bench."[10] In fact, Bell is far more important as the innovator who assembled many inventions into one whole. Innovators often earn the merit of an invention because they're the ones who are able to seal the deal, build a business, and become a "hit maker" to use Thompson's book title.[11]

The prestige of the word "inventor" is anchored in the popular psyche. "Innovator" still fails to carry the same heft as "entrepreneur" or "inventor," even though "innovation" took over "invention" in the 1970s, as shown in figure 3.

This phenomenon tells us that even in a space that has garnered gigantic interest, adopting the word that characterizes the person enacting innovation isn't obvious, which shows that it can take a long time to "break through" existing habits—often the fate of innovations in general.

We love the fact that entrepreneurs take risks and overcome uncertainty, but we can't resist the appeal of the term "inventor," because it conveys a sort of magic. As a result, we continue to amalgamate entrepreneurship, innovation, and invention. Yet, (1) not all entrepreneurs innovate, (2) not all inventors are entrepreneurs or want to be entrepreneurs, and (3) innovative entrepreneurs (or innovators) and inventors have two different perspectives on the world and two different purposes.

TWO DIFFERENT PERSPECTIVES

The distinction between invention and innovation is often discussed by scholars.[12] What I want to stress here is that despite the fuzziness introduced by the history of language, inventors and innovators—albeit sometimes incarnated in the same person, especially in startups—have two different perspectives.

The Inventor's Perspective

Inventors start from the art in their space and see originality or novelty relative to it, and not necessarily relative to a potential market impact. If the invention is at the theoretical level of fundamental science, the impact

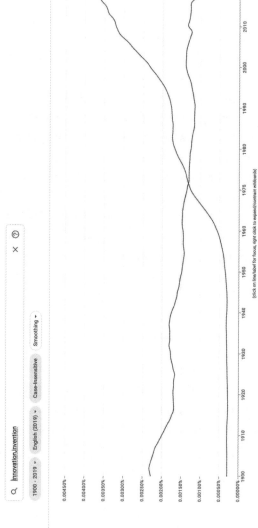

Figure 3. Comparing the popularity of the terms "innovation" and "invention."

Credit: Google Books Ngram Viewer, http://books.google.com/ngrams.

may not even be seen for a long time. For example, if you're interested in the history of aviation, you may wonder why Daniel Bernoulli was inducted into the International Air & Space Hall of Fame at the San Diego Air & Space Museum in 2002, or even wonder who he was.

Bernoulli was an eighteenth-century Swiss mathematician and physicist. One of his works, *Hydrodynamica*, published in 1738, showcased a principle stating, in essence, that a fast-moving fluid (such as the air) exerts less pressure than the same fluid when moving slowly. Bernoulli advanced a line of research on fluid mechanics started by the Dutch mathematician and physicist Christiaan Huygens. Of course, this had nothing to do with airplanes, which didn't exist. Yet the Bernoulli principle is what explains why planes fly. That's what two American aviation pioneers, Orville and Wilbur Wright, needed to understand.

The Wright brothers are usually credited with building the world's first successful motor-operated airplane in 1903, although they failed to become the first commercial airline company.[13] They were versatile experimentalists and had learned a lot from other pioneers, like the German Otto Lilienthal, the American Samuel Langley, or the French Clément Ader and Octave Chanute. Yet, as resourceful as they were, to operate predictably they needed science, and notably the Bernoulli principle, which they learned from Edward Huffaker.[14] Fundamental science may not be visible, but it can condition the reality of many accomplishments.

Time lags between scientific discoveries and their actualization within products are generally well understood. Albeit not always! Sometimes inventors aren't aware of the translation and adaptation processes required to make their invention consumable and how long this might take. As a result, they can be prone to complain about the inefficiencies of the business, especially when their invention is the heart of an innovation. They assume that the hard part of the job is done. They may not realize that innovators must consider a web of internal and external dependencies that have little to do with the invention itself. Inventors are certain of the value of what they have accomplished within their sphere of competency (and it often earns them kudos from their peers). However, they often underestimate the factors that can render that value secondary when presented outside their sphere, that is, to customers who look at the products offered to them from their point of view, with little to no regard for their inventors. At the core of this discrepancy between the certainty of the content of an invention and the uncertainty of its appeal to a market is the fact that there is rarely a direct mapping between invention and innovation.

Take a straightforward device for us today, the computer mouse. Douglas Engelbart began its development in the early 1960s at Stanford Research Institute (SRI). He invented the mechanism to translate the motion of the mouse into a cursor movement on the screen and authored the first patent, called the "X-Y Position Indicator for a Display System," filed in 1967 and issued in 1970. Bill English, then the chief engineer at SRI, built the first prototype in 1964. But it became a marketable object only after years of research and adjustments.

Various organizations worked on their own version of the mouse in the 1970s and early 1980s in order to make it commercially compelling. For example, Logitech—founded in 1981 in Switzerland by Daniel Borel and Pierluigi Zappacosta, two Stanford alumni, and Giacomo Marini, a former Olivetti and IBM engineer—introduced and started to license its mouse, the P4, in 1982. A lot of creativity and engineering were involved in moving the technology from labs to offices and homes. And when this happened, it was all but certain that users would accept the idea that keyboards weren't the only way to interact with a computer screen.

So there can be a difference between what inventors see and what innovators think the market can support, if ever. When entrepreneurs don't explain and justify this gap to inventors, their relationship can be strained: inventors see innovative entrepreneurs as imposters, and innovative entrepreneurs see inventors as moaners.

The Innovator's Perspective

Innovators start from a given market, whose timelines and components are different from inventors'. When or if they see the value of an invention, innovators must work at inserting it into a market, which requires appropriate marketing, sales, and distribution infrastructures; adequate manufacturing capabilities; and so on. Innovators must also make sure that the technologies included in a product don't infringe on existing patents, that inventors aren't incorporating devices for which no explicit authorization of usage was granted, and that developers aren't reusing the intellectual property of another organization. This topic is rife with stories: in addition to the countless patent infringement lawsuits that happen every day, one major incident making the news was the story of a Google employee who left the company in 2016, started his own self-driving truck company (Otto), which was then acquired by Uber for $680 million—only for Uber to realize that it incorporated stolen secrets.[15] Not good!

As previously stated, innovations rarely rest on one single invention. According to Schumpeter, "innovation combines factors in a new way" and "consists in carrying out New Combinations."[16] Look at the iPhone: When it came out in 2007, everybody was eager to look at its entrails—not so easy, because most vendors don't provide detailed information, out of competitive concerns, and they want to cultivate some mystique around products. iFixit disassembled it in twenty-six steps.[17]

Between the packaging, the support of four wireless protocols, the H.264 video decoding, the two-megapixel camera, a touch screen manufactured by a hundred-year-old German company (Balda), the SIM card, the antenna, the headphones, the battery, the Phillips screws securing the logic board to the front panel, and the two-layer logic board with a variety of chips from different provenances, the first iPhone encapsulated a multitude of inventions. Not even counting software. The iPhone combined existing inventions and in the process of combining them created new ones. This merging of dozens of inventions is what made the iPhone *one* major innovation in the history of smartphones. Since 2007, it has evolved a lot, of course, as well as all its components.

Also keep in mind that each of these components has its own history. Among them is an innovation by Corning that is now part of the technology firmament: the alkali-aluminosilicate thin-sheet glass, later called

"Gorilla glass," that now protects portable electronic devices. This was initially intended to be a stand-alone innovation, but it failed.[18] It was meant for use in the automotive industry of the 1960s and had been developed by a material scientist and the first woman PhD at Corning, Ellen Mochel, as well as by fusion process engineers Clint Shay and Stuart Dockerty.[19] When Steve Jobs wanted the iPhone's screen to be made from a sturdy glass, not plastic, someone suggested that he check with Corning. The rest is history.

For innovators, the world is a gigantic store of parts and resources, old or new, to be assembled and often refactored. This need for an assemblage alone creates an element of uncertainty: how evolved and reliable is each of the components involved, and how many additional technologies must be conceived to glue them together? As they do so, innovators *theatricalize* what they have on hand on a stage that must reflect the spirit of the time: How do they see or interpret that spirit of the time and assume that there will be a market fit with potential customers? These are topics I will address in chapters 4 and 5.

For companies relying on inventions, inventors and innovators must join forces to create success. That's why it's meaningful to ask if organizations can better sustain their innovative efforts if their inventor is also the CEO. The short response is "sometimes," provided that they're interested in running a business, which is not always obvious or desirable.

ARE INVENTOR-CEOS MORE LIKELY TO DRIVE AND SUSTAIN INNOVATION?

Do inventors have an advantage if they want to become entrepreneurs? Businesspeople may express reservations about this. Let's put aside the idea that inventors may not have an MBA, because learning the ABCs of business in graduate school is not required to run a successful business. A more fundamental question is this one: If an inventor is running a lab that requires their continuous attention, how well can they delegate critical aspects of the invention processes, and how easily can they see the world beyond their inventions?

What Drives the Success of Inventor-CEOs?

In a 2020 study, Emdad Islam and Jason Zein concluded that companies led by inventors produce more and better innovations.[20] They examined publicly traded high-tech firms on the S&P 1500 between 1992 and 2008 across various industry groups and analyzed the patents earned by their inventor-CEOs. For the 20 percent of US high-tech firms led by inventor-CEOs, they found that these "firms are associated with a greater volume of registered patents, more highly cited patents, higher innovation efficiency, and a greater propensity to produce ground-breaking or disruptive innovations. Such superior innovation outcomes were also reflected in higher market valuations."

They identified several reasons to explain this phenomenon, two of which are notable:

1. Inventor-CEOs are deeply familiar with the company's offerings: as an example, Islam and Zein mentioned former SanDisk CEO Sanjay Mehrotra, who said in a *Forbes* interview, "It's helped me a great deal in understanding the capabilities of our technology, and in assessing the complexities of the challenges ahead. That makes a big difference in determining strategic plans and in managing execution. It becomes easier to focus attention on the right issues."[21] Also, by being more knowledgeable, inventor-CEOs are likely to be more effective spokespersons.
2. Inventor-CEOs' background foster a culture of creativity. Hands-on experience gives them not only "a higher tolerance for failure" but also a credibility to directly engage with the firm's research and development (R&D) teams when needed, thus making the company more agile in adopting new ideas and approaches. "In contrast, CEOs without an inventive streak may focus less on innovation and more on other aspects of a CEO's role, such as reporting, compliance and internal control and monitoring systems."

Although the sample considered is interesting, it's difficult to know to what extent it is reflective of a larger landscape. The 20 percent that Islam and Zein came up with could be on the high side, given that they don't include companies that were acquired or failed, which constitute the vast majority of ventures. Additionally, their use of patents as a criterion may artificially bump up that percentage for two main reasons:

1. Patents can name CEOs despite that they may not be the sole or even the actual inventor and, as a result, include CEOs who should be viewed more as innovators than inventors per se. An example is Steve Jobs, credited with 458 patented inventions and designs. While he is often viewed as an inventor because the word "inventor" sounds better in some contexts, his ability to combine multiple inventions from multiple inventors living at different times to offer huge innovations may be far more important.[22]

2. Patents describe inventions whose breadth varies. It's true that thousands of engineers, scientists, and researchers write patents to protect their ideas and create companies they want to run. However, if you look only at large-scale inventors, you won't find too many inventor-CEOs. Most Nobel laureates have been incubated in universities and national or private laboratories, but few have run companies.[23] Of the twenty-five laureates for 2018, 2019, and 2020 in Physics, Chemistry and Physiology/Medicine, only a handful have ties to commercial organizations. Arthur Ashkin (Physics, 2018), the father of optical tweezers, spent forty years at Bell Labs; Stanley Whittingham (Chemistry, 2019), a key contributor to the development of lithium-ion batteries (winning his prize alongside Akira Yoshino and John Goodenough), worked at Exxon Research & Engineering Company for sixteen years, although safety concerns ended his lithium-ion battery project in 1984. Akira Yoshino (Chemistry, 2019) was employed by a major Japanese chemical company, Asahi Kasei Corporation. Michael Houghton (Chemistry, 2020), who co-discovered Hepatitis C in 1989, started to work at Chiron Corporation in 1982. Frances Arnold (Chemistry, 2018) and Jennifer Doudna (Chemistry, 2020) are among the few who started companies.

In recent times, scientists have increasingly pursued commercial opportunities. The trend is clearer in life sciences than in physical sciences, "where scientists are more likely to view commercially driven research as a hindrance to their academic careers."[24] Unsurprisingly, for the Turing Award, often viewed as the "Nobel Prize of Computing," a significant percentage of the recipients are or have been employed by corporations, albeit not all of them, and more seldomly in a CEO role. Of the seventy-two award winners as of 2020, less than 50 percent were employed full-time by organizations. Among recent recipients, we can mention Yann LeCun, who is chief AI scientist at Facebook, and Geoffrey Hinton, who created a startup that was acquired by Google.

How Business Looks at the Concept of Inventor-CEO

Not all inventions justify the formation of a company. They may be too niche, be of limited interest, or may only make sense as part of a much larger ensemble.[25] The question of whether an inventor is more or less effective at running the business is most relevant when the business primarily revolves around the exploitation of one core invention.

Questions about the value of having inventor-CEOs became raised more frequently after business schools increasingly marked their territory in the 1960s–1970s. Peter Drucker addressed the topic in the 1980s. After admitting that "a great inventor" could also be "a great business builder," citing George Westinghouse as an example, his assessment of Edison was more ambivalent.[26] He considered that Edison succeeded as an inventor but not as a business builder. Why? Are there inventor traits that can get in the way of their success as innovative CEOs?

Was Edison a Poor Manager Because He Was an Inventor?

Drucker mentions Edison several times: "For the high-tech entrepreneur, the archetype still seems to be Thomas Edison," he writes. "Edison, the nineteenth century's most successful inventor, converted invention into the discipline we now call research. His real ambition, however, was to be a business builder and to become a tycoon. He keeps exerting a high fascination for promoting 'the traditional pattern of great excitement, rapid expansion,' or the pattern of 'from rags to riches and back to rags again' in five years.'" However, the reason Edison as an archetype should be taken with a grain of salt is that he was the prototype of "the inventor-entrepreneur who totally mismanaged the businesses he started," so much so that "he had to be removed from every one of them to save it."[27]

According to Drucker, Edison's weakness was his inability to build a professional management team:

> Edison's ambition was to be a successful businessman and the head of a
> big company. He should have succeeded, for he was a superb business
> planner. He knew exactly how an electric power company had to be set
> up to exploit his invention of the light bulb. He knew exactly how to get
> all the money he could possibly need for his ventures. His products were
> immediate successes and the demand for them practically insatiable. But
> Edison remained an entrepreneur; or rather, he thought that "managing"
> meant being the boss. He refused to build a management team. And so
> every one of his four or five companies collapsed ignominiously once
> it got to middle size, and was saved only by booting Edison himself out
> and replacing him with professional management.[28]

Such a harsh indictment shouldn't deter us from asking a simple question: Is it really *because* Edison was too much of an inventor that he didn't bother building a professional management team? After all, many entrepreneurs who aren't inventors can also have a hard time doing so. They maintain a quasi-symbiotic relationship with their organization, believing they can do everything, and end up botching daily operations. This is a common phenomenon, and it's also why creating advisory boards to help them transition from founder to CEO is critical.

So was the problem that Edison—albeit surrounded by businesspeople and financiers, and albeit social and gregarious—couldn't find people who measured up to his standard? It's possible. After all, businesspeople would have to be extraordinarily brilliant to gain the respect and trust of a man like Edison. But does this necessarily denote an intrinsic flaw of the inventor himself? When an inventor fails as a CEO, can't we also look at the other side of the story? I would think that outsize, imaginative inventors also need outsize, imaginative business management talents.

What makes me consider this hypothesis is a remark by a major German economist, Werner Sombart, a contemporary of Edison's: "Mr. Edison was, perhaps, the outstanding example of a man who made a business of invention itself," noting that in Menlo Park and West Orange, New Jersey, Edison employed as many as two hundred laboratory assistants and machinists.[29] Edison's desire to be a business tycoon wasn't fully realized, but his approach of "making a business of invention itself" was a new business model. In 1911 he formed the holding company Thomas A. Edison, Incorporated, which succeeded the Edison Manufacturing Company set up in 1889. But Edison hit a snag: At the end of the nineteenth century and at the beginning of the twentieth, it was hard to implement such a model in the United States. The country's manufacturing infrastructure was not as evolved as in countries like Germany. As a result, Edison had to adopt a mixed model that was a financial pit, all the more so as he created patent after patent (and remained the world's most prolific inventor for almost 150 years). Yet, even though his business model turned out to be muddy, it's not fully historically accurate to declare that his companies collapsed "ignominiously."

General Electric still exists today. Admittedly, it is not "one" Edison company but rather a montage merging multiple organizations. Several companies were grouped under one to form Edison General Electric Company, which subsequently acquired Sprague Electric Railway & Motor Company, and Thomson-Houston Electric Company, started by Elihu Thomson and Edwin Houston. The new entity bought Rudolf Eickemeyer's business of transformers used for the transmission of electrical power (and with it got German-born inventor Charles Steinmetz, who revolutionized AC circuit theory and analysis). In 1896 General Electric was one of the original twelve companies listed on the newly formed Dow Jones Industrial Average. Ultimately, only General Electric had been set into motion by an inventor, Edison—and many of the components included in GE had also been started by inventors.

A more convincing example for Drucker might have been the story of Nikola Tesla, a name resurrected in popular culture largely thanks to Elon Musk.[30] Born in 1856 in a village in Croatia, Tesla had studied electrical engineering at the Austrian Polytechnic in Graz. He went on to work for the American Telephone Company in Hungary and then for Continental Edison Company in France, where he conceived the induction motor and began developing various devices using rotating magnetic fields. These inventions were not of interest to the company at the time, but when his boss, Charles Batchelor, a British inventor and trusted collaborator of Edison, returned to the United States to manage the Edison Machine Works, he took Tesla with him. However, Tesla worked for only a short time there and left to start his own venture, Tesla Electric Light & Manufacturing. His financial investors quickly disagreed with his implementation plan for an alternating current motor and got rid of him. Although he licensed his patents to Westinghouse, thus triggering a "War of Currents" with Edison, he didn't even create a midsize company, although his alternating-current (AC) system won against Edison's direct-current (DC) electric power, and the Tesla coil proved a long-lasting invention. He did continue to invent, win patents (about three hundred), and dazzle the world, but contrary to Edison, he was unable to create a large team of dedicated engineers. A somewhat solitary genius, he died alone in a hotel room at the New Yorker at the age of eighty-six in 1943 and became a sort of alternative cult figure.

Is There a Problem with Inventor-CEOs?

It's legitimate to wonder if inventors are always willing to reduce the amount of time they spend in their lab furthering their invention(s) to be available for the dozens of other tasks necessary to operate an organization. It's just as legitimate to wonder how easily they'll be ready to curb their desire for more inventions regardless of whether or not these will materialize into innovations within a reasonable time frame and a given context or how doggedly they'll cling to their initial idea beyond its prime time or cultural relevance. In both scenarios, the challenge for business colleagues is to channel inventors' perspective into the practical needs of a market where innovation is what people are ready to buy and not what they ought to try in order to be at the forefront of science or technology. So business has to manage two opposite types of profiles and nuances in between:

1. IF THEY'RE EBULLIENT INVENTORS LIKE EDISON: It can be hard to contain their creativity if nobody can help them define an adequate business model or convince them to concentrate on specific areas. That said, they can also show an extreme flexibility and opportunistic openness precious to the business if something doesn't work—or, in the case of Edison, precious to the business of others. Henry Ford admired Edison for giving him valuable advice.

Henry Ford became an engineer with the Edison Illuminating Company of Detroit in 1891 and was promoted to chief engineer in 1893. In his personal time, he started car experiments and worked on a gasoline engine. "Most people, including all of my associates in the electrical company," Ford wrote, "had taken pains to tell me that time spent on a gasoline engine was time wasted."[31] But when he sought Edison's opinion, he got a different answer. To Edison's alleged response—"No one kind of motive power is ever going to do all the work of the country. We do not know what electricity can do, but I take for granted that it cannot do everything"—Ford added, "That is characteristic of Edison. He was the central figure in the electrical industry, which was then young and enthusiastic. The rank and file of the electrical men could see nothing ahead but electricity, but their leader could see with crystal clearness that no one power could do all the work of the country. I suppose that is why he was the leader." Edison delivered practical business advice, not an inventor's harebrained scheme. Knowing all too well that reliable and rechargeable batteries for use in cars were not yet there, he didn't tell Ford something like "Wait, I'll have a battery for you soon."[32]

2. IF THEY'RE SELF-CENTERED: It's challenging to go around authoritarian geniuses. One of the most captivating business failures of a Nobel Prize winner–turned–entrepreneur is William Shockley's. In 1956 he started Shockley Semiconductor Laboratory. Although a division of Beckman Instruments, it was operated as a startup and the first of its kind to work on semiconductor devices in what was later dubbed "Silicon Valley."

Shockley hired incredible engineers, but after a few months these engineers couldn't bear his abusive style. As recounted by Gordon Moore, a group of them, later labeled the "treacherous eight" by Shockley, tried to convince Arnold Beckman to remove Shockley, but to no avail: "What we didn't appreciate is that it's awfully hard to push a Nobel Prize winner aside. Beckman decided (as the result of advice he had received elsewhere) that he really couldn't do this to Shockley. We were told essentially that Shockley was in charge, and if we didn't like it we probably ought to look at doing something else."[33]

Beckman, who had built a large company as an inventor, got blindsided, forgetting that his own company owed its success to growing beyond his own original invention. So the treacherous eight left. By September 1957, they reached an agreement with Sherman Fairchild and formed Fairchild Semiconductor. Robert Noyce became the company's general manager, which didn't prevent him from inventing the first silicon-based monolithic integrated circuit chip in 1959.[34] A few years later, Noyce and Moore didn't like Fairchild's board decisions and started Intel. It's certainly fascinating to think that Shockley, who failed as a businessman, ended up transforming engineers into innovative businesspeople. Robert Noyce was Intel's first CEO (1968–75), Gordon Moore its second (1975–87), and Andy Grove (who wasn't part of the "eight" but had worked at Fairchild) its third (1987–98).

More often than not, the hardest step for inventors is to move beyond their original ideas and credit others for new ones. When they do, they can power long-lasting successes, as exemplified by two members of the Bosch family in Germany:

1. Robert Bosch created the Werkstätte für Feinmechanik und Elektrotechnik (Workshop for Precision Mechanics and Electrical Engineering) in 1886. This was the starting point of a multinational company, dubbed Bosch in 1913. Robert Bosch didn't cling to his initial magneto ignition device, however. He let his leading engineer, Gottlob Honold, invent the spark plug and multiple other devices (such as automotive headlights) and scaled his manufacturing capabilities to produce every possible automotive device, whether or not they were invented by the organization.

2. His nephew was also an inventor-industrialist. Carl Bosch invented the Haber-Bosch process for large-scale synthesis of fertilizers and explosives between 1909 and 1913 with Fritz Haber (Nobel Prize in Chemistry, 1918). In 1925 Bosch helped found IG Farben and was its first head. He received a Nobel Prize in Chemistry in 1931 jointly with Friedrich Bergius in recognition of their contributions to the invention and development of chemical high-pressure methods. Carl Bosch is one of the rare inventor-entrepreneurs personally linked to several Nobel Prizes: his own with Bergius, and, because of his direct assistance to two other recipients, Fritz Haber and Gerhard Domagk. Domagk did his research at the Bayer Laboratories of the IG Farben research institute for pathological anatomy and bacteriology in 1932 and earned the Nobel Prize in Physiology/Medicine in 1939.

Examples don't create rules. Inventors can become great CEOs just as much as disastrous ones. In the same fashion, you'll find exceptional non-inventor-CEOs as well as terrible ones. In all cases, though, even if there is an ideological premium to the positioning of one figurehead, inventor or not, a company is more than one individual. Apple was always and will always remain more than Steve Jobs. Continuous innovativeness supposes that an organization moves beyond its original inventions and innovations. Fusajirō Yamauchi, the founder of Nintendo in 1899, started with a card game, but the company gained international recognition seventy years later thanks to Masayuki Uemura, an engineer who joined in 1971.

Of course, continuous innovativeness also requires consistently investing in research and development.

INVESTING IN RESEARCH AND DEVELOPMENT

Money doesn't generate innovation per se, but if you don't invest in innovation it won't come by magic. The three princes of Serendip made unexpected discoveries because they went through a long pilgrimage.[35] That's what research is about.

In aggregate, according to the National Science Foundation, corporations spent around $490 billion in 2019, with basic research representing around 17 percent and applied research 19 percent; most of the amount, around 65 percent, goes to development.[36] Although numbers and players vary over the years, funds are concentrated; in 2018, for example, about 25 percent of this R&D amount was spent by only ten companies.[37] As noted by John Wu, R&D in the United States may not be quite as strong as it appears, for two reasons.[38] First, Wu notes, "the federal government deprioritized funding for R&D, which reduces the pool of new discoveries that private industry can capitalize on by making additional R&D investments of their own." Second, corporate R&D money tends to focus on later-stage development: "Businesses are steering more of their R&D investments toward product development that has the potential to generate returns in the near term and allocating less for basic and applied research that takes longer to bear fruit." This short-term approach to R&D is not only problematic by itself; it also increases weakening factors, especially two of them:

1. If all efforts are geared toward immediate impact, companies reduce their ability to build corporate knowledge, which, in turn, forces them to continuously resort to ad hoc and reactive product development. This attitude limits their chances of creating larger-scope innovations.

2. As time goes on, organizations have even fewer chances of attracting quality scientists/researchers whose talent may be critical for

longer-term projects, which further diminishes opportunities to retake any form of innovation lead.

Innovating is rarely as miraculous as pulling a rabbit out of a hat. What may come across as a marvel frequently results from large efforts over a longer period of time. Here are a few examples:

- Dennis Gabor was awarded the Nobel Prize in Physics in 1971 "for his invention and development of the holographic method." This discovery in the 1940s, which was the starting point of electron holography, came about as he was improving electron microscopes at the British Thomson-Houston Electric Company.
- Roy Plunkett discovered polytetrafluoroethylene (PTFE) in 1938 at DuPont while attempting to create a new chlorofluorocarbon refrigerant. That's the origin of what was trademarked as Teflon in 1945 and ended up coating satellite components as well as cookware.
- While developing a process for insulating a series of parallel electrical wires using PTFE, two chemical engineers at W. L. Gore & Associates, Walton Gore and his son Robert, discovered that the polymer could expand. This new form of PTFE, named GORE-TEX in 1969, is used for hundreds of medical, industrial, electrical, and sartorial applications.
- Harry Coover was a chemist at Eastman Kodak when he discovered some of the properties of cyanoacrylates. At the time, in 1942, they were deemed too sticky to be of interest. It's only in 1951 that Coover and his team realized their unique adhesive capabilities. In 1958, the adhesive was marketed by Kodak as Eastman 910 and later as Super Glue.

Inventors invent, and it's the job of innovators to make something of it when relevant. Sometimes, inventors see practical applications but not always, because they are often pursuing another goal. This is why people in charge of innovation must walk the floor all the time. If they don't, they risk missing out on opportunities. Of course, it may very well happen that the full potential of an invention cannot be exploited by the organization that invented it. When Paul Hogan and Robert Banks invented crystalline polypropylene and a new process to produce high-density polyethylene at Phillips Petroleum in the 1950s, Phillips commercialized the new plastic under the name of Marlex. But it wasn't the business of Phillips to develop the thousands of consumer and industrial goods that could take advantage of it. I'm sure that nobody foresaw that two graduate students, Richard Knerr and Arthur Melin, who had started a toy company, Wham-O, in 1948, would seize on the potential offered by the new material to transform their business and launch a new product in 1957, the Hula Hoop.

You're able to offer novelties only if (1) you've developed a lot of stuff over the years and (2) you "don't let financial metrics prematurely stifle" the innovation engine.[39] Many patents filed in a development process may not be used down the road, or be used later in a different context (that's why the speculations of patent watchers are often off the mark). If you add to this reality the fact that there are on average twenty-two months between the time a patent is filed and when it is granted (even if there are ways to speed up the examination process), as well as the research time of the engineers who come up with a patentable project, you can't expect R&D to guarantee results today or two years from now.

Many companies don't or can't build strong knowledge repositories. Some prefer to outsource risk through investments in startups that can be written off if these investments don't pan out. In this case, startups act as virtual labs of large organizations. However, they face the risk of losing startup founders quickly after an acquisition if these founders have limited creative freedom or incentives within the acquiring company.

There is logic to the economic idea of disposable inventive and innovative talents. The financial outcomes for all the parties involved may be appreciable. Yet, while this modus operandi is efficient and fits into short-term visions of return on investment, I haven't seen data proving that it's a valid long-term alternative to at least some internal research. Note that large companies with stronger internal R&D are also the winners in the acquisition game: They end up increasing their innovation lead (as I will discuss in chapter 8), and they do so because they value innovative talent and have the means to retain it.

CONCLUSION

Although the word "inventor" is still used more than the word "innovator" by historians to describe icons of the innovation pantheon, it's useful to keep in mind an operational distinction between "invention" and "innovation." Even if inventions and innovations are intertwined, especially in technology-based domains, inventors and innovators start from two different perspectives. Inventors advance their respective domains even if no direct commercial application is in sight, while innovators start from a market that reflects the spirit of the time.

As innovators, we don't sell top-notch algorithms that will secure people's data. We must package them for customers to understand their benefits. In addition, most innovations aggregate several inventions that were not necessarily conceived to work together in the first place. In that case, innovating is not simply presenting one invention to make it consumable; rather, it's creatively orchestrating inventions to produce a product or a service that people will find desirable.

As we will see later, creativity can be expressed in multiple ways, but one thing is clear: key to success is the depth of the relationship between engineering and business—which requires an interdisciplinary mindset. Steve Jobs is an icon for a slew of reasons and comes across as an archetypal innovator. Why? It's because at the base of his success was a deep trust in and from the engineering team, even though he thought he knew better than anybody else, and even if his propensity for "reality distortion field" could drive people crazy. In other words, the multifaceted aspiration treadmill from the top was solidly supported at the base: the Macintosh engineering group made the impossible happen in 1984 with the introduction of a new kind of computer. In the same fashion, although Steve Jobs's NeXT company was a failure, the NeXTSTEP—

created thanks to engineers like Avie Tevanian, Jean-Marie Hullot, and many others—became the source of Apple's new operating systems when Jobs came back to Apple. What made Pixar a stunning success? It's a collaboration with top-notch inventors/creatives such as Ed Catmull, Alvy Ray Smith (who left Pixar in 1991), and John Lasseter.

2

What Is a Typical Innovation Journey?

Give me time and I'll give you a revolution.
—Alexander McQueen

Facebook went public after eight years, Intel after only two, and Apple after three. Does it matter? Yes, to investors. Does it say anything about the innovation journey? Not really. As a matter of course, most empirical observations tend to converge around the idea that companies' success is best assessed after seven to ten years, and sometimes more.

For this chapter, the case study I selected is George Eastman's journey. As the founder of Kodak, Eastman (1854–1932) was one of the most prominent innovators to democratize photography.[1]

Why do I choose to tell his story and not the one of a more recent innovator? First, there are thousands of interviews, podcasts, and books about recent innovators all over the place. Second, as inspiring as they often are, most of them are subject to retrospective simplifications and hagiographic biases. As a result, they tend to underplay the effectuation side of innovating—the fact that things don't always happen as anticipated, that innovators must be comfortable with the idea that a bird in the hand is worth two in the bush, or that they must also be able to improvise and "exploit contingencies rather than predict the future."[2] Nonbusiness biographies often give more accurate narratives of the survivalist's odyssey innovators have to go through and with fewer marketing spins.[3] This chapter doesn't address the downfall of Kodak as a company in the 1970s, decades after Eastman's death, a topic discussed by countless articles that I will briefly address in chapter 12.

ONE STEP AFTER ANOTHER FOR TWELVE YEARS

George Eastman was not trained as an engineer or a chemist. He started his work life in a local insurance company before becoming a junior clerk at the Rochester Savings Bank in Rochester, New York. In 1877, as he was contemplating a vacation (which he didn't take) on the Caribbean island of Hispaniola, he looked for photographic equipment, bought a lot of it, and got absorbed in it—like thousands of people at a time as professional and amateur photography was booming. But he was frustrated by the cost and impracticality of the equipment he had purchased as well as the work involved to develop photographs. So, just like many entrepreneurs, Eastman wanted to solve a problem he'd found.

He kept his job at the bank for three years before formally starting his company, but he dedicated his free time to his new passion. He took lessons from a professional, George Monroe, and followed the expert advice of George Selden, a patent attorney who was also an automobile inventor.[4] He voraciously read all the technical literature that came his way and exchanged ideas with amateurs and professionals. Eastman quickly understood that a way to improve photography was to get rid of the wet-plate process (also called collodion process) that had replaced the daguerreotype and could now be replaced with gelatin dry plates.

Better Dry Plates

Eastman wasn't the first to tackle the subject of dry plates as an alternative to wet plates. Like many others, he was building on an invention by Richard Maddox, an English physician and photographer, whose passion for microphotography had led him to discover dry gelatin photographic emulsion, also known as the gelatin process or dry plate. Maddox had given away his invention by publishing it in the *British Journal of Photography* in 1871, which triggered a variety of additional improvements from countless tinkerers. One of the best known came from Charles Bennett. Eastman subscribed to that magazine in 1878, and the first issue he received was precisely showcasing Bennett's formula. "The English article started me in the right direction," Eastman later said.[5]

Eastman came up with a revised formula and showed it around to fellow photography aficionados. For the English-speaking world, London was the capital of photography. So, in January 1879, Eastman sailed over there. He even filed a patent in the UK for an emulsion-coating plating machine. Although he failed to sell the rights to the machine that he had just conceived, this trip was an eye-opener. He filed his first US patent in September 1879 ("Method and Apparatus for Coating Plates").[6] Back home, he rented a room above a music store to manufacture dry plates on a small scale. He was comfortable enough with his work to look for financial backing, which he got from Henry Strong, who was then running a family-owned buggy-whip-manufacturing company and would become president of the Eastman Dry Plate Company that Eastman formed in 1881.

Eastman began commercial production of dry plates. He was selling a sustaining-type innovation in an effervescent ecosystem with dozens of manufacturers popping up in Europe and in the United States and applying for patents left and right. The Hammer Dry Plate Company in St. Louis, Missouri, already had a great reputation. Two other major heavyweights were E. & H.T. Anthony & Company, in New York City, and Scovill, in Waterbury, Connecticut, with whom Eastman would have frequent dealings over the years, sometimes in a friendly manner but more often antagonistically. In short, Eastman was one of dozens of vendors machine-gunning at each other through products and patents in a world where almost anybody with a little bit of money had a shot at success. Had he been in today's Silicon Valley, he would have been told by VCs that he was starting in a space that was too busy and fragmented or that his idea wasn't "disruptive" enough.

Eastman gained momentum and soon needed more space and more help, but competition was fierce. He also realized that he had to be faster than everybody else. "I have come to think," he later said, "that the maintenance of lead in the apparatus trade will depend greatly upon a rapid succession of changes and improvements," what is termed "continuous innovation" today.[7] Not everything was going smoothly, however. In 1882 dealers complained that the Eastman plates were either registering no image or foggy ones. Eastman recalled them and embarked on no less than 454 attempts at remixing emulsions. After finding a temporary fix, he cut his prices to reenlist the customers he had lost.

Although this calamity was addressed for the time being, he knew he had better diversify. Eastman thought that roll film systems would make glass plates obsolete (except for special high-precision work). In the meantime, he still needed to improve his technology, as many dry plate competitors offered a better product. He had no competitive advantage.

Better Roll Holders and Negatives

Again, the idea of replacing dry plates with film (instead of sheet films) and negative paper wasn't new. As Eastman later indicated, "an exposing mechanism called a roll holder for sensitized paper had been made as early as 1854," his birth year.[8] He was referring to the work of Arthur Melhuish, who, with Joseph Spencer, had designed and patented the first roll film holder and introduced it to the British Royal Photographic Society in 1856.

Numerous professionals and skilled amateurs had followed suit. The most recent improvement had been brought in by a colorful character, Władysław Małachowski, a Polish Lithuanian who had fled Russian repression in Lithuania and lived a double life, one as the head of a group of anarchists and one as an inventor under the pseudonym of Leon Warneke. He had designed the first roll cartridge with negative paper in 1875. His camera first used a collodion process and, after 1881, a gelatin-emulsion. Warneke was a well-known figure and had been awarded the Progress Medal of the Photographic Society of Great Britain in 1882. Eastman also developed a new product at that time, the Eastman Negative Paper. Like many others in the industry, these two men were reviving a type of research that had been initiated by earlier inventors like John Herschel (the first to apply the terms "negative" and "positive" to photography) and Henry Fox Talbot.

Eastman had licensed an 1881 patent related to roll holder film filed by David Houston, a farmer based in North Dakota, before buying it (as well as multiple additional patents).[9] But this wasn't enough for him to make a difference. Two years later, he started to work with a temperamental but skilled engineer, William Walker. Walker had founded a photographic supply business in Rochester and manufactured his own line of dry plates as well as a camera, Walker's Pocket Camera, which he had launched in 1882 with a striking ad copy: "Photography made easy for everybody" and "for ladies it is far superior to sketching." In 1883 he had sold his businesses to the Rochester Optical Company, which became a major player in the 1880s and 1890s before it was acquired by Eastman Kodak in 1903. With Walker on board, Eastman was able to file two important patents in 1884. The first one, titled "Photographic film," was filed in March 1884 and issued in October 1884.[10] The second, titled "Roller holder for photographic film," was filed in August 1884 and issued in May 1885.[11]

Eastman created his own roll film made up of one hundred rolled photosensitive papers, initially called "stripping film" and later known as "American film." The film was sold under the name "Eastman's American Film," which led to the company's name change from the Eastman Dry Plate Company to the Eastman Dry Plate and Film Company. With this, Eastman was ready to tackle the European market. In May 1885, the company participated in the International Inventions Exhibition in London. Walker presented the roll holders under the title "Apparatus for the production of negatives in the photographic camera from continuous rolls of paper." The company won a silver medal and favorable reviews from the British photographic press. Eastman opened an office that year in London, and Walker became its manager.

Eastman also created seventeen standardized roll holder components that were interchangeable. But, once again, things weren't completely rosy. Professional studio photographers and amateurs were not going to drop plates for rolls overnight, so the market wasn't large enough. Additionally, his wares had serious technical problems, and pundits were slamming the company. As proud as he was of the new "permanent bromide paper" he had introduced in 1885 and his upcoming enlarging service, he had serious damage control to do on all fronts.

Seven years had passed: Eastman was now well known, but he was incurring the wrath and sarcasm of competitors who resented his chutzpah. He also knew that he still had a long way to go to reach an undeniable quality level. He had to improve his films, but while doing so he couldn't afford to let other trains pass by without him on board. He had to offer more: a camera capable of exploiting a roll of transparent film.

There were no real Goliaths in the space, but differentiating himself from all the other Davids wasn't a piece of cake either. Even if you believe that innovating is about seeing the light, remember that it may also be the art of persistently groping around . . .

A Better Detective Camera

Combining the roll holder and paper negative film with a handheld camera called a "detective camera" was the next logical move, and not a novel idea either.

The detective camera was one of the crazes of the day, mostly thanks to Thomas Bolas, a professor in chemistry at Charing Cross Hospital's medical school in London as well as a scientific journalist who contributed to important publications such as *Chemical News*, the *Journal of the Photographic Society*, and *Photographic News*. He had become an active member of the Royal Photographic Society in 1875, and in late 1881 he had introduced a hand camera that looked like a box to assist law enforcement. The term "detective camera" caught on like wildfire and inspired multiple do-it-yourself (DYI) enthusiasts until the end of the century, the most famous one being William Schmid's detective camera patented in 1883.[12]

So Eastman joined the pack. In March 1886, he applied for his own version of a patent, written with Franklin Cossitt.[13] It was a box-form hand camera that could be used either with a roll holder or with conventional plates. The result was everything but a success: Manufacturing these cameras was hard and costly. By June 1887, only fifty of them had been produced. Eastman wisely put an end to the disaster. Meanwhile, as he grew increasingly famous, he was also increasingly at loggerheads with the E. & H. T. Anthony & Company, which stole two of his employees, including Franklin Cossitt. It wasn't quite the Wild West, but close, only on the East Coast.

Democratizing Photography: When It All Adds Up

At this stage, Eastman had to shift gears, which entailed getting better control of his company's image and its destiny with better film and a camera that was easier to manufacture.

In March 1888 Eastman filed for a new patent called "Camera."[14] He stated that he had "invented certain new and useful improvements in Cameras," and described in forty-one claims the combination of the different components that constituted his product. This was a turning point that would lead to several cameras, including the "Kodak" and the "Brownie."

What Eastman designated as a "roll holder breast camera" was put on the market in June 1888 under a striking name, the Kodak. The device was advertised with a memorable slogan: "You Press the Button, We Do the Rest." Just as meaningful was the subtitle: "The only camera that anybody can use without instructions." The message was very close to Walker's 1881 "Photography made easy for everybody" but with a stylistic nuance that mattered: Eastman was not speaking of a product or of a genre. He was addressing the user of the product: "You."

"You" could be anybody. Until then, professional and skilled amateurs had been swimming in the same pond. Now Eastman was addressing anybody, with no particular training or skill, who could spend $25. Admittedly, this wasn't quite anybody, since these $25 corresponded to $700 in today's money—or ten-to-twelve days of salary for a person working a skilled occupation at the time. But the absence of knowledge prerequisites greatly expanded the pie of potential customers.

The Kodak was loaded with a film for one hundred exposures. Then, the camera could be returned to the Eastman company to develop and print the picture for ten dollars. The camera was sent back after four weeks with the prints and the negatives and loaded with a new roll of film. Returning cameras was a necessity because daylight-loading cameras with packaged roll films were not yet possible. The mandatory return was, in a way, a forerunner to the novel "razor and blades" business model.[15]

The Kodak was a beautiful object. As a rule, there had always been meticulous craftsmanship involved in cameras, but Eastman exceeded expectations for a lower-priced device by hiring the services of an independent designer, Frank Brownell, a cabinetmaker who had started to make cameras in the early 1880s. Eastman had commissioned him to make parts for the roll film holder in 1885, and Brownell ended up designing most of Eastman's early signature cameras.[16]

Eastman focused on the user experience, a critical component to drive the adoption of any innovation. He was closing in on what he had wanted to do in the first place when he was an employee in a bank—to take pictures—although this had led him to first spend ten years working on how to make and process pictures. Now, he was at a point when he could speak directly to the imagination of the well-paid twenty-something-year-old clerk somewhere who didn't feel like taking lessons to simply enjoy capturing images of his life.

The focus on picture taking led to a critical innovation at this point in time. The camera was expensive, but the value for the customers was to have these pictures, and after three rolls of pictures and hours of pleasure taking them and looking at them, the price of the camera felt psychologically like nothing. This meant everything for the company: recurring revenues. The tight integration of all the components made it obvious to users that the company was in the best position to sell and process the films. In the photography rat race, this approach was an innovative stroke of business genius, and the company was renamed Eastman Kodak in 1892.

Eastman realized that the sale of films, not the sale of cameras, would be the cornerstone of his company's success. So, film quality was paramount. Eastman had started to look for trained chemists, a novel idea at the time. He hired Henry Reichenbach, an undergraduate assistant at the University of Rochester.[17] His task was to continue the experiments to produce a transparent, flexible film, which led to a nitrocellulose material, the first flexible film base. Reichenbach filed a patent for Eastman in April 1889 for the "manufacture of flexible films," something that was much needed because the rolls of photographic film that the company had just launched in 1888 were made of paper.[18] This patent set off a long battle with the Rev. Hannibal Goodwin, who had filed a very close patent for camera film on celluloid rolls.[19] But this was not the end of Eastman's emulsion problems. In 1892 and 1894, sales in cameras and film dropped. Customers were dissatisfied. After an attack by the *Chicago Tribune* in November 1892, Eastman responded, albeit not for publication: "Film photography, while it has been brought to a practical stage, will require several years of experiment and improvement to perfect it."[20]

Despite these hiccups, the Kodak Camera was an enormous success, which led to the improved No.2 Kodak. Eastman added more camera models, like the Folding Kodak, capable of taking rectangular pictures, at a higher price point. His mind was set on taking hold of the entire market spectrum with "Kodaks at any price, $5 to $50." He also marketed his first daylight-loading camera and made packaged roll film available in 1891, which eliminated the necessity of returning the camera to the factory. Competition was so fierce that journalists were often quick to deny Eastman the privilege of being the first in anything. For example, in 1902, a British publication, the *Photographic Dealer*, noted that the idea had been introduced by the European Blair Camera Company in 1893, a firm initially started in Boston and with which Eastman also had a conflicted relationship.[21] Did this matter? No. Being the first is an ego booster but doesn't guarantee whether customers will buy or not, which is the cornerstone of accomplishment.

The "Brownie," designed by Brownell, was introduced in 1900, selling for one dollar and using film that cost fifteen cents a roll. It was a huge hit, as was the No.2 Brownie the following year. It introduced instantaneous photography, that is, a picture with no exposure time, an idea that had been pursued for decades and had been called "snap-shot" by John

Herschel in 1860, a term that Eastman popularized as "snapshot."[22] This time, Eastman was truly democratizing photography. The name, inspired by a best-selling series of cartoons created by Palmer Cox, *The Brownies* (fairies and goblins fashioned after Celtic mythology), was also particularly attention grabbing, which also shows that marketing is not the after-the-fact dressing of innovative endeavors but intrinsically part of it.

By 1900 Eastman Kodak was the largest photography manufacturer in the world, had thousands of employees, and was ahead of competitors thanks to one thing, the only thing that mattered: the company had captured the zeitgeist and become part of the everyday lives and dreams of people. It had even introduced a "Bicycle camera" in 1897 designed to be used while riding! The organization continued to innovate unabated for decades. As a reminder, a Kodak engineer Steven Sasson invented the first portable digital camera in the company's R&D labs in 1975, even though Kodak, at the time, failed to shift toward this novel opportunity, a topic I will discuss in chapter 12.

BIG THINGS START SMALL

Incremental steps define Eastman's innovation journey. Remember what Jeff Bezos said at the end of a PBS *Frontline* episode, "Amazon Empire": "Think about this. Big things start small."[23] The "big picture" and the "next big thing" make us dream of extraordinary end results. But if you want to be more than an urbane futurologist or a failed dreamer, you're better off getting down to brass tacks.

The Art of Micromanagement

What accounts for the success of Eastman was undoubtedly his drive as a founder, his deep knowledge of the history of photography, his extensive personal culture, his extreme attention to keeping abreast of everything that was happening, his listening and questioning skills, his ability to adapt and quickly master the manufacturing and management requirements necessary for the organization, and his capacity to hire and fire people as and when needed. When you combine all of these skills, you find out that great innovators are extremely detail oriented and often prone to micromanagement. Other companies couldn't catch up to the relentlessness and obstinacy of Eastman: he was deeply motivated and involved in pushing his industry faster than most everybody else, and because of that, he could act decisively on the inner workings of his own company and make sure that his organization charged ahead continuously.

Eastman had a kind of big picture in mind, even though this started with a need to solve the practical problems he had experienced after he bought his first photographic equipment. Still, when you think of all the causes for defects and failures that can happen when you start a business, it's healthy to place the "big" picture in the background and, instead, think in terms of "snapshots." Realize that in 1894—that is, almost fifteen years after his first steps—Eastman still had to admit that his Kodak films couldn't keep longer than six months. That's why he hired William Stuber (1864–1959), who had a great reputation as a portrait photographer, spent time studying emulsion techniques, and had invested in a new plate coating machine produced in Zurich.[24]

For Eastman, the big picture wasn't an abstract grand purpose but an entanglement of human, mechanical, and chemical details that demanded sustained attention. The strongest strategies often hinge on details that are context dependent and condition the acceptance of an innovation, a topic I will further develop in chapter 5.

Forget the Tempest and Listen to the "Rustling of the Breeze"

Innovating is a long sequence of missteps and small advances. This was true at the end of the nineteenth century, and it was still obvious to Peter Drucker decades later when he invited entrepreneurs to come back down to earth:

> Successful entrepreneurs do not wait until "the Muse kisses them" and
> gives them a "bright idea"; they go to work. Altogether, they do not look

for the "biggie," the innovation that will "revolutionize the industry," create a "billion-dollar business," or "make one rich overnight." Those entrepreneurs who start out with the idea that they'll make it big—and in a hurry—can be guaranteed failure. They are almost bound to do the wrong things. An innovation that looks very big may turn out to be nothing but technical virtuosity; and innovations with modest intellectual pretensions, a McDonald's, for instance, may turn into gigantic, highly profitable businesses. The same applies to nonbusiness, public-service innovations. In other words, "Grandiose ideas, plans that aim at revolutionizing an industry," are unlikely to work.[25]

So, if "innovative opportunities do not come with the tempest but with the rustling of the breeze," are most people left with small or, I should say, smaller innovations?[26] Yes, until further notice, be they innovators in an established organization or in a startup.

THE SURVIVALIST'S ODYSSEY

As lofty as innovators' goals may be, the daily life of innovators is more like rafting through muddy rivers in which they have to make sure that their boat isn't gutted by a stray tree trunk or an invisible rock. What makes innovators survive is an all-out pragmatism that means changing course when necessary and escaping whirlpools.

Changing Course as You Go

Photography was a hazardous business, where nothing could be established for a long time and ideas were popping up all over. Eastman had a lot of ideas that worked and quite a few that didn't. In one of his visionary moments, he may have been the first to see the potential of paper. Between 1885 and 1887, he became the only American manufacturer of gelatin-bromide developing-out paper (DOP). However, this was ultimately a mistake: By 1889 he had to face the growing demand for printing-out paper (POP) and shift gears quickly. DOP required special equipment to reveal the latent image made by exposure to light, whereas POP enabled forming a visible image directly from the reaction of light on light-sensitive materials and producing warmer tones.[27] As a result, photographers preferred POP and went to a newly formed company, the American Aristotype Company, as well as multiple other smaller businesses. Eastman had to improvise his first offering, Solio, in 1892. Instead of coming out ahead because of his singular idea, he won the paper battle through all sorts of business schemes, like preventing retailers from selling other manufacturers' papers or licensing his patents to archenemies to fix prices, until he acquired the American Aristotype Company in 1901. But again, business schemes are part of the arms race that you have to get into if you want to innovate.

Snatching Victory from Jaws of Defeat

Eastman reaped the benefits of being in the midst of a messy world. Everyone was trying all sorts of methods to come up with better dry plates, better film, better paper, or better cameras, but they were also exposed to selling unreliable goods. The advantage was that they could get away with quality issues provided that they reacted quickly and dodged flak by constantly coming out with fixes and more promising offerings. Innovating was (and still is) not only about coming up with new ideas but also about snatching victory from the jaws of defeat and waging attrition wars with competitors, big or small.

At the same time, entrepreneurs in the industry were faced at all steps of the way with unstable supply chains (e.g., changing a gelatin provider could mean that your entire emulsion was compromised), rubber shortages, trained scientists who lacked the creativity of tinkerers, internal sabotage and political infighting (before leaving, Reichenbach spoiled 1,417 gallons of emulsion), and a serious economic crisis in 1893, to name just a few of the problems that Eastman had to take in stride.

Most clearheaded innovators rarely dream of disruption in the sense of creating a breakthrough product or service that changes the world. They are constantly dealing with frustrating and sometimes trivial disruptions that threaten to derail their efforts. They spend most of their time addressing problems because they know that falling from grace can happen fast.

Navigating Whirlpools

Great companies usually emerge from effervescent environments and rarely from the mind of a genius in the middle of a desert. But this position also means that anybody may be ready to get in bed with anybody else, and that everybody knows, or thinks they know, something about everybody else. It's a whirlpool of people, ideas, and skirmishes.

In Eastman's world (and still today), patents were a big part of the game, as were lawsuits. In fact, everything that anybody did either sneakily or openly infringed on somebody else's intellectual property. The minute a patent was published (and lag times were short), you could be sure that somebody would concoct a workaround. The problem was compounded by the fact that employees were hopping from one organization to the other and often prone to settling scores with their former bosses. For example, one of Eastman's informers warned him that one of his employees was working up a bromide paper in the interest of Anthony. Of course, Eastman responded in kind. By the end of the 1890s, he more or less controlled his business through patents, though.

Are things different today? Of course not! Think of the disputes between Oracle and SAP, Apple and Microsoft, Microsoft and Motorola, Apple and Samsung, Google and Uber, and Apple and Qualcomm or the "dogfight" between Google and Apple.[28] And these are a minuscule fraction of the lawsuits in which companies engage every day to defend their turf. Today, between five thousand and six thousand patent violation cases are filed each year in the United States.[29] No wonder: "The numbers of patent applications and awards have risen greatly over the nation's history. In 1791 a total of 33 utility patents were awarded; in 2015, a total of 298,407."[30]

In parallel, also think of the ubiquitous poaching hiring practices that once happened at a local level and have scaled up to unbelievable proportions because of platforms such as LinkedIn worldwide, Maimai in China, or Xing in Germany, and other generalist social networks!

ACCOMMODATIVE AMPLITUDE AND PERIPHERAL VISION

One of the strengths of innovators is their accommodative amplitude, that is, their ability to have a clear focus whether the goal stands at a far or near point.

The Innovator's Optical Power

I won't dig into what makes us willing to innovate. There are a lot of books that already do that. For example, in *Wired to Create* Scott Barry Kaufman and Carolyn Gregoire develop the intricate and sometimes contradictory characteristics of the creative mind.[31] On the more business-oriented side, Clayton Christensen, Jeff Dyer, and Hal Gregersen in *The Innovator's DNA* emphasize the five discovery skills that distinguish innovative entrepreneurs and executives from ordinary managers: associating, questioning, observing, networking, and experimenting.[32]

I would add that in order to innovate, we must summon in ourselves what American developmental psychologist Howard Gardner called our multiple intelligences: musical, bodily-kinesthetic, logical-mathematical, linguistic, spatial, interpersonal, and intrapersonal, as well as naturalistic, existential, and pedagogical. Although apparently independent, "nearly every cultural role of any degree of sophistication requires a combination of intelligences."[33] Consequently, individuals are as a collection of aptitudes, which are all summoned to some degree as they try to solve problems. The lesson here is that we must develop a full open-mindedness all the time. It's hard, because once we start something, we tend to become mono-maniacal and mono-dimensional.

What makes innovators who they are isn't merely that they have a vision. Everyone can dream. More important, innovators must have the

optical and mental power to deliver on a vision by distinctly apprehend-
ing situations, evaluating their relevance at both the landscape and detail
levels, scanning the periphery, and picking up all sorts of weak signals.[34]
This ability to be keep observing and processing information enables
them to continuously extend and update their knowledge, maintain versatile conceptualization skills, and recursively test themselves in handling
the nitty-gritty. This is all but easy, because our daily lives can be so stress-
ful that we want to believe that we know it all, that our thoughts can be
cast in stone, and that the nuts and bolts are for others. That's also when
even the brightest people can fall victim to myopia and focalism.

- *Myopia, or nearsightedness*: Here, I'm referring to the fact that innovators can be so deeply immersed in their field that they become
  unable to see the relationship between what they do and a parent
  genre. It's as if Jeff Bezos had decided not to sell apparel or cosmetics because his original business was books.
- *Focalism*, sometimes called the focusing illusion: It is the tendency
  for people to place too much focus on one particular piece of information and give it too much weight. As a result, they tend to ne-
  glect other important factors and, consequently, make inaccurate
  judgments or bad decisions.

Myopia and focalism are very close, but there is a nuance. In the case
of myopia, people can't see structural similarities between two apparently
dissimilar activities. In the case of focalism, people refuse to incorporate
new information that would help them make better decisions related to
their topic of focus, either because they're afraid to be wrong or because
they rely on a biased vision of the world.

Myopia's Risks

Everything I read about Eastman made me think that his optical power
was consistent. But I noticed one case in which Eastman could have been
dangerously nearsighted, had he not been advised by his team, William

Walker, William Stuber (who would succeed Eastman as president and chairman of the board in 1925), and his friend George Dickman.

In the mid-1890s Eastman's business was thriving, and despite dozens of problems it was on a continuous growth path. Then, two spaces started to form: X-rays and motion pictures. Eastman exhibited two very different reactions.

X-rays were discovered by German physicist Wilhelm Röntgen (who would win a Nobel Prize in 1901) at the end of 1895. Some six weeks after his discovery, he took a radiograph of his wife's hand. Walker and Stuber brought Eastman's attention to this technology's potential. It was easy to gain Eastman's interest for two reasons: his respect for scientific knowledge and his experience with photographic plates. The latter were a part of the company's DNA and still widely used. In 1902 Eastman acquired the Seed Dry Plate Co., a company founded in 1883 in St. Louis, Missouri, whose dry plates were regarded as the finest in the world. The combination of deep experience and a meaningful acquisition enabled Kodak to quickly gain the reputation for producing the best X-ray product.

However, it was much harder to convince him of the potential of motion pictures. Thomas Edison and William Dickson had created the Kinetoscope, designed for films to be viewed by one person at a time through a peephole, which was followed by the Kinetograph, a motion picture camera. In the 1890s, the space was bustling, a little bit like in the early days of photography, with dozens of inventors in Europe and in the United States. But Eastman first dismissed the genre as a fad, and even though he wanted to democratize photography he looked at this new space as trivial entertainment for the masses. In his mind, photography was an art involving the creative mind of a photographer, whereas motion pictures just offered crowd-pleasing recreation with filmmakers exploiting passive mass gullibility.

He relented upon the insistence of Edison, with whom he had been corresponding since the 1880s, but even more important because of the enthusiasm of his longtime partners in Rochester, as well as the influence of Henry Strong and George Dickman, the trusted man who was now running Eastman-Kodak. George Dickman proved to Eastman that he was already swamped with requests from French filmmakers. Eastman gave in and applied all his business acumen, so much so that by the early 1910s the company had become a major player in the new industry.

Focalism

Innovators must develop an intense focus on what they do. They have to be obsessed and obsessive in order to succeed. However, this very focus can backfire and turn into focalism, if they fear that any new piece of information might destabilize their plans. What's striking about Eastman is his absence of focalism and his extraordinary determination to look at what he knew as an incentive to always know more.

There are quite a few examples illustrating innovators' focalism. And sometimes, this is what causes them to lose in a space that they once dominated or in which they could have expanded. Focalism tricked Edison a few times. As a proponent of direct current (DC), he refused to see that the alternating current (AC) generation and transmission technologies developed by Nikola Tesla were promising.[35] Similarly, he couldn't let go of his early invention of the phonograph.[36] Closer to us, the case of Steve Jobs is also interesting.

In 1981 Apple was a very successful company thanks to the Apple II, which had become the most desirable personal computer. When IBM announced that year that it was getting into the personal computer market, Apple, all wrapped up in the Apple II's great sales, "welcomed" IBM with a full-page ad in the *Wall Street Journal* titled "Welcome, IBM. Seriously," followed by a sarcastic text defying IBM to make a dent in a market that had started without them: "Over the next decade, the growth of the personal computer will continue in logarithmic leaps. We look forward to responsible competition in the massive effort to distribute this American technology to the world. And we appreciate the magnitude of your commitment. Because what we are doing is increasing social capital by enhancing individual productivity. Welcome to the task. Apple."[37] This was a stylish way to throw down the gauntlet . . . but also playing with fire!

Apple wasn't happy to find out how ready for a duel IBM was. Apple had not taken full measure of the acumen and efficacy of the people who created the PC computer division of IBM: Bill Lowe and Don Estridge (whom Jobs unsuccessfully tried to hire later).

Estridge, who was an Apple II user, ensured that his team operated quickly and enrolled third-party hardware and software left and right from the beginning. By underestimating competition and dismissing market research and statistics, Steve Jobs didn't give the Macintosh the best possible chances of success. There was a downside to what Bud Tribble famously called Steve's "reality distortion field." Reality isn't always "malleable," and may speak loud and clear: by the end of 1986, the PC platform had passed the 50 percent market share mark, reaching 84 percent in 1990, while the Macintosh stabilized at approximately a 6 percent market share. In other words, not only could a venerable and bureaucratic organization like IBM breed internal entrepreneurial mavericks, but it could also coin a deal with an external genius, Bill Gates.

Focalism often feeds on enduring stereotypes, like the assumption that large organizations can't innovate. This is almost always a major miscalculation: while it's true that large companies may wither away from failing to rejuvenate, thousands of younger ones can collapse from failing to analyze why it's difficult to break through. My advice to innovators is this: surround yourselves with people who have the guts to debias your intellectual modus operandi and remind you every day that regardless of your strength in your space, change is the only constant.

INNOVATION IS NOT A ZERO-SUM GAME

As soon as a new space emerges, a lot of people step into it. It was true in the nineteenth century, just as it is today. Think of the thousands of food delivery, fintech, artificial intelligence, augmented reality, virtual reality, drone, blockchain, or robotics companies that pop up every single day all over the world. Will a winner take all? No.

Innovation isn't so much defined by the urge to anachronize prior products as it is characterized by the eagerness to alter, deform, transform,

or recombine prior art. Innovation is first and foremost driven by the desire to create some novelty that will resonate with an audience. The phenomenon of anachronism, which happens progressively, is only an effect
that isn't necessarily under an innovator's control. It's our customers who
decide if and how and when innovations fit in their world.

The history of innovation is not a zero-sum game. Many companies
didn't survive the aggressive business acumen of Eastman Kodak. But
we can look at this in two ways: Did they fail because Eastman was too
good, or did they fail because they weren't good enough? The debate is
open. Meanwhile, however, their disappearance doesn't mean that they
weren't innovative at one point or another. Actually, they all contributed to
the buildup of the effervescent environment that propped and bolstered
the emergence of new players. The existence of Eastman Kodak would
have been impossible without the hundreds of people who tinkered with
wet plates, dry plates, emulsions, roll films, and papers. This collective
rivalry is what made Eastman keep an all-out alertness, employing his
optical powers, adaptability, and tenacity to ultimately outmaneuver his
competitors.

We can also see that by constantly morphing the photography market,
he encouraged new and older businesses to try their luck in the remod-
eled space. In the United States, Ansco surfaced from the merging of two
of Eastman's main enemies, Anthony & Scovill, which had combined in
1901, and the Goodwin Camera & Film Company. Ansco merged with
German company Agfa in 1928 to form Agfa-Ansco. Thornton-Pickard,
founded in 1888, remained popular in the UK well into the 1920s. The
Flemish Gevaert & Co, which started in 1884 as a dry plate company,
only merged with Agfa AG in 1964. Agfa itself had been founded by Paul
Mendelssohn Bartholdy (the second son of composer Felix Mendelssohn)
and Carl Alexander von Martius in 1867 as a manufacturer of dyes and
stains, introducing X-ray plates and film products in 1898 and producing
cinematographic film by 1903. At the same time, the maturing field of
photography led to an acceleration in related domains, like optical manufacturers. Leica, founded by mechanic and self-educated mathematician
Carl Kellner in 1849, first produced microscopes and added photography

when Oskar Barnack created the prototype of his 35mm camera in 1913. This is of course true as well for Zeiss, also in Germany (started in 1846), or for Nikon (started in Japan in 1917).

Although Kodak did command close to 90 percent of the film and camera sales in the United States until the early 1970s, it succeeded not because it had a monopoly but because, along with others, it was part of a world that was both shaping and leveraging new behaviors. For example, the popularity of amateur photography changed the way people perceived their own identity. They modified their demeanor for a world in which they could be photographed. They knew that their image could be shared, so they wanted to be at their best, which impacted the world of fashion and cosmetics. Photography also opened up people to the world: pictures from the World War I trenches taken by the American soldiers who carried their Brownies on the French front transformed the war into a visceral, personal experience.

Is all of this still true today? Yes, it is, but maybe not for the reasons we assume. The increased pace of change could first and foremost be the effect of an ever-increasing number of geniuses in the world at large—which means that innovators in every single country today must accelerate their iteration processes and, in some cases, use artificial intelligence systems to more efficiently model them.

CONCLUSION

The history of the early years of Kodak illustrates several key aspects of the innovation journey:

1. Innovators rarely start from nothing and are not necessarily the first to tackle a space. They insert themselves in an environment with prior foundations, whose characteristics, whatever they are, they must experience for themselves through intense learning. They must analyze and also react with open-mindedness to everything that's happening around them.
2. The space they operate in is dynamically altered by other players,

which requires continuous and opportunistic adjustments to novel conditions. While many aspiring innovators all come at the "right time" and insert themselves in the same "window of opportunity," their understanding of the environment can greatly vary (two topics that are closely related and that I will address in chapters 4 and 5).

3. All participants in a given space can be innovators on their own terms, and whatever they do can add to the dynamics of the ecosystem, even if larger innovations end up diminishing their historical value by causing progress to accelerate. But this too is temporary. Innovation is never a zero-sum game even at the time it's established, let alone as time moves on.

4. Innovative entrepreneurs must be as detailed oriented as visionary. Being a visionary primarily means the ability to see and thus maintain an accommodative amplitude at all times, and to use your optical power in order not to miss the details (let alone the big trends) that might destroy you. While often presented as an example of "disruption," the story of Eastman illustrates the opposite. As I will discuss in the next chapter, the disruption terminology may offer a broad-brush depiction of how innovations come across in retrospect but doesn't convey the haphazardness of the innovation journey and the fact that innovators are players in a collective game that's much bigger than who they are individually.

3

Do You Need to Be Disruptive?

In order to carry out a positive action we must develop
a positive vision.
—The Fourteenth Dalai Lama

Do you buy an Apple watch because you want it or because it disrupts the Swiss watch industry? It's likely the former. Today's popularity of coupling the words "innovation" and "disruption" is largely a consequence of the success of Clayton Christensen's books (written by him or in collaboration with other authors).

What can you really make of his theory of disruptive innovation? Can it help you to conceive a product or service that will be perceived as innovative? Should it influence your thought process and your understanding of what innovating entails? How descriptive is it of the innovating process or its outcome in general, and of yours in particular?

When we make a principle our own, it's useful to know where it's coming from, the circumstances under which it was adopted, the scope of its applicability, and how it fares when tested for verifiability or falsifiability. This chapter explores the overall context in which the disruption lexicon appeared. If you don't know where a theory about innovation comes from and yet it is presented to you like gospel, what makes you think that it could be a guiding principle? When we want to innovate, it's precisely because we don't take at face value everything we see or hear; we look at the world differently, applying our optical powers with an open mind. We question even sacrosanct opinions, because it's when we don't that we can't figure out if, when, or why we might be going in the wrong direction.

THE THEME OF DISRUPTION BEFORE
CHRISTENSEN'S BOOKS

Ideas, just like products, don't appear out of thin air. To understand why Christensen's disruption lexicon caught on like wildfire, it's useful to remember the backdrop in which it emerged: a zeitgeist that generated extensive research in the epistemology of sciences and a wealth of innovation studies conducted by academics. Both started in the 1960s and flourished over the two following decades.

The "Age of Discontinuity" Zeitgeist

Peter Drucker's *The Age of Discontinuity*, originally published in 1969, captured the zeitgeist of the 1960s.[1] Subtitled *Guidelines to Our Changing Society*, the work presented a new epoch shaped by the advent of new technologies and major changes in social and economic life, and it assigned a new role to knowledge. The purpose of the book was not to project trends but to respond to this question: "What do we have to tackle today to make tomorrow?" In a way, it was spelling out foundational aspects of the "New Frontier" that John F. Kennedy had heralded in his acceptance speech in the 1960 US presidential election.

At the time, epistemologists of sciences, philosophers, and sociologists highlighted the irregular paths of history. They exposed that novelty in the arts, sciences, and society often rise from dismantling established truths operating as "epistemological obstacles," to use an expression that French philosopher Gaston Bachelard (1884–1962) had coined in 1938 to designate preconceptions that can prevent us from augmenting our knowledge.[2] Bachelard impacted countless writings in the 1960s, notably, research around the fact that the history of sciences and societies is punctuated by ruptures frequently overlooked by evolutionary-oriented narratives. In the United States, a similar perspective was developed by Thomas Kuhn in his 1962 landmark book *The Structure of Scientific Revolutions*.[3] Largely influenced by the history of physics, especially Max Planck's first quantum revolution, he too emphasized the nonlinear progression of scientific domains and showed how the cumulative effect of anomalies to accepted laws undermines existing paradigms and sooner or later topples them.[4]

Kuhn's book was an enormous success, but it was also often distorted by people who hadn't read it. Kuhn was too knowledgeable to ever contend that the history of sciences is only about changing paradigms. Instead, he emphasized that it's just as much about looking into what he called "normal science" to actually understand how "puzzle solving" gradually leads to paradigm shifts that change a scientific community's perspective and redirect its attention. Shifts happen when too many exceptions deviate from an existing rule. Yet Kuhn never implied that older paradigms are immediately trashed. Instead, he demonstrated that revolutions aren't so much about violently overturning prior visions as they are about "moving away from" conceptions whose operative value has reached its limits.[5] In the business sphere, this is an aspect that was well understood by Robert Foster's *Innovation: The Attacker's Advantage* (1986), where he explained how limits encountered in a technology genre call for a different course.[6]

Christensen's idea of disruption fits into the spirit of the second part of the twentieth century. However, he abstracted it from its context. Scientists, philosophers, and sociologists were working on societal shifts, discontinuances, displacements, rearrangements, and discontinuities at a macrolevel. They didn't say that epistemological ruptures were caused by one event or one person that would suddenly turn everything upside down. Even a giant like Max Planck, whose quantum theory revolutionized physics, acknowledged that new models don't take hold overnight, no matter how transformative they are: "An important scientific innovation rarely makes its way by gradually winning over and converting its opponents: it rarely happens that Saul becomes Paul. What does happen is that its opponents gradually die out, and that the growing generation is familiarized with the ideas from the beginning: another instance of the fact that the future lies with the youth."[7]

So what made Christensen believe that one company or a group of companies might single-handedly operate miracles with a disruption mindset as a magic wand? It's unclear, but the economic context of the mid-1990s probably helped. After some unsteadiness at the end of the

1980s, the American economy recovered and the Clinton era displayed strong economic performance. Consultants left and right exhorted companies not to miss out on the opportunities the decade was promising, as was clear from an article that Christensen wrote with Joseph Bower in early 1995 titled "Disruptive Technologies: Catching the Wave."[8] "Catching the wave" of growth was a rallying cry, and the idea of "disruptive technologies" was positioned as a differentiator between companies—as well as between management consultants. This article reads like an introduction to the books that followed.

Christensen began the article with the statement that large companies are in a bind. The same "processes and incentives that [they] use to keep focused on their main customers [and that] work so well also blind [them] to important new technologies in emerging markets." However, these new technologies will eventually spread, traditional companies will be outpaced, and their customers will desert them in favor of pioneers. So the solution for companies is to free themselves from the pressure of their existing base, avoid the pitfalls of confining themselves to only "sustaining technologies," and move ahead with "disruptive technologies." Christensen enjoined corporations to move out of their comfort zone, restructure their workforce, define new trajectories, and eventually start a disruptive-technology business as an independent organization.

In essence, Christensen was brandishing the advice-to-management torch with a new wording for a common predicament in liberal economies since the early 1800s. If a business continues to do what it's used to doing and if competitors propose novel products or business models, the business will dwindle. How such a truism ended up being hailed as illuminative and granted an intellectual blank check is another story . . .

Studies on Innovation Conducted by Academics around That Time

Christensen's disruption lexicon also sits against a backdrop of academic studies started in the 1960s. Scholars were classifying innovations based on a variety of macroeconomic or company-level criteria, which often led to multiple sets of categorizations: regular versus radical, niche versus architectural, nondrastic versus drastic, incremental versus breakthrough, incremental versus radical, routine versus radical, evolutionary versus revolutionary, and so forth. How an innovation was placed in one category rather than in another depended on the frame of reference adopted by researchers.[9]

Of particular interest is a 1985 model proposed by William Abernathy and Kim Clark.[10] They analyzed the competitive implications of innovation and more specifically "the capacity of an innovation to influence the established systems of production and marketing," a capacity they called "transilience." They created a framework illustrating the "transilience" of different innovation types (regular, niche, revolutionary, architectural) for selective automotive innovations at Ford, GM, and Chrysler.

A turning point in the innovation literature, this model was one of the first to articulate how some innovations may conserve/entrench existing competence or linkages or, on the contrary, disrupt existing linkages / create new ones or disrupt/obsolete existing competence. It also showed that different kinds of innovations tend to be associated with different competitive environments as well as with different kinds of organizational and managerial skills.

The Abernathy and Clark paper is remarkable for its nuances: "Our application of the transilience map to the history of the auto industry shows that all four kinds of innovation have shaped the industry's development in subtle and diverse ways," which can vary across players. For example, "while GM and Chrysler (and others) were at work on new concepts in suspensions, brakes, transmissions, and bodies, Ford's development efforts were largely focused on the cost of manufacture." Also, the history of automobile showed that these four innovation models could be operated within one firm at the same time: "While one part of the product line may be in the regular phase of development, the firm may try to introduce a revolutionary development in another, and may try to develop new niches in a third."[11]

A few years later, the same Kim Clark, this time with Rebecca Henderson, complemented this paper by elaborating on the aspects of architectural innovation and the risks incurred by companies that would fail to assess them.[12] After explaining that characterizing innovation as either incremental or radical was incomplete and potentially misleading, Henderson and Clark showed that major architecture changes in products do not necessarily imply changing their components. That's why Sony's radios displaced RCA with a technology licensed from RCA itself.

Christensen followed a less analytical path. He caught the attention of a business community by implicitly lumping his idea of disruption with Schumpeter's popular "creative destruction" phrase discussed in *Capitalism, Socialism and Democracy*, a book often mentioned but more rarely read.[13] Christensen's disruption was and still is often perceived as some scaled-down version of the idea of "creative destruction." Except that it's a stretch. Schumpeter had explicitly excluded such interpretation when he elaborated on "the Process of Creative Destruction."[14] This process is, in actuality, "creative." It's a self-reconstructing global evolutionary process that characterizes the capitalist engine at large and doesn't apply to individual initiatives: "Since we are dealing with an organic process, analysis of what happens in any particular part of it—say, in an individual concern or industry—may indeed clarify details of mechanism but is inconclusive beyond that."

Christensen distanced himself from the contexts in which the idea of disruption originated, which affects his validation. Does it matter? If you have an academic background, it might. To be fair, however, we could argue that Christensen was innovative by importing ideas from the epistemology of sciences and academic research spaces into a business sphere, where validation criteria are less rigorous. But then, some questions we can ask are the following: Does exhorting large companies to disrupt themselves in order to innovate allow one to infer that innovation is about disruption? Is the disruption lexicon a useful descriptor of innovation as a process or its outcome? How representative are the examples chosen to shore up the theory? These are topics we will examine in the rest of this chapter.

WHAT IS DISRUPTIVE INNOVATION FOR CHRISTENSEN?

Christensen contributed to making the words "disruptive" and "disruption" fixtures of the business discourse. As shown in Google Books

Ngram, the terms picked up in the 1970s and 1980s and now occupy a stable plateau (figure 4).[15]

Christensen warned against misinterpretations of his theory but with moderate success. Its inflationist use was too good of a business. Given that his position is usually well known, I will only focus on some of its fundamentals as well as the pitfalls that they encapsulate.

Christensen's Definitions

An innovation is said to be disruptive when it messes up an existing market and/or an existing value network and creates a new market and/or a new value network. There are two types of disruptive innovations starting from two different places, the low-end foothold and the new-market foothold.[16]

The low-end foothold: This is when an entrant comes up with a more cost-effective solution, which undermines the current cost-benefit structures of incumbents. The example of Southwest Airlines mentioned by Christensen is still relevant today: it forced high-end airlines to enter that market with low-cost offerings.

The new-market foothold: Disruption creates a new market and transforms nonconsumers into consumers. An example is the history of photocopying technology, that is, the Xerox case also analyzed by others.

Disruptive innovation doesn't necessarily refer to a product that makes such a sensational entrance that it brings ingrained markets down, even if it's often interpreted this way, a distinction that lifts some of the ambiguities attached to the idea of disruption in popular culture. Christensen's reasoning is subtler. In the case of a low-end market disruption that targets an unaddressed or poorly addressed market segment, the disrupter offers a cheaper product that's easier to use and more convenient. That product may not have all the bells and whistles you could imagine, but it has the features at a price point that make people want to "hire" that product: "Disruptive innovations don't attempt to bring better products to established customers in existing markets," Christensen writes. "Rather

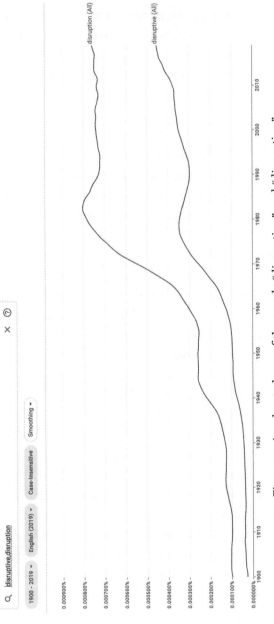

Figure 4. Accelerated use of the words "disruption" and "disruptive."

Credit: Google Books Ngram Viewer, http://books.google.com/ngrams.

they disrupt and redefine that trajectory by introducing products and services that are not as good as currently available products. But disruptive technologies offer other benefits—typically they are simpler, more convenient, and less expensive products that appeal to new or less demanding customers."[17]

An important part of Christensen's rationale is that established companies tend to discard disruptors because the latter serve a market with smaller margins. In addition, when established companies notice new entrants, they may still adopt a head-in-the-sand attitude, stick to their current cash cows, their margins, and the overall equilibria that define the routine of their organization or move up-market as much as they can. Then, they realize, too late, that customers aren't swayed by the new features continually being pushed on them, because they've started to pay attention to other players that offer a different value proposition.

Over time, Christensen attempted to put his terminology into perspective by emphasizing its relativity and thus restricting its use in two ways:

"Disruption is a relative term."[18] What is disruptive to some may just be sustaining to others. As a result, to assert that your innovation is disruptive, "you need to define an opportunity that is disruptive to *all* the established players." Consequently, by Christensen's standards (at least here), of the hundreds of thousands of companies that surface every year, only a handful of them—if that many—could reasonably claim to be disrupters. Christensen's followers seem to have ignored the high bar he set and continue to use disruption as an absolute term.

"Disruption is a process, not an event."[19] Christensen didn't say that new entrants come like lighting out of the blue, succeed overnight, and guarantee a quick exit to their investors and founders, especially as a disruption may not even be immediately recognizable: "Disruption is a process, not an event. The forces are operating all the time in every industry. In some industries it might take decades for the forces to work their way through an industry. In other instances, it might take a few years." By this standard, however, the scope of applicability of the concept by entrepreneurs becomes limited. How could you possibly claim at the beginning of your journey that you are disruptive? This leads to a broader question:

When and who can actually say that an innovation is disruptive? When all bets are off? So is disruption just an observation in retrospect?

The Case of the iPhone

Christensen's clarifying attempts didn't have the intended impact. While most everybody can understand that disruption is a process or that the disruptiveness of a company should not be assessed based on a product's or service's financial success alone, the disruption framework can come across as arbitrary. Basically, if you're neither in the low-end foothold nor in the new-market one, the concept of disruption shouldn't apply. On the basis of this premise, Christensen declared that Uber didn't fit in the disruption model and that the iPhone fit only partially. Isn't this somewhat paradoxical? As far as I'm concerned, a restrictive framework should not prevent anyone from considering that somehow Uber, Lyft, and others did disrupt the taxi market.

His explanation as far as the iPhone is concerned strikes me as an exercise in splitting hairs:

> The product that Apple debuted in 2007 was a sustaining innovation in the smartphone market: It targeted the same customers coveted by incumbents, and its initial success is likely explained by product superiority. The iPhone's subsequent growth is better explained by disruption—not of other smartphones but of the laptop as the primary access point to the internet. This was achieved not merely through product improvements but also through the introduction of a new business model. By building a facilitated network connecting application developers with phone users, Apple changed the game. The iPhone created a new market for internet access and eventually was able to challenge laptops as mainstream users' device of choice for going online.[20]

Christensen's analysis provokes a few simple questions:

- Does this mean that you can't be deemed disruptive if you attract customers that incumbents failed to convince? Why resort to such an absurd argument to enforce the purity of a theory? Let's be pragmatic here: customers are customers. You can't infer that a product is innovative from its great sales, but you can't infer that it isn't either!

- What's wrong with being adopted thanks to "product superiority"? Why would being "better" be a secondary quality? New products may not have all the "bells and whistles" that older ones have and still be innovative, but why exclude products that do have more features, which was the case of the iPhone?

- Was the iPhone really disruptive because it "created a new market for internet access and eventually was able to challenge laptops as mainstream users' device of choice for going online"? There's no doubt that the iPhone transformed online access, but why position this plus on the basis that it "challenged" laptops? The laptop market reached its peak only at the end of 2011—four years after the launch of the iPhone, and, truth be told, the top PC vendors weren't hit as hard by shrinking sales as the little guys.[21] So was the iPhone disruptive mostly because, one thing leading to another, it hurt the small fish selling laptops?

The disruption theory has a hard time explaining why the iPhone was a major innovation, a topic I will discuss in chapter 7. Does the iPhone disturb Christensen's framework because it was an innovation brought about by a multibillion-dollar and then thirty-year-old company?

Ultimately, Christensen's attempt to position the iPhone as a sustaining innovation in the smartphone market when it debuted betrays the inadequacy of looking at the creation of innovative products through the sustaining-disruptive lens. Or, if we accept that "sustaining innovation" describes the early days of the iPhone, common sense tells us that this might be the way to go if you want to hit it big—which makes the disruptiveness story sound like a mediocre financial bet. But I am aware that questioning the relevance of one case may not invalidate a theory, so let's see a few more of them.

Additional Examples in *The Innovator's Solution*

Christensen provides examples of what he considers to be disruptive companies in his various books. Many of them are displayed as "examples of companies or products whose roots were in disruption" in a table displayed in *The Innovator's Solution* discussed in an extensive appendix.[22] The table features three types of players:

- Spaces: flat-panel display, unmanned military aircraft, steel mills, credit scoring in consumer lending, etc.
- Groups of companies: Palm Pilot / RIM-Blackberry or Kmart/Walmart/Target, etc.
- Individual companies: Kodak, Sony, Microsoft, Cisco, eBay, Amazon, Google, Salesforce, etc.

I know that this table doesn't pretend to offer more than "examples." But allow me a simple point: when you give examples, you want them to be representative of your theory, but you may also provoke serious questions.

Christensen created this table mostly for an American reader and from an American perspective, with a few notable Japanese companies because the rise of Japanese manufacturing was an obsession at the time. In some cases, however, he ended up with a distorted landscape. Henry Ford unquestionably revolutionized the car industry in the United States (although William Durant and Charles Mott, who created General Motors in 1908, also propelled a powerful business model), but nobody will claim that Ford invented the automobile. So should we assume that because this innovation was a long process, it wasn't disruptive, whereas Ford's manufacturing process was, to the point of overshadowing automobiles themselves? I agree that it's not easy to assign one name to the origins of the automobile, but can't Karl Benz be credited with creating the first one in 1885 if the criterion is an automobile powered by an internal combustion engine? Or can we invoke Gottlieb Wilhelm Daimler and his four-wheeled, four-stroke engine? This simple case shows that the disruption canon could be a matter of opinion, and sidelines major innovations. I understand that the development of automobiles over time doesn't fit the disruption model. But when facts don't conform to a conceptual model, shouldn't we argue that what's flawed is the model, not the facts?

Multiple omissions are also baffling. Let me pick just three of them:

- Microsoft (mentioned in the early 1980s time frame) was "disruptive" by Christensen's standards. Fine, but what about Apple? Weren't the Apple II and the Macintosh "disruptive" too? So what happens when you have two "disruptive" companies at once? A big mess? Who is disrupting what? In what sense? The theory can't explain the simultaneous existence of vastly different companies with vastly different visions, a topic I will discuss in chapter 6. Disruptiveness is a poor discriminant that overlooks the fact that innovators operate in a context that's larger than all of them individually.

- How is it that IBM isn't mentioned? Is it conceivable that IBM's innovations never had their roots in disruption if disruption is the primary gauge of innovation? Were the 140,000 patents obtained in the United States by IBM since 1920 all about "sustaining" innovations?[23] You don't need to be an IBM fan to say that this assumption doesn't hold water! Even if the number of patents can't be the only barometer used to assess innovativeness, it can't be discarded either. Sure, IBM has gone through ups and downs since the early 1990s, but who will contend that the day (February 10, 1996) when IBM's Deep Blue supercomputer won its first game against world chess champion Garry Kasparov was meaningless?

- The internet is another interesting case. Isn't it one of the most extraordinary innovations of the twentieth century? Sure, the internet is a set of technologies and isn't associated with one specific commercial company, but it's the brainchild of a major organization, the US Department of Defense, in collaboration with universities and private companies. We can't overlook the simple reality that it has fueled national and international economies for the last thirty-plus years via multiple companies (some of them mentioned in Christensen's table).

Like quite a few writers before me, I'm mystified that this theory continues to be peddled even when the facts that supposedly validate it can be questioned. That's what Jill Lepore emphasized when she analyzed some of Christensen' favorite cases, the disk-drive and mechanical-excavator industries or department stores.[24] As Lepore put it, "Christensen tends to ignore factors that don't support his theory." I came to similar conclusions when I analyzed other examples mentioned by Christensen, such as Kodak, personal digital assistants, the boxed-beef industry, and personal computers. Trying to fit them into a disruption framework obliterates how these innovations actually happened. Creating theories and/or building models is a relatable temptation. But their value is always relative to their comprehensiveness, their explanatory value, and their ability to avoid the highest possible level of anomalies. How well Christensen's theory of disruption really complies with these basic requirements is unclear.

Christensen's books are powerful, as they may compel companies to move out of their comfort zone, but the supposed foundational framework to guide their innovation efforts is nonexistent. Is it more useful for startups or young companies? It's all but certain. The entrepreneurs who believe they can enhance their credibility by clamoring that they're disruptive may throw themselves into a dangerous trap.

DISRUPTIVE-SUSTAINING: THE DICHOTOMY TRAP FOR INNOVATORS

Christensen's purpose was to make sure that leaders realize that it's not because they've built state-of-the-art fortresses that they'll be able to resist the assaults of pirates. So far, so good, but in this persuasion process, here's what happened: in order to emphasize the attractive power of disruption, he trivialized sustaining innovation practices, overdramatized the threat posed by agile startups, and assigned to startups a positioning that may not have served them well.

A Matter of Perspective

The disruptive-sustaining dichotomy presents drawbacks induced by the sheer dynamics of language. When we say that corporate routines will be disrupted by new entrants, we're speaking from the perspective of potential disruptees; they're the ones who might perceive new entrants as potential disruptors. Now, why should entrepreneurs make this perspective their own and see themselves as disruptive or disrupters when such descriptors are first and foremost reflections in a mirror held by incumbents? This is what has happened over the past twenty years, but it's been a mixed blessing for entrepreneurs.

For some entrepreneurs, picturing themselves as disrupters is an ego boost in a megalomaniacal cultural backdrop. Practically speaking, however, entrepreneurs can corner themselves into a dilemma. In order to demonstrate that they'll be competitive, they have to demonstrate that established players are giants with feet of clay. Yet, if they believe that, they incur the risk of showing that they haven't fully grasped these large competitors' strengths, and the internal and external factors that enabled them to accumulate power, and, as a result, they may fail to pin down the often much smaller innovation that would enable them to carve out their place. Furthermore, if incumbents really have feet of clay, what's the merit of destroying faltering figures?

For many other entrepreneurs, "disruption" is a cloak they wear for fear of being perceived as worthless. But by forcing themselves to aggrandize their dream to comply with popular imagery, entrepreneurs can lose sight of smaller opportunities that could lead to big things. Start with selling books and media online if you want to become Amazon, for instance, even if you want to be, as Bezos said in 1995, the "Earth's Biggest Bookstore." Was his motivation to disrupt traditional bookstores? Maybe, but what they could or would do was not under his purview. The important thing is how he proceeded to innovate—and he did so by importing a known mechanism into a new space: Amazon was the internet translation of the mail-order principle of items that customers more generally bought in stores, just as Tiffany had innovated 150 years before by creating the first mail-order catalog in the United States, the "Blue Book." After the postal services scaled up, mostly thanks to transportation progress, the founders of Sears, Roebuck and Company, Richard Sears and Alvah Roebuck, started selling almost anything in 1893.

Boomerang Effects of the Disruptive-Sustaining Dichotomy for Innovators

The disruptive-sustaining dichotomy has boomerang effects that paradoxically play against young companies and in favor of established ones, especially in technology.

If you tell your customers that you're disruptive, you're basically telling them that they're taking a risk. Don't you want to be seductive and reassure them instead? Starting a business doesn't mean that you should relinquish all common sense! Think about how you buy stuff yourself. Are you buying an Oura Ring to track your health or to thumb your nose at Bulgari? You probably don't think about older businesses at all. A notable exception would be businesses whose selling point *is* breaking apart problematic established models to address pollution or human rights concerns, for example. Customers who buy a newly created, reusable product are probably doing so specifically thinking about the wasteful materials they've avoided supporting. In a certain way, however, even these more directly attractive "disruptions" are themselves only a modernized return to traditional methods and therefore an antidisruption stand in their own right.

For entrepreneurs, hyping disruption in order to avoid the "sustaining" stigma may combine in an unwelcome fashion with other clichés, like the "fail fast" principle, which says that if you don't show results quickly, you won't get additional funding. Fine, but here's a typical scenario of what can happen if you try to sell, for example, enterprise software: Customers know that nothing happens in a flash, let alone the implementation of a so-called disruptive technology. They'll have reason to believe that other potential customers will be as cautious as they are. Everybody will wait and see . . . and you'll go belly up because you'll run out of money as a consequence of the application of the failing-fast principle. So, won't companies have reasons to be skittish about buying your product? Don't they have reasons to stick to their institutional vendors longer than they ought to or even would like to? Can you blame them? No, they know all too well that venture capital (VC)–funded startups whose performance is not as fast as expected may close shop and leave early customers in the lurch. The end result is that "sustaining" innovation, despite its official bad rap, may be more reassuring to customers. And customers will happily wait for the big vendor to offer them upgrades or updates now and then.

As entrepreneurs, we don't want to say that sustaining innovation is our mantra because this sounds dull, but trumpeting that we're disruptive can be incredibly naive. As I'll discuss in chapter 8, assuming that startups threaten large organizations is a wild overstatement. If anything, the power of incumbents can be so huge that startups are at a clear disadvantage. "Serial innovation" in established companies is supported by real and efficient methodologies. It's true that they can be caught off guard, but for one David that hurts the Goliaths, there are many more Goliaths eating up the Davids.

MOVING AWAY FROM THE DISRUPTION LEXICON

"Breaking apart" or "into pieces," which is the etymological meaning of "disruption," doesn't say much about innovation. It defines innovation negatively, when innovation's purpose is to bring value to people, not to cause headaches to competitors. Innovations exist relative to a market where potential customers will adopt them. So what matters is what it constructively takes to build them.

Christensen exhorts organizations to shake themselves up. So what? The reluctance, unwillingness, or inability to innovate doesn't just plague large organizations; it's also a widespread disease among midsized and even small ones. When companies are in a space in which they could innovate but don't try to do so, only management is to blame. Period. Lack of imagination, lack of initiative, apathy, inattention, ignorance, and so on are common features of incompetence. Companies don't kill companies. It's the people inside companies who do. They don't do their job. So isn't it absurd to create an explosive innovation doctrine just to wake up an apathetic or incompetent lot?

These arguments explain why many business consultants have distanced themselves from the disruption lexicon and focused instead on the techniques and methodological paths that can help companies develop, expand, or rekindle their innovative spirit. Among them, let me mention W. Chan Kim and Renée Mauborgne, who authored a well-known book, *Blue Ocean Strategy: How to Create Uncontested Market Space and Make the Competition Irrelevant* in 2004.[25] The book provides companies with marketing tools they may need "to reconstruct market realities to open up blue oceans" while overcoming organizational hurdles. Their proposition is on how companies can succeed, not why they fail if they don't turn the whole planet upside down.

W. Chan Kim and Renée Mauborgne's starting point is that if companies want to break out of red oceans, an interesting image to represent the bloody and costly fights that they have to get into if they just want to survive competition, they must "break out of the boundaries that define how they compete." Their advice is that "instead of looking within these boundaries, managers need to look systematically across them to create blue oceans."[26] They reconstruct market boundaries by looking across six areas:

1. across alternative industries;
2. across strategic groups within industries;
3. across the chain of buyers;
4. across complementary product and service offerings;
5. across the functional or emotional appeal to buyers;
6. across time.

Their use of the word "across" in the first part of the book is critical. Innovating is not about creating a fracture, an approach that they
further develop in *Beyond Disruption: Innovate and Achieve Growth without Displacing Industries, Companies or Jobs*, by showing that disruptive
innovation only operates within existing industry boundaries.[27] In actuality, disruptive innovation is a conservative and destructive vision of
innovation, while what they call "nondisruptive creation" builds new markets outside existing industry boundaries and envisions bridges across
spaces and people. As we constructively innovate, we're likely to have to
find solutions to pass barriers or obstacles, as I'll discuss later when we
further examine the beautiful expression "breaking though."[28] No matter
what, we have to move "across" real or apparent divides. We can do so if
we simultaneously see a space as it is, a space as we want it to become,
and the spaces we must traverse or explore to reach our goal. We must develop a perspective that merges "looking at," "looking beyond," and "looking through" into a representation whose rendering will vary depending
on the societal, ideological, or technological zeitgeist in which we live.

Generally speaking, "across" refers to a compounded perspectival system.[29] We spontaneously experience this phenomenon when we look at
paintings. We live in our regular three-dimensional world when we visit
a museum, but we imperceptibly glide into completely different coordinates when we admire J. M. W. Turner's linear and atmospheric perspectives in *The Battle of Trafalgar* and share the epic fight between humans
and nature it conveys, or when we adhere to Pablo Picasso's *Guernica*, in
which a triangle of light illuminates a world of shifting perspectives that
no human can master. We experience a composite perspectival system
when we hear our ancestors speak of a telephone "line" while we live
with our smartphones, whose paradigm denotes the exact opposite, the
absence of line, the elimination of distance, and, instead, the immediacy
of a contact.

"Across" is the ideation axis that connects ideas and domains and,
ultimately, creates multidimensional and multidisciplinary perspectives.
While my purpose isn't to give you a course on creativity and ideation
methods, let me remind you that the semantic field around the word

"innovation" almost always carries some sort of "across" thrust. There are dozens of terms: Interpretation, Imitation, Copy, Adaptation, Changeover, Modernization, Recontextualization, Transposition, Translation, Association, Convergence, Mash-Up, Amelioration, Optimization, Automation, Transformation, Personalization, Customization, and so on.

Not all innovations are game changers for everybody, or not in the same way, but behind almost each one, there is the power of the generative intelligence of a simple question: What if?

What if you changed the look and feel of your product to make it so simple and pleasant to use that even a stern person in some IT backroom would enjoy it as much as their Fitbit? What if you looked at your business "as a service," added robots to your restaurant, or reimagined skis? Would adding a module, creating an abstraction layer, or retrofitting a device make a difference? Would decomposing, recomposing, deconstructing, reconstructing, dematerializing, stripping off, integrating, or remodeling have an impact? We have to look at things from a different angle to see the way forward.

The ideas we import from other domains are rarely direct transpositions. You can end up turning them upside down. For example, we owe our three-point seatbelt to Nils Bohlin, a former aviation engineer at Saab who had designed an ejector seat. He was persuaded by Gunnar Engellau, then chief executive of Volvo, to design the opposite, a device that would keep drivers in their seat during a collision.

What if you talked with people around you, listened to what they do or the kind of dreams they have, even if they are completely different from your perspective? Samuel Morse was a famous painter coming back to the United States from Europe on the *Sully* when he met Charles Thomas Jackson, a physician who was well versed in electromagnetism. They discussed the possibility of sending messages through wires, and even if there later were multiple lawsuits about who had invented what, the result is that the world rapidly had the key components of the electric telegraph. And speaking of Morse, maybe you never realized that the Morse code inspired a small innovation that revolutionized commerce: barcodes.[30]

When we ask, "What if?" we are ready to explore and create bridges across domains. Edison was not being facetious when he declared, "I never had an idea in my life. My so-called inventions already existed in the environment—I took them out. I've created nothing. Nobody does." What he was referring to is that the world around offers infinite combinatorial possibilities. That's what you realize if your passions have enabled you to discover multiple domains and build up an interdisciplinary mindset. That's what you realize when you see generative artificial intelligence in action. You create new images and new texts as well as new knowledge graphs.

CONCLUSION

Why does the disruption lexicon remain so prevalent? The answer is that habits and ideologies die hard . . . even when innovation is discussed.

The disruption storyline has thin academic and theoretical bases and is unable to capture the multiformity of innovations. It's also either too restrictive (by Christensen's standards) or too imprecise (as in common jargon) to be used as a creativity principle. It's even more inadequate when you look into the emergence of most innovations, which often result from the progressive elaboration of a concept through multiple intermediate states and only upset preexisting usage habits over time. Sure, if you are widely successful in your endeavors, some "business as usual" will be affected, but you don't know in advance when and how much.

My recommendation is that you leave to rogue marquesses and cowboys the dream of painting the town red and that you never lose sight of the following: it's hard to innovate, for as convinced as you are that you are on to something amazing, the world rarely welcomes innovators as messiahs.

The initial desire to innovate is definitely the conviction that there must be a "better way." But we have to *make our way* through what's around us and first understand how entrenched habits or institutional requirements impede the rearrangement of the space we plan to change to one degree or another, and deal with all the unexpected stumbling blocks we encounter on our path. As I will discuss in chapters 4 and 5, it is naive to assume that we can break things with a hammer or magically shift paradigms. In fact, by believing that, we might lessen our chances of offering something that people will want to buy. Again, it's hard enough to convince customers to adopt something new, so let's put aside theories that may add an even higher degree of uncertainty into our efforts.

4

When Is the Right Time?

Sometimes, I feel the past and the future pressing so hard on either side that there's no room for the present at all.
—Evelyn Waugh

In a 2015 TED Talk, Bill Gross, a serial entrepreneur, said that his analysis of two hundred companies showed that timing was the factor that accounted the most for startups' success, before team execution, idea, business model, and funding.[1] At a high level, this makes sense. That said, relative to *what* could we be either too early or too late to seize an opportunity? To the state of development of the space we tackle or to the moment when customers will be ready to buy? Is there a first-mover advantage, or is it better to let others bear the brunt of getting customers acclimatized to novelties?

As we ponder the timeliness of our endeavors, we must remember that time is not an absolute notion: time is "not the objective, spatial time that was so famously denounced by Henri Bergson. Rather, it is lived time—time characterized by a quality that both shapes and is shaped by the dynamics of our interactions with the environment."[2] As a result, evaluating the "right time" depends on how we see our environment and interpret the pace at which it changes as well as the measuring instruments and frames of reference we rely on.

WHERE WE START FROM: AN INNOVATION STACK

We always start from an existing terrain. We want to solve problems that prior innovations didn't or couldn't address, or even created. We leverage a preexisting body of information, that is, an evolving set of products and processes that constitute what I call an "innovation stack."

Just as writers create new texts based on existing vocabularies, semantic and syntactic rules, templates offered by other writers, or AI chatbots, we create new products starting from the combination of existing products, patterns, standards, or, what James Utterback and William Abernathy, and others after them, called "dominant designs."[3] They govern our space of interest, and from there we have to identify how to best reshape its history while also having to go around constraints they might impose. For example, if you want to implement at scale a virtual reality world, you can't forget that networking latency is an obstacle that won't disappear overnight.[4]

As imaginative as we may be, we operate within boundaries. As much as we want to think "outside the box," we must reckon with it even if our goal is to do away with it altogether. We create new pieces from initial givens and iterate from there, which broadly defines the generative recursion mechanisms that feed our creativity.

When we hear about spectacular successes, we tend to forget the details of the innovation stack that made them possible. For example, Facebook is part of a broader innovation story enacted by dozens of players.

The internet is the father of all social networks, even before it was publicly known as the "Internet."[5] Early internet forums and newsgroups were themselves inspired by multiple initiatives that took place as early as the 1970s. Usenet, publicly established in 1980, enabled reading and posting messages. Then the World Wide Web, created by British computer scientist Tim Berners-Lee at the Conseil Européen pour la Recherche Nucléaire (CERN) in 1989–90, drastically accelerated computer-mediated social networking.

The first modern social media site, SixDegrees (1997) by Andrew Weinreich, enabled users to upload their profile and connect with other users. The concept was loosely based on the "six degrees of separation," an idea started by Hungarian writer Frigyes Karinthy in his 1929 short story *Chains*, which triggered research studies from sociologists and mathematicians and led to Stanley Milgram's 1967 "small-world experiment." SixDegrees also made history because of its patent issued in 2001.[6] It detailed the structure of a social media platform as well as the mechanisms enabling users to connect and interact. SixDegrees was acquired in 1999 by YouthStream Media Networks. Auctioned in 2003, the patent landed in the hands of Reid Hoffman, who co-founded LinkedIn in 2002 (and had prior experience in the genre with SocialNet in 1997), and Mark Pincus, who created Tribe.net (before starting the gaming company Zynga in 2007).

In the early 2000s, dozens of social networks sprang up left and right. Some were primarily social, like Ryze (2001). Friendster (2002) may have been one of the first sites to reach 1 million members. hi5 (2003) targeted the teen and twentysomething demographic and claimed to have over 40 million members in 2006.[7] James Currier's e-Mode.com (1999), later named Tickle, focused on personality tests and later added a dating service. Makeoutclub (2002) attracted a youth subculture aligned with the music scene. Launched in 2003, MySpace stole market share from everybody. Multiply showed up in 2004, as did Piczo; Bebo came out in 2005, as did Squidoo, TagWorld, and many others.

In parallel, blogging was flourishing, as were photo sharing and gaming. Napster (1999) pioneered peer-to-peer music sharing and closed down in 2001, but its founder, Sean Parker, went on to start Plaxo (2002) before becoming Facebook's first president in 2004. Facebook built on this ambient innovation stack, illustrating Schumpeter's organic process by which "every piece of business strategy acquires its true significance only against the background of that process and within the situation created by it."[8]

The evolution of an innovation stack is not always fast, nor is it always linear or homogeneous. Most innovation stacks are composed of elements from multiple innovation stacks, which evolve at different speeds. For example, in order to exist, cell phones needed multiple elements, such as the metal-oxide-semiconductor-field-effect-transistors (MOSFETs), invented by Mohamed Atalla and Dawon Kahng at Bell Labs at the end of the 1950s, and the formation of commercial cellular networks, the first one being in Japan at the end of the 1970s. Also, an innovation stack may branch out to form other stacks that delineate the contours of new spaces, as illustrated by Tony Fadell when he recounts how the iPhone (which he co-designed) helped him to bring out the Nest thermostat. He had been frustrated with thermostats in his homes or hotel rooms forever, but transforming a domain that was sold and installed by HVAC technicians was all but obvious for decades. Things changed with the iPhone: "The success of the iPhone drove down costs for the sophisticated components I couldn't get my hands on earlier. Suddenly high-quality connectors and screens and processors were being manufactured by the millions, cheaply, and could be repurposed for other technology."[9] Fadell started Nest, which initiated a new space with new sections of stores dedicated to connected home products, which in turn created a space not only for Nest but for the burgeoning smart home ecosystem that was starting to spring up all around.

When we characterize some innovators as "category creators," what we often refer to is the fact that they have been able to merge mature enough components belonging to different stacks into a new genre. That said, this is something that doesn't happen every day. Innovation stacks grow through phases and at various tempi thanks to the efforts of other innovators who are just as impressive as the "category creators." This is what I will discuss in the next sections.

PHASES IN TECHNOLOGY LIFE-CYCLES

What we can do depends on when we step into the life cycle of a genre. Russian Nikolai Kondratiev (1892–1938), whose work was rediscovered in the 1970s in Western countries, was probably the first economist to segment technology life-cycles into four phases: R&D, ascent, maturity phase, and decline. I will focus on the first two, as they best reflect the innovation bustle we are thrown into.

Buzz Creation: From R&D to Early Successes

Many innovations appear at the same time in the same space. This phenomenon was first described by Francis Bacon's *Novum Organum* in the early seventeenth century and, since then, emphasized countless times.[10] Singletons are less frequent than multiples. What we perceive as singletons is often due to the fact that other contemporary accomplishments have been forgotten or outshone by other players. The Edisons of history overshadow hundreds of innovators working on the same innovation stack at the same time.

Potentially new fields attract a bunch of irruptive birds that look for ground where they can settle and tinker with new ideas. They then discover technological, economic, or societal dependencies that condition their materialization and are often faced with choices that make them branch out toward different directions or redirect their efforts. During this phase, it's unclear how or when their respective efforts will pan out—let alone who will win.

For example, how can we create live images? This idea attracted dozens of entrepreneurs in the late nineteenth century as it stood at the intersection of several innovation stacks—electricity, telegraphy, telephony, photography, cinematography—as well as new discoveries such as X-rays or cathode rays. The dream of inventing television, a word coined by Russian scientist Constantin Perskyi when he presented his research study at the first International Congress of Electricity in 1900, was in progress. In his address, Perskyi referred to experiments by German engineer Paul Nipkow, the creator in 1895 of the Nipkow disk, an image-scanning device that became a component of mechanical televisions. In 1925, after years of trial and error, John Baird transmitted the televised image of a ventriloquist's dummy. In 1926, he gave a demonstration at Selfridges Department Store in London of what he called a "televisor." In 1929, the BBC used his technology to broadcast its earliest television programming. Is Baird the father of television, then? Yes and no.

At the same time, another direction established what became "electronic" television—and won. It utilized and expanded on Ferdinand Braun's 1897 invention, the cathode ray tube (CRT). By 1927 the all-electronic CRT television began to show its potential, thanks to Kenjiro Takayanagi in Japan, Russian-born Vladimir Zworykin, and American Philo Farnsworth. This was the beginning of a frantic race and multi-million-dollar investments. Between 1928 and the end of the 1930s, there were multiple "firsts" in both mechanical and electronic television.

Mechanical television broadcasting ended in 1939. That said, as an innovation, it had a major impact in the acceleration of the overall innovation stack. The longevity of a given innovation doesn't affect its reality as an innovation. Sometimes, a short-lived innovation can inspire different innovation stacks. Time-sharing of computer resources among many users, a concept developed by John Backus in 1954 and implemented by John McCarthy in 1958 on an IBM 709, is an example. Its purpose faded with the advent of personal computing, but the concept survived through indirect emanations: commercial time-sharing services and the internet. Large commercial time-sharing started mostly with CompuServe in 1969. The idea inspired multiple companies, like America Online (AOL), started in 1983 and expanded in 1985 by Steve Case and Jim Kimsey. Meanwhile, and separately, the pursuit of what J.C.R. Licklider dubbed a "Galactic Network" in 1962 was under way and dozens of technologies later, the internet arrived.[11]

Ascent and Spreading Phase

By the end of Phase 1, the buzz has intensified and technologies have reached a sufficient level of maturity to attract new contenders, both start-ups and established companies. That's when you realize that pioneers' first-mover advantage can be brief: "When industry knowledge matures, copycats will catch up. Because later comers often inherit a lower cost structure without the legacy assets, they exert competitive pressures on industry pioneers," Howard Yu writes.[12]

Newcomers appear quickly and, in today's world of pervasive communication, in a matter of weeks. It's frustrating for innovators and the reason they hope to secure their advantage through patents. But here is one of the paradoxes of innovating: we want them to be unique and protected while also hoping we'll get a wide reach. This structural bind was already highlighted by Jean-Baptiste Say: "Nothing can long escape publicity, least of all what people have a personal interest in discovering, especially if the secret be necessarily confided to the discretion of a number of persons employed in constructing or in working the machine."[13]

The very same economic system that values innovation also makes imitations and copies unavoidable. An example is an innovation that transformed the textile industry in eighteenth-century England and became one of the symbols of the first Industrial Revolution, the spinning machine powered by water, called the "water-frame," created by Richard Arkwright.

Arkwright earned several patents starting in 1769. These patents were challenged by Thomas Highs, who was the brain behind James Hargreaves's spinning jenny that Arkwright was improving. At the end of a legal battle (1785), Arkwright lost, but his company—started in 1771 in Cromford, Derbyshire—was thriving anyway, as were several mills built under license, notably in Lancashire. He became the richest untitled man in England but also kicked off copycat empires in Germany and the United States.

In Germany: German Johann Brügelmann, born in a family of wealthy merchants at Elberfeld (now part of Wuppertal), had a friend, Carl Delius, himself part of an influential family in the textile industry, smuggle a water-frame model out of England in 1782 along with a skilled worker who knew how to operate it. At his death in 1802, Brügelmann was one of the richest men in the Rhineland. Many members of the same powerful yarn-processing guild followed suit. They went on exploration trips in England—just like people from all over the world now come to Silicon Valley. Among them was Friedrich Engels Sr., father of the coauthor, along with Karl Marx, of *The Communist Manifesto* (1848). He visited Manchester in 1837 with Peter Albertus Ermen and built the Victoria Mill in Salford (now part of Manchester) in 1837; when they returned to Germany in 1838, they founded Peter Ermen & Co, later renamed Ermen & Engels, about eighty kilometers from Wuppertal. Engels Sr., wanting his son to follow in his footsteps, taught him the business and sent him to Manchester to learn. Engels Jr. had no plan of abandoning the political ideas he had formed in the Hegelian circles where he had studied. But he did live in Manchester between 1842 and 1844, started a lifelong relationship with an Irish woman who worked in the Engels factory, and wrote an extremely well-informed study, *Die Lage der arbeitenden Klasse in England* (*The Condition of the Working Class in England*), which was published in 1845 and impressed Karl Marx.[14]

In the United States: Arkwright's design was imported in America by British-born Samuel Slater. In 1782, aged fourteen, Slater had started an apprenticeship with one of Arkwright's partners in Belper, England. Since 1774, textile workers had been banned from traveling to America, but American newspapers were offering bribes to English workers for their knowledge. In 1789, having memorized the new practice of cotton spinning as well as the machinery that supported it, Slater, now twenty-one, arrived in America. In 1793 he opened his first factory in Pawtucket, Rhode Island. He also designed a factory system called the "Rhode Island System," which included the mills' systems as well as small towns providing company-owned housing, stores, and schooling to employees. Slater was so successful that President Andrew Jackson dubbed him the "Father of American Manufactures," while England called him "Slater the Traitor."

Fifteen years later, Francis Cabot Lowell, fascinated by Slater's success, traveled to Lancashire and examined the spinning and weaving machines operated by water or steam power. Given that he could not buy a model of the power loom created by Edmund Cartwright in 1785 nor other pieces of machinery, he studied the equipment and memorized it. In 1814 he established the Boston Manufacturing Company (BMC) in Waltham, Massachusetts, and hired a creative machinist, Paul Moody, to help him build and improve cotton-spinning and cotton-weaving machines based on the British models. In 1815 they were awarded a patent for their power loom. When BMC exhausted the waterpower of the Charles River, it moved north and created a new city along the banks of the Merrimack River that became known as Lowell. Moody developed a system of leather belting and pulleys to power the machinery, which became a standard for American mills.

American entrepreneurs got off the ground by ripping off British innovations that they improved and adapted to the local water supply, and, lo and behold, did everything they could to protect their market. Lowell successfully lobbied Washington, which established tariffs protecting US-manufactured items from overseas competition, including cotton cloth coming from Great Britain and its colonies. The Tariff of 1816 was the first tariff passed by Congress.

The ascent phase expands, accelerates, and dynamically reconfigures an initial innovation stack. Arkwright was inspired by John Kay's flying shuttle and James Hargreaves's spinning jenny, among other devices, and started a new innovation stack, which subsumed the previous one while shedding parts of it. What we see here is that epoch-making innovations operate as hinges between innovation stacks that speed up the advent of new products, new methods, or new services within their own specialty but also across multiple branches. For example, James Watt adjusted his steam engine to the needs of the new textile industry, which led to considerable improvements.[15] The iron industry was accelerated, as were England's coal mines in Lancashire, Yorkshire, Nottinghamshire, and Derbyshire. Of course, the textile clusters also impacted transportation, workforce management, and recruiting practices; precipitated the shift from a rural to an urban economy; and inspired new thinkers—and one of them was as directly tied to the textile industry as he could possibly be, Friedrich Engels.

But how fast does an innovation stack evolve? Our assessment depends on our perception of what it encompasses and of the scope of our interdisciplinary knowledge at any given time as well as our ability to remain coolheaded when we are in the thick of it.

MULTIPLE TEMPI OF "TIME"

Our sense of time varies based on the frequency of events around us. When a lot of events happen, time seems to contract. When fewer things occur, time seems dilated. In other words, we experience time as different tempi. We can feel the *accelerando* (speeding up) of the innovation bustle especially if we are in it or, oppositely, bear with its *ritardando* (slowing down). This ritardando can be caused by distinct phenomena that may combine, that is, the ability of our target customers to absorb innovation as well as dependencies on other technologies (which themselves have their own timelines).

Accelerando and Ritardando for Emerging Technologies

When we start a company in an emerging technology area, time seems to fly because an incredible number of events rush in within short intervals. Innovators collectively generate a world of their own—a bubble. They live on the fast track as illustrated by the ascending curve of the "Technology Trigger" of the famous Gartner hype cycle of emerging technologies before experiencing the descent and pangs of the "Trough of Disillusionment."[16]

Gartner Hype Cycle

The Technology Trigger indicates "a potential technology breakthrough [that] kicks things off. Early proof-of-concept stories and media interest trigger significant publicity. Often no usable products exist and commercial viability is unproven." Entrepreneurial eagerness begets a hyperactive bubble where entrepreneurs try to outpace each other. At the top of the curve, the "Peak of Inflated Expectations" shows that "early publicity produces a number of success stories—often accompanied by scores of failures."[17]

The peak doesn't last, and the *accelerando* is over. The downward curve toward the Trough of Disillusionment reflects the fact that "interest wanes as experiments and implementations fail to deliver. Producers of the technology shake out or fail. Investments continue only if the surviving providers improve their products to the satisfaction of early adopters." Some trends disappear or merge with other currents, while others will materialize with variable time frames—two, five, ten years, or even more.

This hype cycle shouldn't be too hastily read or interpreted. Although the downward curve appears like an inversion of the upward curve, we are dealing with asymmetrical arcs that represent different data sets with distinct tempi.

The Trough of Disillusionment features in reality the circumstances whereby innovators leave the innovation bubble to experience the narrow and adverse road into the real world: Will their product work and will people buy it? In the upward curve, they live within their own logic (sometimes with early adopters who become part of their bubble). However, the pace at which solutions evolve from the point of view of innovators is not necessarily synched with customers' consumption pace, their hierarchy of needs, their situation, or even their comprehension capabilities. So the descent of the curve toward the Trough of Disillusionment does more than illustrate a deceleration of the entrepreneurs' activity; it also shows a collision between two different tempi, the innovators' tempo and the tempo that governs the real world, which is much slower. Customers enforce their own tempo.

"Lazy Customer Behavior" Syndrome

A collision between tempi appears when innovators tackle topics that potential users may not even have been thinking about. For example, if you had asked a German farmer on the road between Mannheim and Pforzheim if he would like to try the car that Bertha Benz was driving in August 1888, his reaction would have been that he was fine using his horse to get to the village nearby.

However, this collision also takes place even when innovators address a problem that potential users know they have. But here is what happens: customers and innovators may initially agree that there is a problem, but by the time we get closer to a solution, both constituencies belong to two dynamic systems that have not necessarily evolved in sync. That's why customer discovery is a far tougher job than it sounds and building a minimum viable product (MVP) is the cause of countless headaches.

As innovators tackle an issue, they come up with different perspectives on that issue and are often drawn into adding various twists and differentiators mostly under competitive pressure. But when customers

see the solutions, they also see more of the problem as well as new an-
gles to solve it, and so they have different options to consider. Innovators
then realize that there is no exact one-to-one correspondence between
an opportunity and the way(s) to exploit it, or between a problem and its
solution(s). So, coming back down to earth and meeting its tempo, they
experience serious headwinds. Terra firma is, well, firm. That's when entrepreneurs understand that for an innovation to have a chance to drift
into the mores, it's not enough just to solve a problem customers have.
Customers want novelty provided they won't feel rushed. They live at their
own pace following their own schedule—whose components we may discover when we design our MVP, albeit not always. Customers must also
see the value of this MVP based on their own value system (which can
include multiple parameters, as I will discuss in chapter 5) and validate
the intent of the company. This explains why Guy Kawasaki suggested
that we add two "Vs" to the MVP acronym and think "MVVVP," spelled
out as Minimum Viable Valuable Validating Product.[18]

Many thinkers and consultants have developed problem-solution
frameworks and methodologies aimed at delineating technology adoption life cycles and mapping out customer behaviors.[19] These analyses
all provide valuable information but they rarely discuss head-on the time
equation, controlled by what Mikael Collan and Franck Tétard labeled the
"lazy customer behavior" syndrome.[20]

After analyzing choices of mobile devices or services in the early
2000s, Collan and Tétard concluded that when offered a selection of solutions, customers tend to follow the principle of least effort: "The effort
demanded by the solution is the amount of time, money, or energy (or
a combination of these) used to fulfill the need and the user selects the
solution that will fulfill the need with the least effort."[21]

The authors' purpose was not to declare judgmentally that customers
are slackers or reactionary. Their perspective "is based on the assumption
that what is the path of least resistance in physics and the theory of least
effort in informatics, can be applied to user solution selection to fulfilling
a need, from a set of possible solutions."[22] The path of least resistance is

what eases customers into adopting a solution. We have to accept it even if our customers' timing can feel incredibly anticlimactic compared to our excitement when we create new products.

Accelerandos and Ritardandos within Extended Timelines

The innovation stack rarely evolves through a regular pattern. Instead, it's frequently fraught with stop-and-go because of interactions with and dependencies on other technologies, which themselves have their own timelines. So for the same line of products, accelerando and ritardando effects can alternate like a Scottish shower. Interestingly enough, potential customers can also be the ones getting impatient—lamenting, for example, that there is still no cure for cancers, and only treatments for some of them. They are the ones who dream of accelerated tempi.

The history of autonomous vehicles provides an example of continuously heightened-and-dashed expectations. The dream of self-driving cars started early in the history of automobiles because of the high number of accidents caused by drivers' errors. Innovators in the 1920s were already looking into how progress in aviation, like Lawrence Sperry's gyroscopic stabilizer and artificial horizon indicator or radio guidance systems experimented by the US military, could benefit cars. From the aim of addressing safety, the concept of driverless vehicles transformed into the image of a better tomorrow and encouraged new designs for highways as well as urban planning initiatives.[23] The General Motors Pavilion for the 1939 New York World's Fair, known as Futurama, fired up imaginations. Yet, despite decades of technology prowesses, most experts estimate that autonomous cars today are still only at Levels 2 and 3 (with Level 5 defining full autonomy).[24] As Bryan Reimer at the MIT Center for Transportation and Logistics put it in 2019, "there's an incredible amount of confusion in the general public around the context of self-driving. In our survey data here, about 23% of respondents believe that a self-driving vehicle is available for purchase today. And a lot of that has to do with

statements by Elon Musk and others talking about the driverless capabilities and self-driving capabilities of vehicles."[25]

In 2017 looking at the state of the industry, one of its pioneers in
Japan, Sadayuki Tsugawa, was reportedly unimpressed. He expected the
industry to be much further along and stated that despite progress, he
didn't expect fully autonomous vehicles to come within his lifetime but
only after 2050.[26]

The goal is the same as one hundred years ago, to prevent accidents,
as Waymo's then-CEO John Krafcik declared in 2019: "Ninety-four percent of accidents happen because of human error, and there are 1.35 million lives lost on the roads each year . . . We're not building cars, we're
building drivers."[27]

The goal is ambitious, and the path to get there remains complex.
Deals, alliances, and acquisitions happen every week; billions flow left
and right; timelines keep floating around; and every year you hear cautious predictions about who will win the self-driving race. Dozens of new
aiding technologies continue to feed the hype cycle.[28] Many are still in the
making, as are necessary measures to make driverless cars mainstream:
road designs, security decisions, cohabitation with nondriverless cars,
weather conditions, administration, and so on. Innovations, especially
major ones, recontextualize existing environments, but while doing so
they have to solve the novel issues that arise from this recontextualization, thus feeding the generative recursion pump as well as redefining
timelines.

DO ENTREPRENEURS ACCELERATE A SPACE'S
INNOVATION PACE?

All entrepreneurs at any given time in the innovation cycle have more or
less the same data. They are all present at what we abstractly call the "right
time" to address the same problem. They all contribute to the buildup of
the innovation stack. Then, how is it that some happen to offer more
long-lasting solutions and accelerate a space's pace more than others?

Don't jump too fast to the conclusion that some innovators have more genius, more money, or more luck, or more of anything than others—geniuses can fail, and idiots can succeed. A more important factor is the innovators' understanding of time and what "time" actually holds, which depends on the instruments and frames of reference they choose. We can see this phenomenon when we analyze the different fates of two contemporary products, Goto.com and Google, in the late 1990s.

A Problem to Solve: Search Results Quality

To facilitate access to the internet, Tim Berners-Lee offered the first web browser in 1991; its source code was put in the public domain in April 1993. In September 1993, the popularity of the web soared thanks to Mosaic, a browser created by Marc Andreessen and Eric Bina. As John Markoff put it in the *New York Times*, Mosaic made it possible for people to have a "map to the buried treasures of the Information Age."[29] Subsequently, lots of developers wanted to facilitate this treasure hunt. Dozens of search engines became available, each contributing to the innovation stack.[30]

A major challenge was how to ensure that search results wouldn't be distorted by spam. Initially, search engines ranked pages based on the text they contained, which enabled spammers to fill their pages with commonly searched keywords that marred search results. Both GoTo.com and Google worked at solving the problem.

Bill Gross, whom I mentioned in the introduction to this chapter, pioneered paid search in February 1998 as the founder of GoTo.com. The company went public in 1999 and survived the dot.com bubble burst. Larry Page and Sergey Brin registered Google as a domain name on September 15, 1997, and incorporated the company in September 1998. They got angel money from multiple prestigious sources and raised $25 million in 1999. Perfect timing for both companies.

Bill Gross proposed a paid search engine allowing websites to gain top placement on GoTo.com results page for a given keyword, a solution that was more effective than just buying ads. As reported in its 1999 financials, the GoTo.com marketplace had over 21,000 paying advertisers, with approximately 15.5 million unique users for the month of December

1999.[31] GoTo.com changed its name to Overture in 2001 and ended up focusing solely on running its ad network—and not on becoming a general search engine. Yahoo! acquired Overture for $1.63 billion in 2003, as it wanted to expand contextual advertising throughout its network to beat Google, by then itself in the advertising business.[32]

As for Google, Page and Brin started a research project as PhD students in Stanford in 1996. Their goal was to create a search engine that would return reliable results based on the authority and influence of the site offering them—which would sideline spammers, whose sites had no depth whatsoever. As explained in their 1998 paper, they drew from extensive prior art to create the search algorithm they named "Page Rank" (after Larry Page's last name) and distanced themselves from the ad model that, according to them, misled automated search engines.[33] They summarized their approach this way: "Google is designed to be a scalable search engine. The primary goal is to provide high quality search results over a rapidly growing World Wide Web. Google employs a number of techniques to improve search quality including page rank, anchor text, proximity information. Furthermore, Google is a complete architecture for gathering web pages, indexing them, and performing search queries over them."

GoTo.com/Overture disappeared. GoTo.com and Google had the same timing, but they interpreted the needs and potential of the time they lived in differently and, as a result, had a different take on what the market would reward. When interviewed by Slate in 2013, Bill Gross wholeheartedly admired Google's accomplishments.[34] He was justifiably proud of his paid-search model but elegantly gave to Caesar what belongs to Caesar: "I wish I had come up with the Google idea," he said. "The Google idea was the idea for organizing the world's information. Mine was just an idea for making money."

Two Perspectives on Time

What Bill Gross said, in essence, is that both companies had the same *timing* from a chronological standpoint, but because they had different *perspectives* on how and *why* people would perform a search, their under-standing of what "timing" entailed differed vastly.

For GoTo.com . . .

When Bill Gross says that his company was "just an idea for making money," he isn't being glib. He emphasizes the fact that the source of his site's value was a short-term mechanism based on a short unit of meas-ure, the *clicks* that made people react or not react to advertising. Its cli-ents were the advertisers. GoTo.com addressed end users only as people whom advertisers would influence to buy products within a golden hour of sorts. The scope of the innovation was narrowly circumscribed to what a click could carry. The growth of the company was predicated on a basic calculation: the number of websites and unique visitors during a given period no matter how many times they visited a site during that period. This approach made sense: the number of websites between 2000 and 2001 grew from 17,087,182 to 29,254,370; that is an increase of 71 percent.[35]

For Google . . .

Google back then was looking at search from the point of view of end users, with no assumption as to who they were or what their purpose was when searching.[36] So people weren't narrowed down solely to potential advertisement consumers. Neither were they expected to follow a preset usage pattern, such as navigating the web starting from predefined cate-gorizations of content as set by Yahoo!, given that they wouldn't cover all topics, let alone "esoteric topics."[37]

For Google, the company's success was based on users' probabilistic behavioral scenarios (search rather than navigation) and dependent on an open-ended number of searches performed by people with unknown expectations arising from the multiple dimensions of their lives. Between 2000 and 2001 the number of searches grew from 9,238,200,000 to 27,474,600,000, a 197 percent increase.[38] In other words, the pace of the number of searches was almost *three times faster than the increase in websites.* Two different scales and very different potentials. To deliver on its goal, Google had an imaginary large mathematical number as a unit of measure, the "googol."[39]

Time Elasticity

GoTo.com was a perfect fit at the perfect time for a perfectly defined purpose, and the company illustrates most traditional approaches in market positioning. Google was also a perfect fit but with a different approach and with entirely different acceleration and scalability powers.

What we see here is that the notion of time is elastic. Our vision of the reach of an innovation is influenced by our perception of growth, but this perception of growth is relative to the reference systems we select to evaluate the pace at which things happen around us. Google's perspective was based on verifiable observations such as the exponential growth of documents on the web and an increasing number of people searching, as well as progress in adjacent domains like the augmentation of hardware processing power:

> As of November, 1997, the top search engines claim to index from 2 million (WebCrawler) to 100 million web documents (from Search Engine Watch). It is foreseeable that by the year 2000, a comprehensive index of the Web will contain over a billion documents. At the same time, the number of queries search engines handle has grown incredibly too. In March and April 1994, the World Wide Web Worm received an average of about 1500 queries per day. In November 1997, Altavista claimed it handled roughly 20 million queries per day. With the increasing number of users on the web, and automated systems which query search engines, it is likely that top search engines will handle hundreds of millions of queries per day by the year 2000.[40]

These data points provided reference frames for accelerated tempi.

Google didn't have a business model at the beginning, but it had a lot of money, which let the company figure out what it could do. It was building an audience whose trust could be leveraged in various ways "whenever," and relying on a *multithreaded timeline*. While for GoTo.com a moment was just a point in time calling for one specific action (a click) generating one specific result (money), for Google, time contained several possible threads that could be unwound at "any time" and incarnated in various ways—and the fact is that Search became a springboard for multiple products. For large-scale innovators, "the present is big with the future, the future could have been read in the past, and distant things are expressed in what is nearby," to use a phrase by German philosopher Gottfried Wilhelm Leibniz.[41]

Is Accelerating the Innovation Cycle Being "Ahead of One's Time"?

We like to say that innovators are "ahead of their time" regardless of their success or failure. The expression, though, is misleading and doesn't say why they differ from futurologists.

We all live within given spatiotemporal coordinates and see into the future from these. Futurologists highlight the arsenal of possibilities that they observe at any given time based on various trends in multiple domains, and they express their vision of how the interaction or combination of these trends might push forward the agendas of various spaces. But they don't have to implement these insights, and even if what they say can be perceived as extraordinary visions when their predictions pan out, they can also be castles in the air, which is actually the most frequent scenario for a number of reasons.[42] Their perspectives can inspire and sharpen innovators' minds and imagination, but they aren't the ones who have to pass the here-and-now execution test that substantiates or dashes innovative endeavors.

Innovators don't jump ahead of time per se. They don't even skip steps or "jump curves." As I showed in chapter 2 and here with the Google example, their optical power allows them to apprehend situations differently and pick up different simultaneous signals, with some of them having higher accelerating and predictive capabilities than others.

In an interview of Kevin Kelly, founding executive editor of *Wired* and author of multiple books, James Currier says that "by necessity, founders are rooted in the 'here and now' mental framework required for

launching a new startup" but that "*great* founders do something different at the same time: They are obsessed with what will endure 10 or 50
years from now."[43] What I like about this remark is the expression "at the
same time." What's key here is that "greater" innovators have the ability
to live on several timelines simultaneously, a timeline originally dictated
by their space with the short-term and practical needs that enable their
business to survive, while also factoring in the pace at which different
domains (directly or indirectly related to theirs) evolve.

This is not a capacity proper to innovators only. In fact, we all live
on several time scales at once without really thinking of it: we live in
our memories, the tempo of our weekly family chores, our personal daily
tempo, our work schedule, our larger plans for the future, and so on.
What often happens to entrepreneurs is that because they are told to focus on one thing, they tend to block everything else and thus run into the
risk of falling victims to myopia and focalism. Yet innovative creativity
requires that we keep abreast of what happens in different areas with different tempi, because it's also what enables us to identify convergences
or kinships between some of them and our area of expertise.

Innovation, just like science fiction, "is not about the future; it uses
the future as a convention to present a significant distortion of the present."[44] But contrary to sci-fi authors, innovators don't really "distort" the
present. They insert into their space the present of different domains
whose faster tempi can be used as idea generators and growth models.
When we say that some innovators are "forward thinking," we don't mean
that they achieve the daunting (and impossible) task of seeing ahead to
a future on one fixed timeline. *Forward thinking is, in actuality, flexible,
multi-timeline thinking.* Timeliness for innovators is the ability to be "on
time" at different moments "in time" because they have a multithreaded
vision of time in the first place.

IS INNOVATION FASTER TODAY?

The sense of time and of its speed is relative to an observer's environment. The first Industrial Revolution created a sense of acceleration that

has traversed all subsequent revolutions. By now, we should all be used to this two-hundred-year-old feeling, but we aren't, because the sense of acceleration is relative to previous experiential states. The higher the number of new things coming our way, the more striking time acceleration seems to be if we haven't had "time" to adjust to a prior acceleration. One of the distinctive traits of the fourth Industrial Revolution—the merging of the physical, digital, and biological worlds—is that this acceleration is all the more perceptible, as far more entrepreneurs from far more countries contribute to the innovation world and have a larger reach because of the dramatic expansion of communication channels. This observation, however, shouldn't prevent us from checking what exactly is being measured when we read or hear that innovation is faster today.

Reading Sample Data

We read the same data differently depending on the markers we select. For example, Jean-Louis Prévost and Frédéric Batelli discovered that small electrical shocks could induce ventricular fibrillation in dogs in Geneva in 1899, but the first implementation of an implantable cardioverter-defibrillator (ICD) only happened at Sinai Hospital in Baltimore in 1969. So in this case, we could say that a unit of measure applicable to that space's speed could be expressed in decades. Yet if we factor in intermediate innovations, the unit could be a few years and sometimes a few months. Depending on the markers we choose, we can see the pace of innovation in defibrillation as slow or fast. While historians sometimes take the liberty of skipping stages they deem minor, innovators can't overlook the stepping stones displayed in the past, especially the ones closer to them.

As proofs of a faster innovation spread (which means adoption rather than creation), I've noted the recurring mention of a 2008 graph published by the *New York Times* and an abstract from a 2015 report co-produced by Citi and the Oxford Martin School at the University of Oxford. They're interesting but only if we look at them carefully.

New York Times *Graph*

The purpose of the *New York Times* article in 2008 was to help understand why consumption is a better guideline of economic prosperity than income.[45] Even though the graph created by infographic designer Nicholas Felton showed that the adoption pace of some newly commercialized technologies accelerated between 1900 and 2005, it may be somewhat misleading to issue blanket statements such as "The Pace of Technology Adoption Is Speeding Up."[46] In order to avoid misinterpreting data, you must contextualize them and keep in mind the following:

THE LOCATION OF THE DATA SET: The graph focused on appliance consumption in the United States. So an important question for you as an aspiring innovator to ask is why Europeans didn't buy dishwashers and home appliances quite as quickly, although Europe's first domestic dishwashers with an electric motor were produced by Miele in 1929. What factors made Europe so different from the United States? Confirmation biases may get in the way of understanding the actual conditions for the adoption of innovations.

THE START DATE: The first commercially successful dishwasher (mechanical) was created by Josephine Cochrane in the late 1800s. Why was its adoption slow until the end of World War II? As an innovator, you must identify the technical or sociological obstacles that prevented mass production and mass adoption.

DEPENDENCIES ON OTHER INNOVATIONS: It took decades for the telephone to reach 50 percent of households, but cell phones picked up in no time. This is true. Again, why? That's when we must remember that many rural areas in the United States couldn't possibly have telephones before 1930 because most weren't electrified.[47] In contrast, color TV took off like a rocket. Why? It's because black-and-white TVs already existed. Desktop computing accelerated internet adoption. Technology innovations trigger or reinforce other innovations and can do so exponentially. This course of things was true in the twentieth century. This is true also in the twenty-first century.

SPECTACULAR GROWTH ISN'T PARTICULAR TO OUR EPOCH: One of the most striking growth curves of the twentieth century is radio in the 1920s, when broadcasting started. Given that a household's average size was between four and five persons, radio covered almost the entirety of the US population in record time. In the same fashion, when speaking about appliances used in households, realize that demographic structures are part of the story: from 1900 to 2000, the total US population increased from 76 million to 281 million, an increase of 270 percent. By comparison, the total number of US households grew from 16 million in 1900 to 105 million in 2000, an increase of 561 percent.[48] In a society where home appliances are a must because households' numbers increase, sales increase is a foregone conclusion.

Citi and Oxford Martin Report

In the same fashion, the 2015 Citi and the Oxford Martin School report *Technology at Work: The Future of Innovation and Employment* shouldn't be read too hastily. Its initial goal was to analyze the impact of technology innovation and employment. However, a small section of it is what has been the most peddled: the time it took for a number of consumer products to reach 50 million users. It took seventy-five years for the telephone to do so, thirty-eight years for radio, thirteen years for TV, four years for internet, three and a half years for Facebook, and only thirty-five days for the video game *Angry Birds*.[49] We could add that it took two months for ChatGPT to reach 100 million users.[50]

Here again, data set analysis is critical. Why should 50 million users be a yardstick? How pertinent would it be if applied to electric vehicles? They have been in the making for three decades, and yet how many people have one? Between 1908 and 1927, Ford built around 15 million Model T cars—but in 2022, the International Energy Agency indicated that "the total number of electric cars on the world's roads to [be] about 16.5 million, triple the amount in 2018," in a world whose population is four times larger than in 1930."[51] So let's sober up!

Facebook had 50-million users after three and a half years, but how well does this compare to the use of Nivea Crème, a product created in 1911? You could buy it all over the world three years later, and so it probably passed the 50 million-user mark in a world whose population was 20 percent of what it is today.

Angry Birds? Its average reach of seventeen people/second at its viral height seems like an unprecedented exploit. But let's compare it with "the Gadget," the nickname of the most famous implosion-design plutonium device. The first test happened on July 16, 1945. On August 6 it landed on Hiroshima and killed an estimated 140,000 people. On August 9 it landed on Nagasaki and killed an estimated 74,000 people.[52] Not included are tens of thousands who died later. Given that it takes around ten seconds for the fireball from a nuclear explosion to reach its maximum size, the Gadget hit between 7,400 and 14,000 people per second. I am, admittedly, comparing creations more disparate than apples and oranges, but they remain human innovations that affected lives—and, in the case of nuclear deployment, ushered in a radically new vision of power and a cultural shift that were far more wide reaching than *Angry Birds'* virality. If you want killer examples, don't overlook actual killers, as terrible as they may be.

Pacing Our Sense of Acceleration

When illustrating the rate and importance of change, it's disingenuous to favor certain examples and decontextualize data sets. Journalists can get away with this. Aspiring innovators can't, for they incur the risk of misunderstanding the environment on which they hope to have an impact. They must deconstruct blanket notions of change to focus on *what* changes, at which *level* and at which *pace*. They must adopt a more analytical approach to how innovations infiltrate and reshape our environment. We don't live in a continuous earthquake, even today.

Innovations are accelerated by other innovations that act as amplifiers. For example, electricity triggered a gigantic arsenal of innovations in a world that was much smaller than what it is today. As did the internet. Today, technology amplifiers such as AI, robotics, blockchain, sensors, quantum computing, and so forth are also converging to accelerate the pace of change. I agree with Peter Diamandis and Steven Kotler that "the future is faster than you think," not because it's a projection but because it's actually taking place and shaping innovation stacks as we speak.[53] So, as important as it is to recognize such accelerations or even consider Ray Kurzweil's idea of a "the Law of Accelerating Returns," it's still critical to realize that our world is not a homogenous whole with layers swimming in synchrony—even if layers model each other.[54] Innovations don't merge toward a mono-directional path, because the spaces in which these innovations happen don't necessarily follow identical, let alone straight, lines.

CONCLUSION

We have to start at the "right time," provided that we are aware of the various velocities that define the multiple components of the space we tackle. So remember what David Tennant as Doctor Who stated: "People assume that time is a strict progression of cause to effect, but actually from a non-linear, non-subjective viewpoint it's more like a big ball of wibbly wobbly timey wimey stuff."[55]

What's critical for aspiring innovators is to assess the different units of measure (as well as their variations) that may structure the evolution of their space. The choices they make and their chances of bearing fruit depend on the data they select as reference points.

It's so exhilarating to be in a hot space that we are tempted to rush everything for fear of being left behind. Yet we also have to learn how to pace ourselves and establish firm milestones before hoping to "blitzscale" our company, something we can consider only if we address existing markets that can be restaged and expanded thanks to already widely adopted technologies.[56]

In all cases, keep away from excessive generalizations about the accelerated pace of change. Maybe we do have to make believe in order to believe we'll make it. Maybe we must have faith in exponential growth to scale up our endeavors or reflect on Moore's Law coming to an end to think that we'll overcome roadblocks.[57] Yet we still have to deal with them. We need an acute sense of what gives us an advantage that we can sustain on the arrows of time in a space that reorders itself as we work at redefining it.

Finally, remember that the history of the objects that structure our vision of time in our domain or domains related to ours is part of a larger world. We see the "window of opportunity" open into a complex environment whose entangled characteristics can both propel and hold back our efforts. This is the topic of the next chapter.

5

What Is a Window of Opportunity?

Though we see the same world, we see it through different eyes.
—Virginia Woolf

Of all the expressions that we frequently use, "window of opportunity" is perhaps the most complicated one as well as one of the richest. The word "opportunity" comes from the Latin expression *ob portum veniens*, which means "coming toward a port." It is commonly defined as a time or set of circumstances that makes it possible to do something. So we're speaking of an event that's not only timely but also adapted to an environment, with some kind of a good wind blowing our way. Yet how much of that "opportunity" do we *see* through that "window"? And we must realize that "seeing" can be relative. . . . For example, when you look at God's and Adam's hands almost touching in Michelangelo's *Creation of Adam* on the Sistine Chapel ceiling, do you see their closeness or a gap between both hands alluding to a bigger story, Adam's fall?

Whether it's a crack or a large aperture, the window may thrust us into an environment whose characteristics we don't initially suspect. The makers of electric bicycles in the early 1900s thought that they had a shot given the success of regular ones. They were wrong. So why didn't they benefit from the same window of opportunity? This example shows that we have to keep in mind that any opportunity we believe we discern is part of a larger whole, which I will call "innovation kairos." It is an entangled environment of ideological, societal, cultural, political, economic, and human layers in which an innovation will either remain unheeded or, conversely, will *break through* to drift into the mores, eventually reconfiguring some of the layers that compose our environment and sometimes even the way we live.

FAILURE OF E-BIKES A CENTURY AGO

How is it that electric bicycles, or "e-bikes," which appeared in the 1890s, didn't benefit from the success of regular bicycles at the same epoch?[1] The first response is that battery technologies were too limited. This is doubtful. French physicist Gaston Planté had invented the rechargeable lead-acid battery in 1859, and enhancements shortly thereafter showed that technology would be good enough to power a bike. In fact, bicycle stores sometimes added batteries to standard bicycles. So what prevented electric bikes from catching on? Mostly the bicycles themselves.

Bicycle Craze at the Turn of the Twentieth Century

Philipp Moritz Fischer, a German musical instrument maker, is most likely the designer of the first bicycle with pedals, the Tretkurbel-fahrrad, in 1853. Over the next thirty years, multiple companies began offering two-wheelers. The first commercially prosperous one was Pierre Michaux's velocipede in the early 1860s. It then took about twenty more years to get to what made the bicycle a smashing success, the "safety bicycle." Created in 1885 by John Kemp Starley in Coventry, England, it is the first direct parent of modern bicycles.[2] It inspired dozens of innovators, and bicycles took off. In France there were 50,000 of them in 1890, 980,000 in 1900, and 3,559,000 in 1914 (about one bicycle per eleven inhabitants). In the US, 1,182,850 bicycles were produced in 1900 alone.

The safety bicycle shifted the perception of bikes from being a sport for well-off younger men to a personal means of transportation for both men and women. It was easy to learn how to ride, cost effective, and almost maintenance free. Bicycles became a symbol of individual independence and even of women's liberation.[3] Most bicycles and then roadsters with step-through frames accommodated women's clothing and accelerated changes in fashion, like a wider adoption of bloomers even in France where trousers for women remained frowned on.[4] Bikes didn't abolish sexism and racism, but women and African Americans attempted to circumvent barriers by creating their own clubhouses.[5]

Why Electric Bikes Didn't Benefit from the Bicycle Craze

Having the word "bicycle" in common didn't mean that regular and electric bikes were associated in the people's mind. They belonged to different psychological, sociological, and institutional territories.

DIFFERENT AUDIENCES AND EMOTIONS: When bicycles reached the masses, curiosity for additional developments dropped. The electric bicycle addressed technology fans or spectators in special exhibitions.[6] While over 1 million bicycles were produced in the United States in 1900, only 159 "motor bikes" were made.[7] The motor bike was more expensive and conflicted with a transportation appliance whose appeal was simplicity. Also, engine-powered bike fans and manufacturers mispositioned their devices: they often demonstrated that they were faster than horses. People didn't care. The horse wasn't the criterion. Personal freedom was the value.

IDENTITY PROBLEM: The electric bicycle had the shape of a bicycle, but because it had an engine, it was part of a multientry category: vehicles with two wheels, three wheels, or four wheels. Electric two-wheelers became a poor relative in a space where interest for electric cars was high.[8] However, when electric cars lost their appeal, mostly when Ford started to mass-produce internal combustion engine vehicles that were cheaper, interest for electric bikes waned even more. In parallel, motorcycles (with no pedals) outgrew their bicycle origins to start an independent genealogy.

INCOMPATIBLE REGULATORY FRAMEWORKS: The main feature of the bicycle was its human-powered factor. Legislative authorities discussed where the innovation belonged, and very soon it was deemed to be a mechanical mount, not a vehicle. The electric bike was a vehicle and, as such, subject to a different regulatory framework.

SPORT AND LEISURE: In addition to being a utilitarian means of transportation, cycling became a source of entertainment. Started in 1903, the Tour de France was successful from day one. Bikes became a weekend and vacation device in Europe: cyclo-touring took off after World War I, and railway companies quickly accommodated passengers' desire to take their bikes with them, which obviated the need for a car.

A SHORT-LIVED ATTRACTION FOR BIKES IN THE UNITED STATES: A massive push from US vendors saturated the market quickly after 1900, and when the attention moved to cars, bike sales dropped. After World War I bicycles were increasingly viewed as toys for kids.

E-bikes weren't seen as part of a solution to the huge pollution problem caused by horse manure, a topic at the center of the first international urban-planning conference convened in New York in 1898.[9] Gasoline cars turned out to be. This is ironic from our current standpoint, as today e-bikes *are* a solution to pollution and urban traffic and part of micromobility strategies everywhere in the world.[10]

The context in which e-bikes existed wasn't conducive to showing their potential. This is true, except that speaking of "context" is too vague. A context is what enables us to join or weave things together. Here, what we see is the coexistence of disjointed realities. This story illustrates that an environment is not a homogeneous whole but is, instead, composed of multiple layers that have their own logic and that these layers do not necessarily evolve in sync, let alone combine. Knowledge brokering and transfer between layers aren't automatic. We could say that people should have *connected the dots*. Sure, yet connecting dots is all but obvious, because our perception of reality is itself determined by categorizations that can prevent such synergy. Think of wearables today, for example. You have two closely related categories that have evolved on separate paths on different layers: commercial ones (Apple Watch, Fitbit, etc.) and prescribed wearables (AliveCor, Withings, Philips, etc.). The former are easier to use, but they don't have medical-grade status, which involves liability risks that consumer tech companies aren't interested in taking.[11]

The complex texture whose entangled characteristics can both propel and hold back our efforts, in which some innovations *break through* while others may stay dormant or fail, is the "innovation kairos."

THE INNOVATION KAIROS

Rather than one context, the innovation kairos is a loose assemblage of layers. Rather than one time, it's the floating swaddle of tempi that each have their multithreaded pace as I described in chapter 4. Rather than one zeitgeist, it's an imbroglio of habits, prejudices, and aspirations. It's more than one ecosystem; it's an imbrication of environments with disparate linkages. At its root, it's a linear adaptive recursive neural network seeking the optimal result but rarely finding it. And that's what we're venturing into when we want to innovate.

Why I Chose the Word "Kairos"

The reason I chose the term "kairos" is that it carries a triple meaning: temporal, spatial, and linguistic. This ancient Greek term, *kairos* (καιρός), doesn't have a direct equivalent in English, nor in any European language as far I know. Liddell & Scott's nineteenth-century *Greek-English Lexicon*, mentioned by British classicist Richard Broxton Onians, offered various equivalents that combine "happening at the right place," "the season of action," and "to assist anyone at the right time."[12] In antiquity, the term was used in a wide array of domains (medical, political, military, artistic, etc.). In Aristotle's *Rhetoric*, kairos refers to "the appropriateness of the discourse to the particular circumstances of the time, place, speaker, and audience involved" and more specifically to the moment when an argument is the most persuasive, a topic vastly developed by the Sophists, whom we could view as the opinion peddlers and marketers of the Ancient Greek World.[13]

Kairos involves more than a quantitative measure of time, contrary to the word *chronos*, which gave us "chronology." It includes a collection of qualitative and situational features as well as the intent of effecting an action with an impact that people can understand—which is why we can persuade them to buy into what we say or do. It places the notion of opportunity within the time-space-human-coordinates of a social and cultural milieu.

Kairos reflects the mental landscape to which French philosopher Michel Foucault applied the term "episteme" in *The Order of Things:* "In any given culture and at any given moment, there is always only an *episteme* that defines the conditions of possibility of all knowledge, whether expressed in a theory or silently invested in a practice."[14] This episteme doesn't necessarily come to our conscience. It is an invisible fabric that operates as a background for our actions and worldviews. Likewise, the innovation kairos designates a sociocultural texture and its motley open or tacit rules, knowledge, know-how, or institutions into which a product must insert itself. The glass of what we call a "window of opportunity" is all but transparent.

The Innovation Kairos: A Multilayered World

Have you ever used graphics software that allowed you to place objects or images at different layers/levels? If you have several layers, you can get lost, and even more so when you merge layers or partially obscure some of them to let an image appear in a translucent manner within another image or multiple images at different layers. Now look at our world and all the objects that populate it. It's a gigantic, complex project. It's composed of multiple layers with multiple objects, each with their own timelines, and to which our customers attach conscious and unconscious thoughts, ideas, or emotions. This is the kairos into which innovations have to make their way.

The Multilayer Maze

As innovators, we are quick at seeing big trends. They seem to propel us toward a different future, but we often underestimate how long it takes for them to worm their way within the kairos. In 2008 everybody was talking about the "sharing economy," an expression coined by Lawrence Lessig to designate free or for-profit assets mutualization.[15] Airbnb, founded in 2008, is a successful illustration of this trend. Today, the company holds a large slice of the vacation rental industry market share, but, just as its alternatives, it still has to deal with a desultory world of various layers.

Airbnb and traditional hotel chains remain on a collision course. However, Airbnb's competitor is not hotels only. It's a tangle of layers of housing policies and politics. Airbnb is consistently accused of affecting housing costs, and hosts can be fined for breaking local housing regulations even when they pay the required transient taxes. At times, housing regulations are used by hotel lobbies and associations entrenched in local politics to protect their own business—even though, by doing so, they slash thousands of jobs and economic benefits that Airbnb hosts create in their communities, which contradicts local job development efforts.

Even innovations with a major impact don't change the lay of the land quickly. In fact, the reorganization and redistribution of layers within the kairos rarely show a vanishing point where all the lines of a landscape might converge, but instead generate new complexities and contradictions.

Vaclav Smil illustrates a similar phenomenon when he analyzed the meaning of engine dematerialization.[16] "In the early 1920s the dominant Ford Model Y had a mass/power ratio of 15.3 g/W, while nearly 100 years later the best Ford engines had a mass/power ratio of less than 1 g/W, a very impressive reduction in less than a century." Yet here is what has also happened: "This gain has been negated by the growing average power and average mass of American cars. The Model T had power of 15 kW, but the average power of new U.S. vehicles has been above 150 kW since 2003 and in 2015 it reached a new record of 171 kW, making the average car of the second decade of the 20th century nearly 12 times as powerful as the Model T—and erasing all relative dematerialization." Does this mean that "dematerialization" is a hollow term? No, because even if the gain is negated when we compare these two data sets, innovations haven't been stalling when seen from the vantage point of users who want a car more powerful than the Model T.

The kairos is messy and often puzzling. As we innovate we have to keep in mind that we often create a host of side effects directly in our space or adjacent spaces that change dynamics and that we generate im-

balances that compel us to further create to counterbalance new or existing innovations. That said, as we create balances and counterbalances, we
potentially add to the layers consumers must mentally traverse when evaluating what we do. Given that acceptance by customers is the ultimate validation of innovations, we also have to break through their mental layers.

The Multilayer Maze in Our Customers' Minds

As innovators, we hope that our "Eureka! moment" will translate into a
"Wow moment" for customers. That's not what necessarily happens, as
we can experience ourselves when we look at other innovators' products.

When we conceive new products, we have to think of how we ourselves adopt anything new and not assume that our customers will beat
down our door. We may be impressed by a novelty, but we don't necessarily buy it. Oftentimes we dither, not because we're indecisive but
because a new product summons to our minds several layers that may
collide instead of reinforcing each other. The decision "buy / don't buy"
isn't a binary choice between a "yes" or a "no" but rather the consequence
of conscious (or subconscious) reconfiguration processes in our mental
layers. When we weigh our choices, we're doing more than comparing
one thing to another; we're trying to reconcile fruits that bear the marks
of different orchards.

Here's an example: Almost every smartphone brings some innovation. You love technology. You can afford a new phone every six months.
Will you do this? Most likely, you won't. You may be concerned with the
fact that only a fraction of this smartphone's components are recyclable.
So, your passion for gadgets and your economic capabilities clash with
your desire to save the planet. Result: if your belief system prevails, you
won't buy a smartphone every six months. Not only that, but you may even
wonder whether it makes sense to buy a new one every two years and conclude that buying one every four years might be good enough. Add other
considerations, like the country where the phone is manufactured, the
salaries of the workers in these plants, and so on. But then, another layer
might surface: the image you'll convey if owning the latest smartphone
is a status symbol. Now, you're conflicted! So, imagine what happens if

everybody goes through similar processes: The great feature X offered by manufacturer Y will infiltrate the kairos at a slower pace.

That's the type of scenario we have to keep in mind when we innovate. . . . Remember, startups primarily die because they haven't reached one of the mental planets where their customers live. We segment our market, but our customer segmentations are rarely as reliable as we might hope. When we look at our data, we often find that they don't quite fit the profile we had identified when we initiated our customer discovery. So we adjust and refine our positioning(s) and yet we may still experience that people aren't buying as fast as we thought they should even when they say they love our product. After months of conversations, they may come up with odd questions that send us back to square one. They may even tell us they saw a competitor who did something similar—even if it's only remotely akin to what we offer. When you sell a new product, pay attention to the maze of comments and objections: they reflect an acclimation process that hints at more past experiences or past traumas than you can even think of. Our market segmentations customarily miss the complexity of our multilayered world.

When we start, we expect to see some validation of Everett Rogers's adoption rate curve: First come "innovators" (2.5%) and "early adopters" (13.5%), then the early majority (34%), the "late majority" (34%), and finally the "laggards" (16%).[17] But what's the difference between an early adopter and a laggard? It's not always as simple as assuming that the former is forward thinking whereas the latter isn't. In fact, if you place the curve back in its context, especially in later editions of Rogers's book, you realize that the difference between early adopters and laggards is less related to personal psychological traits and more to how they abide by their social or cultural reference systems. One of the many examples offered by Rogers is the failure of the diffusion of a water-boiling initiative in a Peruvian village. The reason was that this innovation was perceived as culturally inappropriate by the villagers. This led Rogers to a clear and simple definition of the diffusion of innovation as "a process by which an innovation is communicated through certain channels over time among the members of a social system."[18]

I experienced firsthand that what distinguishes early adopters from laggards isn't what I initially believed when I was selling the first graphical relational database for Apple's Macintosh computer at the end of the 1980s and early 1990s. I expected that our early adopters would be Macintosh fans until I realized that my strongest customers were more of the IBM type, especially in the United States. Typical Macintosh customers used their Mac to create documents. The users I needed wanted to manage their data. Both categories of users lived on different wavelengths and had different decision processes and criteria. Customers choose on their own terms, and I had to accept it!

As innovative as we may think we are, we have to incorporate into the design of our innovations the fact that we're addressing people who go about their lives in a multilayered kairos that rarely reads like an open book. They don't randomly adopt or reject innovations; they adopt them when it's convenient to them. That's why the true litmus test for innovation success is adoption by *both* laggards and early adopters.

If we focus too much on the people we believe are trailblazers, we won't have much of a business anyway. We must realize that to reach a wider audience, we'll have to "cross the chasm."[19] But don't misunderstand what that "chasm" actually represents. It's the discrepancy between our frame of reference as a vendor and our addressees' mindsets. That's what makes marketing a tough job. As intrinsically innovative as we believe our product is, customers are the ones who validate our claims. The innovation kairos is their world too, a complex one where new paradigms drift more than they shift.

Paradigms Drift

When we speak of paradigm shifts, we primarily speak from our point of view as producers of innovation hoping to bring about change rapidly. While it's true that some innovations change the direction of an industry, these "shifts" seldom translate into abrupt turns. As I mentioned in chapter 3, paradigm shifts in science result from the gradual anachronism of previous paradigms, which means that a new paradigm must drift into a community and become accepted knowledge—until another one emerges, but this is relatively infrequent. The same goes for innovations. They drift into a community, as though metabolized by it.

The adoption of innovations is more akin to what German American anthropologist and linguist Edward Sapir called "language drift." Language drift reflects the gradual and often unconscious changes in natural languages. This drift translates into new words, new grammatical forms, new patterns of expressions, and sometimes new behaviors. "The drift of a language is constituted by the unconscious selection on the part of its speakers of those individual variations that are cumulative in some special direction."[20]

New paradigms, just like new linguistic forms or words, drift into the kairos. There isn't always an immediate or even clear demarcation line between a "before" and an "after." In fact, neither linguistic forms nor products flatly erase the past. Cars and agriculture mechanization didn't kill horses. They *displaced* their use from labor to recreation. In other words, innovations reconfigure the kairos by reassigning previous products to a layer different from the one they originally occupied—until that layer eventually dissolves into oblivion.

Innovations often have to speak to more than one layer of the kairos—for example, layers that want something better as well as layers that preserve some real or imaginary pristine feel of past experiences or, on the contrary, skirt a bad taste attached to past experiences. Sheila Minton and Jag Padala at TAGNOS, a platform orchestrating surgical operating rooms, reminded me that hospital personnel still remember what they had to go through when they consolidated patient data into one Electronic Health Record system twenty-five years ago. So sometimes, what we have to overcome when we sell our products is not related to what we offer but to a memory related to something completely different. The "once bitten twice shy" syndrome can be a fierce enemy.

PARADIGM DRIFT SCENARIOS

In 1898 Gabriel Tarde, usually recognized as the first theorist of innovation, asked the question to which all innovators would like to have a response: "Why, among 100 diverse innovations simultaneously imagined . . . [do] only 10 of them spread into the public while 90 fall into oblivion?"[21] Tarde and then generations of researchers after him have tried to identify the causes facilitating or thwarting the diffusion of innovations and provided methodologies to improve chances of success—but we still have to reckon with the fact that innovating remains somewhat of a gamble. After-the-fact rationalizations of successes or failures and retrospective predictability are one thing, but living through the dynamic context in which we actually innovate is a different tale. So, as much as we want to drive the innovative process when we identify an opportunity, we may also be driven adrift in a world that doesn't expect us.

Not All Innovations Drift into the Mores in the Same Fashion

If there were one formula to predict the success of any innovative endeavor, we would all know it by now. Yet the success of some types of innovation is more probable than others, which led Peter Drucker to try to qualify the "discipline of innovation" as "a diagnostic discipline: a systematic examination of the areas of change offering entrepreneurial opportunities."

Drucker identified seven sources of changes, which can appear either within the precincts of an enterprise or industry or, in contrast, outside them because they are triggered by changes in social, philosophical, political, and intellectual environments.[22] Logically enough, according to Drucker, sources identified within an enterprise or industry lead to more predictable outcomes because of a de facto correlation between an identified change and the ability for entrepreneurs to take advantage of it. This is not true for outside "sources of opportunity," among which Drucker singles out "knowledge-based innovations," which "are almost never based on one factor but on the convergence of several different kinds of knowledge." These "knowledge-based innovations" have long lead times and convergences, which, he says, give them "their peculiar rhythm." As a result, he adds, "for a long time, there is awareness of an innovation about to happen—but it does not happen. Then suddenly there is a near-explosion, followed by a few short years of tremendous excitement, tremendous startup activity, tremendous publicity. Five years later comes a 'shakeout,' in which few survive."[23] You'll see this phenomenon when we discuss the history of personal digital assistants in the 1990s (chapter 7).

As intent as Drucker was on guiding managers and entrepreneurs by classifying sources of change, he also asked them to keep in mind a more fundamental reality: "The lines between these seven source areas of innovative opportunities are blurred, and there is considerable overlap between them."[24] However, he didn't elaborate on the topic, for want of an overarching concept reflecting the complex and dynamic space-time environment where innovations happen and can be adopted: the innovation kairos. The reason sources of innovative opportunities are "blurred" is that few of the spaces where innovators apply their ingenuity are free of dependencies, and also that innovations drift through layers at discrepant speeds and resonate diversely with potential adopters. Based on my knowledge of history and empirical observations, I am inclined to suggest these points:

- The drift is faster for innovations delivered within a layer/context where there is direct or indirect preexisting understanding between innovators and consumers.
- The drift is slower for innovations that touch behavioral or emotional layers. People may acknowledge these innovations and yet resist. So the role of marketing isn't about reaching rational buy-in layers; it's about identifying slumbering layers that might facilitate transitioning between the old and the new.

Adoption through Direct/Indirect Understanding within a Layer

It's easier to get our message across when we and our addressees share a common vocabulary—communicate in the language of the customer— for a well-defined topic in a given space. People understand what we're talking about and see the plus of an innovation. They know why they need a product (now or at some point) or why they don't. Adoption is based on experience, either directly acquired or through trusted change agents and influencers.

When Innovations Meet Existing Patterns or Mindsets

Drifting within a specialized community can be faster because the innovation blends in with existing patterns or mindsets. As soon as the web became mainstream, users and applications needed a way to access updates to websites in a standardized way, which necessitated a common format. The RSS format was readily adopted by webmasters, who weren't deterred by the ongoing heated technical discussions among its designers—Dan Libby, Ramanathan Guha, and Dave Winer—or the 2006 RSS Advisory Board. Many innovations become normal additions to people's toolboxes. Likewise, since the early 2000s, USB flash drives have had different storage capacities but they've always been used in the exact same fashion.

When the original usage layer disappears, either the product disappears or it can move to a different layer with a similar usage: Duct tape is an example. We take it for granted as a base product, but it was originally created in 1943 in a particular context. Vesta Stoudt, a factory worker packing ammunition boxes at the Green River Ordnance Plant in Dixon, Illinois, noticed that the way ammunition boxes were sealed made them difficult to open for soldiers in a hurry; so she suggested that the army adopt the waterproof, tearable cloth tape she had created and tested. The Ordnance Department approved the change and tasked Revolite, then a division of Johnson & Johnson, to create the product. Duct tape left the confines of the army after World War II because its usage was transferable.

Some innovations can be extremely complex technologically but still gain adoption relatively quickly. Cloud computing under its multiple forms is one of the transformative sets of technologies developed over the past thirty years. It powers access to most of the information we consume. Yet people easily went from working off their hard drive and local network to working off the cloud. Resistance was higher within the IT space, mostly for security and data sovereignty reasons, but the problem could be addressed. What accelerated adoption was that although the cloud metaphor was new, many of its concepts could be mapped to multiple previous IT notions and operations.

Accelerated Adoption through the Network Effect

We can learn by osmosis. If somebody I respect uses a product, I'll get what it could also do for me. Friends are implicit situational translators. They are people "like me." Many innovations are adopted through contagion or network effects.

Network effects operate in multiple ways and via different media, but the general idea is intuitive.[25] An innovation sees its user base grow faster if its usage involves more than one person. You aren't going to do much with TikTok if nobody uses the app. In other words, the more structurally contagious a product is, the faster it can spread. Today, we're used to mentioning dozens of companies as network-effect powerhouses, but we shouldn't forget older, structurally viral platforms. Railroads spread fast because friends and friends of friends used them. The success of Kodak's Brownie cameras was also remarkable: 245,000 were made between February 1900 (when they were introduced) and October 1901 (when they were discontinued).[26] Given that people distributed their pictures, it's highly probable that at least 1 million people held a photo taken with a Brownie in their hands within a year!

When Innovations Touch Behavioral, Emotional, or Ideological Layers

Adoption is more complex when innovations require behavioral changes or touch sensitive layers that evolve at a slower pace. Here, I'll explore different cases: How easy is it for people to understand the expression "easy to use" or overcome their personal feelings, and why is something like birth control a recurring subject?

How Easy Is "Easy to Use"? The Power of Habits and Emotional Layers

When using the phrase "ease of use," we hope to shorten learning curves and demonstrate benefits faster. We see ease of use as a magic key that will open doors. Yet even though it's often true that ease of use is a relevant demarcation criterion between older and newer products, we can unknowingly touch layers of ingrained habits.

Cumbersome stuff is straightforward when we're used to it. Steve Ballmer, then Microsoft's CEO, famously laughed at the iPhone in 2007, declaring to *CNBC*'s Scott Wapner, "That is the most expensive phone in the world. And it doesn't appeal to business customers because it doesn't have a keyboard, which makes it not a very good e-mail machine."[27] He explained later that he was wrong, but his remark at the time wasn't as silly as it sounds. Ballmer, like many people, was conditioned to physical keyboards, and the iPhone was dematerializing a habit that many wanted to hang on to.

Another example of how innovations can come up against ingrained mindsets is virtual reality. Tom Furness started as an airplane cockpit developer and built virtual interfaces in the 1970s. Spatial computing and metaverse models are used today in hundreds of applications in transportation, manufacturing, retail, healthcare, fintech, and education.[28] But broad adoption of virtual reality and the "metaverse" may remain elusive for much longer than usually believed. Here again innovators will have to overcome emotional layers, similar to Juanita's in Neal Stephenson's *Snow Crash*, who considered that "no matter how good it is, the Metaverse is distorting the way people talk to each other, and she wants no such distortion in her relationships."[29]

Progress in data analytics can hit affective layers, like our sense of personal identity. Many people both want and fear artificial intelligence (AI). AI-based medical devices, for instance, can tailor treatments to a specific individual by learning from others' data. It's because AI products can process the data of millions of people that they can understand a person individually and deliver situationally relevant information. But here's the catch: How enthusiastically can people embrace essential technologies they fear might impinge on their personal privacy? People understand the benefits of AI and that ubiquitous knowledge underpins individual empowerment, but as much as we want to know everything for ourselves, we're terrified at the idea of being watched. Nothing new here. Some re-

sorts banned the Brownie in 1900 because visitors didn't want to be photographed; journalist Sarah Slocum was attacked in a San Francisco bar
for wearing Google Glass in 2014.[30]

When Breaking Through Requires Continuous Efforts: Birth Control

Making one's way into the kairos can be a complex journey if you think
of the history of "birth control," an expression that we owe to Margaret
Sanger, who opened the first birth control clinic in the United States and
founded the American Birth Control League in 1921, renamed Planned
Parenthood in 1942. To what would you attach championing birth control
if you lived in the 1910s? To free sex, eugenics, Neo-Malthusianism, population control, women's health, women's freedom, or family planning?
Birth control has been caught across multiple layers and reflected through
ideological, political, and religious prisms from the get-go, a plight that
has never stopped.

It took ages to get reasonably effective intrauterine devices (IUDs).
The first published paper on IUD insertions was made by Richard Rich-
ter in 1909 in Germany, and multiple solutions came after that, starting
with Ernst Gräfenberg's in the late 1920s. The concept of the birth control
pill started much later. Many scientists worked over decades to create its
chemical components. Carl Djerassi and his team (George Rosenkranz
and Luis Miramontes) synthesized a progestin called norethindrone,
which became the key ingredient of the pill, at Syntex Laboratories in
1951. In 1952 Frank Colton, who had joined Searle, synthesized the progestin norethynodrel (an isomer of norethindrone). Yet Colton had not
been working on synthetic progesterone for birth control but on a miracle drug that would be as lucrative as cortisone. In fact, drug companies
weren't eager to venture into the minefield of birth control for fear that its
opponents would boycott their other products.

The big move was powered by Sanger's relentless activism. At a
dinner, she met Gregory Pincus, a biologist who had founded his own
laboratory. She convinced Katharine McCormick, heir to a part of the Mc-
Cormick family's fortune (her stepfather had revolutionized agriculture

with the McCormick Reaper), to fund the work he was pursuing with Min
Chueh Chang. When Pincus, who had a prior working relationship with
Searle, contacted the drug company about his birth control research, he
had to overcome the company's resistance. As stated in a PBS documentary series, "throughout the early 1950s, the drug company kept a very low
profile about their involvement with the Pincus birth control pill trials."[31]
Gynecologist John Rock played a major role in testing, and the FDA approved the distribution of the first hormonal birth control pill, Enovid,
which G.D. Searle and Company began marketing in 1960.

What we see here is that breaking through multiple layers requires
an amazing amount of talent and courage from all the people involved
but also that when innovations touch sensitive ideological layers in the
kairos, victories are never a done deal regardless of when we believe the
"window of opportunity" is as innovators. The reality today for American
women is that reimbursement for contraceptives is regularly challenged.
Simple examples like these help temper generalist grandiloquent talks
about innovation.

The very existence of some innovations as well as their survival can
require that we continuously fight for them. Sometimes, it's one thing
to innovate and meet success, and it's another to sustain the existence of
that innovation.

When Breaking Through Requires Transitional Experiences

We never really know to what extent we will hit emotional layers when we
innovate. We hope to activate in our customers the fear of missing out
(FOMO), avoid their delay tactics for a better option (FOBO) or their fear
of doing anything.[32] But more generally and even most of the time, what
we must do is to help customers reconfigure their own mindset. People
often need a transitional experience more than a culture shock. If users
know they won't lose their data, it's easier for them to switch phones. It's
a small thing. Yet it has a big psychological impact.

While innovators are understandably tempted to overemphasize the
newness of their offering, they should preemptively address the possible trauma caused by the displacement of their customers' psychological

comfort and, for that, leverage past behaviors and perception as an ally rather than simply see them as punching balls or obstacles. In fact, the endurance of the old is also what gives time for the new to seep into the minds and mores. Even if we live in a consumer world with accelerated obsolescence rates, gasoline and diesel vehicles won't die out tomorrow, but their slow decline operates as an acclimation process to something else.

The past can act as a pedagogical support. As I'll further discuss in chapter 7, one of the most remarkable product introductions I know is Steve Jobs's launch of the iPhone.[33] Listen to the first four minutes of his presentation. They're all about what we knew back then, from which he jumped off to the point: "What we want to do is to make a leapfrog." And that's exactly what he did. In the game of leapfrog, the first participant rests their hands on their knees and bends over, which is called "giving a back." What already exists gives innovations a base from which they can get going. The seemingly most iconoclastic innovators often pay extreme attention and an indirect tribute to what they're attacking. Game changers start with a game, whose rules they have to know to be able to bend them.

Whether we introduce a new product into an existing market or a new product into a new market, or resegment a market as a low-cost or a niche entrant via new business models or processes, we can't assume that customers are homogenous or can be rushed. We must prod them into novelty. That's where great marketing comes in. Great marketing subdues the cultural and emotional "wait-a-minute" layers, and it creates the Wow or Aha moments that pull up buy-in layers associated with a sense of personal agency. As I'll discuss in chapter 6, one of the reasons for the failure of the original Macintosh launch advertising was a sectarian tone that turned down many people. Key to the success of the 1997–98 "Think Different" campaign was a broad-minded style that brought up a variety of human traits. Similarly, why do so many people like Subaru ads about love? It's because they reach deep-rooted layers of positive emotions. They alleviate the uncertainty often attached to innovations and thus enable people to more serenely examine the characteristics that will help them jump on board: relative advantage, compatibility, complexity, trialability, and observability, to use Rogers's terms.[34]

Drift Modifiers: Wars and Crises

Exogenous factors, notably, wars and crises, can have an exception effect on the drift of innovations within the kairos, accelerating certain innovations while decelerating others.

Once the United States entered World War II, factories stopped producing most home appliances and switched to producing equipment for the war. In parallel, the war effort accelerated the development and adoption of dozens of technologies and products such as jerry cans, jet engines, radars, computers, and the scaled production of synthetic rubber and penicillin with the help of new processes. World War II hastened an emphasis on the power of science and technology. Hundreds of brilliant minds from dozens of labs, universities, and companies contributed to the success of the US initiative. This ebullience trickled down to the general public and made people crave new stuff right after the war.

The role of Vannevar Bush in the war effort, often overlooked today, was critical.[35] As one of the most influential advocates of science in the United States, he did not only marshal US wartime technology but also pushed the US innovative spirit well into the twentieth century. Having graduated as an engineer in 1913, he obtained his first job in that capacity at General Electric. He then enrolled in the MIT electrical engineering program for his doctorate. While he was involved with the American Radio and Research Corporation (AMRAD), he joined the MIT Department of Electrical Engineering, participated in multiple inventions, co-founded Raytheon in 1922, and constructed an analog computer (the Differential Analyzer) with Harold Hazen between 1928 and 1931. He taught binary algebra, circuit theory, and operational calculus and inspired hundreds of students, including Claude Shannon, often seen as the father of information theory. He became dean of the MIT School of Engineering in 1932 before being appointed president of the Carnegie Institution of Washington in 1938. By then, Bush was not only one of the most knowledgeable scientists of the first part of the twentieth century; he was an influencer for research policy in the United States and advised the government on scientific matters. The same year, he was appointed to the National Advisory Committee for Aeronautics (NACA), of which he quickly became vice chairman. He utilized his position to boost what would become known as Silicon Valley, when NACA established a new aeronautical research laboratory in Sunnyvale, California.

Bush was extremely influential during the Roosevelt and Truman administrations. His power later waned to the point that the United States was caught off guard when the Soviet Union launched the world's first artificial satellite, Sputnik 1. Just as much as the Pearl Harbor attack, Sputnik 1 created a gigantic crisis of confidence. The Cold War made the United States resume considerable federal investments in research and development, education, and national security. In February 1958, Dwight Eisenhower authorized the formation of the Advanced Research Projects Agency, which became the Defense Advanced Research Projects Agency (DARPA), with a mission of accelerating the development of new technology for the US military. Six months later, Eisenhower signed the National Aeronautics and Space Act, thereby creating NASA. Very soon after that, Congress passed the National Defense Education Act (NDEA), a four-year program that poured billions of dollars into the US education system. The Sputnik crisis considerably boosted innovation through a powerful cooperation between public authorities, universities, and the private sector. The US human spaceflight programs powered advances in avionics, telecommunications, and computers, inspiring countless future engineers as well as the general public.

Just like wars, crises refocus large innovative endeavors. COVID-19 rekindled research on vaccines and new therapies. Internet-based video-conferencing services that had started in the 2000s became mainstream. Zoom, founded in 2011, became a household name in the span of a few days, which shows, by the way, that the window of opportunity and the potential it holds can shift drastically between the time you start and the time you hit it big. Zoom's focus on simplicity, high-quality video, and stability encompassed the right combination of capabilities to seize the moment and grab the zeitgeist. Food delivery services became essential services for millions of families. COVID changed the way we work, where we work, where and how we shop, and how we interact with others and will speed up the desire for immersive experiences and the buildup of Web3 protocols.

Crises throw the spotlight on several aspects of the kairos at once and reveal its weaknesses or inconsistencies. For example, while over the past decades it has become customary for Western countries to outsource manufacturing to reduce production costs, the COVID-19 pandemic may encourage them to reconsider some aspects of the globalization of the economy as well its efficiency criteria—and to pay closer attention to the consequences of their declining share in manufacturing value chains. COVID-19 was an opportunity for Western countries to ponder the lopsidedness of their global value chains and realize how dangerously it may affect their innovation potential in general. A European analysis shows that "the EU's global share in electronics has fallen even more than in total manufacturing, without evidence that specialization in other segments of this value chain could significantly mitigate the trend."[36] The same reckoning could happen in multiple other domains, from artificial intelligence to 5G broadband cellular or digital currencies. Will there be a Vannevar Bush of manufacturing? I don't know. The fact is that former Intel CEO Andy Grove had sounded the alarm about manufacturing in 2010 but to no avail.[37] Gross domestic expenditures on R&D show that China has surpassed Europe and is close to surpassing the United States.[38]

Crises and wars trigger warning shots that reshuffle the cards. The interesting phenomenon is that once they pass, the kairos doesn't revert to its previous state. Instead, more or different innovations, or refreshed takes on existing ones, tend to remain once the dust settles. As Emmanuel de Maistre, a pioneer in the use of drones, told me, COVID impacted this market. In early 2020, the market for commercial drone solutions was growing only at a moderate pace. When the pandemic hit, enterprise customers paused their drone initiatives, but once the economy showed signs of potential reopenings, the appetite and need for drone technologies rebounded. Drone solutions themselves didn't change much, but customers realized their value in the newly constrained environment caused by the pandemic.

THE GLASS COLOR OF THE WINDOW OF OPPORTUNITY

We love "accidental" innovations like the Slinky, Post-it Notes, Viagra, and many others because they seem to embody the instantaneous magic of creativity. Yet, as unexpected as some of these seem to be, they aren't that "accidental." Their originators had backgrounds enabling them to come across these products and had enough understanding of the kairos to figure out whether they might be accepted. Am I saying that innovations are always brownfield innovations of sorts? Yes. Does that mean that blue-sky, greenfield, or white space innovations are more fancy constructs than anything else? Also yes.

Blue-Sky, Greenfield, or White Space Innovation

Can we create anything if nothing around us gives us the idea? Is there really something like blue-sky science, seemingly unrelated to any specific line of research? There aren't too many examples illustrating that ignorance is the mother of invention or innovation. Are we better off believing that greenfield innovations—innovations whose adoption wouldn't be conditioned or constrained by prior work—are more frequent? Not really. In real estate, it refers to development in rural areas or in cities' outskirts. Yet success is still dependent on other factors (roads, electricity and gas availability, soil surveys, etc.). In software, it refers to programs not constrained by backward compatibility with other software or file formats, but again, in order to accelerate adoption of these alleged greenfield innovations, you have to find ways to draw people to them. Does the idea behind white space innovation have more breadth? Unsure. The concept is to identify a gap in an area that's been left out or untouched by competitors. Fair enough, but isn't it the basic thought process that always drives us when we want to innovate? And where is the gap? In the brown(field) space we live in.

Brownfield Innovation

Brownfield innovations are defined as innovations that must deal with what exists, such as technical infrastructures, economic interests, habits and behaviors, regulations, and political considerations. But doesn't that describe all innovations to one extent or another?

Was Edison's electric lighting a blue-sky innovation? If you ignore the history of electricity. Was it a greenfield innovation? If you ignore that there were other ways to light houses and streets. Was it a white space innovation? If you forget forty years of prior work on incandescent lamps. It was really a brownfield innovation, and this is also what made it adoptable. As emphasized by Andrew Hargadon, "in the 1880's, Edison was forced to compromise his electric lighting technology to integrate it effectively within the existing market and regulatory environments of the time that favored natural gas over electricity use."[39] Was it really a "compromise" or was it the best thing that happened to Edison? I'd opt for the latter.

Most innovations begin with some preexisting infrastructure or expectations. Prima facie, older industrialized nations are at a disadvantage compared to newer economies. That's why Hargadon writes, "In the 1990's, China was able to leapfrog the construction of traditional copper wire telephone network, moving directly to cellular communications in the 1990s and they are now pursuing the same opportunities in rail and energy infrastructure, embracing high-speed rail, and nuclear and solar power." Yet I would argue that the absence of older infrastructures doesn't eliminate the challenge of integrating innovations into an environment with other habits and mores. As noted in a 1991 report on China for the US Congress, technology progress is "changing the attitudes and escalating the demands of the country's citizens. Given the magnitude of these challenges, instability would threaten any government in Beijing during the 1990s."[40] This concern may still hold true today. In all cases, what we see through the window and how we interpret what we see depend on our perspective grids.

Reading the Kairos

As amply discussed by Steve Blank, we must proceed to a full customer discovery.[41] It's no less important to add marketing and communication perspectives expressed by Brian Solis, Ethan Beute, and many others. The more we understand that customers are people first whose mindset is shaped by a specific sociocultural environment, the better. That said, we must realize that as innovators, we too are people who see the world through our own grids. Notably, when we define who our customers should be, we may want to check how our own notion of "customer" is formed in the first place. For example, we can believe that grocery customers are grocery customers . . . until we discover that they are only under certain conditions and realize that the attributes of our customer concept can vary considerably. The story of Webvan, a dot.com company in the grocery business, which is usually discussed as a typical example of dot.com folly in 2000, is actually far more interesting than that and a good example of the mistakes we can make when we take our own constructs for granted.

Webvan started in 1996 and shut down in 2001 after customers' behaviors vastly differed from what the company had anticipated.[42] At the base of the Webvan initiative was the assumption that the same people already buying books on Amazon (started in 1994) or all sorts of items on eBay (started in 1995) would also purchase groceries online. The trouble, though, is that book customers and groceries customers were two fundamentally different entities. Customers in the grocery sector remained shaped by noninternet habits for much longer. In fact, it took a pandemic to dramatically shift habits around purchasing groceries online.

As entrepreneurs, we like to focus on the reasons customers will buy into our solutions, but it's even more critical to diagnose the possible components of the kairos that will prevent them from doing so. On the encouraging side for Webvan, the percentage of the US population on the internet was growing fast, going from 14 percent in 1995 to 46 percent in 2000. However, although the gender gap on the internet had virtually

disappeared by 2000, women, the main grocery shoppers, were less intense users. This factor combined with other data points, such as age, demographics, socioeconomic status, education, type of community, other
channels' competition, and relationship to food consumption (also composed of a host of emotional, health, and cultural aspects all extremely
hard to measure). So, just as the concept of "movement" has a different meaning depending on the theory of physics in which it's used, your
concept of customer is conditioned by the framework that guides your
own perception of reality. This is something we often forget when we
use words that we believe are easy to understand. In reality, a "customer"
is a construct whose components can vary depending on our reference
system.

For us in the twenty-first century, it's hard not to smile at the fact
that the best solution to address the horse manure problem in large cities
in the early 1900 was the use of automobiles, not bicycles. So were people in the early twentieth century idiots? No. They interpreted their surroundings through the knowledge grids they had at their disposal. Were
Webvan's marketers as reckless as many analysts were tempted to declare
after the company's failure? No. The founders and investors of Webvan
saw the world through their lens. In 1996 the internet had the wind in its
sails; online businesses were popping up left and right. The company had
huge financial means, and the "first mover advantage" as well as scaling
to "get big fast" mantras were on everyone's mind. Allegiance to many of
the internal rules of the innovation ideological ecosystem prevailed over
what we see after the fact as an assessment of who and where customers
were—and the very definition of the word "customer."

Again, not all layers of kairos move at the same speed. When we don't
realize this fast enough, our company is heading straight for disaster, especially when the company is new. When the company is well established,
innovators can adjust their course of action and have a greater cushion for
errors. For example, the fact that the giant game maker Ubisoft faced vo-
cal backlash from gamers for exploring the blockchain and nonfungible
token (NFT) space in 2021 made Didier Genevois, Ubisoft's blockchain
technical director, admit that this major change would take some time.[43]

CONCLUSION

Our sense of agency makes us start. But reality quickly shakes our certitudes. The innovation kairos can throw us into a maze. We believe we can hold on to something, but as we address people we believed should be "our" customers, we may find out that they ignore us for a host of reasons that may not even add up. The innovation kairos operates very much like a grinder that only spares the pieces that serve its durability more than our predictions.

As we innovate, we have to be familiar with the ABCs of entrepreneurship to keep our company afloat while admitting that the mission that made us start the company could remain a moving goalpost for some time because the rules or criterion for success do change as the multiplayer innovation game progresses within the kairos maze. As entrepreneurs, we want as much operational predictability as we can, while as innovators we have to be aware that we embark on a treasure hunt for which there is no certain positive outcome. Is there a solution to this dilemma? In practice, yes, at least to some extent. It's to start small, look at each setback as a rebounding opportunity and at each success as a building block toward a larger project.

By the same token, the complexity of the kairos is also structurally the "opportunity." As challenging as it may be to "break through" the multiple layers of the kairos or even occupy a tiny spot on one of them, it's also why what happens in one or some of its layers can inspire us if we cultivate the multidisciplinary brain needed to connect dots. It's also what makes us understand why competing innovations can coexist (chapter 6) with comparable brilliance, even if its internal dynamic makes it hard for us to stand out (chapter 7) or sustain our organization's innovative drive (chapter 12).

6

Can Competing Innovations Coexist?

Undoubtedly philosophers are in the right, when they tell us that
nothing is great or little otherwise than by Comparison.
—Jonathan Swift

There's no one way to navigate the kairos, which allows for the coexistence of dissimilar products with identical goals. At the end of the 1970s, putting computers in the hands of nonspecialists was one of the big ideas. Who won? Many, among them Apple and Microsoft.

This case study starts with how personal computing was perceived within the genealogy of computing.[1] One hypothesis was that it would upset the primacy of large systems. Did it impact the competitive positioning of one of the first huge successes, the Apple II? Not really. Did Steve Jobs's assumption that the world would be a better place if Big Blue / IBM was smashed into pieces when he launched the Macintosh work out as expected? No, and the Mac almost died. Microsoft's opposite approach did prevail, while also leveraging the new capabilities the Mac was bringing.

This journey into this tranche of computing's chronology shows how the rules at play within the multilayered kairos can determine the products' destiny just as much as what their initiators believe they do. It also shows why the binary thinking that makes us wonder whether innovation is a revolutionary endeavor or an evolutionary process doesn't say much on why innovations seep into the mores or don't.

PERSONAL COMPUTING IN THE GENEALOGY OF COMPUTING

As I discussed in chapter 4, comparable or related innovations show up at the same time. Large trends emerge subsequent to a combination of factors shaping up new domains. For example, the bacteriology space came about from the convergence of various factors: contagious diseases that plagued the nineteenth century, new economic and urbanization structures caused by the Industrial Revolution, improvements in instruments (like the microscope), legislative measures, and, of course, research linking diseases and microorganisms, like Ferdinand Cohn's sterile culture mediums; Robert Koch's identification of tuberculosis, cholera, and anthrax; or Louis Pasteur's growth of microorganisms.

By the 1970s, modern computing, that is, digital electronics, was in full swing. It grew out of dozens of antecedent milestones, such as the first working germanium-based transistor created by John Bardeen and Walter Brattain in 1947, followed by other critical inventions such as Jean Hoerni's planar process to build and connect individual components of a transistor, Robert Noyce's monolithic integrated circuit chip, Mohamed Atalla and Dawon Kahng's MOSFET, the development of the complementary MOS (CMOS) process by Frank Wanlass and Chih-Tang Sah, and the continuous expansion of the number of transistors included in each chip.

The first commercial microprocessor chip (Intel 4004) was co-designed in 1971 by Ted Hoff, Stanley Mazor, Federico Faggin (who also led the development of the Intel 8008 and 8080), and Masatoshi Shima.[2] The microprocessor war had begun. Faggin left Intel to found Zilog in late 1974. He conceived the Z80, which compelled Intel to accelerate the development of its 8086 and 8088, the processor used in one of the most influential microcomputers of the 1980s, the IBM PC, which also spurred the ascendency of Microsoft's operating system. Motorola released its 6800 in August 1974, and MOS Technology offered the 650x family of processors, designed by a former member of the Motorola team, Chuck Peddle. The most famous model of that series was the cost-effective 6502, used in the Apple II, which sealed Apple's reputation.

The emergence of personal computing is a key chapter in the history of technology innovations. However, this emergence can also be read through a different grid: the human landscape that enabled vendors to reach a new audience.

After the Watergate scandal, many people withdrew from politics, and the activist groups that continued to fight for expanded social and political rights also strengthened desires for a more personal sense of liberation. As a result, the kairos harbored a line of thought that wasn't about extolling breakthroughs in microprocessor technology but more about how personal computers would be a means to empower people. People from all walks of life, who didn't have access to large computers and were hoping to be more than clerks sitting in front of a mainframe terminal, wanted to remove computing power from the priesthood of the few.

Personal computing symbolized the future, which cast mainframes (and later smaller versions, then called "mini-computers") as mainstays of the past. So, while there was a continuity at the technology level, the generational insurrection lexicon stressed an ideological discontinuity and, with it, a straw man of sorts that had to be knocked down.

In 1984 David Sanger, then a twenty-four-year-old reporter for the *New York Times*, crystallized this zeitgeist when he announced that "the nation's computer industry should pass a remarkable milestone this year: For the first time, the value of desktop, personal computers sold in the U.S.—computers that were almost unheard of only eight years ago—will overtake sales of the large 'mainframe' machines that first cast America as the leader in computer technology."[3] Indeed, desktop computer sales were expected to jump to $11.6 billion in 1984, up from $7.5 billion in 1983, while mainframe sales would drop to $11.4 billion from $11.7 in 1983.

Yet new desktop computer fans were reading numbers from their own observatory. Mainframe companies had been going downhill for a while, but IBM, which owned the lion's share of the market, hadn't. In fact, IBM was already exerting a critical role in personal computing thanks to its contracting the young Microsoft in November 1980 for the creation of an operating system that was to be called MS-DOS.

Engineers often had reasons to be somewhat indifferent to the ideological noise around the desktop computer revolution that they were making. Many had honed their skills on large systems in major organizations or universities. These intrepid engineers loved programming these systems and were also having fun creating computer games. For example, in 1951 British computer scientist Christopher Strachey (one of the fathers of "time-sharing") developed a game of draughts ("checkers" in the United States) on the Pilot ACE, which was a reduced version of the Automatic Computing Engine designed by Alan Turing. In 1952 Sandy Douglas created OXO (noughts and crosses for the Brits and tic-tac-toe in America) for the EDSAC computer at the University of Cambridge. Also for the EDSAC, Stanley Gill's game was a dot approaching a line in which one of two gates could be opened.

The same tradition had developed in the United States. Computers galvanized what was probably the first US hacking group, the Tech Model Railroad Club (TMRC), started at MIT in 1946. Its fame reached new heights after Digital Equipment Corporation (DEC), founded by Harlan Anderson and Ken Olsen in 1957, donated a PDP-1 computer to MIT. Students from TMRC worked on serious stuff such as the LISP programming language designed by John McCarthy, but in 1961 they also developed *Spacewar!*, a video game inspired by Marvin Minsky's Minskytron or "Three Position Display." One of the authors of the game was Steve Russell, the same Steve Russell who explained to Bill Gates and Paul Allen how to use the DEC PDP-10 when they were part of the programming group of Lakeside School (Seattle) in 1968. Nolan Bushnell was one of many computer science students of the 1960s who played *Spacewar!*. He and Ted Dabney formed Syzygy to produce a *Spacewar!* clone, and in 1972 they founded the arcade game company Atari.

This is the overall landscape in which Apple and Microsoft entered the innovation scene and became key actors in the desktop computing revolution. They each handled the mainframe straw man very differently.

- For Apple in the Apple II era, the mainframe straw man wasn't really a factor. It was the business space of corporations. This was the prevailing view of the makers of the first generation of personal computers, notably, Apple's co-founder Steve Wozniak. This separatism may, in retrospect, seem somewhat shortsighted given that the killer app on the Apple II was a business application, the spreadsheet.

- For Apple in the Macintosh era, the straw man was what Steve Jobs saw as a nefarious reality: IBM symbolized corporate and human oppression. Jobs's perspective as a "disruptor" when he positioned the Macintosh didn't pay off. The Mac almost failed because Jobs's optical powers discarded other environmental signals.
- Microsoft didn't view the mainframe as a straw man. Mainframes and personal computers were on a continuum that catered to the world of business users. With the immense power of its IBM partnership, Microsoft had the wind behind its sails. This approach paid off big time.

THE APPLE II: DIFFERENTIATION IN THE LATE 1970S

Apple has been one of the most innovative companies of the past forty-plus years. So let's take a more precise look at two of its early innovations: the Apple II (or Apple][) and the Macintosh. Which one was an innovation success? We tend to say that it's the Macintosh, mostly because the Apple II no longer exists. However, when I ask *when* the Macintosh proved to be a successful innovation, younger people are hesitant. They're even more surprised to find out why the Apple II immediately succeeded while the Mac didn't. Yet the Apple II was a major innovation whose success inspired the IBM PC to a large extent and a massive personal computer industry outside its grasp. And, while the Macintosh failed to be a successful product at first, it inspired a revolution with its graphical user interface (GUI) and mouse input device and transformed the entire personal computer industry.

You Don't Need to Be the First or the Only One

Immediately following the Apple-1 in 1976, the 1977 Apple II joined a cohort of early personal computers. The Altair 8800, designed in 1974 by MITS, is usually recognized as what sparked the microcomputer revolution even though it's not the computer that spread it.[4] As Jeremy Reimer summarized in Ars Technica, "the concept and form factor of desktop computers, with add-on boards that plugged into a standardized bus, the concept of third-party software, and the idea of retail computer dealers and dealer expositions were all pioneered by MITS."[5]

The Altair 8800 inspired enthusiasts, including the habitués of the Homebrew Computer Club.[6] Many of them would create important software and hardware companies. They were part of an ebullient technology innovation ecosystem often connected to or influenced by the counterculture of the 1960s.

Various magazines hailed the microcomputer revolution. Byte, for example, touted the "1977 Trinity"—that is, the Commodore PET 2001, the Tandy TRS-80, and the Apple II—because they were three personal computers that didn't need to be assembled like the Altair 8800. They were ready to run. All three were innovations in their own right, even though each had a different fate. The Tandy TRS-80 was discontinued in 1981, and the Commodore PET 2001 in 1982, whereas the Apple II lasted sixteen years. The IBM PC, which came out in 1981 and would ultimately influence the whole space, flooded the market pretty quickly, along with a plethora of IBM PC compatibles and other famous computers such as the Commodore 64 or the popular Atari 8-bit family. The ecosystem triggered an explosion of novel pieces of hardware and software.

The Appliance That Won the People's Hearts

How do you create a darling that captures the hearts of consumers? Innovative products tap diversely into our personal or collective unconscious. More often than not, the very newness that prompts Aha moments also activates a wide set of older signals in our brain (emotions, feelings, understanding, memories, actions, etc.). Sometimes, recall and innovation don't cohere in the public consciousness, but they coexist and vary depending on people's history. For example, Elon Musk's Cybertruck, unveiled in November 2019, was allegedly inspired by the 1982 science fiction movie *Blade Runner*, but it first reminded me of an old model construction Meccano kit.

The "1977 Trinity" seized the technology moment, but Apple tapped into additional layers of the kairos. It not only fit right into the breakneck evolution of the hardware and software space and often surpassed it thanks to Steve Wozniak's genius, but it also imposed the appliance metaphor and, with it, the idea that computers could be just as accessible as household items. The fact is that in April 1977, a few weeks before the Apple II shipped, *Byte* noted, "It may be the first product to fully qualify as the 'appliance computer.' An 'appliance computer' is by definition a completed system which is purchased off the retail shelf, taken home, plugged in and used."[7]

Apple was the first computer company to associate its product, a new and still-enigmatic object for many, with a humanized and familiar environment—and give it a compelling appearance. This feature became an essential part of Apple's design philosophy during Jobs's time at Apple. Reportedly, while "haunting the appliances aisles at Macy's," Steve Jobs was struck by the style of Cuisinart's food processors, a company founded in 1971 by Carl Sontheimer.[8] This impression made him want a sleek case made of light molded plastic. He offered Jerry Manock $1,500 to produce such a design, thus starting one of the most striking hallmarks of Apple's products but also emphasizing the fact that interface and design quality aren't just cosmetic tricks; they are also mechanisms that stage innovations on the societal scene and thus allow customers to connect with them.

In this energetic zeitgeist in which vendors competed for price and technical capabilities, Apple struck a latent nerve that was irrelevant to most technologists but existed in people: the human cords of kindness. This concern was reflected in the friendliness of the Apple logo (then a multicolored striped apple with a bite) designed by Rob Janoff and "The Apple Marketing Philosophy" penned by Mike Markkula, Apple's marketing and business guru of the early days, who emphasized empathy as well as the positive psychological impact of a quality design.[9]

Apple II won the hearts of its customers, as lyrically expressed by Steven Levy after he acquired an Apple II Plus (the second model of the Apple II series, sold between June 1979 and December 1982):

> There are machines that do some of the things I do with an Apple II a
> bit better than I can do them with my Apple, but none of those machines
> can sit on my desk and be an Apple, which just by sitting there says, "I'm
> a computer. Touch me. I can do amazing things." . . . The secret every
> Apple owner knows is that in this world some of us are passengers and
> some of us are pilots. People who own IBMs are passengers in ambas-
> sador class. First-class riders buy Hewlett-Packard. Epson folk have res-
> ervations in coach, and Commodore 64 flies stand-by. Kids at half price
> own Ataris. Up in the cockpit, scarves tossed to the wind, are the Apple
> owners. All Apple owners see themselves as pioneers, and appreciate the
> original personality in a computer as well as its foxy looks."[10]

Yet were Steve Wozniak and Steve Jobs the only gods in the kairos? Of course not.

Who Was *TIME*'s "Person of the Year"?

Steve Wozniak and Steve Jobs were part of a personal computer galaxy captured by *TIME*; its San Francisco bureau chief was Michael Moritz, who would become one of the most celebrated venture capitalists in the world. In January 1983, the magazine explained why it didn't elect a "man of the year" but a "machine of the year": "There are some occasions when the most significant force in a year's news is not a single individual but a process, and a widespread recognition by a whole society that this process is changing the course of all other processes. That is why, after weighing the ebb and flow of events around the world, *TIME* has decided that 1982 is the year of the computer."[11]

But was the machine story the only relevant one? No. Bill Gates and Paul Allen weren't addressing the new era from a hardware perspective. After attracting attention for their 1975 Altair BASIC programming

language, they were well on their way to transforming the microcomputer software industry (hence the name Microsoft, established in 1975).
By displacing the first meaningful mass-market operating system CP/M,
created by Gary Kildall in 1974 for Intel-based microprocessors, with what
would soon become MS-DOS, they were the force behind the success of
the IBM PC introduced in August 1981.

In February 1982, pioneering computer magazine publisher David
Bunnell had prophetically dubbed Bill Gates a "Software Guru" in an interview with a full-page portrait.[12] He was "The Man behind the Machine,"
that is, the IBM PC, with a pragmatic perspective and clear plans on how
to deliver on customers' expectations given that it was already obvious to
him that "people are buying a solution, not a computer." Gates's pitch was
a business-oriented message addressing practical needs, not any form of
sentimental connection between people and their computer.

What became the Apple-versus-IBM and the Apple-versus-Microsoft
battles stem from the exact same environment, and determining which
company was the most innovative is a matter of perspective. The innovation kairos can hatch very different products. The market and, of course,
history do eliminate a lot of them, but this doesn't mean that they were
less instrumental in shaping the world where others survived better.

The elimination of many ideas is often triggered by random phenomena (internal company issues, financial shortcomings, market desatura-
tion effects, etc.) and not always because they're less innovative. Look at
what happened with the first iteration of Atari: the company was unable
to survive the video game crash of 1983, but nobody can forget that it pioneered electronic arcade games and made history with Pong. In the same
way, we can't overlook that Steve Wozniak built Atari's Breakout arcade
video game (aided by Steve Jobs) or that Bushnell introduced Steve Jobs
to Don Valentine, who had founded Sequoia Capital in 1972 and invested
in both Atari and Apple. After all, and perhaps most strikingly, the innovation kairos is also a highly collaborative environment where friends, foes,
or frenemies operate hand in hand, willingly or unwillingly, and where
success can be evaluated from diverse perspectives.

THE MIXED RECEPTION OF THE MACINTOSH

If there's one archetypal product that illustrates how perplexing it can be to evaluate an innovation and figure out its fate within the kairos, it's the Macintosh. When the Macintosh came out, there was no doubt that it was the computer of the future in the minds of many. The story, though, is more complex. The Macintosh got a mixed reception to say the least.

Steve Jobs's Grand Expectations

By 1980 Apple was already a formidable company. Its initial public offering (IPO) prospectus, published in December 1980, reported that sales had grown from $774,000 in 1977 to $118 million in 1980, "a pace which would inspire envy in any 21st-century unicorn," as tech journalist Harry McCracken puts it.[13]

Given that we were in the early days of personal computing and that competition was coming from everywhere, pressure was high for Apple to maintain its presence in the limelight. So, by the end of 1978, development work had started for the Apple III as well as for the Lisa, which used the more advanced Motorola 68000 processor and had a graphical user interface. In 1979 Jef Raskin had initiated the Macintosh project, which Steve Jobs took over after he was thrown out of the Lisa development team. Jobs viewed the Macintosh as his revenge and magnum opus.

Jobs was intent on revolutionizing the entire computer industry. In his 1984 speech introducing the Macintosh, he posited that the new machine would become "the third industry milestone product," the first two being, according to him, the 1977 Apple II and the 1981 IBM PC. Jobs forgot about the Commodore 64, which was outselling everything at the time.[14] His line of fire was the IBM PC equipped with Microsoft MS-DOS. He was also repeatedly adamant about how the success of the Macintosh would be assessed: "Apple offers no compromise to the IBM standard with the Macintosh," he declared. "If it fails, we deserve to fail. If it succeeds, no compromise will be necessary."[15]

By Jobs's own standards at the time, the Mac failed. It sold well in 1984 but not so well in 1985, and never in its history did it come close to unseating the IBM PC/clone industry.

So, what stood in the way of the adoption of the Macintosh? Steve Jobs overlooked three important forces at play within the layers of the kairos:

1. the loss aversion factor;
2. the advertising gap instinct trap;
3. the uniqueness trap.

The Loss Aversion Factor: The Mac's Limitations

The development of the Macintosh is a fascinating saga, reported in details by Andy Hertzfeld in *Revolution in the Valley: The Insanely Great Story of How the Mac Was Made.*[16] The effervescent 1980s demanded newness, and the Macintosh was undeniably a treasure trove of technological and artistic prowess as well as a brilliant interpretation of a host of novelties and experiments produced by Xerox Palo Alto Research Center (PARC) starting in 1970.[17]

The Macintosh was the first personal computer designed around a fully fledged GUI and using a mouse destined to a wide audience. Because of a tight integration of the hardware and system software, it was much easier to make it work than any other machine. Yet the same part of the kairos that calls for novelty also grows its own rules for what that novelty ought to be—hence the onslaught of criticism that plagued the neonate.

For the general public, the Macintosh was a mixed bag. The friendly "hello" greeting users on the screen wasn't cutting it. The Macintosh came out with hardly any software, shipped with only 128K of memory, was slow, had no hard disk, was a closed system, lacked color, had a minuscule screen, and was expensive—to name a few of its flaws. Jobs was present at the right time and place but misread the market and shipped an exciting, innovative product that lacked sufficient capabilities to be a practical choice for people. The various layers of the kairos were not aligned.

Most problems could have been avoided had Steve Jobs heeded the remarks of his own team. Many issues were addressed in September 1984, when Apple released a model with 512K; then, in 1985, the combination of Apple's LaserWriter printer, Adobe's PostScript, and the publication of Aldus PageMaker gave the Macintosh a powerful niche by starting a genre that became known as "desktop publishing," an expression often attributed to Paul Brainerd, the co-founder of Aldus in 1984—later acquired by Adobe, founded in 1982 by John Warnock and Charles Geschke. Unfortunately, first impressions can create big damage, especially in a fiercely competitive environment. As a result, the Macintosh failed to upset the makeup of the personal computing market of the 1980s.

The basic lesson here is that as innovative as we want to be, we can't just push aside popular expectations and hope that people will only focus on what's new. As loaded with fascinating features as the Macintosh was and as promising as desktop publishing was, what the Macintosh didn't have (and particularly PC compatibility) was perceived as a major obstacle to adoption. No matter what innovators think, what the general market believes becomes the law of the land. Innovators can't unilaterally forgo basic human behavioral traits, especially not what psychologists and economists call "loss aversion" or "endowment effect." The "Compatibility Craze" was here to stay.[18]

People love the idea of acquiring something new (objects, knowledge, relationships, etc.) only if they're sure that they won't miss what they already have or have heard is a must-have.

The Advertising Gap Instinct Trap

Steve Jobs had created gigantic expectations. As Hertzfeld put it, "the marketing campaign that launched the original Macintosh was almost as imaginative and innovative as the product itself. . . . The basic idea was to create a perception of the Macintosh introduction as an epochal event."[19] It was, indeed, but it was also double-edged.

In his ambition to go for dominance, Jobs displayed a rather sectarian worldview. As much as we can hail the 1984 Macintosh commercial directed by Ridley Scott as one of the boldest creations in advertising, it also demonized and almost ridiculed millions of new personal computer users. They didn't necessarily see themselves as the victims of Big Blue (IBM), Big Brother, or of any Orwellian totalitarian leader, for that matter. Often the opposite: in the early 1980s, many users felt they had overcome their distrust of computers and were thrilled by all the new things they were learning.

The 1984 commercial illustrates what Hans Rosling called the "gap instinct," which is the tendency to "have a strong dramatic instinct toward binary thinking, a basic urge to divide things into two distinct groups, with nothing but an empty gap in between. We love to dichotomize. Good versus bad. Heroes versus villains."[20] But where does such an approach leave normal people? Sometimes, it's unclear: "The stories of opposites are engaging and provocative and tempting, but they rarely help understanding."[21] Were those who had read Orwell's *Nineteen Eighty-Four* inclined to see themselves as part of the helpless "proles"? No.

The series of commercials that presented the Macintosh as "the computer for the rest of us" was similarly ambiguous.[22] The intent was to democratize computing. Jobs had the wild hope that intellectuals often exhibit when they believe they can orchestrate proletarian revolutions. But intellectuals are often mistaken: Who wants to be part of an undifferentiated bulk? Who wants to be part of the masses rather than the classes?[23] And if you were happy to be part of the masses, could you afford a computer whose initial price was $2,495 (almost $7,000 in 2022), that is, 11 percent of the median household revenue in 1984 in the United States? The Commodore 64 was priced at $600 and selling about 2 million units per year.[24]

To top it all off, this "rest of us" weren't exactly painted generously. The star wasn't even the user; the Macintosh was the one with all the wits: "The real genius of Macintosh is that you don't have to be a genius to use it," the ad declared, and this, at a time when computer literacy was promising all sorts of new job opportunities. So, at the very moment people were feeling empowered, a major vendor was telling them they'd wasted their time acquiring new skills, because now technology would do all the heavy lifting. Or, was the Mac targeting the ignorant? Not quite . . .

In his presentation introducing the Macintosh on January 24, 1984 (heard only by a happy few), Jobs indicated that the Macintosh would target the 25 million "knowledge workers," a growing buzzword designating people sitting behind desks at smaller companies as well as college students, the "knowledge workers of tomorrow."[25] So was the Macintosh for those who felt part of an elite of sorts? In many respects, it was. By the same token, then, it may not be surprising that it didn't immediately garner the market share originally anticipated.

The Uniqueness Trap

Innovators want to bring something unique. But here is the paradox of innovations that I mentioned earlier: The uniqueness that may protect us can also push us into a corner. Innovations inspire clones. The Mac was inspired by innovations created at Xerox PARC and the Stanford Research Institute (SRI), and both combined inspired Microsoft's Windows. But Windows won because it also powered a gigantic PC clone industry inspired not by Apple but by the IBM PC, which itself had been partly inspired by the Apple II. Innovations inspire imitations and copies, which are often, whether we like it or not, a proof of their substantive importance. The Macintosh had a few clones but often partial and unauthorized, and the phenomenon was by no means close to what happened in the PC industry.

The first PC clones appeared as soon as IBM launched its IBM PC and before the Mac even was out. Criteria to meet to deserve the "title" of clone were also established quickly, as tech journalist Corey Sandler then emphasized: "And finally, the 'PC Work-Alikes.' To achieve this first cousin status, a computer must accommodate the user who takes a disk from an IBM PC, walks across the room, and plugs it into a 'foreign' machine. We shall award the title 'clone' only to those micros that meet this rigorous standard."[26] IBM could not resist the flood of clones. To be part of the emerging market, the company had broken away from its traditional proprietary technology approach and offered a personal computer made of parts from established companies and, importantly, didn't have exclusive rights to Microsoft's operating system. Although IBM moved very fast in a market where demand was high, it could not deter Compaq from creating a clone in 1983—as well as many others. When IBM tried to reclaim the market with new proprietary technology, the clone makers (Compaq, Dell, HP, Acer, etc.) resisted the idea of paying any licensing fees to IBM. "To this day," computer industry analyst Tim Bajarin noted, "the clone makers standing up to IBM is considered one of the greatest business coalitions to preserve what turned out to be one of the first open hardware architectures."[27] Imitators became the engine of the personal computer innovation stack.

By fall 1984, the dominance of IBM and clones was unquestionable: "The array of IBM [compatible] personal computers is now formidable," a *Byte Magazine* editorial asserted, adding that "Apple's Macintosh offers a superior user interface that attracts passersby."[28] By 1985 the prospect for the wide success of the Macintosh was gone.

THE MACINTOSH SURVIVAL PHASE

Why did the Macintosh survive? The short response is paradoxical for a product that was supposed to ignite a revolution. The Mac survived thanks to the slow tempo of durable sentiments that developed between September 1985, when Steve Jobs left Apple, and December 1996, when he returned. So it survived for twelve years as Apple struggled to regain its edge. If Apple had been a small company, the Macintosh would have disappeared.

The history of the Macintosh illustrates that when "disruption" pomposity fails, everyone can be thankful that a company has the possibility of adopting a "sustaining" innovation strategy to save the day. By 1997, 20 to 25 million Macintosh users had become a movement of people speaking the same language, and this for various reasons:

1. Apple progressively delivered on Steve Jobs' early promises.
2. Macintosh fans remained unrelenting evangelists.
3. The Macintosh's foothold in education trained a generation.
4. Windows was trying everything it could to speak Macintosh too . . .

Apple Progressively Delivered on the Early Promises of the Macintosh

Innovations rarely come as fully formed bodies ready to wage and win wars. Many die because they come from organizations with insufficient resources and, as a result, don't have the means to improve their initial version. After Steve Jobs's departure, Apple did ensure the survival of the Macintosh by adding features, mostly under competitive pressure.

The Macintosh Plus, released in early 1986, was a welcome evolution; in 1987, Apple delivered the Macintosh SE and the Macintosh II. Through multiple iterations, the Macintosh did reasonably well until 1995. Of course, it was unable to compete with PCs, which had become much easier to use with the release in 1992 of Windows 3.1, which mimicked the Macintosh user interface. Nonetheless, the Macintosh rose from 1.3 million units in 1990 to 4.5 million units in 1995.[29] By 1996, however, prospects were starting to look grim, with severe revenue losses and grave management issues. The Macintosh seemed like it might be doomed, along with the company.

Apple got a new lease on life with the purchase early in 1997 of Steve Jobs's failed computer company, NeXT. Despite its failure, the NeXTSTEP/OPENSTEP operating system was amazing, and it would become the foundation of a new generation of Mac operating systems. Jobs progressively regained full control of the company, accepting the job of interim CEO in September of 1997. As expected, he slammed everything that had been done while he was away, but luckily for him he still had the Macintosh to restart from. He cleaned up the product line, and the iMac, released in August 1998, with its gumdrop looks and its translucent plastic case, blew people away. It was a Macintosh appearing in new clothes.

The Fans' Unrelenting Evangelism

The initial Macintosh users were far more than early adopters meant to validate/invalidate a new product. Thanks to the Macintosh evangelists (Mike Boitch, Alain Rossmann, and Guy Kawasaki) in the United States and Apple executives abroad (like Jean-Louis Gassée, initially based in France, or Sören Olsson, in Sweden), people believed in the Macintosh as fervently as did Steve Jobs. The Macintosh base were more loyal fans than customers, a force-multiplying layer that brands or products rarely achieve.

The Macintosh granted people a sense of social status. Even when they had boring jobs, they didn't see themselves as paper pushers. Using a Macintosh made them feel superior and more creative, and for good reasons: Mac-compatible software generally created slicker, neater work in comparison to the PC alternative.

The Mac emboldened a composite community of intellectuals, artists, designers, independent developers, mavericks in corporations, and so on, and spurred the creation of powerful Macintosh user groups. Berkeley Macintosh User Group (BMUG), for example, had a sort of double mission. On the one hand, it was a resurgence of the 1960s counterculture with "roots in The Hacker Ethic and Berkeley Radicalism," as Stephen Howard and Raines Cohen put it.[30] On the other, it was a pedagogical platform, as Reese Jones explained: "There is a tremendous need for a source of objective and realistic advice to the user and to the potential computer user."[31]

The Macintosh's Foothold in Education

Almost from its inception, the Apple II had been successful in the K–12 education market. It took the strong will of Macintosh product marketer Joanna Hoffman to convince Jobs that it made sense to also put together a plan to sell Macs in higher education. Her tenacity led to the formation of the Macintosh consortium run by Dan'l Lewin, which provided discounted Macs for students and faculty.

In an environment where success was a sprint often followed by a fall, an educational program was placing the Macintosh in position for an endurance race, and its efficacy partly illustrates Max Planck's statement that important innovations must wait for their opponents to gradually die out, as discussed in chapter 3.

In his first big public comeback keynote at the August 1997 Macworld Expo, Steve Jobs emphasized that "Apple [was] the single largest education supplier in the world: 60% computers in all of education are Apples. What an incredible foundation to build on!"[32]

The Success of Windows Established the Macintosh as a Standard

Much has been written on how to interpret Steve Jobs's statement that "good artists copy; great artists steal," but one thing is clear: the products built on other products' back can also help the copied products.[33] The fact is that the success of Windows validated the Macintosh interface, in part lifted from Xerox PARC and SRI, and helped it to drift into the kairos.

The Macintosh interface was a new way to create a dialogue between users and electronic devices. Windows ultimately validated it as the language shaping the relationship between human beings and digital devices. It also became the substratum for a power business agreement. In August 1997, Microsoft purchased $150 million of nonvoting Apple stock, and the companies settled all the pending lawsuits between them. The resolution was in both vendors' interest, of course Apple's, which was in dire shape, but also Microsoft's, which was close to being threatened by antitrust laws. It is also part of the twists and turns of what's happening in the kairos and shows how intertwined its layers can become.

THE MACINTOSH REVIVAL: "THINK DIFFERENT" (IT'S THE SAME)

The survival of the Mac between 1985 and 1997 undermines the myopic visions of what timeliness means when we speak of innovations. The 1984 kairos wasn't identical to that of 1997, but this doesn't mean that they were incongruous eras either.

Innovative products truly "made to stick" can stick for a long time, sometimes for what they are intrinsically as products but more frequently for the long-lasting emotions they trigger.[34] That's what gives them migratory capabilities. Oracle founder Larry Ellison put it eloquently: "I have been using a Mac since 1984. . . . Apple is the only lifestyle brand in the computer industry, the only company that people feel passionate about. You know, my company Oracle, it's a huge company. IBM is a huge company, Microsoft is a huge company, but no one has incredible emotions associated with our companies. Only Apple is really a lifestyle brand."[35]

The 1997 Mac wasn't the same as the 1984 128K . . . except that it was still a Macintosh, a continuity that Jobs insisted on in his 1997 keynote, while also launching the "Think Different" campaign.[36]

"Think Different" tapped into most people's desire to feel and think "different" and was also a tribute to an existing base shaped by the typical '80s counterculture style, that is, "the crazy ones, the misfits, the rebels, the troublemakers, the round pegs in the square holes, the ones who see things differently," and so forth. But the ad didn't play the confrontational hand of the "1984" commercial. Just the opposite: The iconoclastic side of the message was counterbalanced by the image of seventeen long-lasting role models of the twentieth century (Albert Einstein, Bob Dylan, Martin Luther King Jr., John Lennon, Muhammad Ali, Mahatma Gandhi, Jim Henson, Maria Callas, Pablo Picasso, etc.). This campaign had a cross-generational appeal.

An ecosystem doesn't disappear just because "time flies." In fact, time doesn't fly, because the kairos is a combination of contexts that self-rearrange, often imperceptibly blending into each other, pushing some realities into the background and eventually into oblivion while pushing others into the limelight—so much so that the Macintosh was de facto positioned as a favorite in the new internet era. Nearly two-thirds of all websites were created on a Macintosh at the time.

The May 6, 1998, event introducing the iMac marked a turning point for Apple. The colorful iMacs reanimated a moribund Apple, and the rest is history. Apple's marriage of hardware and software became the foundation for a transformation of the music business, the mobile phone industry, tablet computers, the app market, the gadget scene, and even the brick-and-mortar world. The Macintosh never had a dominant market share, but it was the foundation that underpinned every subsequent product and made Apple a gigantic brand.

TAKEAWAY: TWO VISIONS OF INNOVATION

Steve Jobs optimistically focused on promises that fit his worldview, his aesthetic palette and vision for creating products that elicit an emotional connection, while Bill Gates stuck more practically to what customers were most likely to purchase based on the state of an industry. I would guard anybody from making any judgment on which is the better one. They are simply two different understandings of the same kairos. One exploits a situational logic that shows innovation as an evolutionary process (Gates) dealing with known factors. The other exploits an aspirational logic that sees innovation as a revolutionary movement (Jobs) dealing with new perceptions. Gates started from a Karl Popper–type principle of rationality (you know where you're going).[37] Jobs implicitly adopted a sort of popular "creative destruction" philosophy (you know what you're destroying, but you can't know whether what you create will survive).

Situational Logic: Innovation as an Evolutionary Process

Bill Gates didn't start with the prevailing ideology that personal computing would destroy mainframes and minicomputers. IBM was what it was, but by all accounts it was a serial innovator since its inception. So his alliance with IBM was a thoughtful move.

While it's clear that computers sitting on desktops were different from mainframes, IBM entering into the fray was a turning point in the history of the young personal computer industry. It reduced the uncertainty of its adoption and accelerated the speed of its usage. In corporations, personal computers were addressing users whose needs were well defined. Scores of middle managers of all stripes with no access to mainframes had been managing almost everything manually and had had to wait weeks on end to get the most basic reports related to their own group or department. So, they had reason to welcome personal computers, and especially a piece of software that was running on them, spreadsheets. The VisiCalc spreadsheet, conceived by Dan Bricklin and Bob Frankston in 1979, initially for the Apple II, was the first "killer app."[38] Yet Apple didn't take full advantage of its significance. The company was selling computers and often saw software mostly as a prop for its hardware. VisiCalc became multiplatform, and other companies developed spreadsheets. Microsoft developed Multiplan (1982) to compete against VisiCalc, and Lotus 1-2-3 (1983) launched on the IBM PC. Ten years later, Microsoft Excel became the industry standard for spreadsheets on all platforms.

Bill Gates took a global view of the market faster than anybody else with the implacable logic of a pragmatic and cerebral statistician. Albeit new, personal computers were de facto situated within the bounded precincts of corporations. Consequently, he fast-deployed a two-pronged strategy: on the one hand, he gained control over the operating system of the IBM PC as well as PC compatibles, and, on the other, he accelerated scalable software development and project management techniques to produce key multiplatform applications under the guidance of Charles Simonyi (a XEROX PARC veteran, who, like a few others, disseminated his experience across the new industry).

When managed with a strong hand, innovation seen as an evolutionary process indexed on situational rationality is as transformational as innovation seen as a revolutionary movement. In this regard, I like the analogy that Robert Cringely drew between Bill Gates and Henry Ford in *Accidental Empires*.[39] Ford didn't invent cars. What made him a formidable innovator was an understanding of people's needs and the design of novel supply chain processes allowing for fast and cost-effective mass production.

Aspirational Logic: Innovation as a Revolutionary Movement

In 1981 Steve Wozniak, the brain behind the Apple II, was badly injured in a plane accident, which led Jobs to take control of the technology future of Apple. Wozniak's goal was to make a computer that people would love. Jobs's goals were more aspirational: to change the world.

Steve Jobs illustrated what Abernathy and Clark had described as "the revolutionary mode of innovation . . . dominated by 'technology push'" in a climate that encouraged "a sense of competitive assault."[40] Jobs combined the Macintosh as a technology novelty with the dream of novel organizational and social frameworks. His ambition was to deliver "imagined futures," to use the title of a book by Jens Beckert, that is, to allow people "to move beyond inherited thought patterns and categories and [access] an as-if world different from the present reality."[41] Jobs's phenomenal storytelling bolstered that dream, which, in many ways, was irresistible. You wanted to believe in his cause, all the more so as Apple had extraordinary evangelists. They were extremely effective at relaying Jobs's belief system and at amplifying it via user groups that drew in droves of people.

But, as Beckert states, "making fictional expectations credible and obtaining support sufficient to even begin the task of attempting to transform them into concrete reality is a formidable challenge."[42] It was indeed. Why would people rush to buy an expensive Macintosh for the future that was of limited use in the present given the small number of applications available and poor performance when it first came out?

Bill Gates and Steve Jobs leveraged different aspects and velocities of the kairos. Gates banked on the predictable tempo of companies' budgets, whereas Steve Jobs relied on the slower pace of deep individual aspirations: creativity, freedom, empowerment, and an aesthetic relationship to one's environment. The problem with slower time velocities is that they can indifferently trigger impulse or delayed buys. Their advantage, however, is that when and if users accept the uncertainty of the dream, they'll stick around and fight for it as long as there's a chance of any delivery on the promise.

When you look at the history of the Macintosh, you can also see the paradox of revolutions. When they're not well prepared, they flop, something that political history has shown countless times. They come across as short-lived insurgencies because they had assumed a convergence between societal layers that didn't happen. Successful revolutions are the apex of an evolutionary (and often meandering) process that builds a progressive alignment of layers. Absent this preliminary course, the objectives pursued by revolutionaries die, unless they are taken over by other innovators, like Bill Gates in this case.

CONCLUSION

The kairos harbors a range of options that pan out because of a variety of factors that exceed what we usually gather when we perform competitive analysis. Its complexity allows for the coexistence of competing innovations that tap into different layers and seep into the mores following very different customer development patterns and curves (which consequently may also require from innovators very different financial capabilities).

Over the years, a change has occurred in the evolutionary-revolutionary opposition between Microsoft and Apple and maybe, at the same time, in a dichotomic type of reasoning anchored in the nineteenth century and still regularly relayed by most twentieth-century ideologues and business theorists.

Microsoft still emphasizes a smooth business continuity and the idea of taking users where they are to move them toward new capabilities. For example, Microsoft's CEO, Satya Nadella, albeit convinced that virtual reality will become a big thing, "expects the metaverse concept to begin seeping into Microsoft's various products and businesses."[43] Thus, "Teams is going to have Mesh meetings, so these immersive meetings which will start on 2D screens whether it's PCs or smartphones, and then lead up to immersive experiences where you'll wear your AR or VR goggles."[44]

Apple abandoned the provocative style of the 1980s. In fact, it's Steve Jobs himself who did it first with the iMac, then the iPod and even more so with the iPhone. Although the company continued to use the "revolutionary" lexicon, instead of looking at revolution as a dream, it did start to position its innovations as the apex of an evolutionary process and as a natural response to frustrations experienced by users over time. So instead of romantically waving the liberty flag leading the people, Apple started to operate more as a "Velvet Revolution" orchestrator, reconciling and subsuming trends scattered across the layers of the kairos.[45] With the iPhone, Steve Jobs didn't push a dream but pulled disparate expectations together and gave a masterful presentation of the art of "standing out," which is the topic of the next chapter.

7

Why Is Standing Out Challenging?

But the cloud never comes in that quarter of the horizon from
which we watch for it.
—Elizabeth Gaskell

To be noticed, we need the right product for the right market with the right business model, the right competitive positioning at the right time, the right team and the right funding, and so on. We all know that, but such awareness is not enough to make us stand out as an innovator. As much of a captain we believe we are, the complex dynamics of the kairos can rock our boat so ruthlessly that it can be hard for us to keep our head above the water.

As I mentioned earlier, when a space opens up, aspiring innovators rush in to exploit its potential. Many get into the race, but few survive and sometimes almost none, as was the case for personal digital assistant (PDA) companies in the 1990s.[1] I selected this case for two reasons: (1) their story hasn't been distorted by recent marketing spins and (2) it's a genre to which all of us, as smartphone users, are hugely indebted today.

These companies surfaced against the personal computer industry backdrop and became the stepping stone for a major innovation, the iPhone, and modern smartphones in general. They surfed the converging waves of personal computing miniaturization, portability, and mobility. Many of them came to prominence yet only for a short while, not because they weren't good but because it's extremely difficult to have control over all the inertial forces and layers traversing a space in the making. Then, an entrant standing by or back, a late mover, can show up, redirect the innovation course, and take the spotlight. This phenomenon happens frequently, which makes innovating both a gripping and terribly frustrating game. As an innovator, you start believing you'll be a star, only to realize that no matter how much money you'll make, you'll have to be content with only being a meteor momentarily moving across in the innovation skies.

PDAS: THE QUEST FOR COMPUTING AT YOUR FINGERTIPS

PDAs belong to the personal computing rhizome. Once personal computing took off, the dream was to place small devices in everybody's hands. The atmosphere was favorable, and many companies sprouted up, but the euphoria didn't last.

Standing against the Personal Computing Rhizome Backdrop

The idea of devices connected to people through a quality user interface started in the 1960s. For example, Ivan Sutherland conceived the "light pen" to allow a user to point at and interact with objects displayed on a screen as discussed in his 1963 dissertation, "Sketchpad: A Man-Machine Graphical Communications System."[2] Research was no less active in California. In 1957 Douglas Engelbart joined SRI and first worked for Hewitt Crane on magnetic devices and miniaturizing electronics.[3] Then, he built his own lab at SRI to create multiple interface elements familiar today, such as bitmapped screens, the mouse, and a model for creating and using linked content, which became known as hypertext with Ted Nelson (who also coined the terms "hypertext" and "hypermedia").

In 1968 Alan Kay, who had worked with Ivan Sutherland and would join Xerox PARC, offered the novel concept of the Dynabook, which, as he formulated in a 1972 paper, would be "A Personal Computer for Children of All Ages."[4] It would be portable, weigh no more than two pounds, have a flat-screen display, and recognize handwriting. For him, the Dynabook was "A Dynamic Medium for Creative Thought."[5]

The landscape was set. Although the Dynabook remained a concept model, the book metaphor inspired innovators for years. It was on Steve Jobs's mind even before he launched Macintosh: "We want to put an incredibly great computer in a book that you can carry around with you and learn how to use in twenty minutes. That's what we want to do and we want to do it this decade."[6] Steve Jobs didn't do it in the 1980s. After he left Apple, he created, instead, the NeXT computer, a black cube with one-foot-long sides aimed at the higher-education market. Apple, though, used the metaphor in 1991 with its PowerBook 100. When he came back to Apple, Jobs reused it at Apple's Macworld 2008, presenting the MacBook Air as "the world's thinnest notebook," one year after the iPhone was introduced.

The Dynabook concept triggered intense activity, spanning several products across over two decades in pursuit of smaller, better, faster portable devices: portable personal computers, notebooks, subnotebooks, netbooks, message pads, organizers, personal communicators, PDAs, pen computers, tablets, smartphones, and more. It inspired the Xerox NoteTaker of 1976, which was never commercialized but influenced subsequent products such as the 1981 Osborne 1, the 1982 GRiD Compass (one of the first laptop computers), and the 1987 Linus Write-Top, the first to include handwriting-recognition software, among others. The 1989 Compaq LTE was one of the first devices to be widely referred to as a "notebook computer." The 1989 GRiDPad, created by GRiD Systems Corporation, was the first commercially successful tablet with a touchscreen interface and a stylus. It was created by Jeff Hawkins, who later founded Palm, a pioneer in PDAs.

By the early 1990s dozens of innovators were challenging each other, eagerly announcing their specs (processor, memory, display, weight and size, battery, applications, GUI, form factors, functionalities) and emphasizing certain sets of features rather than others, depending on their target markets. Many of the technologies or concepts coming from the US Defense Department research environments and academic or corporate laboratories working on enhancing human-computer interaction were finding their way into this new world of increasingly smaller, more powerful, and cost-effective devices. Virtually every major computer manufacturer had a portable computer, a pen-based device, or a tablet in its portfolio or its plans. It's in this exhilarating climate of device diversity that PDAs tried to shape their identity.

It's Hard to Stand Out in a Space in the Making

When a genre has the wind in its sails, there are still basic questions to ask, like: How can you stand out when customers are not be quite here? Which capabilities will determine their choice? Which direction will the space ultimately take?

One of the most fascinating hotbeds of research and development was General Magic, which, although secretive, was famous throughout Silicon Valley. It was founded by Marc Porat in 1989 with stars of the original team that developed the Macintosh, including Andy Hertzfeld and Bill Atkinson, soon joined by Joanna Hoffman, Dan Winkler, Phil Goldman, and Susan Kare. By the end of 1993, the company revealed its Magic Cap digital communications platform, which is sometimes viewed as a precursor to the iPhone software, but the company eventually folded in 2002 without realizing its vision.[7] Multiple additional companies had their moment of glory, and some of them fared considerably better than others, notably, Palm and BlackBerry.

Nobody had an easy ride. The entrants were faced with questions that originated directly from the backdrop they leaned against. One of them was formidable: Who would the customers really be? The obvious response was anybody wanting to do some form of portable personal computing. Sure . . . but these potential customers were confused by the plethora of products with various form factors and functions.

In fact, identity indeterminateness and abundance of features were part of the genre from the minute PDAs took the stage, notably, at the 1992 Comdex computer expo and trade show. IBM demonstrated its Simon Personal Communicator, which combined several technologies and functions: telephone, email, voice, address book, calendar, world clock, notepad, and more. The final product came out in August 1994, but its distribution ended in February 1995. Just as much of a short-lived hit was the 1993 EO 440, a phablet (a portmanteau of phone and tablet) elegantly fashioned by Frog Design.[8] Apple also launched its Newton PDA. At about the same time, the expression "smart phone" was coined by Pam Savage to describe the AT&T PhoneWriter Communicator (released at the 1993 Comdex).[9]

PDAs straddled categories, organizer and tablet devices, on the one hand, and mobile technologies, which were heating up fast, on the other. In 1996 Alain Rossmann, also an Apple veteran from the Macintosh team, started Libris, which became Unwired Planet and then Phone.com. He developed mobile client software and end-to-end mobile network solutions for internet access and web browsing. In 1999 he launched the Wireless Application Protocol (WAP), whose goal was to move various wireless technologies toward a standardized protocol. The camera phone business was also surfacing. In 1997 Philippe Kahn connected his fliptop Casio phone to his camera and laptop and ripped off a speakerphone from his car to complete an apparatus that enabled him to take and send a picture of his newborn daughter, Sophie, in real time. Kahn refined his prototype, and in 2000 Sharp used his technology to release the first commercially available integrated camera phone with a 256-color display in Japan, the J-SH04.

As we got closer to the end of the 1990s, PDAs were becoming smartphones of sorts and cell phones were adding PDA features. As early as 1996, the Nokia 9000 Communicator was a cellular phone with PDA functions. Japan was ahead of the rest of the world, but by the early 2000s new versions of the Nokia Communicator, the Ericsson R380 and the Kyocera 6025, showed that cell phones were making headway everywhere.

In the face of the evolution of cell phones, PDA vendors reacted. Companies like Blackberry leveraged the convergence of technologies, adding cellular telephony to their PDA. But the identity crisis evolved for the worse. PDA companies continued to bolt on functionality, but sales started to slide in 2001 and continued to do so over the following years: "While PDA shipments have fallen, smartphones and cell phones with PDA have taken up the slack."[10] By the end of 2006 PDAs were on an endangered list: "Right now, smartphones are the new hotness and PDAs are old and busted."[11] Both categories of products followed asymmetrical bell-shaped curves, but both were to be displaced by the new generation of smartphones heralded by the iPhone.

PDAs successfully stood out against the backdrop of personal computing but ended up being destabilized by pre-smartphones that brought the different dynamics and history of telecommunication services. In a developing market where innovative endeavors are running wild, it seems that the kairos is running wild too. It took until the iPhone in 2007 to align the kairos in ways that stabilized the PDA-smartphone industry, and it was on its way to putting a powerful computer-and-phone in the hands of billions of people around the world.

Standing Out in the Flow—and Withering in the Ebb

How is it that the most prominent PDA companies didn't stand out for a longer time and didn't survive their space's transformation? PDA innovators displayed an amazing amount of ingenuity. But what happened to them can happen to any innovator in any space. It's simply hard to realize how much the space you are building can force you to re-create yourself, because you are in the thick of it. You believe you're one of the front-stage actors, while in reality you're at risk of becoming an extra on a wider stage you can't control. That's also what's happening in 2023 for many entrepreneurs working in generative artificial intelligence, for example.

While benefiting from a collective momentum, innovators are pressured to add differentiating features as quickly as possible. In the speed race, however, these features allow them to stand out only temporarily because everybody catches up with everybody else in a matter of weeks or even days. So, as differentiation is continuously erased, innovators are compelled to always add more, and, as a result, they fall prey to a "featuritis" syndrome by which features pile up without necessarily adding up smoothly.[12] This can create irrelevance and confusion. Here are two examples related to our case study:

Irrelevance: The stylus/pen craze sidetracked many players because the technology didn't improve as fast as people had hoped. In 1991 the

Momenta Pentop had received significant press coverage but failed to succeed. So many tried to do better . . . but also failed. Apple's Newton became the topic of endless jokes because of its handwriting recognition errors. That's why, in his 2007 presentation of the iPhone,[13] Steve Jobs found complicity with the audience when he derided pen computing—and replaced it with something just as intuitive as a pen, the fingers that hold a pen, and a virtual keyboard.

Confusion: When you're in the thick of things, you may have a hard time assessing the real scope of trends and are tempted to metabolize as many of them as possible into features of yours. PDAs and smartphones displayed overlapping features, and users became confused.

When he described the slowing of PDA sales in 2005, Eric Bangeman recounted his own experience:

> When my last cell phone contract was up in 2003, I ditched my aged
> Palm V and Motorola flip-phone for a Kyocera 7135. It performs both
> functions adequately, but I'm already thinking ahead to this summer
> when my current contract expires. Having said that, I'm not all that
> excited by any of the options out there—to me, the smartphone sounds
> great in theory, but all the implementations seem to be lacking in one
> way or another. I may just pick up a cheap cell phone and sync my con-
> tacts and calendar to my iPod.[14]

PDAs and pre-smartphones were eating each other in a world in flux.

The iPod, which was not a PDA, had been released at the end of 2001, and Bangeman's last sentence reflects an interesting and prophetic hack. Like him, users wanted everything but above all a cohesion and cohesiveness that nobody was really delivering. The features race had been driving all devices toward becoming Rube Goldberg machines of sorts, in which each capability was relevant but when combined made it cumbersome for users to perform any given task.

The PDA space was imploding, and the quantitative increase of features created a viability threshold that generated the desire for a qualitatively different experience, a phenomenon that sociologist Morton Grodzins called a "tipping point." The expression had been applied to the analysis of racial dynamics by economist Thomas Schelling and was later exported into the business sphere by Malcolm Gladwell.

Especially in the early stages of a genre, many companies stand out with innovations that quickly dissolve into commodities. They all contribute to the innovation stack that forms the bedrock of the innovation dynamics, but they're rarely recognized as the paragon of a landmark innovation. The flow helps them rise. The ebb makes many of them dry up on the beach—and later movers can pick up the debris.

THE LATE MOVER ADVANTAGE

We're prone to believing that new players are the ones who move a space to the next level. In a way, they do: new companies breathe new life into an existing space by reexamining the ledges of gold that lie unexploited in their landscape. But are they always the ones who stand out at the end of the story? Not necessarily. Clearly, this wasn't the case for PDAs. In 2007 Apple's iPhone won a battle initiated by the Dynabook concept. Apple was a thirty-year-old company, not a fresh startup.

Steve Jobs leveraged some of the typical mechanisms that enable late movers to establish their dominance, including

1. taking an insider/outsider perspective;
2. leveraging an existing customers' stack;
3. positioning an idea/product within a platform approach;
4. building a collaborative support and alliance system;
5. reigniting the innovation engine.

Taking an Insider/Outsider Perspective

Apple was an insider. The company had lived through the PDA adventure with its Newton. Steve Jobs shut down the division when he came back; he knew firsthand the shortcomings of both the product and the genre. Apple actively stepped into the development of the iPhone in 2004, when PDAs were nearing the end of their course.[15] Jobs roped in multiple engineering stars capable of delivering on the technical challenges that combining a host of features in new ways would entail. One of these stars was Tony Fadell, who was the senior vice president of the iPod division. He also had a background in the PDA space from his time at General Magic before moving on to Philips Electronics, where he had led the development of Windows CE–based handheld services the Velo and the Nino.

Apple had also acquired a deep knowledge of small electronic devices with the 2001 iPod, which revolutionized the music industry. If you listen to Steve Jobs's launch presentation of the iPhone at Macworld San Francisco in 2007, you'll be struck by his emphasis on the iPod.[16] This extraordinary gadget alleviated users' frustrations caused by their Sony Walkman, Sony Discman, Sony MiniDisc, and other audio devices thanks to its design. The iPod redefined portability and became a status symbol with a pervasive echo within the kairos. In 2003 Apple launched the iTunes Music Store, which sold over a million songs in its first week, and also released iTunes (originally on Macintosh only) for Windows.

As he proclaimed the virtues of the new iPhone, Jobs exposed the irreversible irrelevance of PDAs and the first generation of smartphones, which, he said, were not so "smart," and derided the user interface of the Moto Q, Blackberry, Palm Treo, and Nokia E62. He applied his deep understanding of the kairos to ensure that the iPhone would meet the moment. Although he used his familiar lexicon ("revolutionary," "breakthrough," "leapfrog," "reinvent," "unbelievable," "pretty doggone gorgeous," and "change the entire industry") in his presentation, you can notice how he was bringing users with him and helping them transition toward his new product by connecting them with familiar gestures and expectations. He was operating a "Velvet Revolution" of sorts in a kairos that was ready for it.

Jobs once said that "Innovation is saying no to 1,000 things," but he could have also indicated that it's saying "yes" to hundreds. While reinterpreting prior advances, Apple reset the PDA and smartphone categories at once. The iPhone brought additional innovations that powered their convergence, such as expanding multitouch functionalities by an order of magnitude, an onscreen keyboard, a glass slate, and alliances with a telephone services provider. The iPhone delivered more features than PDAs and early smartphones combined but merged them all in a completely different fashion, restaging usage patterns and reinitializing both genres through a new usability paradigm: touch.

Jobs redefined the digital world metaphor registry. As prevalent as the "book" metaphor had been, and as important as it still was to be able to hold a small device in the "palm" of your "hand," the new smartphone was first and foremost about being *in touch* with anyone, by phone, email, or text message, and accessing whatever you wanted on the internet.

Leveraging an Existing Customers' Stack

We tend to look at Gartner's and Rogers's adoption curves from our individual standpoint. Understandably, we want to attract the "innovators" (2.5%) and the early adopters (13.5%), get out of the trough of disillusionment toward the slope of enlightenment to reach an early majority (34%), followed by a late majority (34%), and finally convince the laggards (16%). We all know that identifying and gaining early adopters are daunting tasks early in the technology cycles that fashion innovation stacks.

Later movers can take a different perspective—that is, take an aggregate view involving all the players who have participated in the innovation stack buildup and rely on the fact that this innovation stack has also generated a customers' stack—which means that the time and effort required to educate and attract a customer base are compressed.

The iPhone skipped the first part of the Gartner hype curve as well as the descent toward the trough of disillusionment, and, as a result, its own internal Rogers bell curve could start at the beginning of "the slope of enlightenment." The iPhone leveraged the customers' stack of early adopters formed by PDAs and the first wave of smartphones. These early customers were frustrated by what they had in their hands, and it's precisely why they were ready for something else. They were open to the concept of the iPhone, and even more so if they were familiar with the iPod, which, in 2007, was at its zenith. The end result was spectacular. Announced in January 2007, the iPhone was released in the United States on June 29, 2007, and rose like a rocket: from Q3 to Q4 of 2007, Apple's share of the US smartphone market went from 19 to 28 percent, putting it ahead of both zombie Palm (9%) and Microsoft (21%).

First movers may have a great idea, but innovating is not just about having a great idea or even the "right" idea. It's making it work in a world that doesn't expect them. More often than not, first movers are the budding artists who warm up the audience for the stars. The "hockey stick growth" they all dream of is far easier to achieve for late movers.

Positioning an Idea/Product within a Platform Approach

Many innovations survive better when they are part of a larger set. The innovation is as though choreographed within an ensemble that touches several layers of the kairos. Edison was an extraordinary innovator, but it is often overlooked that most of his accomplishments were incorporated into larger environments or necessary in multiple situations. This versatility is even true of innovations of his that are lesser known today. For example, as an automobile fan, Edison, who had noticed that lead-acid storage batteries were inefficient at powering cars, started to develop an alkaline battery. The project took ten years. His innovation missed the car market because gasoline-powered cars were on their way to winning the race, but it may have been one of his best money-makers by providing lighting for all sorts of equipment, from railway cars to maritime buoys or miners' lamps.

The iPhone, in addition to being better than a PDA-plus-phone, was a close-up on a wider panorama. As I mentioned in chapter 6, when Steve Jobs came back to Apple, he loosened the ties between the Macintosh and the computing industry. The purpose was no longer to make it an "industry milestone product" but to offer a "lifestyle brand," to use Larry Ellison's description of Apple in 1998. Since the iPod, the Macintosh operating system (Mac OS) has become a foundational platform for other products and services. The iPhone was another piece in a vertically integrated business that included several products and services connected by the same philosophy, similar usage patterns, and aesthetic.

The iPhone became part of a global service-oriented and user-centric ecosystem. Such integration within a larger ensemble is difficult to achieve for younger companies with inevitably smaller footprints. As I'll discuss in the next chapter, new companies can be extremely innovative, but as Davids of sorts they rarely have the levers they need to bolster a continuous standing-out strategy. As a result, many are gobbled up by Goliaths or crushed beneath their weight.

Building a Collaborative Support and Alliance System

The Steve Jobs who launched the iPhone was not the same as the one who had launched the Macintosh. After selling Pixar to Disney (and becoming Disney's largest shareholder), he had become a star in multiple genres. The iPhone was, from the beginning, a lifestyle device, and one of the critical factors of its success was an alliance with a telephone carrier. Alliances as part of an innovation stack aren't always emphasized, but they are often crucial.

The success of the iPhone was all the more irresistible because of its five-year exclusive partnership with Cingular Wireless. Cingular Wireless had become wholly owned by AT&T in December 2006 and was, at the time, the largest wireless carrier in the United States, serving 58.7 million customers.[17] This move changed the handheld device industry by changing the relationship between manufacturers and carriers.

Vendors had been struggling for years with an industry whose business models and ideology were curbing the development of handhelds. After lengthy negotiations, Jobs and Stan Sigman, then president and CEO of the wireless division of AT&T, metamorphosed two industries at once: handhelds and wireless carriers. One of the clearest accounts of the impact of this transformation was provided one year after the first release of the iPhone by Fred Vogelstein in a *Wired* article.[18] "As important as the iPhone has been to the fortunes of Apple and AT&T," Vogelstein writes,

> its real impact is on the structure of the $11 billion-a-year U.S. mobile
> phone industry. For decades, wireless carriers have treated manufactur-

ers like serfs, using access to their networks as leverage to dictate what phones will get made, how much they will cost, and what features will be available on them. Handsets were viewed largely as cheap, disposable lures, massively subsidized to snare subscribers and lock them into using the carriers' proprietary services. But the iPhone upsets that balance of power. Carriers are learning that the right phone—even a pricey one—can win customers and bring in revenue. Now, in the pursuit of an Apple-like contract, every manufacturer is racing to create a phone that consumers will love, instead of one that the carriers approve of.

Jobs was a relentless negotiator who wouldn't quit until he had his way. But we can't underestimate the exceptional acumen of Stan Sigman—and Jobs didn't. In October 2010, when Sigman was inducted into the Wireless History Foundation Hall of Fame, Jobs attended the ceremony. Jobs and Sigman did far more than transform their respective industries. They accelerated them both.

Building effective alliances that expand the stage where innovative products can shine is easier said than done. For younger companies, building up a wider stage for their innovation (thanks to a platform or through alliances) can be somewhat trying, but they can also adopt other solutions. For example, you can open your product to connect with others and allow other products to connect to yours. You can also develop users' communities using various platforms (Discord is one of them for certain audiences) as well as contribute to the definition or establishment of industry standards.

Re-igniting the Innovation Engine

Major innovations are both an endpoint relative to innovations that preceded them and a starting point stimulating more innovations. When he introduced the iPhone, Jobs claimed that Apple was "five years in advance" of competitors. We can hear this statement as typical Jobsian swaggering braggadocio, of course, but also as a call to competitors to catch up with him and force him to work to maintain his lead. Large innovators can have competitive instincts similar to those of athletes.

Jobs was well aware that he wasn't the only one rethinking the space. Since the end of 2003, Andy Rubin had been building a mobile operating system dubbed Android, leveraging open-source software, notably Linux. He too had worked at General Magic (starting in 1992), and he too had experience with PDAs as a lead engineer for the Motorola Envoy released in 1995 (and based on General Magic's operating system, Magic Cap). Android was acquired by Google in 2005. By the end of 2010 Android already controlled 10 percent of the worldwide smartphone market and had overtaken Windows Mobile as well as Symbian, the operating system then used by Nokia, Samsung, Motorola, and Sony Ericsson.

In 2022 Android was the leading mobile operating system worldwide, with over a 70 percent market share.[19] The first Android-based smartphone, the HTC Dream released in 2008, didn't threaten the iPhone, but the iPhone sent multiple vendors back to the drawing board. As a result, Apple is challenged every year to compete both against itself and others.[20] While Apple's global market share for the iPhone is under 20 percent, it's collecting 80 percent of all the profit in the industry with its aspirational, premium product.[21] It's an example of how Apple defines the kairos in its own terms—and aligns its layers to its advantage.

Today's major players in the smartphone industry are enormous companies with extensive platforms. Samsung is a gigantic conglomerate started in South Korea in 1938 with a diversified horizontal platform, after moving to the forefront of the global electronics industry in the 1980s. Founded in 2010, Xiaomi made it onto the Fortune Global 500 list for 2019 as the youngest company. OPPO, launched in 2004, is a subsidiary of another Chinese conglomerate specializing in electronics, BBK Electronics Corporation, started in 1998. Vivo, founded in 2009, is also a Chinese company and in 2020 established a long-term strategic partnership with legendary German manufacturer of optical systems and optoelectronics, Zeiss.

The financial strength of each of these companies allows them not

only to innovate but also do so continuously, that is, to develop fierce serial innovation game plans and remain indomitable titans gnawing at the
market share of all other contenders.

It stands to reason that great achievers want to gain some form of
monopoly even if they can't claim it too loudly for fear of awakening antitrust laws, but they also know that when they try to limit competition
through business schemes rather than through superior technologies or
services, they aren't in the innovation game any longer.

CONCLUSION

Innovations more commonly happen in bustling spaces with so much
activity that they have the potential to power the emergence of new ideas
that eventually split into multiple expanses. Then, innovators step in with
the conviction that they'll be able to leave their mark. As they participate
in the flurry, they also experience how difficult it is to survive, let alone
to stand out. But they do leave a mark. The entrepreneurs who developed
PDAs didn't try to no avail. As spectacular as the iPhone may be, Apple
owes a debt to a multitude of PDA and pre-smartphone entrepreneurs.
They were *trailblazers* in the true sense of the term because they cleared
the rut, identifying the potholes, the dead ends, and a host of unforeseen
obstacles. And some of them were able to convert their failures over years
into successes later. You can also say that they were *pioneers*, which originally designates the foot soldiers preparing the way for the army.

Even renowned innovators can operate as trailblazers or pioneers and
can start a lineage without being the first to benefit from it. Google Glass
in 2013 or Snap Spectacles in 2016 were intriguing initiatives, but they
were missing one thing, the fact that eyewear is an established genre
and making it "smart" didn't have to make it odd or sci-fi. That's why the
2021 Facebook/Ray-Ban glasses were an important step in acquainting
more people with augmented reality despite its limited capabilities. As
rightfully noted by Harry McCracken, "while Ray-Ban Stories [the videos
you can create with these glasses] are no epoch-shifting breakthrough in
themselves, they might ratchet Facebook that much closer to its goal of

creating AR glasses [by] getting the world acclimated to eyewear that packs sensors, computing power, and connectivity."[22] Mark Zuckerberg himself did acknowledge that "there's a bunch of work that still needs to be done." Although such humbleness is rather unusual in the often-bombastic Silicon Valley world, what's again highlighted here is that innovations don't come all fleshed-out nor out of the blue from one single company. The innovations that stand out as emblematic market successes rarely started it all.

Again, innovating has nothing to do with zero-sum thinking, because innovations aren't slices of a pie with a predetermined size. Even though only a minority of companies or people are remembered, they're never the last nor the first. The innovation game is a multiplayer game that isn't based on scarcity but on the dream that more or better is indefinitely possible—a dream that is fostered by the very nature of the kairos, where layers converge, diverge, or intersect, often unpredictably. As Joyce put it in *Ulysses*, his protagonist Bloom had "to reflect that each one who enters imagines himself to be the first to enter whereas he is always the last term of a preceding series even if the first term of a succeeding one, each imagining himself to be first, last, only and alone whereas he is neither first nor last nor only nor alone in a series originating in and repeated to infinity."[23]

8

Can David Thrive in Goliath's World?

And the child smiled on the Giant, and said to him,
"You let me play once in your garden, to-day you shall come with
me to my garden, which is Paradise".
—Oscar Wilde

Entrepreneurs are flooded with pep talks that make them feel like special underdogs, or to use a nobler image, like Davids on a mission to dispatch Goliaths. But if you want the credit for cutting off Goliath's head, make sure you know what you're up against. Many established companies are serial innovators and have developed a wide antidisruption arsenal. As convinced as they are to herald new ways to do, consume, or see things, startups must temper their biases against larger corporations.

Fortune's public and private companies represent over two-thirds of the US GDP. They too innovate. So, as determined as aspiring innovators are to "think big," they should never underestimate that there are already big fish out there with a massive influence on the innovation kairos—which also dispels romantic visions of what innovating is about.

REALITY CHECK: WE START, BUT THEY CONTINUE

Large organizations don't "die off as the deer flies do towards the end of August," to use Saul Bellow's expression in a letter to Philip Roth.[1] So, you shouldn't misinterpret Credit Suisse's report on corporate longevity showing that companies don't stay on the S&P 500 as long as in the past.[2] Sure, the longevity peak on the index was high in 1958 (companies stayed there for about sixty years); it went down to thirty in the 1960s (with a spike in 1976 that resulted from the S&P committee removing forty industrial, transportation, and utility companies and replacing them with financial stocks), to twenty to fifteen years in the 1990s, and it stands today in a twenty-year range. This doesn't mean that companies are ousted faster because of some accelerating gale of disruptive technologies.

What the report describes is not the life expectancy of companies in general but their presence on a particular index. The removal from or addition to the S&P 500 is managed by a committee whose primary goal is to provide a tool for investors, not to confirm or invalidate theories about innovation. Despite a general sense that corporate longevity is shrinking, the data offer "a more nuanced picture." In fact, "longevity has lengthened in recent years," the report says.

After exploring the annual turnover in the Fortune 500, Credit Suisse observed that "on average, there are 32 changes per year, representing turnover of roughly 6 percent, above the S&P 500 at about 4 percent."[3]

Strikingly enough, the average age of the companies listed is over sixty-nine. For companies listed by Fortune 500 in 2019, it's over seventy. In 2019 *Forbes* indicated that the average age of the top ten largest private American companies was seventy-five.[4]

INSTITUTIONAL POWER OF INCUMBENTS

As I discussed in chapter 3 the disruption frame of reference carries a false symmetry between incumbents and new entrants.

In Latin, the verb *incumbere* means to "recline on" or "rest on" something. Incumbents are established and are more than just organizations with products. They exist within a complex structure that includes customers, implicit or explicit balances of power with competitors and "coopetitors," alliances, professional organizations, and lobbies. Large companies are, in fact, institutions within the kairos. They have an ideological weight that allows them to operate covertly or overtly as regulative, standardizing, supervising, bargaining, or governing bodies. They often are, whether we like it or not, innovations' referees.

Incumbents' Regulative Influence

Governments establish public policies. However, many implicitly delegate these regulations to the corporations they're supposed to regulate, based on the assumption that commercial actors know the market. As a result, large companies tend to recommend what's good for them. That's true in most industries. The pharmaceutical industry is a prime example.

Business Insider once published an article provocatively titled "Pharmaceutical Companies Are Backing Away from a Growing Threat That Could Kill 10 Million People a Year by 2050."[5] Their point was that the variety of new drugs brought to market has decreased without necessarily leaving the field open for new initiatives from new entrants. Why so? Established companies partially fund the institutional bodies, like the drug certification program within the US Food and Drug Administration (FDA) that regulates them.[6]

Nick Hanauer of *Pitchfork Economics* along with Priti Krishtel and John Arnold also describe how the intricate patent laws system and practices in the United States not only favor incumbents but also discourage new entrants and contribute to the high cost of drugs.[7] Of course, that's not the only way for large companies to control the course of innovation.

A study performed at Yale on a data set of over 35,000 drug projects for the US market from 1989 to 2011 showed that pharmaceutical companies are free to perform "killer acquisitions" that eliminate competing therapies under development.[8] It estimated "that 7% of the acquisitions were killer acquisitions; if such deals did not take place, the number of drugs continuing development each year would increase by 5%." In other words, killer acquisitions may be holding back a substantial number of innovative medical treatments.

Even though the word "innovation" carries the dream of change, its actualization is always relative to a context. The regulative clout exerted by large organizations is not anti-innovation per se, but it displays how they intend to fashion the kairos, something that can be extremely frustrating for new companies.

Incumbents' Shepherding Impact

We like to think that companies go under because they didn't innovate, and we keep harping on the reason ice companies didn't invent refrigerators was that they couldn't escape from their past. Fine. But we shouldn't forget that there are many exceptions to this alleged rule. One of them is General Motors, which, along with other automobile manufacturers, defined what America's competitiveness should be in the car industry for decades.

In the 1890s Durant-Dort Carriage Company, based in Flint, Michigan, was a leading manufacturer of horse-drawn vehicles. Despite his skepticism about the future of the car industry, William Durant started General Motors (GM), which was the first automobile company to hold multiple simultaneous brands. GM subsequently came to such prominence that President Eisenhower nominated Charles Wilson (president of GM between 1941 and 1953) as his secretary of defense in 1953.

During his Senate confirmation hearing, Wilson declared that for a long time, he had come to think that "what was good for our country was good for General Motors, and vice versa." He created somewhat of a stir, but what he was saying is also what Ford would have said in his place.[9] The Big Three (GM, Ford, Chrysler) spoke in one single voice on the national scene, and everybody believed them . . . until their tentacular influence adversely impacted the competitiveness of the United States in the 1980s. US companies had innovated at their pace, but they had been outpaced by more nimble competitors: Japanese imports were sending doubts about the quality of American cars.

The automobile lobby was so confident about its power that everyone in the auto industry has discarded the help of one of the most effective thinkers in manufacturing, W. Edwards Deming. He almost single-handedly reshaped the industry's speedometer by designing and

implementing a new process methodology called total quality management (TQM). Think of him as a David, offering process innovation that
could accelerate corporate growth, but he had to bear the brunt of a cor-
porate-driven national shortsightedness.

Expressed in fourteen points, TQM methodology explained to managers how to transform their management style in order to optimize productivity while offering customers better quality products and services.
Deming's approach, later summarized in a book, *Out of the Crisis* (1986),
wasn't simply a set of recipes made up by a management consultant.[10]
Deming had studied the application of statistical methods to industrial
production and management from Walter Shewhart, employed by Bell
Telephone Laboratories from 1925 to 1956, and was known as the father of
statistical quality control. Deming understood how these methods could
apply to manufacturing processes as well as all the internal processes
of an organization. During World War II, Deming was a member of the
five-man Emergency Technical Committee that designed the American
War Standards and taught statistical process control methods to workers
involved in wartime production. The whole initiative had been a success.

But wartime discipline vanished after World War II because of a huge
demand for American mass-produced products. Deming settled for an academic position as a professor of statistics at New York University's graduate school of business in 1946. Corporate America wasn't interested
in his expertise, but Japan, in the midst of full reconstruction, was. As
a result, in 1950, Deming trained countless engineers, managers, scholars, and leaders (including Akio Morita, Sony's co-founder) in statistical
process control and demonstrated that quality control not only reduced
downstream expenses but also improved productivity. By 1951 Japan had
already instituted the Deming Prize for industrial achievement. As Hobart Rowen put it a few days after Deming's death in 1993, "American executives [had] scoffed at the foolish idea that any other country, especially
Japan, which had a post–World War II record of producing shoddy goods,
could compete."[11]

America was in love with its Big Three and remained so until it was forced to wake up. The Big Three, which owned an 89.6 percent domestic market share in 1966, were seeing the rapid erosion of their national and international impact. Ford was one of the first American corporations to seek Deming's assistance, when the company's sales dropped sharply in the early 1980s.

Did process innovation succeed in changing how companies operated? The response is "yes" in Japan. In the United States, the response is a mixed bag. As Rowen noted, "The full meaning of Deming's wisdom hasn't been absorbed in America." America was blaming its trade deficits with Japan on its "unfair" trade practices, not on what was at stake, product quality. When threatened by outside innovation, American car manufacturing largely defaulted to racist and xenophobic assertions of their international competitors' inherent inferiority, blaming their nefarious practices rather than learning from their actual value. Deming's process innovation was finally adopted but only as a defensive tactic to protect American exceptionalism and not as the proactive strategy to prove it, let alone extend it. It was a stopgap approach supported by protectionist sentiments—shared by corporations and unions alike.

Yet Deming's impact materialized in unexpected ways. Competition accelerated so much that the United States started to entice automakers from all over to come in, following a strategy of Sun Tzu: "Keep your friends close and your enemies closer." According to Reuters, between 1976 and 2017 "the U.S. states [vied] for new auto plants, with 17 states granting $17 billion in tax breaks, job training funds, infrastructure development and other incentives to woo investment from both domestic and foreign automakers."[12]

By helping foreign manufacturers, states looking to boost their economies and create jobs changed the trajectory of the auto industry in the United States. They ultimately adopted an innovative legislative stand that relaunched its innovation dynamics and that would also help new entrants down the road, including Tesla Motors. Founded in 2003, the company was heavily financed by venture capitalists, and before launching its initial public offering in June 2010, it received a $465 million loan from the US Department of Energy (repaid in 2013). The various government subsidies received by Tesla and its related companies have been the subject of much writing.[13] Tesla stated in a 2018 CNBC video report that the company "has succeeded in spite of government subsidies, not because of them" while pointing to competitors receiving more.[14] This statement sounds like a lack of gratitude for the taxpayers who ponied up huge amounts of money, but what it also highlights is how quickly an organization can adopt an entitlement approach.

Corporate Welfare and Entrepreneurial Poverty

Incumbents have the advantage of having become emblematic figures within the kairos. Despite continuous pleas from multiple organizations to authorities to better support innovation from small organizations, funding from agencies such as the US Small Business Administration is a fraction of what is often called "corporate welfare," that is, the special and favorable treatment granted to larger corporations in multiple forms such as grants, subsidies, incentives, tax breaks, trade initiatives, and regulatory decisions.[15]

The lobbying power of large organizations is considerable. For example, in 2017 the action of internet service providers and tech companies such as Google successfully dismantled federal internet privacy rules. The innovation flag floats in a highly texturized world.

Large organizations can use their ability to innovate or their vision of what innovation means as part of their bargaining power. Startups have little bargaining power. Government grants represent a tiny portion of their funding sources, less than 5 percent. As far as subsidies are concerned, "there's a galling mismatch between how governors and other state officials characterize their support for small businesses and what they actually spend," said Greg LeRoy, executive director of Good Jobs First. His 2015 analysis of 4,200 individual subsidy awards showed that "90 percent of dollars and 70 percent awards [were] going to big businesses—even though the programs examined were open to companies of any size."[16]

INCUMBENTS' MODULUS OF RESILIENCE:
ANTI-DISRUPTION MECHANISMS

Goliaths survive for multiple reasons. Many of them are serial innovators. In addition, they can leverage various business instruments—including platformization, concentric diversification, horizontal diversification, vertical integration, and acquisition strategies—that can constitute antidisruption mechanisms, enabling them to remain relevant players and build dominant market positions.

Serial Innovation

Various organizations offer lists every year of what they deem to be the most innovative companies based on diverse criteria. For example, the Boston Consulting Group (BCG) has been ranking large organizations since 2005 by evaluating the strength of their innovation approach based on their responses to topics such as innovation ambition, innovation domains, innovation governance, performance management, organization and ecosystems, talent and culture, idea-to-market fit, project management, funnel management and portfolio management, and, more recently, green growth.[17]

The list changes over time, showing newcomers not previously ranked in the top 50 or companies that return after a temporary absence. Yet quite a few companies have made it to the top on a regular basis (like Apple, Microsoft, Sony, IBM, Samsung, Alphabet/Google, etc.), providing "clear evidence that companies equipped with the most productive innovation engines know how to stay on top of the innovation game."[18]

According to the BCG, "committed innovators" invest more money in innovation than do their competitors, but they also invest more time and are more patient. As a result, they outperform their peers.

Startups often underestimate the ability of large players to innovate, a cliché reinforced by disruption theories. Yet don't bury them too fast, and stay informed. For example, every year, *Fast Company*'s editors and reporters honor businesses and organizations with their "World-

Changing Ideas" and "Innovation by Design" awards, and you can easily see that large companies aren't lagging behind!

Platformization

The word "platformization" aggregates two main concepts:

- A set of technology components and services linked by a common underlying architecture, which itself allows for the rapid incorporation of new services.
- A business model that strengthens network effects and leverages or accelerates interdependencies. For example, Amazon created an end-to-end platform for ecommerce: I can buy a book, toothpaste, and watch a movie all on the same platform.

In all cases, a platform is a service-based ecosystem that orchestrates resources and integrates them transparently. When they move toward a platform approach, companies strengthen their position, which explains, for example, why Salesforce remains a thriving company today. The concept of customer relationship management (CRM) started in the 1970s, expanded in the 1980s, and boomed in the 1990s. Marc Benioff, Salesforce's founder, rejuvenated the genre by being the first company to deliver CRM as a service twenty-five years ago. What made the company endure and grow isn't simply that it was cloud based but the fact that less than ten years after it started, it effected major architectural changes capable of accommodating the mobile revolution and powering an application development environment and marketplace; these developments allowed customers to build and buy apps based on their needs across every industry.

Whether a platform operates as an à la carte service in a specific space or more as a general store, it embeds growth opportunities hard to achieve with a pipe model.[19] As a unified backbone, a platform allows customers to access the same product or different products with few encumbrances—which can often make it hard for a new offering to penetrate a space. The "platform revolution" has transformed our economy and powered new monopolies. For example, the Apple App Store and Google Play are gatekeepers for millions of smartphone apps, creating a barrier to entry for potential insurgents.

Concentric Diversification: The Bibendum Effect

Concentric diversification refers to a company developing or acquiring new products derived from or expanding on its core competency. It's more than creating products with specific usages; rather, it's creating a synergistic relationship between these products, where the positive image of one reflects favorably on the others. They share the same artist's hand. Of course, if one or two products are lousy, the whole house may suffer.

Let me illustrate the principle with the history of the second-largest tire manufacturer in the world: Michelin. It's an interesting example of a company that went from the hodgepodge diversification common in the nineteenth century to a powerful concentric diversification just before the twentieth and is now strengthened by a twenty-first-century digital transformation.

Founded in Clermont-Ferrand, France, in 1832 by Aristide Barbier and Edouard Daubrée, the original company, Etablissements Barbier et Daubrée, manufactured all sorts of products: farm equipment, machinery for the sugar industry, water or drainage pumps, and so on. It added, somewhat by chance, the production of small vulcanized rubber products (belts, valves, balls, pipes) under the influence of Daubrée's wife, Elizabeth Pugh Barker. She was the niece of Charles Macintosh, the Scot who invented the waterproof raincoat named for him in 1824. Macintosh's invention consisted of placing a solution of rubber in naphtha between two layers of fabric. His process was perfected by his business partner, Thomas Hancock, in 1843, thanks to a new method for vulcanizing rubber (sulfur vulcanization), which he patented.[20] That's how the rubber industry started in this unlikely place in France, a country where there was no natural rubber whatsoever. Multiple companies in Clermont-Ferrand

followed suit. After the death of the founders, respectively, in 1863 and
1864, the company went downhill and was in dire shape when Aristide
Barbier's grandsons André Michelin (an engineer) and Edouard Michelin
(an artist/painter) took over the family business in 1886 and renamed it
Michelin in 1889.

For a short while, the newly minted entrepreneurs sold whatever they
could opportunistically, until in 1891 a British cyclist who needed to repair a Dunlop tire showed up at their plant.[21] At the time the wooden
wheels of a bicycle were placed into rubber sheaths filled with air, which
made repair a cumbersome process. That's when Edouard had the idea of
a removable pneumatic tire with an air chamber. He patented his invention in France and England in 1891 and soon after in the United States.[22]

That's when the rubber met the road for Michelin. The brothers focused their business on rubber and diversified concentrically into all ver-
ticals, from bicycles and motorbikes to cars, trains, and, later, to aircrafts.
They innovated in each of them. In 1900 they published the first *Michelin
Guide*, originally a promotional book that provided cyclists and the small
number of car owners at the time with information on things like repair
shops, doctors, maps, and, while they were at it, sites worth seeing. Four
years later, the guide began listing hotels.

In a concentric diversification strategy, the products of a company
congregate around a common theme (here, transportation), and they all
conspire to build an irresistible brand. Michelin embodied the expression
of its brand in a mascot, Bibendum, also called the "Michelin Man."[23]
Introduced at the Exposition universelle, internationale et coloniale in
1894, it is one of the world's oldest emblems for a commercial enterprise
still in existence.

Thousands of companies have adopted this type of concentric diversification. One of the first companies in the high fashion business
to understand its value was Coco Chanel. Before World War I, she was a
milliner designing hats in Paris. She then opened a boutique in Deauville
(1913), where she sold casual clothing for leisure and sport. Soon after, she
added another one, in Biarritz (1915). After the war, in 1919, she changed
course and established her "maison de couture" at 31 rue Cambon. Two

years later, her name was attached to a perfume, Chanel N°5. She was the first fashion designer to ally clothing and perfume almost immediately, and, of course, she had bags and accessories from day one since she was designing with her own needs and interest in mind.[24]

Concentric diversification starts from a core competency that enables the creation of products that differ but are all intrinsically connected by a meaning that echoes throughout various layers of the kairos. Their innovations are staged within a larger environment. Consequently, it's much easier for companies with a concentric diversification strategy to become influential, recognizable brands, as illustrated by Nike or the Walt Disney Company.

Horizontal Diversification

Just like in finance, the purpose of horizontal diversification is to reduce exposure. Positive performances in one business branch offset possible problems in another. For young companies, it's hard to have more than one iron in the fire, so horizontal diversification often comes across as a dispersion of their efforts.

Horizontal diversification is rarely an easy process and works better when efforts are meted out under a general umbrella, as is the case for large pharmaceutical and biomedical conglomerates such as Johnson & Johnson, Roche, Pfizer, or Bayer, to name just a few. They often accumulate so much power that it's almost impossible for new players to destabilize them. Also, they can quickly acquire smaller innovative firms to further expand their reach.

Historically, horizontal diversification has often happened through a loose one-thing-leading-to-another process or association of ideas as well as acquisitions. Siemens (founded by Werner von Siemens and Johann Halske in Germany in 1847) built the first long-distance telegraph line in Europe (1848) and over the decades expanded its reach across multiple industries from transportation to medical equipment. So did Philips, started by Gerard Philips with the production of carbon-filament lamps in 1892.

The success or failure of horizontal diversification largely depends on the ability of an acquiring company to integrate both the culture and the product(s) of the one acquired and delineate clear strategies. There are myriad good and bad acquisitions in this realm, and the same company can experience both. For example, Microsoft's acquisition of phone maker Nokia was a flop, but its acquisition of Skype, a video communications platform, was a success. The acquisition of Motorola by Google was a flop but its acquisition of the Android mobile operating system in 2005 a resounding success. It turns out that finding the seam between horizontal and concentric diversification yields the best results.

Vertical Integration

In theory, in a vertically integrated business, a company controls or owns its supply chain (suppliers, distributors, and/or retailers) basically from the purchase of the raw materials to the final product delivered to customers. The model has obvious advantages, like reducing supply chain disruptions, higher delivery predictability, or better cost controls at all the steps along the way. But the disadvantages can also be significant, even in optimally managed systems: high capital expenditures as well as rigidity if a product innovation requires new types of skills, especially if competitors have easier and faster access to more agile sources. The two most common methods of vertical integration include backward integration (when a company expands into the manufacturing side) and forward integration (when a company expands by controlling the distribution or supply of its products).

Vertical integration serves the needs of the most diverse types of companies and requires innovation throughout the business model to derive benefits from this more inclusive approach. Target has its own store brands and manufacturing plants. Netflix, which was originally a platform distributing films and TV on DVD, expanded by creating its own original content. The merger of Ticketmaster and Live Nation in 2010, and numerous acquisitions since then, has transformed Live Nation Entertainment into a formidable organization controlling the artistic chain, from the management and representation of artists to the production of shows and ticket sales.

Acquisitions

Not only can large companies be serial innovators, but they also can add to their internal innovation capabilities. They can also buy new entrants with quasi-similar capabilities to make sure they won't be snatched up by a competitor or they can adopt the strategy of "acqui-hiring," a portmanteau coined around 2005 to designate buying out a company for the skills and expertise of its staff.

Regardless of their motives, big players such as Apple, Microsoft, Alphabet/Google, Amazon, Meta/Facebook have acquired hundreds of companies and continue to do so to increase their innovative firepower. Do they stifle innovation? It's a complex subject. Their scaling capabilities can accelerate the adoption of innovations, but they can also build direct or indirect monopolies, harming the overall innovative dynamics of an ecosystem. This has become a problem serious enough that the Federal Trade Commission issued "Special Orders" to five large technology firms, requiring them in 2020 to provide information about prior acquisitions not reported to the antitrust agencies under the Hart-Scott-Rodino Act.[25]

The power of some large companies is further augmented when they also own an investment arm. Dealing with them is often a double-edged sword for startups. Companies can get enough inside intelligence to clone what you do, to put it charitably. For example, the *Wall Street Journal* stated that Amazon appeared to have used the investment and deal-making process to help develop competing products.[26]

CAN THE "ENTREPRENEURIAL STATE" INDIRECTLY HELP DAVID?

Government providing funding and resources to businesses for driving economic growth is a potential source of support for the Davids. Of course, a die-hard libertarian would yell, "no way." The topic is an ideological landmine. That said, the government can help the Davids through its own innovative initiatives and through its legislative power.

When Governmental Initiatives Help the Davids

Countries support their innovation ecosystems diversely, but governmental initiatives do matter, even in free-market economies. Major initiatives have been powered by national and international organizations and have facilitated the emergence of a host of Davids. For example:

- A huge number of large platforms we use today are directly beholden to the Department of Defense, which lifted the last restrictions regarding the use of the internet to carry commercial traffic in 1995. Amazon started in 1994, as did Yahoo! and Sabre Corporation; eBay started in 1995, as did Craigslist and Angie's List (now part of ANGI Home Services with HomeAdvisor); Yelp came in 1996, as did Booking.com (now Booking Holdings, which includes many sites such Priceline, KAYAK, Cheapflights, Momondo, and OpenTable, to name a few) and Expedia; Netflix started in 1997, as did the Japanese Rakuten and the Chinese NetEase. In 1998 yet another big collection of companies launched, including Google, PayPal, Tencent, and Zynga and, in 1999, Alibaba and Salesforce. With the internet, the US administration opened up a gigantic new playing field where innovators developed their game and created the basis of the modern worldwide network economy.
- The European Telecommunications Standards Institute (started in 1983) gave us the Global System for Mobile Communications (GSM) and Short Message / Messaging Services (SMS). The Global Positioning System (GPS) was initiated by the US Department of Defense in 1973 and was allowed for civilian use by President Reagan in the 1980s. Smaller innovations like Caller ID didn't start with one vendor descending from Mars but with a service defined in 1993 by the oldest global international organi-

zation, the International Telecommunication Union, whose origin dates back to the mid-nineteenth century.

The role of nation-states in innovative economies can't be understated, as is clear from the remarkable monograph by Mariana Mazzucato, *The Entrepreneurial State: Debunking Public vs. Private Sector Myths.*[27] This doesn't mean that the economy should be nationalized, but, as analyzed by Nobel Prize–winning economist Joseph Stiglitz, the abdication of governments in favor of international consortiums for the management of the globalizing economy has created gigantic scars in the human texture of society.[28]

This abdication can be puzzling when it ends up contradicting a country's interests. Large corporations do cover a lot of ground, but the idea that they can cover everything through the market's dynamics is illusory. Were companies asking for the internet because they needed it? Not too many, to my knowledge. They leveraged it when a noncommercial organization built it.

Liberal economies are always eager to slam nationally controlled ones, which is more about a war of words and ideologies than about reality. Most of the time, large corporations exert disproportionate control over economic models, whatever they are. More structural discrepancies come to light when strategic choices involving longer-term futures are at stake. No single company can address global warming. Isn't it a little naive to think that all the initiatives needed to address the problem will miraculously converge toward a solution thanks to some serendipitous agreement between corporate stakeholders? It's not the business of private companies to define projects that are of national interest, even when they can serve them. Now and then, countries experience the limits of innovativeness embedded in free-market economies. For example, how is it that the country that invented the internet has only thin control over 5G?[29]

Governments are welcome when they open up new spaces. They can seriously help Davids, but once these have turned into Goliaths, they become antigovernment if governments try to leverage their legal arsenal like applying antitrust laws.

Legislative Power and Sherman Antitrust Act: Boxed Beef Industry and Others

Among Clayton Christensen's stories with roots in disruption, one is called "Boxed Beef." I didn't think that I would ever venture into this space until I saw how tragically employees in the meatpacking industry had been exposed to COVID-19. I was curious to learn what Christensen found disruptive about the meatpacking industry. What I saw is how various legislative actions restructured the space several times and facilitated the arrival of Davids, one of them being Iowa Beef Packers (later called Iowa Beef Processors and then IBP), founded in 1960 by Currier Holman, a cattle buyer, and A. D. Anderson, a pork plant owner.[30]

The meatpacking industry developed at scale at the end of the nineteenth century and became a repository of horror stories: abominable slaughtering practices and working conditions for employees, with unacceptable levels of squalor and health hazards. Upton Sinclair's 1906 novel, *The Jungle*, was famously influential in the adoption of the Meat Inspection Act the same year the book was published. Government intervention suppressed some of the worst practices, but this didn't change the configuration of the space. What finally shook up the meatpacking industry was the application of the Sherman Antitrust Act.

As early as 1905, The "Big Six" (Swift, Armour, Morris, Cudahy, Wilson, and Schwartzchild & Sulzberger), who dominated the meatpacking industry, were hit on antitrust grounds by the Sherman Act for engaging in a conspiracy to fix prices and divide the market for livestock and meat in order to preserve higher prices, margins, and profits. Government surveillance and a series of decrees subsequent to the action of multiple advocacy groups (like the Humane Slaughter Association) consistently sent shockwaves throughout the space.

By the 1950s the "Big Six" were the "Big Four" (Armour, Swift, Cudahy, and Wilson). But they still owned 40 percent of the fresh beef trade with vertically integrated packinghouses near large urban livestock markets. Antitrust regulators made them give up control over stockyards, transportation, and retail marketing. This regulation, combined with restructurings in retail channels after World War II and the growing habit of households of purchasing prepared or prepackaged foods, changed the food-processing landscape.

One of the first companies to take advantage of this reconfiguration was Iowa Beef Packers. By 1974 they had surpassed all rivals and become the largest beef packer in the world. David had become Goliath in no time. In a 1981 article, Thomas Friedman summarized the success of IBP by saying that the company did for the "American meat-packing industry what Henry Ford did for automobile assembly."[31]

IBP, Friedman added, innovated by deconstructing and then reconstructing the meatpacking process. He also noted that IBP ran into the law along the way. In the early 1970s, it couldn't market its boxed beef in major metropolitan areas like New York, where unionized meat cutters attempted to ban the product. In 1974 IBF and Currier Holman were found guilty of conspiring to bribe meat and supermarket executives. After that, the company and three other meatpackers were named in a lawsuit charging them with conspiring to fix meat prices. Later, in 1988, as reported in a PBS documentary, the Occupational Safety and Health Administration (OSHA) fined IBP for exposing workers at its plant in Dakota City to cumulative trauma disorders resulting from highly repetitive meat cutting.[32]

IBP did grow quickly thanks to novel business processes for that industry and a wider adoption of technology. But this is only one aspect of the story. Government action is what changed the entire landscape. Even though the "Big Four" didn't collapse overnight—partially because way before the 1950s, they had already diversified—they lost their dominant position.[33] They didn't fail to act (it wasn't rocket science to imitate IBP), but they could hardly move anyway. Armour, Swift, Cudahy, and Wilson were hampered by antitrust regulations, and by the time some of these regulations were amended (1980), they had lost too much momentum.[34] Two of them survived through various mergers. The meatpacking side of

Armour was acquired by ConAgra in 1983, which had become a major player in beef packing before divesting most of their refrigerated meats businesses to Smithfield Foods in 2006. Cudahy was sold to management in 1981, renamed Bar-S Foods Company, and acquired by the Mexican packer Sigma Alimentos in 2010. Swift was purchased in 2007 by JBS USA Holdings, Inc., the wholly owned subsidiary of JBA, a Brazilian company that is the world's largest processor of fresh beef and pork. IBP itself was acquired by Tyson Foods in 2001.

New spaces don't surface because of sudden earthquakes. Here, a major operator of the emergence and dynamics of the new space was the application of antitrust laws, which made it possible for new players to appear. The Sherman Antitrust Act is a powerful tool for governments, which explains why very large platforms worry so much about its application. It can decelerate their growth and permit the arrival of new players.

For example, the fear of potential antitrust actions pushed Bell Labs to license its transistor technology to various companies directly or indirectly. One of the licensees in 1952 was Texas Instruments. The company wanted to expand from its geophysical and seismic services toward semiconductors. It ended up creating the first low-cost commercial silicon transistor that powered the first transistor radio in partnership with Regency Division of I.D.E.A. in 1954. The popularity of portable radios (and in the early sixties cassettes introduced by Philips) drastically reduced the role of jukeboxes in music distribution.

All the companies formed on the shoulders of the internet are in a position to defend their turf with monopolies or quasi-monopolies just like older companies. Whether Facebook/Meta, Google/Alphabet, or Amazon should be sued under antitrust laws is an ever-recurring theme. The US government has a hard time proving that these companies, despite their de facto market dominance, harm consumers. Additionally, all these big tech companies now pour fortunes into lobbying activities as well as into think-tank groups that strengthen their position—sometimes causing internal havoc.[35]

It's certainly ironic that many contemporary tech giants flaunt a libertarian antigovernment attitude, claiming that it's an anti-innovation force even though the existence of their business was made possible thanks to government research in the first place, and even though they deem it indispensable to spend enormous amounts of money to monitor its decisions. The same Eric Schmidt who brandished antimonopoly clauses against Microsoft when he was the CEO of Novell (and won) challenged the idea that Google might abuse its dominant position in internet search as Google's chairman.[36] In any case, it's not news that incumbents want the help of the government when it serves their interests but not when it acts as a referee.

Where Does the Antigovernment Narrative Come From?

The antigovernment narrative is triggered each time the stakeholder of a company feels threatened by any action that a government might take and is part of the somewhat paradoxical folklore attached to innovation.

States in liberal economies have been innovation capacitors for private enterprises at least since the eighteenth century. So where does the idea that states would be a structurally anti-innovation force come from? It probably originated with the "laissez-faire" economics advocated by French Physiocrats during the eighteenth century as they fought against trade restrictions imposed by French kings' administration. After that, the idea became a popular political and economic doctrine in the nineteenth century independently from its original context, mostly under the influence of John Stuart Mill in his 1848 *Principles of Political Economy*, before it regained steam during the twentieth century, notably through monetarist economists such as Milton Friedman.

The notion of free individual enterprise came out of a resistance to an overarching power. But why this overarching power should necessarily be viewed as anti-innovation is a different story. It was one thing to fight the abusive power of kings; it's a whole different one to assert that they were opposed to innovation. In fact, they weren't. Minister of state Jean-Baptiste Colbert's mercantilism in the seventeenth century was innovative, and the state basically operated as a mega-corporation. Colbert wasn't anti-innovation. Simply, he didn't want innovations that would imperil the innovations he deemed important to maintain the economic dominance of the royal enterprises. In fact, the idea of governments as anti-innovation forces was primarily the transfer onto secular power of religious systems that actually did dread change in general, as analyzed by Benoît Godin.[37]

This anti-innovation label of government colluded with the multiple left- and right-winged forms of libertarianism that developed over the course of the nineteenth and twentieth centuries, often loosely associated with a Nietzschean vision of a superman defying institutions. This type of mythology was exemplarily peddled by the pulp novelist and philosopher Ayn Rand in the United States in the 1960s and 1970s. In *Atlas Shrugged*, she portrayed the United States as a nightmarish landscape where entrepreneurs are smothered by bureaucrats and government officials. Her books and conferences became a cult for engineers. This view is still incredibly pervasive, even in a relatively intellectually sophisticated environment like Silicon Valley. It survives because the kids of the 1970s are now established players, Goliaths of sorts. But, as we all know, the very apostles of change can hold firm to the immutability of some credos even when they don't pass the smell test.

CONCLUSION

A 2016 survey showed that large and very small companies both contribute to innovation: "Approximately 60 percent of private-sector innovations originate from businesses with more than 500 employees, and 16 percent originate from firms with fewer than 25 employees."[38] There is no reason to believe that things have changed dramatically since then. So, generally speaking, the odds are stacked against Davids. Most Goliaths are here to stay, and startups constitute only a fraction of the world's GDP.[39] I know I depict a challenging landscape for startups, but we must remember that what characterizes innovation isn't simply the fact that it's something new. It's something that we have to market in a kairos that doesn't expect us and is largely influenced by organizations that have the wherewithal to defend their own innovation turf. Persisting in this environment entails the following actions:

- Perform extensive analysis of the full landscape into which you're setting foot. It's tempting to start from the pluses of your products instead of examining the reasons people have been able to live without you and ponder in earnest all the reasons you might fail, including the existence of Goliaths. It must be part of any premortem analysis recommended by business consultants.[40]

- Build a team with hands-on experience in the space you want to address. Despite the mythology around innovators as lone rangers, entrepreneurs often need to surround themselves with professionals coming from larger organizations. I'm not suggesting that you poach the VPs of sales, marketing, or business development from one of the large companies in your line of fire but that you look at people at a senior manager or director level. That's the level where people have to be competent and knowledgeable—and are often frustrated to see that their ideas are not implemented as quickly as they would like.

- Gather as many mentors and advisers able to introduce you to some of the space's important recesses that aren't directly part of marketing or financial reports.

- Don't underestimate the money and time you need to accomplish your goals. Especially not the money. Be ready to knock at the door of dozens of venture capitalists. It's not fun, but when you can't bootstrap, that's what you have to do.

9

Where Is the Right Place?

*For the strength of the Pack is the Wolf, and the strength of the
Wolf is the Pack.*
—Rudyard Kipling

While it's true that Steve Jobs and Steve Wozniak initially tinkered in the garage of Jobs's father, we must remember that this garage was located some fifteen miles away from the Menlo Park home of Gordon French, who played a key role in the Homebrew Computer Club that influenced the microcomputer revolution, and some twelve miles from Stanford University. Even though there were still orchards in Silicon Valley at the time, hundreds of great companies had been thriving within a thirty-mile radius for decades and well before it was called "Silicon Valley." In addition to starting at the right "time," they were in the right place, or at least one of them.

Kairos is a broad and complex expanse with a lot of windows opening on lots of opportunities, but from where can we discern them best? In other words, what's the right place? In reality, there are many of them. The "geography of genius," to use Eric Weiner's expression, is composed of multiple places, often called "business clusters," which, for a variable period of time, coalesce dominant trends of the kairos in particular domains.[1] They are both observatories and scale models of the kairos that help entrepreneurs and large companies alike to navigate the complex environment in which they operate as well as identify areas ripe for change, key drivers, and new industry directions.

Along with the multiplication of these geographical hubs, we also see a globalization and virtualization of business through a combination of various technologies. This phenomenon fosters de-clustering trends that may reduce the relevance of being part of physical groupings. But it also reminds us that we are citizens of a larger world, that is, performers in a large distributed orchestra where our individual chances of accessing the coveted part of becoming a noted soloist may become even more improbable.

BUSINESS CLUSTERS: THE "GEOGRAPHY OF GENIUS"

Hotbeds of creativity have popped up all over the world throughout history. These are energizing microsystems that make you feel in the thick of it. If you're in technology, this may mean being in places such as Silicon Valley, Shenzhen, Beijing, Tel Aviv, Seattle, London, Berlin, San Diego, New York, and so on. In short, you want to be in an ecosystem bubbling with ideas.

In the Ancient World these ecosystems often formed around harbors and ports for trade reasons. The Hanseatic League was a vastly distributed hub of artisans and merchants for northwestern and central European towns with its own legal system and armies. Generally speaking, in the preindustrial world business clusters developed along trade routes. For example, Aït Benhaddou, in Morocco, owed its wealth to being part of the trans-Saharan exchange system. In the same fashion, the Silk Road was a network of itineraries, which started with the Han dynasty in China in the second century BCE and lasted until the early eighteenth century, with thriving business centers along the way.[2] Even in our virtualized world, some of these ecosystems keep a high symbolic and inspirational value, as evidenced by the modern Chinese initiative of a "New Silk Road" between China and Europe. In the course of the nineteenth century, business clusters formed more around industrial specialties. Today, even when they leverage the infinite internet cartography, they haven't necessarily abandoned all physical approaches or components.

Drawing from British economist Alfred Marshall's description of industry clusters, Michael Porter popularized the notion of "business clusters" in his 1990 book *The Competitive Advantage of Nations*.[3] Their definition is intuitive:

> Clusters are geographic concentrations of interconnected companies and institutions in a particular field. Clusters encompass an array of linked industries and other entities important to competition. They include, for example, suppliers of specialized inputs such as components, machinery, and services, and providers of specialized infrastructure. Clusters also often extend downstream to channels and customers and laterally to manufacturers of complementary products and to companies in industries related by skills, technologies, or common inputs. Finally, many clusters include governmental and other institutions—such as universities, standards-setting agencies, think tanks, vocational training providers, and trade associations—that provide specialized training, education, information, research, and technical support.[4]

Clusters bolster the innovation engine in multiple ways. They drive its pace and direction, stimulating the formation of new businesses and enable aspiring innovators to soak in the overall mood of an industry and learn what's going on almost by capillarity. Clusters are social learning accelerators. You meet people in both formal and informal events. You can sense whether or not you're in the loop and draw inspiration from what you see and hear. This is what "music scenes" represent for musicians.

Analysts and economists categorize clusters diversely—by geography, sector, type of expertise, and so on—but in all cases, a cluster is present when a region or city shows overrepresentation in a specialization compared to other regions or the rest of the country.

THE FORMATION OF CENTERS OF GRAVITY: SILICON VALLEY

The birth of business clusters is a slow process, even today. Their formation is often preceded by a combination of circumstances and people that end up placing an entire area at the forefront of innovation. This is what happened in an emblematic business cluster, Silicon Valley.

For a long time, the computer industry's most influential cluster in the United States was on the East Coast, mostly in the Boston area, until Silicon Valley took over in the second half of the twentieth century. However, Silicon Valley didn't rise out of nothing. The prosperity of this small area between the southern part of San Francisco (and now including San Francisco) and San Jose started early in the twentieth century, with strong military roots and a deep involvement in wireless telegraphy and ham radio. In 1908 Australian-born Cyril Elwell, a graduate of Stanford University, had founded the Federal Telegraph Company (FTC); it developed, based on a technology created by Danish Valdemar Poulsen, high-powered transmitters used for long-distance radiotelegraph communication and installed the US Navy's first global scale radio communications system. Lee de Forest, a young inventor who had created the first practical electronic amplifier, the three-element "Audion" triode vacuum tube in 1906, joined the company after unsuccessfully trying his luck in various companies on the East Coast. FTC attracted and trained countless engineers and even helped external scientists, like Ernest Lawrence from the University of California, Berkeley, who invented the cyclotron (Nobel laureate in 1939). As noted by David Laws, "FTC bred other startups and trained engineers and technicians for a growing industry cluster around San Carlos, California, manufacturing radio transmitting and receiving vacuum tubes in the late 1920s and '30s."[5] Among them, San Francisco–born and Stanford graduate Charles Litton, who joined FTC in 1927 as its company's chief engineer, developed a glassblowing lathe that enabled mass production of vacuum tubes before he founded Litton Engineering Laboratories in 1932.

The history of Silicon Valley is well documented, even though its foundations are often overlooked.[6] Yet these foundations are the bedrock for an accelerated transformation into the beacon that Silicon Valley remains today through two main catalysts:

- Fred Terman and the foundation of Stanford Industrial Park (now Stanford Research Park);
- the founding of Fairchild Semiconductor.

Fred Terman and the Foundation of Stanford
Industrial Park

Fred Terman was born in 1900 in Indiana. His family moved to California when his father, psychologist Lewis Terman, joined the Stanford faculty.[7] He got his undergraduate degree in chemistry and his master's degree in electrical engineering, both at Stanford. For his doctor of science in electronic engineering, he went to MIT, where his adviser was Vannevar Bush.

Bush was an inspirational figure to Terman. Before he was thirty-five, Bush had demonstrated the power of transparently merging theoretical knowledge and practical application as well as the advantages of establishing close collaboration between academic organizations, private companies, and public institutions. He was also the iconic example of a dyed-in-the-wool entrepreneurial spirit capable of raising money to make things happen. What an ideal mentor and mindset to plant in the orchards and vineyards of Northern California!

Fred Terman joined the Stanford engineering faculty in 1925. He quickly set up a vacuum tube laboratory and hired Karl Spangenberg and Charles Litton. This initiative turned out to be a critical move for Terman to institute Stanford as a major knowledge center.

A fan of ham radio since his childhood, he also wrote a best-selling textbook on radio engineering that came out in 1932 and was followed by a greatly enhanced version in 1937 and two additional editions after World War II. As one of his students and later colleague Oswald Garrison Villard put it, "Fred was not a distinguished inventor like the University of California's Ernest Lawrence, whom he greatly admired. Terman had a remarkable ability to understand complex material and to present it in books, articles, and teaching in such a way that his readers found it easy to grasp."[8]

Terman became president of the Institute of Radio Engineers in 1941 and was the first national president of that organization west of the Mississippi River.[9] His personal impact was amplified when, in 1942, he became the head of an eight-hundred-person secret laboratory on the

Harvard campus, the Radio Research Laboratory, whose mission was to develop the Allies' electronic warfare arsenal to counter the Axis powers' radars and communications. This appointment must have had Bush's blessing given that the lab was a spinoff of MIT's Radiation Laboratory, whose funding by the National Defense Research Committee (headed by Bush) was arranged via Alfred Loomis, who was a polymath, inventor, and major philanthropist (and whose personal laboratory in Tuxedo Park, New York, became a meeting place for the most celebrated scientists of the time). By the end of the war, Terman was part of the US national defense inner circles, which gave him additional access to funding and other resources.

He continued to encourage students to become entrepreneurs, something he began doing in the 1930s. As the head of the Stanford Department of Electrical Engineering, Terman was concerned by the limited employment opportunities for Stanford engineering graduates in California. Many had to go to the East Coast. This had been the case of one of his students, David Packard, who upon graduation in 1934 had taken a job at General Electric in New York. This could have been the case of Bill Hewlett, who had received his bachelor's degree from Stanford in 1934, and his master of science degree in electrical engineering from MIT in 1936, and who in 1937 was pursuing a Stanford electrical engineer degree. Terman played a seminal role in bringing Packard and Hewlett together. He shared with them a new idea in electronics, an audio frequency oscillator that could help control audio equipment. Terman also gave them a list of potential customers, including Walt Disney Studios, which ended up purchasing eight oscillators in 1938. Hewlett and Packard operated in a one-car garage on 367 Addison Avenue in Palo Alto, California, and incorporated their company in January 1939.

Terman helped numerous young engineers. One of them was Edward Ginzton, a graduate from the University of California (Berkeley), who couldn't find a job. He had shown up at Stanford because there was an opening for an assistant for Joseph Carroll in high-voltage engineering. Ginzton didn't have the right profile, but Carroll sent him to Terman, who both gave him a research assistantship and connected him with another professor, William Hansen. Ginzton got involved with Hansen as well as Russell and Sigurd Varian in the development of a major project, the klystron tube, the first powerful source of radio waves in the microwave range. Ginzton—along with Hansen and the Varian brothers—was one of the original board members of Varian Associates, a major electromagnetic equipment manufacturing firm founded in 1948.

Terman became the dean of engineering when he returned to Stanford in 1946, and its provost from 1955 to 1965. As time went on, he gained more than power. He was so knowledgeable in so many areas and such an efficient connector between people that his ideas always seemed to be poised for success. A major one was the creation of Stanford Industrial Park in 1951. The goal was to have a high technology hub close to the university. In 1951 Varian Associates signed a lease, and in 1953 the company moved into the first building in the park. Then came Eastman Kodak, General Electric, Admiral Corporation, Shockley Transistor Corporation, Lockheed, Hewlett-Packard, and many others. In parallel, Terman transformed the university's chemistry department by attracting important chemists, like William Johnson (Lemieux-Johnson oxidation and artificial production of steroids) and Carl Djerassi (oral contraceptive pills), who brought in one of his colleagues at Syntex, Alejandro Zaffaroni, who would later start several biotech companies.

Terman was a major societal innovator in nurturing an environment that fostered new ideas. He created a sense of growth, reshaping most of the science and engineering departments, encouraging students to start their own companies and faculty members to advise them. He also operated as a powerful connector between eras, generations, and lifestyles directly or through his students. For example, Myron Stolaroff, a former student, provided Alexander Poniatoff, who had founded Ampex in 1944, with critical ideas for the Ampex Model 200, which was based on a German Magnetophon modified by the audio engineer Jack Mullin. Stolaroff worked with Harold Lindsey, initially at Charles Litton's company—and Poniatoff was Litton's neighbor and friend. With Bing Crosby's financial support, the Ampex 200A went into production, and subsequent products reshaped American broadcasting, show business, film audio production, and the recorded-music industry. Ampex, as a company, then generated multiple entrepreneurs. Memorex, started in 1961 by selling computer and then disk packs, became the home of multiple Ampex engineers. Ray Dolby founded Dolby Laboratories (in England in 1965 until he moved the headquarters to San Francisco in 1976). Larry Ellison and Bob Miner left the company to co-found along with Ed Oates (ex-Ampex and ex-Memorex) Software Development Labs in 1977—later renamed Oracle.

Extraordinarily efficient at attracting federal government research funding and countless private sponsors, Terman was an essential node in a hyperactive rhizome of entrepreneurial talents that expanded independently from him.[10]

Fairchild Semiconductor

By the early 1950s, the whole region was poised to become the center of the semiconductor industry with the founding of Fairchild Semiconductor in 1957 and later, in 1968, with Intel, which kickstarted Silicon Valley's large venture capital (VC) network.

As I mentioned in chapter 1, William Shockley was unable to keep key people in his pioneering semiconductor company. In 1957 eight of them resigned from Shockley Labs: Julius Blank, Victor Grinich, Jean Hoerni, Eugene Kleiner, Jay Last, Gordon Moore, Robert Noyce, and Sheldon Roberts. One of them, Eugene Kleiner, whose family had fled the Nazi persecution of Jews in Austria and settled in New York, contacted his father's broker. Arthur Rock, the young analyst working for that broker, convinced his boss to meet with the team in San Francisco. As a result, team members got in touch with Sherman Fairchild, the son of IBM's largest shareholder and the founder of multiple companies, including Fairchild Camera and Instrument. Before the end of 1957, Fairchild Semiconductor was formed as a division of that company and based in San Jose, California.

Fairchild Semiconductor was very successful, but part of the original team left when Fairchild Camera and Instrument's board diverted

profits from the division outside the semiconductor industry.[11] Robert
Noyce and Gordon Moore then founded Intel in July 1968. That said,
the semiconductor industry spawned by Fairchild Semiconductor's "children" changed the makeup of what became known as Silicon Valley in
1971.[12] In 1997 *Business Week* provided a graphical representation of
twenty-seven major companies that were the direct descendants of Fairchild Semiconductor.[13] In 2014 Rhett Morris, then director of Endeavor
Insight, reported that of the more than 130 Bay Area tech companies trading on the NASDAQ or the New York Stock Exchange, 70 percent of these
firms could be traced back to the founders and employees of Fairchild,
and that these 92 public companies were worth about $2.1 trillion.[14] Note
that the first investor in Apple, Mike Markkula, had been a marketing
manager for Fairchild Semiconductor and Intel, and that Apple alone
reached that market capitalization in August 2020.

The founding of Fairchild Semiconductor spurred another major innovation that operated as a machine to support aspiring innovators and,
ultimately, their innovations: the financing of young companies via venture capitalists.

Venture Capital wasn't invented in California but in Boston in 1946,
when French-born immigrant Georges Doriot, who had served in the
US Army as the director of the Military Planning Division, founded the
American Research and Development Corporation (ARDC). The original
goal of this first private equity VC firm was to stimulate investment in
businesses run by returning World War II veterans, but Doriot quickly
supported multiple new companies along Route 128 in Massachusetts.
Many showed tremendous growth, often driven by technology coming
out of MIT and Harvard. Doriot's first success was funding the Digital
Equipment Corporation (DEC). That same year, Doriot also founded a
business school, INSEAD.

The formation of Fairchild Semiconductor in California attracted
East Coast investors, starting with Arthur Rock. Eugene Kleiner left engineering to co-found the firm Kleiner Perkins with Thomas Perkins in
1972 (nabbing Frank Caufield and Brook Byers). The same year, Don Valentine—a New Yorker whose career in sales had led him to Raytheon,

Fairchild Semiconductor, and National Semiconductor—set up Sequoia Capital. These three funds financed hundreds of companies whose entrepreneurs and executives themselves financed companies as investors. These entrepreneurs were part of companies such as Sun Microsystems, and later Netscape and PayPal, which in turn spawned investment firms such as Khosla Ventures, Andreessen Horowitz, and 500 Startups.

Silicon Valley has inspired the development of multiple technology clusters around the world and provided a model of cluster effectiveness. This effectiveness is predicated on the combination of at least these ingredients: R&D funding and support provided by public authorities and private organizations, collaboration with higher education organizations, an initial dominant specialty (which can evolve over time), venture capital availability, regional incentives, and measures to accelerate regional employment and retain the relevant workforce.

THE DYNAMICS OF CLUSTERS

Over time, business clusters can strengthen their influence or, oppositely, may lose their edge. As an example of a thriving cluster, I'll take the California wine industry and then explain what contributes to the vulnerability of business clusters.

The California Wine Industry

Not all business clusters are about technology. You can have what's called "factor endowment clusters," that is, clusters associated with particular geographical characteristics that support specific activities. This characteristic is the case with wine production areas, like the California wine cluster, whose clout has kept growing over the decades.

When Michael Porter described the California wine industry in the early 1990s, it included 680 commercial wineries as well as several thousand independent wine grape growers. He also mentioned the various complementary industries supporting both winemaking and grape growing, including suppliers of grape stock, irrigation and harvesting equipment, barrels, and labels; specialized public relations and advertising firms; and numerous wine publications aimed at consumer and trade audiences. A host of local institutions is involved with wine, such as the viticulture and enology program at the University of California at Davis, the Wine Institute, and special committees of the California senate and assembly. The cluster also enjoys weaker linkages to other California clusters in agriculture, food and restaurants, and wine-country tourism.[15]

Not all clusters continue to thrive just because they're in the right natural area. They must remain relevant as the rest of the world evolves. Since Porter's analysis three decades ago, the California wine cluster has grown considerably. It was the leader in the United States in terms of wine production as of 2021, with over 4,200 wineries.

Wine can be seen as a slow-moving genre because even though it's true that consumers' tastes vary over time, they do so at a much slower pace than other senses. When we drink wine from the Monte Bello vineyard in the hills above Cupertino, California, in the 2020s, we want to experience the same gustatory pleasure we had in 2000—the era of the Nokia 3310 and so many other once-promising technology starlets that became relics thrown off the deep end of our memory. The strength of the California wine cluster is due to its ability to conciliate very different velocities in the kairos, the slow-moving rhythm of taste on the one hand and societal changes on the other.

My friend Mark Vernon, CEO of Ridge Vineyards, one of the most prestigious brands in the world and co-founded in 1959 by four engineers at the Stanford Research Institute (SRI), summarized some of the multiple reasons the California wine cluster has strengthened its hold through continued adjustments to the times.[16] "The move to organic and biodynamic farming has triggered a lot of innovations in the past ten years," Vernon says.[17] Several new devices allow for mechanical weed control used with tractors—with most having sensors so that they can till the ground up close to the vine without hurting it. Machines take care of tasks previously done by hand for harvesting, sorting, trimming, or removing leaves for more sunlight. Drones are used to plan vineyard plantings, determine irrigation patterns, and identify diseased vines. New environmentally safe products protect them from insects, and new recipes for compost provide vine nourishment in an organic way. Another area of innovation relates to methods for water management, also used in Australia. Sap flow sensors measure vine water uptake. This technology is combined with a software infrastructure that looks at weather conditions together with other variables predicting vine water needs as well as the vines' reaction to irrigation.

"Ridge has been very effective in water use improvements," Vernon adds. "We have invested heavily in technology to recycle the water that we use in our wineries for vineyard irrigation. For example, at our Monte Bello vineyard we have an advanced reverse osmosis membrane-based filtration system that gives us very pure water for use on our vineyards."

At the same time, the California wine cluster has spurred numerous business innovations adapted to consumers' expectations, like direct or online sales and improvements to the tasting room experience. In parallel, the cluster was extremely effective at urging the loosening of the regulatory environment, even if there is still work to do there. "We can sell wine to individual consumers now in about 15 countries due to work done by FedEx to allow these shipments to quickly clear customs and collect the needed taxes and duties. In fact, from California I can get a bottle of wine delivered to a customer in Tokyo faster than New York," Vernon says.

The California wine cluster even includes virtual wineries. You can create a wine brand with nothing more than a phone and an internet connection. This has been made possible by the availability of contract service providers at every step of the wine business. While it was always possible to buy grapes from growers, you still had to make your own wine if you were going to go into the business. Now that you can do everything on a contract basis, barriers to entry have fallen and, as a result, the number of wine brands has exploded. However, if you control the best vineyards, "you still stand above most of these virtual producers in terms of quality," Vernon concludes.

The reasons for the sustained success of the California wine cluster isn't simply that it produces great wines. It's also because of a continuous adaptiveness to multiple aspects of kairos, ranging from technology improvements to consumers' new behavioral patterns. In other words, this cluster has evolved in sync with transformations within multiple layers of kairos.

The Vulnerability of Business Clusters

While the raison d'être of a business cluster is its ability to bring promising trends to the forefront, there can be companies that have become conservative within that cluster. That's fine if the entropy they create is offset by the energy input from others. When that's not the case, however, a cluster can glide toward its demise. So if you choose to integrate a business cluster, you may want to check on the exact ratio of companies that stand at the forefront of new trends.

Clusters can't be static entities. They're a specific emanation and interpretation of the kairos and must evolve and pivot with it. The British nineteenth-century Lancashire cotton textile industry didn't survive the evolution of trade, and dozens of mills had to close. The beginning of the end of clusters starts when they believe that they're a scale model of a kairos frozen in time.

Clusters wither when they turn into groupthink bodies living by their own norms and view themselves as a prescriptive group that can unilaterally influence the rest of the world. They lose their actual connection with the kairos they initially represented. They become islands of sorts and lose their ability to reflect the real kairos. In short, "[they] are at least as vulnerable to internal rigidities as they are to external threats," as Porter said when he analyzed the fall of the automobile cluster in Detroit.[18]

Multiple books and research papers explain the failure of the American auto industry after 1970. What's less frequently analyzed is the fact that the Detroit automotive industry also hurt the American automotive industry at large. This cluster imposed its norms, ranging from what American consumers would buy to how large industrial complexes should be managed—which led, for example, to strong positions against labor or a sharp decrease of manufacturing jobs with the extension of outsourcing practices to reduce labor costs. As I mentioned in chapter 8, because of its power and its lobbying capabilities, the cluster impacted a number of policies at the national level, so much so that when it started to wither, an entire segment of the American economy was at risk. This happened in the 1970s and then again in the 2000s, so much so that the auto industry had to be bailed out by the US government.

Booming clusters usually present fast-evolving segments of the kairos. However, even when they're continuously forward thinking, they're not immune to parochialism. As prestigious and financially successful as Silicon Valley is, it's not the ultimate temple of all things technology. Silicon Valley isn't at the forefront of the 5G revolution and isn't really poised to drive the 5G economy, which includes everything from indoor and outdoor wireless broadband to augmented reality, as well as the Internet of Things (IoT), like asset tracking, energy monitoring, or autonomous vehicles.

Silicon Valley, just like any cluster, has its rules, from the way its major venture capitalists manage their portfolios to their returns on investment criteria. But as obvious as it was to say that "software is eating the world" in 2011, as a major Silicon Valley venture capitalist, Marc Andreessen, wrote, it's also somewhat perilous to believe that the world could only feed and live on software.[19] During the COVID-19 crisis, Silicon Valley didn't exactly shine. In 2020 the same Andreessen rang the alarm bell in a post that sounded like an appeal à la Andy Grove, advocating for a major infrastructure overhaul:

> Our nation and our civilization were built on production, on building. Our forefathers and foremothers built roads and trains, farms and factories, then the computer, the microchip, the smartphone, and uncounted thousands of other things that we now take for granted, that are all around us, that define our lives and provide for our well-being. There is only one way to honor their legacy and to create the future we want for our own children and grandchildren, and that's to build.[20]

History shows that business clusters can be vulnerable, some more than others, especially when they evolve around one specialty. Also, innovation geographies change. Now and then, we hear that Silicon Valley might be losing some ground. It's true that it doesn't have the monopoly it used to have, because of the boom of tech clusters around the world. In fact, the share of all VC money flowing into American startups in general has declined from 84 percent two decades ago to less than half. As a result also, and although unicorns should not be viewed as a barometer but only as a financial indicator that isn't necessarily associated with a specific innovation, it's useful to note that about half of them reside outside America.[21]

DE-CLUSTERING BUSINESS CLUSTERS

Joining a cluster is important in industries where knowledge of state-of-the-art practices or products is paramount to the success of their endeavors. Today, aspiring innovators have multiple choices that aren't mutually exclusive. They can join physical clusters but also virtual clusters.

Joining a Physical Cluster

If you have capital and few encumbrances, you can set up business almost anywhere you want, though in practice you might encounter difficulties such as not getting work visas easily or being as fluent as you need to be in a new language.

I'm often asked by entrepreneurs whether moving to Silicon Valley is a must. Invariably, my response is that it depends on what your business is about. Silicon Valley presents unique advantages and touches a vast number of sectors, but you must realize that it's not the only business cluster in the United States, let alone in the world. Choosing one may be the delicate part of the equation.

As attested by William Kerr and Frederic Robert-Nicoud when they analyzed characteristics required for an important tech cluster, ranking clusters is a complex task, even though it's generally agreed on that "a distinguishing feature of tech clusters is their cultural celebration of innovation that has the potential to change the world."[22] It's still hard to define sets of criteria in stone, but a high level would include a combination of critical components like VC funding, patents, and employment in R&D-intensive sectors or digital-connected occupations that allow for a relevant hierarchy between clusters.

A large number of countries have developed powerful clusters that obviate the need for international entrepreneurs to start in the United States, even in technology. They help their startups with public funding, and more VC firms have popped up throughout the world. Also, many US venture funds are now open to investing not only in their geographical area but anywhere in the United States as well as abroad.

Note that rankings vary depending on the criteria and over time. Various organizations, such as the Startup Genome, provide updates or new information. Also, many countries are working diligently at forming new clusters around a large number of smaller cities. For example, in 2014, Steve Case launched "Revolution's Rise of the Rest" to accelerate the development of dozens of startups in various regions of the United States.[23]

Of course, selecting one country or city doesn't preclude you from always checking on what's going on around the world. I can only suggest that you keep a close eye on what's happening in Asia, especially China, which has become a world leader in patent grants and has emerged as a forerunner in many technologies. The "Chinese government has pledged to convert the nation into an international innovation leader by 2030."[24] This deadline is all the more realistic as the country has consistently been gearing its efforts for at least twenty-five years.

Cluster De-clustering: Blockchain and Cryptocurrency

Do we always need to be part of a physical business cluster? This is debatable, especially when a space is represented across multiple physical and virtual business clusters. The blockchain and cryptocurrency space illustrates a fragmentation that, although dictated by the nature of this type of businesses, could also be indicative of a larger trend.

The topic of the extent of possible choices for entrepreneurs in blockchain and cryptocurrency came up in a conversation with Thomas France, who started as an entrepreneur (he was a co-founder of Ledger in

Paris) and has become a venture capitalist in California. To the question, "Where can you find the talent, money, legal advice, stimulating encounters, etc.?" which are the main reasons for joining a business cluster, his response was "in many places around the world."

Talent is everything. So where do you find it? Anywhere. California universities like Stanford and Berkeley offer remarkable courses, but multiple other campuses do too all over the United States as well as the rest of the world. They're serving an industry that's both decentralized and global and has to leverage talents everywhere. So while Silicon Valley may remain an excellent option because of its accumulated history, the rest of the world is also a gigantic playground for all sorts of innovations across all areas of blockchain and cryptocurrency: underlying blockchain technologies, standards and regulatory practices, cryptocurrency exchanges, hardware and software wallets, and integration with traditional financial services or development of applications offering blockchain as a service (BaaS). As a result, it's no surprise that many specifically focused blockchain startup accelerators and incubators have popped up throughout the world—from the Iconic Lab Accelerator in Berlin to the Tribe Accelerator in Singapore—that latter of whose government is intent at creating a leading think-tank for blockchain research and technology at the Crystal Centre of Computing, which is part of the National University of Singapore.

The birth of Ethereum is one of the many examples of this talent blowout phenomenon. The founders of Ethereum are an international lot. Russian Canadian Vitalik Buterin studied at the University of Waterloo for two years and was an assistant to an assistant for famed cryptographer Ian Goldberg.[25] An hour away, Toronto was home to another co-founder, Anthony Di Iorio, who studied at Ryerson University. While two of the founders are Canadian (with a third one, Joseph Lubin, from Princeton University, joining early on), the others hail from different countries: Charles Hoskinson (alma mater University of Colorado Boulder) is American, Mihai Alisie is Romanian (Lucian Blaga University of Sibiu), Amir Chetrit is a US-Israeli national (Sami Shamoon College of Engineering in Beersheba), Gavin Wood is British (University of York), and Jeffrey Wilcke is Dutch. Although not an Ethereum co-founder,

Jutta Steiner, who served as the foundation's original chief of security, is German (University of Bonn). She co-founded Parity Technologies with Gavin Wood, with offices in the UK (London and Cambridge) as well as in Berlin, with developers spread across multiple countries. Today, the Ethereum Foundation is a Swiss nonprofit organization headquartered in Zug (about thirty minutes away from Zurich), dubbed "Crypto Valley" by Mihai Alisie. The view of Zug as a blockchain global center was initiated by Johann Gevers after he moved his cryptofinance startup Monetas there in 2013. Since then, Crypto Valley has attracted dozens of companies, organizations, and foundations that not only produce great technologies but are also helping to sort out the labyrinth of regulatory environments around the world.

That said, because of their intrinsic nature, blockchain and cryptocurrency software is largely decoupled from physical clusters—so much so that companies can even do away with the concept of "headquarters," a phenomenon accelerated by the COVID crisis. Originally started in San Francisco, Coinbase, a cryptocurrency exchange, announced in February 2021 that it would be "a decentralized company, with no headquarters."[26] Brian Armstrong, the CEO and co-founder of the company, provided the rationale for that decision: First, "remote-first has been working really well," he said, mentioning that "94% of employees believe that the benefits of remote-first outweigh the drawbacks, or that the benefits and drawbacks balance each other out. In particular, they appreciate the autonomy, flexibility, the ability to focus, and reclaiming commute hours." Second, he added, "It has helped us attract top talent." This remote-first approach has allowed them to "cast a much wider net. Over the last nine months, we've onboarded hundreds of employees from locations outside of the commute range of any of our existing offices. In Q1 of 2020, only 28% of new employees lived outside of California. In Q1 of 2021 to date, 58% of our new hires are from outside of the state."

Of course, such de-clustering best applies to businesses with a high software component operated by white-collar workers, and it shouldn't lead us to the conclusion that we can do away with physical business clusters altogether. The blockchain and cryptocurrency industries themselves do rely on heavy-duty data-center infrastructures, manufacturing of high-efficiency chips, or optimization of power plants.

Physical business clusters, no matter how prestigious they are, do not reflect all innovation activities. What the World Wide Web has made possible over the past thirty years is an extended innovation virtual map that continues to expand. Large, open-source development platforms of all types are already effective virtual business clusters, as are to some degree digital distribution platforms and vendor-led marketplaces that federate all sorts of businesses. New technologies combine to build up different worlds and energize the kairos. For example, in South Korea familiarity with micropayment has accelerated the popularity of cryptocurrencies, integrating with a pervasive adoption of video games, outstanding internet speed, and high-performing telecommunication systems.

CONCLUSION

The right place is ultimately any location from which you can best apprehend the diversity of the kairos, along with the various directions toward which some of its layers may evolve.

Since their early existence, business clusters have primarily centered on a region or city (and this is what the industrial revolutions of the nineteenth and the twentieth centuries have primarily focused on), but we shouldn't forget they were often only stops along routes across nations. Historically, one of the most complex networks of routes, of course, was the Silk Road, which operated as a gateway between countries whose relationships were facilitated by people meeting face-to-face. Among the most successful traders along the Silk Road were the Sogdians, an Iranian civilization that occupied territories in Uzbekistan, Tajikistan, Kazakhstan, and Kyrgyzstan. While many middlemen on the trade route tended to be local, the Sogdians established the longest trading network, an innovation route across from Sogdiana to China, where they established communities in strategic outposts in the Northwest, notably in Gansu and Ningxia. As a result, the Sogdian language, now extinct, was de facto the lingua franca of the Silk Road.

Today, many innovators must be Sogdians of sorts with English as their lingua franca. Although physical business clusters still constitute key economic attraction poles for regional or national authorities that claim global reach while defending some form of balkanization advantages, entrepreneurs have to see them as ad hoc outposts along an innovation route that traverses multiple geographies.

The impact of COVID-19 has widely demonstrated that we can operate in a highly distributed world in which interpersonal relationships and trust aren't exclusively predicated on face-to-face contact. Fast progress in virtual reality technologies enables us to simultaneously process the physical and digital, sit next to each other from across the world, and be anywhere we want or need to be. The right place for innovation may be anywhere in both the real and virtual worlds. In all cases, though, we have to be connected, because ultimately innovation is about being part of networks of people—as I will discuss in the next chapter.

10

Do You Need to Be Connected to Succeed?

Any fact becomes important when it's connected to another.
—Umberto Eco

In his short story "Chains," Frigyes Karinthy explained, "Planet Earth has never been as tiny as it is now" and staged an imaginary conversation about how easily one could be connected with a riveter at the Ford Motor Company "who could then assemble a new automobile for me, should I need one."[1] This isn't fantasy. The vast majority of innovators belong to traceable and intertwined networks that make up the intellectual, financial, and social connective tissue supporting their endeavors both at any given time and over time.

Business clusters, be they physical or virtual, aren't abstract places. They're inhabited by people who are members of circles, organizations, companies, laboratories, educational institutions, and so on, and they form genealogies of knowledge and affinities. At the heart of the innovation kairos are people who mark the routes driving innovations. This idea may sound somewhat contrary to the individualistic mythologies that geniuses are solitary, fringe creatures who suddenly appear and show off their magic. But history tells a different story.

Yes, we must be connected, and it's more than amassing thousands of contacts on professional and personal social networks. That's only addressing the surface. Networks are two-dimensional. We see the horizontal side of them pretty easily, but we shouldn't forget their vertical depth, the lineages that strengthen kinships sometimes spanning across several generations.

Many innovations that seem unrelated when you look at them on a timeline can stem from the same root, and many innovators that live decades apart can belong to the same cultural rhizome within the kairos. Think of it as genealogy stacks within innovation stacks. To illustrate this phenomenon, I'll start with a case study that associates two seemingly disparate innovations, baking powder and dynamite, and from there, expand on the open or subterranean networking structures that underpin the innovation scene. For aspiring innovators, the best course of action is to make sure that you connect to these genealogies.

CASE STUDY: THE BAKING POWDER AND DYNAMITE FAMILY

Alfred Nobel invented dynamite—a new type of explosive made of nitroglycerin, sorbents, and stabilizers—in Sweden in the 1860s. The American Eben Horsford developed the first double-acting baking powder that we still use today, Rumford Baking Powder, at about the same time.

What do these two men have in common? Their innovations can be traced back to one of the founders of organic chemistry, Justus von Liebig (1803–73), the same man who gave his name to the beef stock cube sold under the OXO brand. Liebig was a prototypical outsize inventor and contributed directly and indirectly to many innovations in multiple spaces.

Liebig's career path is important.[2] After studying in Bonn and Erlangen, he went to Paris in 1822 for a year to study with the French chemist Joseph Louis Gay-Lussac. Gay-Lussac was himself connected to one of the fathers of modern chemistry, Antoine Lavoisier (guillotined in 1794), via a key disciple of his, Claude-Louis Berthollet. Liebig didn't meet Berthollet, who had just died, but Gay-Lussac, who had been his assistant, was carrying out his tradition of experimenting in a laboratory. That year in Paris also immersed Liebig into a group of monumental thought-leaders, two generations of scientists that made up the Société d'Arcueil.[3] It included direct participants of the Age of Enlightenment who had advocated the conciliation of theory and practice and a younger generation determined to apply these principles in real life. This approach meant taking seriously the intersection of scientific research and industrial applications as well as adapting educational systems to the demands of the beginnings of the Industrial Revolution.

When Liebig came back to Germany, his goal was clear: building a research laboratory to practice chemistry, adapting modern teaching methods, and devising practical applications. At twenty-one, he was appointed professor *extraordinarius* at the University of Giessen with the recommendation of Wilhelm von Humboldt and the vetting of the European chemistry elite.[4] As a professor between 1824 and 1852, he transformed chemistry education, encouraging the seven hundred students he trained to continuously experiment.[5] He built close relationships with industrialists and chemical manufacturers in various countries. For example, an important industrialist friend of Liebig's was the Englishman James Muspratt, who sent his daughter, Emma, to Liebig's home to study German in 1853. It's when Emma fell ill that Liebig created the beef stock extract that made his name popular. He wasn't just an inventor and professor; he was also an innovator, co-founding the Bayerischen Aktiengesellschaft für chemische und landwirtschaftlich-chemische Fabrikate, the first German fertilizer manufacturer, in 1857. Liebig's impact was extraordinarily wide ranging. In the 1860s he published an article on substitutes for maternal milk, and he inspired Swiss-German Henri Nestlé to venture into the production of food for babies in 1867.

Liebig was such a central figure in the nineteenth century that the link between Eben Horsford and Alfred Nobel becomes more logical. After discovering one of Liebig's books, Horsford went to Germany to work in Liebig's lab (1844–45), where he focused on the analysis of the nitrogen content of grains. Then, when Horsford later taught chemistry and conducted research at the Harvard Lawrence Scientific School, the textbooks he used had been authored by two former Liebig assistants: Heinrich Will and Carl Remigius Fresenius. Over the years, Liebig had developed ideas on new bread-making processes. But it's Horsford who published *The*

Theory and Art of Breadmaking in 1861 and ended up designing the artificial yeast commercialized under the name Rumford Baking Powder. The name didn't mean much to most people, but it had a high symbolic value. The company was named after the Rumford Chair of Physics, an endowed professorship established at Harvard University in 1816 under the will of Benjamin Thompson, Count Rumford. And who was Thompson? He was a reputed physicist who had married, in 1804, Marie-Anne Paulze Lavoisier, the widow and close collaborator of Lavoisier. Horsford shared his formula with Liebig, who spread the information, always giving him credit. Production in Germany was somewhat rocky, but in England the baking powder based on Horsford's formula was sold as Horsford-Liebig Baking Powder.[6]

Alfred Nobel belonged to a younger generation. He was born in 1833, whereas Horsford was born in 1818. But they belonged to the same sphere: Nobel's private chemistry teacher, Nikolai Zinin, had studied with Liebig. Thanks to him, Nobel, aged only seventeen, was able to join the private Paris lab of Théophile-Jules Pelouze, who had himself started as a laboratory assistant to Gay-Lussac. Pelouze had also been a colleague of Liebig in Giessen and now ran the largest private laboratory in France, training a new generation of chemists and physiologists (including Claude Bernard, who introduced experimental methodologies in medicine). It's there that Nobel met another student of Liebig's, the Italian chemist Ascanio Sobrero, who had discovered nitroglycerin in 1846. After Nobel's father's company went bankrupt subsequent to the end of the Crimean War, Alfred was searching for new products, and Zinin reminded him of the potential of nitroglycerin.

In 1864 Nobel began its manufacture in a small plant outside Stockholm, where an explosion killed several people, including his youngest brother, Emil. Nobel then worked on developing a safe nitroglycerin explosive, first inventing the blasting cap and then discovering that a siliceous sedimentary rock earth (kieselguhr) would stabilize nitroglycerin. Nobel started a new industry, and within ten years, sixteen factories producing explosives had been founded in fourteen countries with Nobel as shareholder or co-owner.[7] In the United States, the DuPont Company would later buy the rights to manufacture dynamite, which ties us back to Lavoisier. The originator of DuPont, Éleuthère Irénée du Pont de Nemours, who immigrated to the United States in 1800, had been Lavoisier's student at the Régie des poudres, which had worked on improving the manufacturing of black powder and new explosive-production techniques and had been run by Lavoisier until 1792.[8]

Liebig built a powerful network of chemists and industrialists spanning geography and time. Each member became an active messenger of and contributor to genealogies of knowledge linked to an industry segment (chemistry), specialties within that segment (agricultural, industrial), and organizations (universities, laboratories, manufacturers, etc.) as well as relationships between individuals (similar interests, friendships, etc.) and financial groups. Combined, they changed chemistry while impacting multiple other domains—such as medicine, pharmacology, manufacturing processes, and nutrition—as well as agriculture, as emphasized by Karl Marx, who mentions Liebig several times in *Capital*.[9]

This snapshot about Liebig, which covers only a small fraction of his contribution to the history of chemistry and of the laboratory movement in Germany, illustrates the importance of networking structures that enable inventors and innovators to become relevant players within an ecosystem—because they belong.[10]

NETWORKING STRUCTURES

Innovators belong to at least one network, and often several of them, explicitly or implicitly. These intertwine and create apparent coincidences, that is, a concurrence of events with no direct causal connection. But such coincidences emerge because of these shared structures. They're an archaeological foundation of sorts, in which we operate even when they escape our awareness.

For example, Steve Jobs idolized Edison. Did they belong to completely disparate worlds? Not really. They shared a cultural ethos transmitted by people. One of Edison's early employees, Arthur Kennelly, was an engineer and experimentalist at Edison's West Orange laboratory in New

Jersey before becoming a professor of electrical engineering both at Harvard and MIT, where Vannevar Bush was his doctoral student. Then Fred Terman was Bush's doctoral student at MIT. When Terman moved to Stanford, two of his students were David Packard and William Hewlett. When Steve Jobs was twelve, he cold-called Bill Hewlett to request leftover electronic parts to build a frequency counter. Hewlett not only gave him what he wanted but also offered him an internship that summer.[11] Meanwhile, two other Terman students were Russell and Sigurd Varian. Among the early employees of their company, Varian Associates, there was a bookkeeper, Clara Jobs, Steve Jobs's mother. This story doesn't even include the fact that Steve Wozniak was designing calculators at Hewlett-Packard (HP) when he conceived the Apple 1.

Many network structures canvass the kairos. I'll focus on three of them: laboratories, schools, and companies. They are environments where innovators meet and build relationships as well as benefit from knowledge accumulated over time. These hubs serve as the conveyance belts in genealogies of talents, which themselves combine to generate all sorts of subnetworks (financial institutions, accelerators, incubators, influence groups, professional organizations, etc.).

Laboratories

The history of labs is closely linked to the history of chemistry, but the concept expanded beyond this discipline and touched other industrial segments during the second part of the nineteenth century.[12] Labs considerably accelerated the pace of production of the inventions that shaped the innovation landscape.

Early University Labs

As in Europe, the lab approach in the United States originated in universities.

The Sheffield Scientific School at Yale established two professorships in 1847, in agricultural chemistry (held by John Pitkin Norton, who had visited Horsford in Giessen) and in practical chemistry (held by Benjamin

Silliman Jr., a noted chemist who was the son of Benjamin Silliman Sr., the first person to distill petroleum in America).

A similar phenomenon happened at Harvard. Horsford became the third Rumford Professor, and his appointment coincided with the foundation of the Lawrence Scientific School in 1847. Unsurprisingly, Horsford accelerated the adoption of a practical curriculum synched with the needs of local chemical industries. As a result, when a graduate of the Lawrence Scientific School, John Trowbridge, became an assistant professor of physics, he brought with him a recognition of the importance of lab research to the future of physics, which led to the dedication of the Jefferson Physical Laboratory in 1884.

Education associating scientific knowledge and practical applications became the craze. Peter Cooper (who built the first American steam locomotive in 1829) founded the Cooper Union for the Advancement of Science and Art in 1859. Edison enrolled in a chemistry course there in 1872 and took advantage of its lab.[13] Many universities that had been founded earlier or were getting off the ground (such as MIT in 1861) oriented studies toward ensuring a stronger connection with the industrial world. Although the majority of labs and research centers at MIT started after World War II, the first physics lab, the Rogers Lab, opened in 1869 and was designed and managed by Edward Pickering, a physicist and soon a major astronomer. Computer research at MIT began much later, of course, mostly when Vannevar Bush became the first dean of the school of engineering. Then, the wartime MIT Radiation Laboratory and multiple postwar initiatives and research in artificial intelligence began in the late 1950s, sealing the already high reputation of the school, which now offers dozens of programs.

Early Industry Labs

The first industrial labs in the United States were not immediately related to the chemical industry, but they still involved a lot of chemistry as part of the analysis of materials.[14]

One of the first large industrial labs that turned into an important ecosystem in a major industry of the nineteenth century was the Department of Physical Testing created by the Pennsylvania Railroad Company in 1874 in Altoona. There, the chemist Charles Dudley, who had been trained at the Yale Sheffield Scientific School, championed the rigorous testing of all materials used in the railroad industry and the development of standards for steel (which infuriated steel makers), fuels, lubricants, paints, and even locomotives. He also published his findings and later became one of the founders of the American Society for Testing and Materials (ASTM). The lab developed a number of test machines and new products and was the most prestigious one for this space in the country.

What accelerated the idea of an industry-driven research lab in the mind of the American public was Edison's lab, which opened in 1876 in Menlo Park, New Jersey, promising to produce "a minor invention every ten days and a big thing every six months or so."[15] The Pennsylvania Railroad even organized excursions to this "village of science." Crowds longed to see "the Wizard of Menlo Park" experimenting with his phonograph. In 1887 Edison's laboratory moved out of Menlo Park into a much larger facility in West Orange, New Jersey. This is where Edison spent the rest of his life, improving on earlier inventions and creating new ones. Edison's key collaborators were all familiar with the constructing-and-testing, trial-and-error, and iterative models that supported his invention methodology—of which today's concept of minimum viable product could be seen as a modern iteration. Unsurprisingly, they exported this approach to where they later worked. For example, John Kruesi, who participated in multiple Edison's experiments, pursued this methodology at General Electric.

Formally founded in 1901 by Charles Coffin, the GE Laboratory kept some parts of Edison's approach, but it incorporated deeper theoretical knowledge derived from the German university model under the influence of Charles Steinmetz, whose first important work was a new technology for a three-phase alternating current generator that placed General Electric ahead of Westinghouse. The first éminence grise of the lab was Willis Whitney, who had earned a Bachelor of Science at MIT and later studied at the University of Leipzig under one of the founders of the field of physical chemistry, Wilhelm Ostwald, a former student of Carl

Schmidt, himself a student of Liebig in Giessen. Later, in 1932, one of the lab researchers, William Coolidge, became its director: he too had studied with Ostwald.

The GE Lab didn't just produce a large quantity of innovations.[16] It also generated countless alumni who spread the message throughout the United States. The lab was also socially forward thinking and probably one of the first to hire a woman to work as a scientist, Katharine Burr Blodgett, in 1918. She became the inspiring aunt of another major female scientist, astrophysicist Katharine Blodgett Gebbie, the founding director of the Physical Measurement Laboratory of the National Institute of Standards and Technology (NIST) and head of its two predecessors, the Physics Laboratory and the Center for Atomic, Molecular and Optical Physics. During her twenty-two years at the helm of these institutions, four of their scientists were awarded the Nobel Prize in Physics.[17]

By the turn of the twentieth century, virtually every larger company had a lab. Two decades later one of them, Bell Telephone Laboratories, or Bell Labs, is of particular importance.[18] Started in 1925 Bell Labs contributed to major inventions of the twentieth century in a wide range of areas, including radio astronomy, stereophonic sound, an early hearing aid, the first encrypted communications systems (A. B. Clark, assisted by Alan Turing, 1942), the transistor (John Bardeen and Walter Brattain), the metal-oxide-semiconductor field-effect transistor (MOSFET), communication satellites, the laser (Charles Townes and Arthur Schawlow in 1957), the carbon dioxide laser, a charge-coupled device that became a crucial component of digital cameras and scanners (Willard S. Boyle and George E. Smith in 1970), the Unix operating system (Dennis Ritchie, Ken Thompson, Douglas McIlroy, and Joe Ossanna, Brian Kernighan, Peter Neumann and various programming languages, including C++ in 1979 (Bjarne Stroustrup).[19] Nine Nobel Prizes have been awarded for work completed at Bell Labs, as well as nine Turing Awards and over twenty Institute of Electrical and Electronics Engineers (IEEE) Medals of Honor, as well as multiple Emmy, Grammy, and Academy Awards.

Bell Labs' influence expanded throughout the industry. Its employees became important knowledge vehicles in a highly connected environment. I discussed in chapter 9 the case of Shockley, who contributed a lot to the formation of Silicon Valley's semiconductor industry. Let me mention a few more names:

- Gordon Teal, who had worked with the Shockley group, was hired by Patrick Haggerty to create Texas Instruments Central Research Laboratories in 1953, which he modeled after Bell Labs. The lab delivered multiple notable inventions. One of them, in 1958, was Jack Kilby's first integrated circuit, which translated into spectacular innovations like the radio transistor or the pocket calculator.
- Charles Litton, who had experimented with new techniques and materials for building vacuum tubes in the 1920s, pursued the Bell Labs culture when he created the tube research lab at Stanford. He recruited David Packard. When Packard and Bill Hewlett started their company, they hired the prolific inventor Bernard Oliver, a Bell Labs alumnus, to found the HP Labs, which he led for four decades until his retirement in 1981 (while also heading the HP calculators development team).
- In more recent history, Bell Labs alumni abound. It's at Bell Labs that Steven Chu, the US secretary of energy under President Obama, carried out his 1997 Nobel Prize–winning laser cooling work. Marian Croak (vice president of engineering at Google) joined AT&T at Bell Labs in 1982 and advocated for switching from wired phone technology to internet protocol. Eric Schmidt, who later became the CEO of Novell and Google, was an intern in 1975. Corinna Cortes, now VP at Google Research in New York City and working on a broad range of theoretical and applied large-scale machine learning problems, spent more than ten years there. Jon Hall, now the board chair for the Linux Professional Institute, also worked at Bell Labs (among other companies), as did two of the "Godfathers of Deep Learning," Yoshua Bengio (who co-founded Element AI, a Montreal-based artificial intelligence incubator, in 2016) and Yann LeCun (now chief AI scientist at Meta/Facebook).

R&D culture and labs developed all over, before, during, and after World War II, both in privately and publicly funded organizations.
Invention-innovation factories emerged that allowed creativity with relative autonomy and faster authorization and decision processes, while
observing stealth mode practices. Many of them had (and still have) a
"Skunk Works" mentality about them, to use the nickname of Lockheed
Martin's Advanced Development Programs (ADP), which initiated the development of several aircraft in 1939.

The combination of collaborative work and covertness is often the
secret sauce of great labs. It was an obvious necessity for defense-oriented
labs like the Los Alamos National Laboratory, which started in 1943 to work
on nuclear weapons under the Manhattan Project, or the Argonne National
Laboratory (1946), which was building on Enrico Fermi's work on nuclear
reactors. The invention-innovation factories working in stealth mode are
also a competitiveness imperative. We can't expect the Chinese Academy
of Sciences, which provides advisory services to the Chinese government,
to unveil much about the work of their sixty thousand researchers spread
across over one hundred research institutes. Yet, as little as they may di-
vulge, their scientific papers have been representative enough to have
them now ranked among the world's leading research organizations.

Large labs and research institutes have to disclose enough of what
they do to earn the street cred that enables them to attract and breed
talents, but their secrecy can also occasion frustrating collisions. For example, the attribution of the Nobel Prize to Emmanuelle Charpentier, at
the Max Planck Unit for the Science of Pathogens, and Jennifer Doudna,
of the University of California, Berkeley, for CRISPR (genome editing),
may have been somewhat disappointing for Feng Zhang at another lab
working on genome editing, the Broad Institute.[20]

Belonging to a lab or having worked in a lab can be a tremendous asset and credibility builder for innovators, as their mission is to anticipate
what comes next given the state of the art in a specific domain. While in
many cases the goal is to come up with products that could be commercialized, an important guiding principle is also to allow the rapid gener-

ation of many ideas. With more flexible agendas, labs accumulate a deep knowledge and allow for fast iteration processes, which enable them to always be one step ahead and ready to seize on new market opportunities. Engineers trained in important labs at companies like IBM, Microsoft, and Google—or more generally in labs that claim major distinctions and industry award winners—are less likely to believe that the Moon is made of cheese, and they're also more likely to be trusted entrepreneurs.

Educational Organizations

The eighteenth-century Age of Enlightenment had a huge impact on educational programs. Europe began to envision schools that would associate theoretical and practical purposes. The trend was inaugurated in France with the creation of the École Polytechnique in 1794, whose first director was the famous mathematician Gaspard Monge. At the same time, Wilhelm von Humboldt was taking part in the debate regarding the direction of national education in Germany; he later founded the University of Berlin in 1809. The École Polytechnique and the l'École normale supérieure, as well as the notoriety of Humboldt's University, influenced new educational approaches in the United States, whose institutions scaled the Age of Enlightenment ideal to proportions commensurate with the size of the country. They formed a huge invention and innovation foundry through the sheer effect of numbers: the number of people connected through strong alumni associations and enormous fundraising activities, as well as the number of companies started by alumni.

When we think of the content of inventions and innovations, we see the accomplishments of individuals. We forget to frame these individuals as members of a much larger system that directly or indirectly influences the nature and the rate of both inventions and innovations. Even though we can't postulate that everybody is a genius, we can assume that the greater the number of people you attract in a highly intellectually charged environment, the more chances you have of sparking new ideas, inventions, and innovations.

Over the decades, the American university system has been an extraordinary force de frappe, creating hundreds of thousands of students starting companies (sometimes even as students). Compilations offered by PitchBook show how some universities have "a truly exceptional track record of producing future entrepreneurs."[21] Many of these universities want to be at the forefront of state-of-the-art research, a knowledge that percolates through alumni, who themselves have the ability to connect with other networks. They power extensive knowledge and support networks. The larger these networks, the higher the chances for aspiring innovators to enter the innovation kairos. This network effect is amplified by the intense marketing carried out by many of these universities.

Western countries tend to take their educational system for granted to the point of neglecting it or often making it unaffordable to people, especially in the United States. That said, we shouldn't forget that a significant component of the rise of China commenced with Project 211, initiated in 1995 with the goal of creating one hundred national universities in order to prepare for the twenty-first century. It was followed by Project 111 in 2006 subsequent to the Ministry of Education of the People's Republic of China's announcement that it would create one hundred innovation centers. According to Statista, in 2021, "around 35 million undergraduate students were enrolled in degree programs at public colleges and universities in China. 19.1 million of them were studying in bachelor's degree programs, while the other 15.9 million were enrolled in more practically oriented short-cycle degree programs."[22] As a reminder, "there were approximately 18.99 million college students in the U.S. in 2020, with around 13.87 million enrolled in public colleges and a further 5.12 million students enrolled in private colleges. The figures are projected to remain relatively constant over the next few years."[23] Given that the ability to innovate is largely a matter of numbers, trends may not be that favorable to the United States—and even less so when you factor in that young people entering the workforce can shy away from the idea of starting companies or joining startups due to the burden of student loans, as discussed in the section "Self-Made People, Mavericks, Dropouts, Geeks, Nerds, and the Like."

Companies

Companies breed companies. As we saw in the previous chapter, the Fairchild children formed a tribe of entrepreneurs and venture capitalists who, in turn, generated more entrepreneurs and more venture capitalists. On a smaller but still impressive scale, Linkabit, a telecommunications contractor started in 1968 in Los Angeles by three MIT graduates—Irwin Jacobs, Andrew Viterbi, and Leonard Kleinrock—spawned dozens of direct or indirect companies in Southern California and more specifically in San Diego, the largest one being Qualcomm, co-founded in 1985 by Jacobs and Viterbi.

Companies form a powerful affiliation network. Many large organizations have alumni networks that allow former employees to stay connected. For example, the Procter & Gamble network includes thirty-five-thousand-plus+ members, according to their LinkedIn page, and "every two years [holds] a global conference that draws P&Gers from many walks of life together for camaraderie and learning."[24]

Companies' alumni networks don't just provide contacts and chains of contacts. They also bestow references and credentials that have a multiplying effect when alumni found their own companies, and they do so in droves. For example, as of February 2023, according to Crunchbase, former Google employees created 2,292 companies.[25] Crunchbase listed 2,413 companies founded by Microsoft alumni.[26] IBM alumni founded 1,332 companies.[27] Apple alumni founded 976 companies.[28] Marc Benioff, the founder of Salesforce, is one of the 856 Oracle alumni.[29] Examples of Amazon alumni include Dan Lewis (who also worked at Microsoft and Google), who started Convoy, or Apoorva Mehta, who started Instacart in 2012.[30] What's often called the "PayPal mafia" is also a major network. PayPal, originally called Confinity, was founded in 1998 by Max Levchin, Peter Thiel, Luke Nosek, and Ken Howery. In 2000 it merged with X.com, an online banking company founded by Elon Musk. The "PayPal Mafia" is a group of some twenty-five men who became investors in, founders of, and executives in multiple companies, including Geni (acquired by MyHeritage), Yammer (acquired by Microsoft), YouTube (acquired by Google), LinkedIn (acquired by Microsoft), Zynga, Palantir Technologies, Addepar, Square, Slide (acquired by Google), Kiva, Yelp, and so forth. Although occasionally reluctant to be seen as part of the "mafia," Elon Musk, after PayPal, co-founded Tesla, Neuralink, and OpenAI, and founded SpaceX and the Boring Company.

Many founders worked with several organizations before starting their own company. For example, the three founders of NVIDIA—Jensen Huang, Chris Malachowsky, and Curtis Priem—worked (combined) at LSI Logic, AMD, Sun Microsystems, Hewlett-Packard, and IBM. WhatsApp was founded in 2009 by two former employees of Yahoo!: Brian Acton and Jan Koum. Acton had previously been a product tester at Apple and Adobe. Both had applied for jobs at Facebook and been rejected, but they were acquired by Facebook in 2014 for almost $20 billion. OpenAI, which became a household name when its chatbot ChatGPT launched in November 2022, didn't appear out of thin air. It started in December 2015 with Sam Altman (former president of Y Combinator), Elon Musk, Greg Brockman (early employee at Stripe), Reid Hoffman, Jessica Livingston (founding partner of Y Combinator), Peter Thiel, Amazon Web Services (AWS), Infosys, and Y Combinator Research (co-founded by Paul Graham). The organization's chief scientist and co-founder, Ilya Sutskever, who did his PhD (2012) under the supervision of Geoffrey Hinton (recipient of the 2018 Turing Award, together with Yoshua Bengio and Yann LeCun, for their work on deep learning), was a research scientist at Google Brain. Its chief technology officer, Mira Murati, previously worked at Leap Motion and Tesla.

Labs, schools, and companies define the texture of the environment where people create businesses and can combine into subnetworks. Venture capitalist networks, which can be perceived as networks unto themselves, are in reality closely related to companies that had successful initial public offerings (IPOs) or were acquired. Mentorship and advisory networks, incubators, and accelerators are groups of current or former professionals. Many associations are gathering places for people from the same country. For example, Suhas Patil, an Indian American who started Cirrus Logic, a fabless semiconductor company, co-founded a global not-for-profit organization, TiE, to connect entrepreneurs and business owners from India or Indian origin in Silicon Valley.

CAN YOU AVOID NETWORKING STRUCTURES?

Networking structures don't only protect us. They immerse us into the kairos ebullience that underpins innovation. Many people also create startups that remain small or fail—but they still constitute useful networks if they're in the midst of hyperactive clusters like Silicon Valley.

Self-Made People, Mavericks, Dropouts, Geeks, Nerds, and the Like

Business literature can be a rather boring genre. To spice it up, many authors feel they have to romanticize innovators and emphasize their uniqueness. However, while it's true that you have to be somewhat different to even be willing to be an innovative entrepreneur, you aren't necessarily breaking up with existing networks.

Mavericks are unbranded animals, but the reason they can enjoy a certain freedom and wander around without dying of hunger is that they are still part of an environment that can guide their actions. What makes mavericks interesting is their ability to delineate their own paths within a given environment, which demonstrates a high dose of resilience, self-reliance, and initiative, and not so much the negative desire of ridding themselves of any structure. If anything, they tend to mash up various networks into one that suits their goals.

We love self-made people, especially when they become famous. The first person described as a self-made man in America was Benjamin Franklin, one of the most brilliant polymaths in American history.[31] Franklin ended his formal schooling when he was ten, but he learned by working as an apprentice in his brother's printing business; at the age of fifteen, under the pen name of Silence Dogood, he placed articles in his brother's newspaper (initially unbeknownst to him), the *New-England*

Courant, published between 1721 and 1726. When he ran away to Philadelphia in 1723, he worked several jobs, mostly in print shops, and ended
up creating his own network, the "Junto," originally a twelve-member
club of tradesmen and artisans who met Friday evenings to discuss issues
of ethics, politics, or sciences. The club was the starting point of a historic
career. Self-made people are rarely solitary people. They tap into existing
networks, commanding attention and forming their own network.

In the same fashion, famous dropout entrepreneurs only stray from
a course that most people would expect them to pursue, but it's often because they already have a network that's meaningful to them. Bill Gates
dropped out of Harvard, but he was already, as an adolescent, part of
the Lakeside prep school network, where he had co-founded the Lakeside Programmers Group with Paul Allen, Ric Weiland (who would later
join Microsoft), and Gates's best friend, Kent Evans. Gates joined Harvard
in 1973 but took a leave of absence after two years to work with Allen,
who had become director of software for MITS, which had just produced
the first microcomputer, Altair 8800, in Albuquerque, New Mexico. Allen and Gates created their "Micro-soft" partnership in April 1975 and
hired Wieland. Steve Ballmer, whom Gates had befriended at Harvard,
completed his bachelor in applied mathematics, became assistant product manager at Procter & Gamble for two years, enrolled in the Stanford
Graduate School of Business, and then dropped out to join Microsoft in
1980.

Many of the entrepreneurs in the computer industry who skipped
college or dropped out were not only brilliant but were also lucky enough
to be raised in stimulating family environments and attend well-equipped
high schools with access to technology and established networks. In 1995
while still in high school, Sean Parker (who founded Napster in 1999 and
Plaxo in 2002) interned for Mark Pincus's startup Freeloader. Parker was
exposed to a young company funded by major venture capitalists (VCs)
and founded by a person who had graduated from Wharton, had an MBA
from Harvard, and had worked at Lazard Frères and Bain & Co. If you also
win a Virginia state computer science fair that gives you a gig at the CIA at

a very young age, it's not uncommon to have built a lot of relationships before you're twenty. A similar phenomenon accelerated the career of Mark
Zuckerberg, who too was well versed in programming as an adolescent,
joined Harvard, and dropped out. The original product designed there in
2003, "Facemash," attracted the attention of many, and, one thing leading
to another, Zuckerberg got co-founders. Soon after, Parker, who by then
had become a social network expert, took Zuckerberg under his wing by
introducing him to the PayPal Mafia—and got the company funded via
Peter Thiel.[32]

This is the same Peter Thiel who made the news at TechCrunch Disrupt in September 2010 by announcing a fellowship offering $100,000
over two years to students under the age of twenty-two who would drop
out of school to start their company.

The idea behind the initiative is that top universities are overpriced
and that it doesn't make sense to have to reimburse so much debt for
years. Thiel had, and still has, a point. The Kauffman Foundation observed a coincidence between a drop in entrepreneurship and outstanding student loan debt: "Nearly 1 in 6 adults in the U.S. has outstanding
student loan debt. Among those between the ages of 18 and 29, 1 in 3
reported having student loan debt. Meanwhile, the share of new entrepreneurs aged 20–34 declined from 34% to 27% between 1996 and
2019."[33]

Thiel's initiative caused a stir among parents, universities, and some
thought-leaders, yet it will take far more to "disrupt college." It's so hard
to obtain the fellowship that only twenty to twenty-five students per year
out of the thousands who apply get one. The principle benefits people
who might have loved to drop out anyway but could not. This fellowship
doesn't deprive students from their university network entirely (you can
build it in one year), and it offers them valuable networks of business
leaders and venture capitalists, which accelerate chances of success: "Our
network is yours," the Thiel Fellowship website claims.[34] Regardless of
what we think of Peter Thiel's political declarations, this elite group of
entrepreneurs is lucky, to say the least.

The Case of Immigrant-Entrepreneurs

In theory, you can set up your company in any business cluster of your choice, provided that you have the financial means to do it, obtain the right to work in the host country, and know its language. In practice, however, you may experience the invisible obstacle of not being fully part of it. I say "invisible obstacle" because very few people will tell you that you aren't "one of them." Yet you'll be treated like a stranger. Should this statement be tempered given that very active business communities like Silicon Valley welcome entrepreneurs from all parts of the world? Probably yes, but maybe not as easily as one might believe.

Advocates for immigration go at length to expound on the number of companies founded by immigrants and explain why the United States should have better immigration policies—and they're right. Extensive research and data analysis by William Kerr and Sari Pekkala Kerr show the success of many prominent immigrant entrepreneurs.[35] For the period they covered (1992 to 2008, with additional empirical datasets until 2014) and the eleven states they focused on, they found that 24 percent of all entrepreneurs were immigrants (although immigrants account for only about 15% of the population) and that this percentage had been growing over the years.

While there is substantial heterogeneity in immigrant entrepreneurship, it's clear that high-skill immigration does have an impact on US innovation, even if more data would be needed to see if immigrant founders produce types of innovations that differ from the ones offered by American-born founders. Even if, for VC-funded companies, the authors "do not observe greater business survival, better employment outcomes, or higher likelihood of going public for firms founded by immigrant entrepreneurs," what matters is that immigrants add to the overall innovation dynamics. A National Venture Capital Association study showed that "immigrants have started more than half of America's startup companies valued at $1 billion or more and are key members of management or product development teams in more than 80% of these companies."[36]

However, my question here is the following: Do immigrants succeed *because* they're immigrants or *because* of their ability to fit into an environment that has fostered the creativity of American-born entrepreneurs for decades? In other words, are chances of success for immigrants impacted negatively if they don't belong to the networks that canvass the US innovation landscape?

To my surprise, I found that the majority of the immigrants listed on immigrant-founded companies reported by the various National Foundation for American Policy's reports were actually connected to typical US networks. They often complemented their studies abroad with a US degree, or worked for a US company, or created the company with an American-born co-founder, which facilitated their immersion into the US ecosystem. Also, it's customary to mention Google as an immigrant-founded company; however, I agree with the Kerrs that although it's true that Sergey Brin was born in the Soviet Union, Google hardly qualifies. Sergey Brin was six when his family emigrated and was schooled in a US environment (with the advantage of parents highly educated in Moscow).

Multiple analysts have emphasized that immigrants are almost twice as likely as native-born Americans to become entrepreneurs. Great, but can we conclude that Americans might be less entrepreneurial or innovative? No. The comparison is based on asymmetrical data sets. The entrepreneurial immigrants who come to the United States are a minuscule fraction of the population of the countries from which they come. In many cases, they come to the United States primarily because they hope to become innovative entrepreneurs and are willing to do whatever it takes to belong. If you take 100 American-born entrepreneurs and 100 immigrant entrepreneurs, the 100 American-born entrepreneurs represent 100 of 360 million of the American population, whereas the 100 immigrant entrepreneurs may represent 100 of the 7 billions of the aggregated population of their countries of origin. The way you read data matters.

If you are an immigrant who is not connected to the US educational system, who is not connected to a US company, and has no American co-founder, don't assume that you'll have an easy ride, because more likely than not, you won't. So you must actively build a network with tentacles in institutional networks.

Still, it's clear that immigrant entrepreneurs believe in the American dream and are ready to enact it. The more people you attract into an ecosystem, the stronger it becomes. Invention and innovation are truly a numbers game. The more people try, the higher the likelihood that someone will come up with products that stick and will be viewed as being innovative. In short, the size of the funnel matters.

CONCLUSION

The word "innovation" carries with it an immense field of possibilities, but imagining is one thing, and the ability to innovate is another.

Innovations happen in delineated territories with rules, statutes, and statuses; grants and privileges; governing bodies; and authorities that largely condition your course of action. These territories have entrance keys, that is, pattern recognition signals that take you into the innovation stage.

You can claim to be a revolutionary, a nonconformist, an iconoclast, whatever, but only if you also fit into their cultural milieu. A lot of people or organizations (like incubators and accelerators—which can also be virtual, like One Million by One Million, created by Sramana Mitra) can help you, but you have to work at becoming part of a community to share ideas and opinions.[37] It's not always easy—which explains the challenges met by women and ethnic minorities—a topic I will address in the next chapter.

11

Are Women and Minorities Unwelcome?

*And, of course, men know best about everything, except what
women know better.*
—George Eliot

Asking whether women and ethnic and racial minorities are at a disadvantage in the innovation kairos in the United States (and most countries in the world) leads to a foregone conclusion. Yes. Innovation has been framed within ideological frameworks that have disenfranchised the majority of the population, a group that I will refer to as women and underrepresented communities (W&UC).[1]

Over the past two hundred years, W&UC have had to overcome challenges that show a contrario the role of established networks. The same culture that praises innovation as a growth engine has been slow at diversifying the human chassis producing it. Innovations are part of a global economic process that can leave out many layers of society. While economic literature customarily discusses how workers are displaced or eliminated as a consequence of some innovations, it frequently overlooks the reasons W&UC are more sparsely involved in its production.

Yet the same kairos that has made it hard for W&UC to emerge as innovators has intermittently shown cracks that have enabled them to not only offer new products and services but also generate an innovation of another order, a societal one. Does this mean that sexism, racism, or bigotry will disappear anytime soon? No, so let's not fool ourselves. As optimistic as we want to be, hard facts prevent us from being delusional. Yes, innovating is harder for W&UC.

THE DRAG OF HISTORY

We will progressively recode the traditional genealogies of knowledge and innovate in an inclusive world. But we can't ignore the state of affairs from which we start.

Science and Technology Accolades

Although not all innovations are linked to science and technology developments, we live in a world where almost everything depends on them—so, the low representation of W&UC in these areas gives reasons to pause.

Women

Between 1901 and 2023, the Nobel Prize and Prize in Economic Sciences have been awarded to women parsimoniously. One woman, Marie Curie, was honored twice—once, in 1903, with Henri Becquerel and with her husband, Pierre Curie, in Physics and the second time, in 1911, as a solo recipient in Chemistry. If you focus on scientific disciplines, you'll find five women in Physics (one born in the United States), eight in Chemistry (three born in the United States), thirteen in Physiology/Medicine (five born in the United States), and three in Economic Sciences (two born in the United States). These women represent just over four percent of all laureates for these disciplines.

Only three women received the Turing Award (Frances Allen, Barbara Liskov, and Shafi Goldwasser). In 2014 Iranian Maryam Mirzakhani became the first woman to win the Fields Medal, and Maryna Viazovska from Ukraine was the second one in 2022. Representation of women in the National Inventors Hall of Fame is better (close to 8%). In many cases, they were inducted well after the fact, like actress Hedy Lamarr in 2014 with composer George Antheil for their 1942 frequency-hopping technology, or Evelyn Berezin in 2021 for the first stand-alone word processor in the 1960s.

As of 2019, the US Patent and Trademark Office showed that nearly 230 years after the creation of the US patent system, "women made up only 13% of all inventor-patentees in the United States" and noted that "this persistent underrepresentation of women has created an unnecessary drag on American innovation and prosperity." Leveraging the analyses of multiple economists and societal researchers, they also added that "if women were to patent at the same rate as men, commercialized patents could increase by 24% and per capita gross domestic product—that is, total economic output adjusted for the U.S. population—could increase by 2.7%."[2]

Racial and Ethnic Minorities

Few minorities have been Nobel laureates in Physics, Chemistry, Medicine, or Economics. The only Black man was Arthur Lewis, a Brit from the West Indies who won for Economics in 1979. Among the few Latinx/Hispanic Americans, let's mention Luis Alvarez (second-generation American) in Physics in 1968 and Baruj Benacerraf, a Venezuelan American immunologist in Physiology/Medicine in 1980. There are just over two dozen laureates who identified as Asian Americans. The Turing Award has a few Asian recipients but no recipient of African descent.

Black Americans represent less than 5 percent of the National Inventors Hall of Fame inductees, although they've made up 12 to 13 percent of the total population since 1850. The number of recipients of Latinx/Hispanic descent is also limited. In addition to Luis Alvarez, they include Alejandro Zaffaroni, founder of several biotechnology companies in Silicon Valley; Miguel Angel Ondetti, who synthesized the first angiotensin-converting enzyme (ACE) at the Squibb Institute for Medical Research in Argentina; and Julio C. Palmaz, also from Argentina, who invented the first commercially successful intravascular stent.

For Asian Americans, we find Ashok Gadgil (affordable water and energy supply for people in need), Dawon Kahng (who co-invented

MOSFET), Sumita Mitra (nanocomposite dental materials when she was a chemist at 3M Oral Care). In 2020 three names were added to the list: Ming-Jun Li and Pushkar Tandon shared the honor with Dana Bookbinder for the bend-insensitive ClearCurve optical fiber at Corning. The third one was industrial chemist Margaret Wu, whose work at ExxonMobil Research and Engineering Co has changed how automobile and industrial lubricants are designed and synthesized.

Presence in Educational Institutions

University education has operated as a major network in the makeup of innovation ecosystems, but integration of W&UC has been historically slow.

Women

The education of women started in the nineteenth century in a piece-meal fashion. Ironically, one of the first labs in the United States was the Women's Laboratory, an experiment at MIT in 1876 prompted by the first woman admitted to MIT as a "special student" in chemistry in 1870, Ellen Swallow Richards. The lab's purpose was to respond to this question: "Have women the mental capacity for scientific work?"[3] By the early 1880s, the success of the experiment was clear. In 1883 MIT built a new chemistry laboratory for male and female students, but this doesn't mean that women flocked to MIT or other prominent universities. Women and men were enrolled in American colleges in equal numbers only in 1980.

Starting in the late 1800s, women were welcomed and needed in the workforce but often in lower-paying jobs.[4] Although the idea of facilitating women's education was gaining ground, women were denied prominent roles in corporations or research. Many went for teaching positions. This was the case of Isabelle Stone, the first woman in the United States to receive a PhD in physics (1897), at the University of Chicago, whose Physics Department was headed by Albert Michelson (first American Nobel laureate in Physics in 1907). In 1900 she was, along with Marie Curie, one of two women out of 836 guests to attend the first International Congress of Physics in Paris.

The case of bacteriological chemist Mary Engle Pennington a few years later is atypical. In 1907 she became the chief of the Food Research Laboratory, established to enforce the Pure Food and Drug Act of 1906 by a very progressive man, Harvey Wiley. Men represented 95 percent of American scientists before 1920, even though the small minority of women were more educated, with 63 percent having PhD degrees as opposed to 47 percent for men.[5]

Today, according to the National Science Board, women account for about half (52%) of the college-educated workforce. But there is a caveat: As of 2022, women accounted for 35 percent of physical scientists, 26 percent of computer and mathematical scientists, and 16 percent of engineers.[6] Male professors have acted as role models and mentors for male students, thus engraving most of the knowledge genealogies traversing the history of innovation. The number of female professors in engineering remains too low to power a similar momentum. As of 2021, the number of women faculty members represented 19.2 percent of all faculty, with only 14.2 percent being full professors.[7]

Racial and Ethnic Minorities

Only six African American males earned a PhD in physics between 1876 and 1941. The first one, Edward Bouchet, in 1876 at Yale, was unable to obtain a college teaching position. The first Black graduate of Yale Medical School was Cortlandt Van Rensselaer Creed in 1857, but it took eighty-seven years for the first Black woman to earn an MD at Yale (Beatrix Ann McCleary-Hamburg in 1944).

The first two African American women to earn a PhD in physics were Willie Hobbs Moore in 1972 at the University of Michigan and Shirley Ann Jackson in 1973 at MIT. Patricia Bath, who invented the Laserphaco Probe, a tool used during eye surgery to correct cataracts in 1981, was the first African American to obtain a residency in ophthalmology at New York University between 1970 to 1973. Barely fifty years ago!

Between 1923 to 1947, only eight Black men earned a PhD in mathematics. While the first white woman to earn a PhD in math was Winifred Edgerton (Columbia University) in 1886, the first Black woman to do so was Martha Euphemia Lofton Haynes in 1943 (Catholic University in Washington, DC); the second and third were Evelyn Boyd Granville (Yale) and Marjorie Lee Browne (University of Michigan), both in 1949. In short, Black genealogies in academia started slowly and often quite recently.

Before emancipation, literacy among African Americans was low despite the fact that during their enslavement clandestine schools taught reading and writing.[8] Prior to the Civil War, there was no structured higher education system for Black students, something that was even banned in various parts of the country. It was also only in 1954 that the 1896 principle of "separate but equal" education was overturned.[9] But several public and private historically black colleges and universities (HBCUs), including Howard University and Tuskegee University, started to offer increasingly diversified curricula and thrived outside mainstream networks.

Overcoming the weight of history is a long journey. Black students who want to innovate today won't find many Black mentors within academia. Black Americans represent 2.13 percent of full professors. The percentage of Black people earning bachelor's degrees has hardly increased between 2011 and 2021, from 4.5 percent in 2011 to 4.7 percent in 2021. The situation for Hispanic and Latinx students is not quite as dire but not great either. Faculty members for this group represent 4.1 percent of all faculty.[10]

Asians are far better represented, of course (28%). There is a long history of Asians in the American university system dating back to the 1850s, despite many fluctuations due to geopolitical issues, as has been the case with China, for example.[11] That said, academic presence and performance gaps within the Asian American population (which encompasses diverse groups from the Far East, Southeast Asia, and the Indian subcontinent, representing very different immigration histories and patterns) are as wide as the gaps between white people and Black Americans.[12] The large representation of Asian Americans in Silicon Valley bolstered a "model minority" myth that is not only inaccurate but is also used against them.[13]

In addition, Asian American women are confronted with the "bamboo ceiling," also loaded with stereotyping qualifiers.[14]

Drip-Feed in Corporations

The desire to create companies is frequently triggered by a working environment and through exchanges with friends and colleagues. But for W&UC, joining affinity subnetworks where they can devise their next move is harder. They may feel that they don't fully belong and, because of that, make themselves as unnoticeable as possible to obviate rejection. They may also be afraid of sharing anything with biased people who might think that they're dreaming above their pay or gender-race grade.

Women

Firsts in corporations have happened sparingly.[15] Edith Clarke, generally considered to be the first woman to earn an MS in electrical engineering from MIT, could not find work as an engineer at General Electric in 1920.[16] She had to settle for a position as a supervisor in the Turbine Engineering Department—which didn't prevent her from inventing a calculator. She then became the first woman to deliver a paper at the American Institute of Electrical Engineers (AIEE) and the first female professor of electrical engineering in the United States in 1947 (University of Texas). Elizabeth A. Wood was the first woman scientist at the Physical Research Department of Bell Labs (1942). Beatrice Hicks was the first woman engineer hired by Western Electric (1942). In 1950 she co-founded and was the first president of the Society of Women Engineers (SWE), which started as a grassroot organization.[17] These premieres occurred despite limited rights for women, many of them being quite recent.[18]

Today, women are underrepresented in senior management. While they represent 48 percent of the workforce, they make up only 26 percent of the "C Suite." Women still have to prove themselves more than men, even though discrimination against female bosses seems to be lower among younger workers. But this means that we may still be two generations away from anything that would come close to parity. For example, although 49.6 percent of science and engineering degrees were earned by women in 2018, they comprised only about 29.4 percent of those in science and engineering jobs in 2019. Worse, only 30 percent of women who earn bachelor's degrees in engineering still work in engineering twenty years later—and 30 percent of those who left the engineering profession cited toxic culture as the reason.[19]

Racial and Ethnic Minorities

The same biases that have limited access of Black people to academic tracks have reduced their chances of being part of corporate environments. Lewis Latimer was able to break through in the post–Civil War era but was an exception.

Latimer was pretty much self-taught when he joined the patent law firm Crosby, Halstead & Gould as an office boy in 1865. After his boss recognized his talent for sketching patent drawings, he was promoted to the position of head draftsman. In 1876 Alexander Bell employed him as a draftsman at his patent law firm. Latimer then became assistant manager and draftsman for the U.S. Electric Lighting Company, where he devised a process to make carbon filaments. In 1884 the Edison Electric Light Company in New York City hired him as a draftsman and an expert witness in patent litigation on electric lights. He then wrote the first book on electric lighting and supervised the installation of public electric lights throughout New York, Philadelphia, Montreal, and London. After 1892, with the formation of General Electric, he continued to work in the legal department.

However, the case of Wendell King, a Black student at Union College in Schenectady, New York, in the early 1900s, illustrates a more common story. He had gained popularity as an adolescent by giving classes on the wireless telegraph. At seventeen, as the president of the Amateur Marconi Radio Association, King was more than a big fish in a small pond. He was so competent that he was welcomed as a student at Union College of Schenectady, where Charles Steinmetz, a top researcher at GE, was also a teacher. As a result, in June 1917 King was one of two dozen Union students chosen to intern at GE Schenectady Works. But the presence of a Black intern incensed the machinists, all white. They went on strike. King couldn't expect support from the American Federation of Labor (AFL), which had originally required its affiliates to pledge that their members would never "discriminate against a fellow worker on account of color, creed or nationality" but had reversed its principles and allowed its members to exclude African Americans.[20] The strike lasted a week. George Emmons, vice president of manufacturing in 1916, refused to get rid of Wendell and moved him to another department. Wendell eventually continued to work at GE before joining Bliley Technologies Inc., which manufactured quartz crystals for the amateur radio market. It's only in 1978 that the GE Young Engineer Award was given to a Black person, Greg Talley.[21]

Black people encountered obstacles of all sorts. Think of the inequity of the patent system. Thomas Jennings may have been the first African American to be granted a patent in 1821, for his dry-cleaning method. He could because he was free, but recognition eluded many Black inventors, like Jo Anderson, an enslaved man who helped Cyrus McCormick design his mechanical reaper in the 1830s. Even later in the century, some Black inventors who had their own research companies chose to sell their patents instead of expanding their business, as was the case of Granville Woods, often called the "Black Edison," who sold patents to American Bell Telephone Company, Westinghouse, and General Electric.

Legislative frameworks changed over time, starting primarily with the nationwide opening of defense and other government jobs to all Americans regardless of their race, as enacted by Executive Order 8802, signed by Franklin D. Roosevelt in 1941. But no one can be so deluded as to imagine that laws change mindsets overnight. American corporations added Black engineers only progressively.

John Stanley Ford was the first Black software engineer at IBM, in 1946.[22] Although Ford was passed over for promotions and paid less, he loved his job and helped young Black job applicants, according to his son, Clyde, who became an IBM software engineer in the 1970s.[23] IBM later engaged more Black engineers, like Mark Dean in 1979; he was part of the team that developed the color PC monitor, the Industry Standard Architecture system bus, and the first gigahertz microchip. He was the first African American to become an IBM Fellow, in 1995.

General Electric made it part of its strategy to hire more Black people in the 1960s and early 1970s. Marshall Jones, who pioneered the use of lasers for industrial materials processing, joined in 1974. A few years before, in 1970, GE had hired Lloyd Trotter as a field service engineer; twenty years later, he was named vice president and general manager of manufacturing for the Electric, Distribution and Control division (ED&C). In 1990 he helped found the GE African American Forum, a mentor group for African American GE employees.

Bell Labs added a significant contingent of African Americans. According to William Massey, an expert in queueing theory and professor at Princeton who worked at Bell Labs after earning his PhD from Stanford, "Bell Labs of the 1970s, '80s, and '90s was to black scientists what Harlem of the 1920s was to black writers, artists and musicians. It was a true renaissance." This "renaissance" was primarily due to physicist James West, the acoustician who invented the foil electret microphone in 1962 with Gerhard Sessler and whose principles are behind most of the 2 billion microphones produced every year. When he joined Bell Laboratories in 1957, there were at least seven Black technical workers there, including Lincoln Hawkins (a pioneer of polymer chemistry and the first Black person to join the technical staff in 1942), Ray Story, Charlie Miller, Bill North, and others. In 1970 West co-founded the Association of Black Laboratory Employees (ABLE), one of the first programs of its kind.[24]

As much as we want to eulogize history makers, we must still look at what reality shows today. Major tech companies may claim that they "take diversity seriously," but as data-centric as they are when they sell us advertising, they're nowhere close to showing a comparable efficiency in diversity. Yet, as uneven as progress in diversity has been in STEM jobs, it's still hard to explain why many tech companies in Silicon Valley would have only 1 to 3 percent of their engineers as Black or Latinx/Hispanic.[25]

Venture Capital Funding

There are funds focusing on woman- or minority-led businesses, but these are a minority in the venture capital business. Even though many mainstream firms have tried diversify their partners and portfolios or have entered in partnership with organizations specializing in the advancement of W&UC groups, no radical change has happened. Funding for women and ethnic minorities is so low that it barely registers.

Women

Businesses funded by venture capital are the exception rather than the norm (less than 1% altogether), but women aren't remotely close to occupying 50 percent of that privileged sky. Female-led startups in 2022 received only 2 percent of the total funding, while percentage skyrocketed to 17.2 percent when the team was mixed gender.[26]

So what accounts for such stagnation? A combination of factors and stereotypes. A Swedish study performed ten years ago remains valid today. Researchers recorded conversations showing how VCs talked about female entrepreneurs and questioned their abilities.[27]

Sexism can take many forms, such as "women choose types of businesses that aren't of interest to VCs." So what? When this is true, does this mean that they aren't uninterested in innovations that could matter to 50 percent of humanity? Whatever the reasons, W&UC have a hard time getting into the male-dominated structures and genealogies that VCs rely on. And women are also underrepresented in VC firms (between 12 and 14 percent of the decision-makers depending on the sources).

Of course, there are other sources of funding. In some cases, crowdfunding can be an option. A 2021 study showed the women's share as entrepreneurs on the Kickstarter crowdfunding platform was 34.7 percent but also that "they are concentrated in stereotyped sectors, both as entrepreneurs and as backers."[28]

Racial and Ethnic Minorities

As of August 2022, Black as well as Hispanic and Latinx founders raised under 3 percent of the total funding. They continuously experience rejection from investors "because they do not fit a certain profile."[29] In practice, the "right" profile means education in top universities and/or a work experience in recognized companies and/or an association with non-Black or non-Latinx. It's hard to break out of the vicious circle of social exclusion.

Can entrepreneurs find funding somewhere else? It's not that easy. Mentioning a piece written by Black entrepreneur James Norman,[30] Crunchbase noted that the first check to get started is also more arduous for underrepresented founders: "Receiving $50K, $100K—and sometimes more—from family and peers is not part of the average Black founder's journey. Personal loans, credit and day job salaries often serve as a substitute for readily accessible capital from their social network," Norman said. No wonder, according to Marlene Orozco, the lead research analyst at Stanford Latino Entrepreneurship Initiative, "the lack of funding to Black and Latinx founders is a result of historical gaps in community wealth."[31]

YET THEY INNOVATED: THE SOCIETAL INNOVATION PROCESS

As Matilda Gage—a famous suffragist, abolitionist, and Native American rights activist—said in 1883, "That woman has not been an inventor to an equal extent with man is not so much a subject of surprise as that she should have invented at all."[32] It's true that we can marvel at the fact that women and minorities have even been able to innovate, but what's just as striking is that their history tells us something that transcends the separate innovations they offered: the protracted trajectory of societal innovation.

The fact that the kairos is not a homogeneous whole made W&UC's inroads possible and has allowed for what Erik Olin Wright called "interstitial transformations" (the ability to create cracks within an environment) as well as "symbiotic transformations" (the ability to act on a system from inside by contributing to its growth).[33] As a result, W&UC's initiatives can be read in two ways: both as frustrating efforts to break into institutional frameworks and as a practical progressivism triggering societal reengineering.

Interstitial Transformation: From Frustrating Attempts to Societal Reengineering

Matilda Gage highlighted innovations by women in her days, such as the deep-sea telescope by Sarah Mather, flat-bottomed brown paper bags and the machinery to produce them by Margaret Knight, or Mary Walton's device to reduce the noise produced by elevated railways, a system she sold to the Metropolitan Railroad. But what's striking in her pamphlet is her frustration and what historian Margaret Rossiter, a century later, dubbed the "Matilda Effect," in other words, a lack of recognition or even the obliteration of women's achievements or their downright attribution to men.[34] Think of the woman whom Einstein dubbed "our Marie Curie," Lise Meitner. She was nominated nineteen times for the Nobel Prize in Chemistry between 1924 and 1948 and twenty-nine times for the Nobel Prize in Physics between 1937 and 1965 and never got anything. It's Otto Hahn, her longtime collaborator, who received the Physics Nobel in 1944 for nuclear fission.[35]

Yet W&UC's accomplishments are more than "exceptions to the rule." They delineate a different world. As Wright put it, "Interstitial transformation aims to get on with the business of building an alternative world inside the old from the bottom up."[36]

In the early 1900s, Annie Turnbo Malone and Sarah Walker (i.e., Madam C. J. Walker) revolutionized hair care for Black women, and Walker may have been one of the first female self-made millionaires in America (of any race). Elizabeth Arden supplied the shade of red lipstick to the suffragettes that became a symbol of female emancipation before World War I, and by the end of the 1920s she and Helena Rubinstein had created business empires. George Washington Carver, born in slavery in Missouri, became one of the top agricultural scientists and environmentalists in the country, devising alternative crops to cotton and promoting the culture of peanuts and sweet potatoes as well as methods to prevent soil depletion. He inspired several generations of Black students even after his death, one of them being Lonnie Johnson, who worked at NASA and became famous for multiple inventions, including a best-selling toy, the Super Soaker water gun in 1990.

Interstitial transformation starts as a guerrilla type of warfare through individuals able to sidestep the rules thanks to the patronage or activism of other individuals and associations.

Prominent individuals sometimes embraced the cause of W&UC. For example, when mathematician Gösta Mittag-Leffler convinced his colleagues in the Nobel Prize Committee to award the 1903 prize for Physics to both Marie and Pierre Curie instead of Pierre Curie and Henri Becquerel only, he broke implicit rules. When Booker Washington founded the National Negro Business League in 1900 (renamed National Business League in 1966), he had the support of Andrew Carnegie.

In addition to associations supporting the right of women to vote, women created organizations to advance equity in education (such as the American Association of University Women [AAUW], founded in 1881, or the Alpha Kappa Alpha Sorority, the first intercollegiate histori-cally Black sorority started in 1908) or in business (the first Zonta Club was founded in Buffalo, New York, in 1919). Over the decades women have created countless networks aimed at building a sense of personal and professional belongingness.

Virtually all the sectors of the economy now have organizations (or chapters) whose mission is to close the gender gap and end ethnic dis-crimination. The road to firsts, seconds, thirds, and hundredths has been steep but may have been faster than waiting for institutions to proactively undertake their own remodeling. They have to at some point—when their walls show too many cracks to be ignored. Think of the difference be-tween Rosalind Franklin in the 1950s, on the one hand, and 2020 Nobel Prize winners in Chemistry Jennifer Doudna and Emmanuelle Charpen-tier, on the other.

Rosalind Franklin was the English chemist whose work set the stage for the discovery of the DNA double helix and the analysis of molecular structure of viruses. She was the starting point of accomplishments that resulted in four Nobel Prizes awarded to James Watson, Francis Crick, and

Maurice Wilkins in 1962 for the structure of the DNA and to Aaron Klug in 1982 for his development of the crystallographic electron microscopy and his structural elucidation of biologically important protein-nucleic acid complexes. Since the early 1940s, when Rosalind Franklin pursued her PhD, the number of women in sciences has changed considerably. In 1950 doctoral degrees awarded to women represented only 4 percent of doctoral degrees in chemistry, but in 2020 they were 39 percent.

Black entrepreneurs also produced hundreds of transformative "firsts," and here also we have to appreciate the distance covered.[37] Charles Drew, an American surgeon who improved techniques for blood storage and large-scale blood banks that saved thousands of lives of the Allies during World War II, could do nothing to stop the practice of racial segregation in blood donation, which made him resign from the American Red Cross (that maintained this policy until 1950). Fifty years later, Joycelyn Elders was the first Black person to serve as US surgeon general (1993–94), the second woman to hold that post—the first one being Puerto Rican physician Antonia Coello Novello, from 1990 to 1993.

Symbiotic Transformation: From Consumers to Producers

Interstitial transformation doesn't infiltrate all the layers of society at once but can be complemented by what Wright called "symbiotic transformation," which designates emancipatory changes at the core of a system. They result from a collaboration between parties with opposite interests that ends up serving both, as exemplified by the solution to the traditional Keynesian problem: "Capitalists simultaneously want to pay their own employees as low wages as possible and want other capitalists to pay as high wages as possible in order to generate adequate consumer demand for products."[38] This phenomenon can be transposed to the relationship between women and innovation vendors.

For innovations to survive, they must be adopted by customers—of whom women became an increasingly larger part starting at the end of the 1890s. This was the topic of a 1929 book, *Selling Mrs. Consumer*, by home economist Christine Frederick.[39] She mentioned Henry Ford's bit-ter words: "We are no longer in the automobile, but in the millinery busi-ness." He was, she thought, "chiefly responsible for the rise of Chrysler and General Motors at the expense of Ford's model T, because while Ford arrogantly said 'you can have any color so long as it is black,' Chrysler and General Motors supplied color and feminine luxury and comfort . . . Even the mighty Ford was brought to his knees by Mrs. Consumer's power." Frederick was no feminist, but she was the first to focus on the power of women as buyers of innovations in the new era of "progressive obsolescence."[40]

There's no doubt that gender consumerism reinforces stereotypes and strengthens the dichotomy between women as consumers of inno-vations and males as their primary producers. The same process, how-ever, combined with the snowball effect of interstitial transformations and civil rights, powered the desire among W&UC to become innova-tive producers too. The Wonderbra was created by a man, Israel Pilot; commercialized by a man, Moe Nadler; but vastly improved by a woman, Louise Poirier. Because she had a bad experience exercising in ordinary bras, Lisa Lindahl created the first sports bra (the "jockbra," later renamed a Jogbra) in 1977.

Of course, opportunities to innovate aren't limited to apparel. Women have countless opportunities to identify flaws in innovations designed by men and ultimately for men, be they devices such as seat belts or a whole host of medicines, as expounded on by Caroline Criado Perez in *Invisible Women*.[41] Incidentally, women can transform men's worlds: Linda Zhang is the chief engineer behind the all-electric Ford F-150 in 2021. Central to the development of the Moderna COVID-19 vaccine is immunolo-gist Kizzmekia Corbett, born in 1986. In the same fashion, the Pfizer-BioNTech coronavirus vaccine is the career achievement of Hungarian biochemist Katalin Karikó.

Over the decades, W&UC advances have cumulatively provoked meaningful qualitative shifts in the dynamics of the innovation sphere, even though we are not close to an inclusive world.

Case Study: Women in Computing

Industrial societies evolve because innovations are the engine of their perpetuation. That said, societal innovation can be metabolized in multiple
ways without necessarily conferring equality status to its originators: for
example, huge cultural innovations such as jazz or rap have pervasively
influenced all sorts of music genres without necessarily advancing the
rights for their originators.

As W&UC reclaim their role in the innovation space, the posthu-
mous reevaluation of their contributions can remain a tricky exercise.
For example, is the role of women in the creation of software a footnote
for women by women or a keystone moment in the history of the genre?
When I started a career in a software area that had very few women, I was
understandably inclined to advocate for our role. But to do so, I always felt
that I had to answer a hard question: If women were so important, why
didn't they own the space? I will address the topic by discussing the respective impacts of Ada Lovelace and of "human computers" in the 1940s.

Ada Lovelace

Lord Byron's daughter, Ada Lovelace (1815–52), is often mentioned as the
first computer programmer for describing an algorithm computing the
Bernoulli numbers and lauded for annotating her translation of Luigi
Federico Menabrea's "Notions sur la machine analytique de Charles Babbage." She was undoubtedly extraordinarily gifted, but it may be a stretch
to retrospectively attribute to her the advent of computer programming.

Babbage also wrote multiple algorithms, and his computing machine
never worked. So his efforts, just as Ada Lovelace's, are largely a false start
for a computing genre that we're viewing through contemporary eyes. It
was a failed attempt to expand on calculators—the first one, the Pascaline
created by Blaise Pascal, having been produced and used in the mid-
seventeenth century.

Lovelace can be seen as a visionary anticipating that a machine could
do more than crunch numbers to manipulate symbols according to rules

and create new data (as when she wrote that "the engine might compose elaborate and scientific pieces of music of any degree"), thus advancing the idea of a transition from calculation to computation.[42] Yet, here again, we must avoid revisiting the past based on the present. In fact, her remarks may only be the restaging of a then very famous dream, Leibniz's idea of a "characteristica universalis," that is, the quest for a universal symbolic language that would not only coordinate human knowledge but would operate as an "ars inveniendi," an art of inventing, a generative AI of sorts.

However fascinating Ada Lovelace was, emphasizing her exceptionality may ultimately tokenize her and bestow her a celebrity that relegates her to tabloid tragedies. It's hard to know how her career would have turned out given that she died at thirty-six of uterine cancer. Meanwhile, we also create a new form of historical imbalance and overlook women who advanced the women's cause much further, like the mathematician and astronomer Mary Somerville.[43] She was Lovelace's mathematics tutor and introduced her to Babbage, as well as to numerous other scientists and inventors, including Charles Wheatstone, who created the first commercial electric telegraph, the Cooke and Wheatstone telegraph, in 1837. She was the first woman (with Caroline Herschel) to become a member of the Royal Astronomical Society. She enjoyed a high reputation as a scientist, especially after the publication of her second book, *On the Connexion of the Physical Sciences* in 1834, reviewed by William Whewell, a celebrated polymath, and she remained engaged in scientific debates throughout her life.[44] She was also the first person to sign a major petition for female suffrage initiated by one of the most influential political economists of the time, John Stuart Mill, in 1868.

Women in the Early Days of Modern Computing

From the point of view of innovation, the women of the ENIAC, who invented how to program the first general-purpose electronic digital computer successfully used, are far more relevant.[45] They weren't the only pioneers: Grace Hopper, a PhD in mathematics from Yale and a member of the Navy Reserves, began her computing career in 1944, when she worked with a team led by Howard Aiken on the Harvard Mark I, used during World War II to make calculations for the Manhattan Project.[46] So how is it that women didn't take over a space where they had such a considerable initial role?

The short response would be sexism, but this reproachful label obfuscates the actual mechanisms and circumstances that breed unfairness and oblivion. Most of these women were categorized under the older concept of "human computer" that predated modern computing.

Human computers were hired to perform research analysis and calculations on the vast amount of data that started to accumulate in the mid-1800s, especially in astronomy and navigation. By the 1870s, there were enough women trained in math to become "human computers." What was initially attractive about them was that they were a cheaper workforce and were perceived as more precise and conscientious than men. That's why Edward Pickering used an all-female group who became known as the Harvard Observatory computers.[47] The twentieth century carried over this old habit. Women like Barbara Canright, who joined California's Jet Propulsion Laboratory in 1939 as its first female human computer, and many others at NASA did work that had life-and-death consequences, but their status didn't change.[48] The same goes for the women of the ENIAC.

As remarkable as they were, these women didn't have a status as scientists or engineers. Their position was more akin to clerical activities, a space that had exploded after the 1920s. They were classified at a "sub professional" grade.[49] When World War II came, the need for more human computers flared up but didn't trigger a change in job classification, especially as there wasn't a real shortage of talent.[50] The Moore School of Engineering of the University of Pennsylvania (where the ENIAC was developed), funded by the US Army, hired massively, and especially women (about two hundred, i.e., 50% of human computers) because many young American men were fighting overseas.[51]

While it's true that the women of the ENIAC did more than what was expected from traditional human computers by creating new methods to manage the data on which they had to perform calculations, and thereby inventing programming, the institutional framework in which they operated was not going to grant them special recognition. Exceptional employees do not change job classifications. Their bosses could have been the ones requesting a recategorization. They didn't. Why?

People are products of their environments, no matter how remarkable they may be. John Mauchly and Presper Eckert, the two main inventor-innovators behind the ENIAC, were no exception. They were conditioned to view women within preexisting ideological frameworks. Eckert had studied at Penn's Moore School of Electrical Engineering, which admitted women as undergraduates only in 1954. Mauchly had earned his PhD from Johns Hopkins in 1932 in physics, where women were exotic exceptions. Realize that when future Nobel physicist Maria Goeppert Mayer came to Johns Hopkins with her husband, Joseph Mayer, she was given only an assistantship position in the Chemistry Department.[52]

Female "human computers" were innovative as they built the software for a major hardware innovation—electronic computers—but they remained statutorily something like what the couture industry called *petites mains* (little hands), who sewed priceless dresses and stitched fancy beads. Women had sewn forever, but Charles Frederick Worth, an Englishman who established his fashion salon in 1858, is considered the father of haute couture (and we forget that his wife, Marie Vernet, was the first professional model, and thus powered the *diffusion* of his creations). Women had cooked for centuries, but the role of being "chef" was appropriated by men. The history of female human computers is the carryover of a secular opposition between the "hand" and the "head."

So, when electronic computers came about, there was a collusion between a device called "computer" and a job also called "computer," but the same word covered two different concepts belonging to different layers of the kairos with two different histories. Female "human computers" belonged to a linguistic construct where being acknowledged as an innovator would have been an oxymoron. Programming was later repositioned within an area where men were kings, engineering, as "software engineering."[53]

Although quite a few female human computers did continue as programmers, the repositioning of the genre as engineering excluded them down the road, because companies were starting to look for "engineers." But very few women had this title in the 1950s and 1960s. It's also probable that the women who had graduated in electrical engineering, which was difficult, couldn't have been thrilled by the idea of applying for jobs they had seen as destined for human computers. Language frames the way we see opportunities and people. It's because the term "human computer" has fallen into disuse that we can evaluate the actual content of what the women of the ENIAC and many others (like Katherine Johnson, who worked on the first spacecraft launch in 1961 and the first moon landing in 1969) did, and that we can legitimately reintegrate these women into the mainstream history of innovation. Sometimes, people are forgotten because they are left out of the linguistic structures that shape the kairos at any given time.

Contrary to Ada Lovelace, the women-computers do fully belong to the general history of computer innovation and represent more than a special section about "women in computing." As we render homage to W&UC's contributions, we may not want to lose sight of the fact that the goal is color and gender neutrality, not the formation of identity-based gardens that might ultimately continue to rubber-stamp biases or possibly reinstitutionalize them in a different way.

Diversity, Equality, and Inclusion (DEI) in Innovation Spaces

How close are we to reaching actual diversity, equality, and inclusion in innovation? Closer, but not as close as we may hope given where we're starting from. So, as intent as organizations may be to "close gaps," the weight of history is still here, and evidence of the gaps even creeps back through simple expressions like "unconscious bias" or the observation that companies encounter pipeline problems.

When the facts are available for anybody to see, why do so many people still use the "unconscious bias" phrase? The history of all W&UC constituencies is so well documented that biases can't seriously be blacked out—unless you assume pervasive ignorance or deliberate indifference.

The popularity of the expression sounds increasingly like a way to sweep an embarrassing issue under the rug by shifting the blame to some collective subconscious to be analyzed through endless corporate therapies that enrich the consultants leading them.

While it's clear that each of us is the product of our history—and that it's part of our duty to always investigate our blind spots—facts, statistics, and numbers are strong enough to provoke a significant mental shake-up. Then the real question should be, What can be done in practice? But here again, we're led into another trap. W&UC are underrepresented in a major antechamber of the innovation castle because of an alleged pipeline shortfall for the type of skills companies need. But what if such a statement were some red herring operating as a guardrail destined to maintain the status quo?

When you can't catch fish in your net, could it be because the net is not appropriate to the type of fish you want to catch? Instead of blaming people for not being in your net, you might consider changing your methods of attracting them. The way job requirements are worded or data parsed by an application tracking system may be biased, recruiting teams may be evaluating résumés guided by old criteria, or interview models influenced by norms may be detrimental to W&UC candidates. Hoping to go around that obvious problem, recruiting platforms now advertise that they're AI-driven, as if it were a miracle cure. It isn't. Cathy O'Neill showed how big data algorithms can reinforce preexisting inequalities.[54] Joy Buolamwini, who analyzed algorithmic biases and founded the Algorithmic Justice League, elaborated on what she called the "coded gaze."[55] AI programs aren't magically "objective," just as data aren't inherently either. They're the result of information collected by people, and in most cases the information ingrains accumulated biases. Data, no more than language, are independent from the characteristics of the layers they come from—and they come from a world where W&UC are often invisible or bit players.

Pipelines are created by people; the tools they choose are their responsibility. Their understanding of others is under their control. Right now, the way people are hired at all levels, be they board members or employees, is based on a narrow definition of skills. Basically, companies want "proven" skills and "proven" experience, that is, an experience anchored in yesterday's needs for the jobs of tomorrow in a biased vision of the world. How can this advance diversity in innovation?

Institutions and companies continue to select people who have the "right" profile, meaning streamlined career paths that fit preformatted requirements, using preexisting guidelines. For example, countless organizations make money hand over fist now placing W&UC members into corporate boards, but what they do is simply bringing them up to corporate standards provided that they're already close to the norm. They don't support the vast majority of W&UC who could breathe fresh air into a company but have patchy résumés that showcase a variety of experiences demonstrating more than skills. Leaders of institutions devalue diversity of experience and an ability to learn. Many W&UC don't fit into the talent pipelines designed for "culture fit," a congruence with a nondiverse culture. Unsurprisingly, as an excuse for low diversity, companies will continue to claim that they have a hard time keeping their diverse employees and that attrition rates offset some of their hiring gains. But who's to blame? Innovative and creative W&UC are still regularly perceived as "misfits" even though corporate leaders like to extol insurgents, originals, or nonconformists when they deliver pep talks.

The legislative route would be the fastest way to accelerate societal innovation. A few institutions and states are setting diversity mandates. Yet what's stopping them from demanding strict gender parity and establishing clear guidelines for ethnic and racial diversity? Nothing but the weight of a history and manifest biases that ensure their survivorship through half measures that uphold the very criteria that have always stopped W&UC.

CONCLUSION

Gabriel was a play by French writer George Sand, whose eponymous hero was raised as a boy by his grandfather to make sure that he would inherit the family estate. When Gabriel suddenly discovers that he's a woman, he realizes, "I was a woman; for suddenly my wings got numb; aether closed in around my head, like an impenetrable crystal vault, and I fell, fell . . . and I had around my neck a heavy chain whose weight was dragging me into the abyss; and then I woke up, bowed with grief, fatigue and dismay."[56]

The expression "impenetrable crystal vault" is generally viewed as the origin of the expression "glass ceiling" coined by Marilyn Loden in 1978.[57] The expression is striking yet somewhat restrictive.

It's possible to get out of the room in order to avoid a glass ceiling, look at the sky, and believe that dreams have no limit. What's more difficult for W&UC is handling what's on the ground, getting over the barricades that they encounter along the way. As numerous as they are, to paraphrase Sand's text, their wings are still clipped, and chains still dangle around their necks. Could they foment an all-out strike similar to what women did in Iceland on October 24, 1975, when 90 percent of women in the country decided to demonstrate their importance? Just imagine what would happen if all W&UC members were to stop buying or using the products from any company that isn't truly diverse at all its levels, from its board to its people in the trenches. But of course, that's a pipe dream because it would render them unable to use almost everything that is part of their daily lives to deliver on that goal.

12

How Can Organizations Remain
Innovative?

*The only man who behaved sensibly was my tailor: he took my
measure anew every time he saw me, whilst all the rest went on
with their old measurements and expected them to fit me.*
—George Bernard Shaw

Like all systems, companies tend to degrade. It's called entropy. When
innovation isn't seen as a living organism feeding from a multifaceted
kairos, it dies off. So day in and day out, organizations must work at maintaining their energy level, which means thwarting deterioration by persistently breeding creative energy. But how? Recommendations abound.

Much has been written about the success trap whereby companies
focus on the business activities to which they owe their original success
to the detriment of larger innovations. As a remedy, they seek to become
ambidextrous, that is, exploit what they have through incremental
innovations while exploring new avenues that will ensure longer-term
relevance.[1] Countless books and executive management classes also discuss how organizations can best organize to internally regenerate their
innovation drive or create incubators to do so. In this book, I will only
focus on a foundational element frequently addressed flippantly because
it relates to the often unloved department of human resources: people.

"INNOVATING" IS A VERB THAT REQUIRES ACTORS

Behind every innovation, there are people—people with an idea we'll either adore or discard; people who implement this idea brilliantly or more

awkwardly; people who are able, unable, or unwilling to test the viability of ideas; people who support ideas or, conversely, sabotage or steal others' work. Innovation, regardless of the angle you take, is about them.

It's not companies, as entities, that innovate. It's the people within them who do. So, when you hear about companies having problems innovating because of their corporate structure, translate the problem: Who in companies obstructs novel ideas, and why, given that most CEOs believe that innovation is key to the future growth of their organization? Companies don't fail because they're disrupted by meteorites. They fail because the people who manage them don't leverage talents around them.

From Organizational Structures to "Humanocracy"

Peter Drucker predicted in 1988 that twenty years down the road, companies would have "fewer than half the levels of management and no more than a third of the numbers of managers as their counterparts today" and that organizations would operate more like symphony orchestras with agile, self-directed groups of specialists.[2]

Decades later, bureaucracy hasn't disappeared and has, instead, grown. According to Gary Hamel and Michele Zanini, "between 1983 and 2014, the number of managers, supervisors and support staff in the U.S. workforce grew by 90%, while employment in other occupations grew by less than 40%."[3] At the same time as organizations need to improve employee commitment, they have created guardrails that could make it harder to deliver on that goal, with new positions such as chief analytics officer, chief collaboration officer, chief customer officer, chief digital officer, chief ethics officer, chief learning officer, chief sustainability officer, and even chief happiness officer. We're a far cry from holacratic self-management and decentralized practices![4] Yet, given that companies continue to innovate, we have to wonder to what extent organizational structures really matter and how intertwined management innovation and innovation management actually are.

It is logical to believe that flatter organizational structures are more adapted to the expression of employees' creativity and an innovation ethos. It is also obvious that organizations with complex top-down power structures may choke novel ideas. In a previous book, I discussed why if you see people as cogs in the corporate machinery, they'll be reluctant to contribute to innovative initiatives.[5] I emphasized the value of employee empowerment and what Hamel and Zanini call a "humanocracy."[6]

That said, when we look at the history of innovations throughout the world, we see that they can come from companies with very different organizational structures. So, an actual humanocracy could be relatively independent from one specific type of organizational structure. A more direct question may be about whether or how employees are allowed or encouraged to express themselves within an organization—which doesn't exclude the idea that hierarchical structures might offer clear channels for people to offer and develop new ideas.

In practice, you can design internal innovation networks very diversely. What matters are the ability to communicate, the feedback system, and ultimately the people within a structure and not so much the structure itself. The most common problem CEOs might have to address is the presence of petty tyrants who crush subordinates and whose power game can equally plague hierarchical and flatter organizations. They have to fight what Chris Argyris labeled "skilled incompetence" (basically the art of using all the right corporate jargon while doing nothing of substance), which damages companies from the inside more surely than competition.[7] The quality of the people and processes in all intermediate levels, no matter how many of them exist, are paramount for any company that wants to remain consistently innovative.

Creating a Continuous Generative Circuit

Creating a continuous generative circuit that keeps an innovation mindset alive rests on the idea that innovation can appear anywhere in an organization. As emphasized by Ed Catmull in one of the best books about creativity, imagineering is rank agnostic, and it's incumbent on CEOs to establish a learning organization that both uncovers and begets talent.

Creativity Is Predicated on Building a Learning Organization

While most corporations advertise wanting "creative" candidates, they may not like these individuals all that much. As Isaac Asimov said to researchers in an MIT spinoff, "The world in general disapproves of creativity."[8] The fact is that noncreativity is almost embedded into recruiting habits.

Companies look for ready-to-use people who have the "right skills" or have "done it before," a common wording indicating that they've positioned themselves with one foot in the past. While displaying on their websites that they look for "creative" candidates, they also expose another major failing: They assume that creativity is a natural predisposition. It's not. Creativity exists only if enacted and only if people are placed in breeding grounds where ideas can germinate, be tested and acted out, and in turn fertilize more breeding grounds. Otherwise, creativity talk is just hot air.

If your company isn't a "learning organization," nobody will unearth anything of substance. Managers will just "manage" whatever exists, believe that they know what there is to know, and never ask recruiters to identify people who might bring a different perspective. One thing leading to another, you'll program your obsolescence and realize too late that "today's problems come from yesterday's solutions," as Peter Senge put it.[9]

If you want employees to be willing to participate in innovative endeavors, you probably have to overhaul many of your hiring procedures and put an end to the practice of evaluating "skills" with a fixed mindset aimed at "filling" positions just like you'd fill a hole, one that people can get out of only by leaving the company.

Partially derived from experiments by Robert Wood and Albert Bandura on organizational functioning from the perspective of social cognitive theory, the expressions "fixed mindset" and "growth mindset" were popularized by Carol Dweck.[10] People with a fixed mindset believe that others have a fixed amount of talent and abilities. They cannot change, and their journey through life and work is about avoiding challenges and eventually covering up their failures to save their ego. People with a growth mindset believe in human potential and development, learning, and continuous discovery for themselves and others.

A fixed mindset doesn't encourage innovation in anybody. If you ever created a startup, chances are that you weren't a fixed mindset leader and that you didn't attribute your innovative spirit to your SAT scores or entre-preneurial classes that taught you all you needed to know. So why would you value a fixed mindset when the growth of your organization is at stake and when your ability to sustain your market advantage depends on even more creativity and imagination than when you started?

If you yourself have a growth mindset, why would you lock your em-ployees in the role that they currently occupy and evaluate them with rigid mental parameters? If you want to avoid crippling your company's energy, the solution is to look for people who have the talent and the desire to ex-pand on their competence—in other words, people who, like the servants in the Parable of the Talents in the New Testament's Gospel according to Matthew, will double the value of the opportunity they are given.

If you lament the fact that educational systems don't prepare stu-dents well or fast enough for businesses, you're only expressing a narrow-minded hiring methodology. More than a workplace, your company must be a live university. A learning organization trusts and encourages the learning capabilities of everybody and offers online courses, internal training platforms, peer education, and experience sharing with gurus and mentors. If you hire a marketing manager today, your best recruit won't necessarily be somebody who "studied" marketing and communi-cation. A stronger choice might be somebody who is familiar with video games or loves cinematography, the magic of being immersed in multiple worlds, and is mentally ready to look at your current and future products in both physical and virtual terms. It may not take much time for them to learn what you see today as the required skills for a marketing manager. Existing knowledge can be learned. Innovating is the investigative mind-set that dynamically generates new knowledge. So, hiring for potential is building up the springboard that enables you to remain involved in the innovation race.

A smart company is a network of bridges and gateways, not a lab-yrinth of cul-de-sacs and impasses. You need "skills," of course, but look for cross-disciplinary minds and hybrid skills—in other words, for

Renaissance people of sorts. Don't program the deterioration of your company by endlessly looking for prepackaged goods.

Internal Gig Programs

Internal gig programs are a way to help employees discover and access, or even create, new territories within, adjacent to, or even unrelated to their regular job. The concept regained popularity through Google's "20% time" policy, which founders Larry Page and Sergey Brin described in their 2004 IPO letter.[11] Even though this Google practice has met a diversity of reactions over the years, the takeaway is that something like this exists as an option to stimulate innovative thinking.[12]

The origin of the concept is inspiring. It came from the 3M Company, which creates thousands of products that we use every day, from adhesives to car shampoos. Begun as the "Minnesota Mining and Manufacturing Company" (hence the name 3M), the company was originally a mining venture to extract corundum, a crystalline form of aluminum oxide. The company failed, but thanks to its management and its employees, it reinvented itself by using the corundum to make a new product, sandpaper. In 1948 they created 3M's "15 percent" program, which allowed employees to dedicate almost a full day each week to their own projects. In 1974 one of its scientists, Art Fry, came up with what was going to be the famous Post-it Note.

Even in hyperbusy companies, there are times when employees may not have as much work as usual and may want to develop different skills on the side. This is a practice with which some organizations have experimented. When these projects don't work as well as hoped, it's not because they're intrinsically faulty but because they're often poorly managed, probably just like many other initiatives in the organization.

The message here isn't that you should always have a formal program but that you should always keep in mind that ideas can come from anywhere, no matter what the official job description of an employee may be.

Innovation rarely comes from brainstorming sessions and, instead, results more from an informal gestation phenomenon. If you don't pay attention to your employees' ideas, or if your managers trample them instead of helping them thrive, employees will leave. Even pretty-open organizations can lose great talents by not "expanding their aperture," to borrow an expression by Eric Schmidt and Jonathan Rosenberg when they recount why Google lost Kevin Systrom, who went on to co-found Instagram. "Sometimes we screw this up ourselves," they said. Systrom was rejected from a management training program because it only accepted candidates with degrees in computer sciences, which he didn't have. Although his sponsor argued that he had a "history of working closely with engineers and shipping things," several execs "steadfastly refused to expand the aperture, and denied the transfer."[13]

I-Deals and Management by Exception

Many quitters are replaceable, especially if they only joined the organization for a paycheck. But that's not always the case. So the company must dive into the reasons why employees resign and analyze the content of their exit interviews to determine who left because they didn't have opportunities to do more meaningful work, were uninspired by the company's culture, felt unappreciated, stuck, and so on. Surveys show that "fifty-two percent of voluntarily exiting employees say their manager or organization could have done something to prevent them from leaving their job."[14] What percentage of them were potentially creative? Most companies don't know, because their managers can make sure that nobody will.

Great employees are often the victims of talent hoarding, a practice used by managers to keep them in their current role and prevent them from exploring other opportunities within the company. Talent hoarders tell employees that they are "close, but not quite yet ready" for the next position, limit high-visibility work assignments outside the team, restrict development and training opportunities, or reduce their access to information on internal job openings. According to 2016 Aberdeen research, 50 percent of managers admitted they prevented their best employees from seeking out other roles in a company.[15] Meanwhile, 45 percent of employees who changed companies in 2014 and 2015 said they left because they didn't have advancement or lateral move opportunities.

The sad part is that even growth-minded managers don't always have an easy way to handle employees who could remain in their department while operating under different rules. They are not necessarily authorized by their superiors to design "flexible work arrangements through idio- syncratic deals" or "I-deals."[16] Yet innovation-driven management must always be a sort of "management by exception," that is, capable of taking care of quick and prolific thinkers. Innovating is not carrying business- as-usual. So, we can't think in business-as-usual terms if we want to spot and nurture innovative people. I was lucky enough to realize this early on in my career. Ever since, I've encouraged every single company I've led or advised to find what I called their "Arthurs."

Arthur was one of my favorite employees in my career. Everything about him was different—from his outfits to his florid vocabulary. An early user of my first company's main product, a relational database for Apple's Macintosh, he would storm into our office with the most unex- pected bugs, apologizing profusely for being a pain in the neck, using all kinds of made-up words and poetic metaphors to describe his problem. As exotic as he was, we made the decision to hire him in tech support even though he wasn't looking for a job. We didn't regret this decision. Customers loved him. The interesting part is that after his workday, he would stay at the office focusing on his hobby, databases on large sys- tems, until, one day, he proudly declared that we should create modules connecting our database to all the large mainframe computing systems. The rest of the team was not exactly enthusiastic. First, our realm was the Macintosh, a fairly insular world in the 1990s. Second, we would lose a critical resource in a tech support team that was already stretched. Finally, it was doubtful that large organizations, who at the time were for the most part anti-Apple, would even accept that a Macintosh could be connected to anything.

We dragged our feet for a while, but Arthur wouldn't give up, re- counting what he'd learned with his epic tone every day at lunchtime. Anybody who listened to him would have believed that operating systems like Unix, Ultrix, and OSF/1 were heroes in a comic strip. Finally, to the displeasure of the rest of the team, I bought Arthur a Digital Equipment VAX machine to help him test interface modules connecting our database to larger systems and vice versa. Of course, the system was as unfriendly as you can possibly imagine, but Arthur, installing it and reading through pounds of manuals, was like a kid in a candy store. His passion was so contagious that he roped in other employees, and we created interfaces for all the major mainframe databases. This ended up being a phenomenal move for the company. Corporate accounts couldn't connect their PC databases to their mainframes, but lo and behold, that ugly duckling, the Macintosh, was something they could use, and many customers forgot that it was an Apple product.

So find your "Arthurs," or your "originals" as Adam Grant calls them.[17] They have the imagination, the drive, and, frankly, the dream to turn lead into gold. If you don't pay attention to them, they'll leave. As challenging as these employees may sometimes be, accommodating them is worth the pain—and the reward.

Kaizen Feedback

If you don't have gig-type programs or believe that your managers will be unable to handle i-deals, you can at least set up intelligent "kaizen" feedback processes that enable employees to give feedback (and not simply receive it) and discuss not only the tasks at hand but also the way they are performed and even, sometimes, their relevance.

Originally spearheaded by Toyota, the goal of a kaizen approach isn't simply improving productivity or eliminating waste. It's just as much about leveraging the intelligence and life experience of human beings and inciting them to participate in the enhancement of what they produce. It was the foundation of the Toyota Creative Ideas and Suggestions System (TCISS), which Eiji Toyoda borrowed from a Ford Motor Company plant that he had visited in 1950. Note that neither Ford nor Toyota had flat organizational structures.

Suggestion boxes can take several forms, ranging from fully organized systems to more informal, online conversations. Of course, it's not enough to gather ideas and feedback. The commitment of your employees isn't merely predicated on your ability to listen but also on your determination to respond. So, make sure that employees' suggestions don't disappear in the company's labyrinths. The goal is to transform as many employees as possible into inventors, as was Bill Coughlin's mission when he was overseeing Ford's intellectual property matters.[18]

Employees are key actors of the regenerative circuit that maintains the dynamics of workplaces. Your company won't be innovative just because one person will have one idea. Innovation is a matter of numbers. To build up a culture of innovation, many people must be engaged in generating hundreds of ideas, with the hope that one or two will break through and transform the business. That's common sense, and a topic amply discussed in creativity courses, albeit generally overlooked elsewhere, but it's "the only business metric that matters."[19]

Design Thinking and Design Making

As a professor at MIT and then at Stanford, John Arnold taught seminars in creativity for engineers in the 1950s, following a tradition initiated by Buckminster Fuller. This trend grew in the 1960s and 1970s and gained influence thanks to various parallel movements, notably human-centered design research. It received mainstream recognition with the foundation of companies such as IDEO in 1991, which merged various organizations founded by David Kelley, Bill Moggridge, and Mike Nuttall. IDEO helped popularize Arnold's concept of "design thinking," that is, of new collaborative approaches to context analysis, problem discovery and framing, modeling, prototyping, testing, and other skills.

More often than not, companies resort to design thinking when they believe it's time for them to wake up, although this methodology should be part of a continuous cross-team ideation process. Ideas don't pop up upon request. They result from ongoing mental calisthenics. Why was Edison so prolific apart from the fact that he was a genius? Because he could materialize his ideas by bringing them to his lab and testing them considerably faster than anybody else and thus continuously strengthening thinking exercises.

Not all companies can afford to set up laboratories, but most of them can have a virtual version of it using simulation platforms. AnDi, a simulation platform created by the European company id-sl, for example, helps parties iterate faster, creating a virtual representation of how a concept or process would translate in practice.[20]

It's about Your Human Horizon

Most organizations adopt detailed frameworks (also called "innovation models") to design processes and set implementation horizons. But they can work only if the human beings in charge are up to snuff and comfortable with the simple fact that innovating is never a sure bet. You must have the guts to keep on with projects whose outcome is all but certain, which requires courage. If you don't get rid of executives who can't see beyond the tips of their noses, your timidity will be costly. Here are two archetypal cases of courage and timidity.

Courage: In a 2019 story, Susan Crawford interviewed Claudio Mazzali, a Brazilian physicist who joined Corning in 1999.[21] What's striking about Mazzali's interview is his pride as he discussed the organization's innovation heritage and his reference to the courage displayed by a historical head of Corning Glass Works research, William Armistead. Corning entered the telecommunications space when its researchers got inspired by Charles Kao's work on optical fiber (which earned him his 2009 Nobel Prize in Physics). In the early 1970s, Donald Keck, along with Robert Maurer and Peter Schultz, designed the first optical fiber with optical losses low enough for use in telecommunications. Armistead was skeptical, but he respected his team so deeply that he secured funding for them. They experimented for four years before they produced a commercially viable low-loss optical fiber in 1970. Although it took ten more years for Corning to get its first customers, the company persisted, and today Corning is a leader in this domain.

Timidity: The failure of Kodak in the 1970s is a famous case study, but we often focus too much on the failure of the company and not enough on the failure of people. When Steven Sasson presented the first digital camera as well as its display device to his bosses in 1975, they didn't like it. An all-electronic camera that didn't use film and didn't use paper meant hurting Kodak's analog cash cow. Kodak still patented the camera in 1978, but Sasson was not allowed to publicly discuss it.[22] The patent earned billions for Kodak until it expired in 2007, but when Kodak finally directly embraced digital photography it was too late.

When you read Sasson's words in a *New York Times* article, you realize that the fear of jeopardizing the status quo was, at its base, a human problem: "When you're talking to a bunch of corporate guys about 18 to 20 years in the future, when none of those guys will still be in the company, they don't get too excited about it," he said.[23]

Corporate myopia is human myopia. Companies can be blind, sure, but only metaphorically, because they don't have eyes, ears, or any other senses, for that matter. They are only abstract entities, after all, so what they see, hear, and smell is what their people do. Consequently, if these people see no further than their personal agenda and manage others based on their career path, their understanding and perception of the kairos shrink down to almost nothing, compromising the long-term health of their companies. Innovations are driven by people and overlooked by people.

IBM missed the relational database market by neglecting one person, Ted Codd, whose landmark paper in 1970, "A Relational Model of Data for Large Shared Data Banks,"[24] inspired entrepreneurs, such as Oracle co-founder Larry Ellison and many others. That's the type of poor decision that upsets employees who want to keep abreast of what's going on in the outside world. So, unsurprisingly, when Tom Ehrenfeld profiled former IBM employees who had left Big Blue to become entrepreneurs, he noticed that they ultimately found "much good" to take with them and what had horrified them wasn't "big business" but "bad business."[25] Great for these entrepreneurs but not so great for the organizations that lost them, even if—let's admit it—they had had the acumen to hire them in the first place.

TAKING IN THE KAIROS'S DYNAMICS

The biggest threat larger organizations must reckon with isn't the arrival of new entrants who would suddenly disrupt their comfort because of exceptionally quick and supercharged capabilities. It's not even necessarily the nature of their organizational structure. It can also just be a group-think confidence that prevents them from continuously assessing what's really happening in their space and how the layers of kairos where they sit can be impacted by evolutions in other, sometimes unrelated, layers. Taking in the kairos's dynamics means crowdsourcing intelligence, tapping collective knowledge and ideas.

From Not-Invented-Here (NIH) to Invented-Anywhere

Companies are often legitimately proud of the inventions that support their innovations. So they have reason to coddle their inventors. But there is a drawback. Their inventors can become overly protective of their turf and discard what's not invented in their shop. The "Not-Invented-Here" (NIH) bias tends to create cultures that discredit or dismiss what other organizations come up with, as Dan Ariely explains.[26]

Organizations, just like individuals, can be addicted to their own ideas. They can also lose sight of the fact that there are thousands of inventors, scientists, and researchers out there who have chosen to remain independent from commercial organizations, who want to participate in projects that can serve multiple types of businesses or collaborate on long-term initiatives that don't necessarily immediately materialize into commercial innovations. Remaining closely informed about what non-commercial inventors are doing outside the realm of your enterprise and your competitors' is of paramount importance, widening your innovation aperture and revitalizing your own vision of the world.

Many innovations offered by prestigious companies are beholden to the contributions of thousands of engineers to open standards at the system, hardware, file format, or protocol levels and to various internationally recognized standards bodies: the Internet Engineering Task Force (IETF), the International Organization for Standardization (ISO), and the International Electrotechnical Commission (IEC), to name a few.

The open source movement has changed the world.[27] For example, the Linux operating system software now powers the vast majority of our smartphones or the infrastructure supporting the world's ecommerce leaders, including Amazon, eBay, PayPal, Walmart, and many others. Apart from the internet, it's hard to find a collective invention more pervasive than this one and with more impact on the innovative capabilities of so many companies.

Why do people want to contribute to the open source movement? It's because they need a freedom that can otherwise be curbed by corporate short-term expectations. This explains the reservations about the commercial world that engineers or thought-leaders sometimes express. When Presper Eckert and John Mauchly (who created the ENIAC in 1946) severed their ties to the University of Pennsylvania to start their company, many went ballistic. For example, John von Neumann—one of the most brilliant polymaths of his time—vented his disdain for their initiative. "Eckert and Mauchly are a commercial group with a commercial patent policy," he complained to computer scientist Stanley Frankel. "We cannot work with them directly or indirectly in the same open manner in which we would work with an academic group."[28] Not all researchers would be so harsh, well aware as they are that research is necessarily financed by somebody (state, country, public or private organizations, etc.) and part of an economic system where institutions compete fiercely and protect the intellectual property they facilitated. But it's true that inventors or creative people in general can feel constrained by the often shorter-term needs and policies of corporate environments.

When inventors work in an organization, their perception of the world is swayed by the organization's vision for who they are or whom they want to become. They follow a recursive generation process proper to that company that may not be in sync with recursive generation processes evolving in their industry at large or in other industries that can influence theirs. Why did the engineers at AT&T declare that Paul Baran's idea of packet switching to ensure data communication across a network wouldn't work?[29] Not because they were unintelligent but because their imagination was restricted to what AT&T as a business was expecting from them. Yet packet switching turned out to be a pivotal element in the buildup of the internet.

Corporations tend to view the world from their own observatory. As a result, inventors may prefer to operate as freelancers or be employed on an on-and-off basis. For example, Whitfield Diffie pursued his research in cryptography as an independent researcher. The Diffie-Hellman Public key he co-created revolutionized cryptography—and now underlies the security of internet commerce. Diffie later had a long career at Sun Microsystems (1991–2009).

While popular culture directs our attention toward the companies that produce innovations, we can't lose sight of the fact that many of the inventions that undergird them were cooked up within public organizations or a variety of foundations where inventors are spared some of the constraints inherent to the commercial world, even if they still have to operate within restricted and controlled budgets. Decision-makers and inventors at government-funded agencies contributed to innovative projects more meaningfully than what they would have been able to had they only worked for commercial organizations. Bob Taylor certainly did a great job helping design the MGM-31 Pershing at Martin Marietta, but his impact was considerably larger after he joined NASA and the Information Processing Techniques Office (IPTO) of the Advanced Research Projects Agency (ARPA). In 1966 he initiated no less than the ARPANET project—and he built another inventors' incubator in 1970, Xerox PARC. While many of the inventors who built the internet also developed careers in the commercial world, they will always be remembered for a level of inventiveness that outmatches what any particular commercial organization would have embraced. Vint Cerf and Bob Kahn are forever the inventors of the TCP/IP protocols that interconnect devices on the internet. They are part of the collective who transformed the entire world economy.

If you want to spot inventors, look beyond the precincts of your organization or your competitors'. The numerous US federal agencies devoted to research and development have inspired or triggered thousands of innovations. For example, the National Institute of Standards and Technology (NIST) has been the home of four Nobel laureates in Physics, and dozens of recognized inventors have worked or work at NIST. Another example is the National Institutes of Health (NIH), which has nurtured dozens of scientists from around the world and over one hundred Nobel Prizes.

It's precisely because they knew that research could be the antecham-ber of diverse innovations that prominent industrialists, like Alfred No-bel, started foundations late in the nineteenth century. The first Nobel laureate in Physics in 1901 set the tone: Wilhelm Röntgen stunned the world by not seeking patents for his discovery of X-rays (1895), consider-ing that his work should be available to the public free of charge. The fact is that only a few years after the invention, it was extensively leveraged in medicine, dentistry, and even crazy innovations like shoe-fitting fluo-roscopes in the early 1920s for customers to see how the bones of their feet sat in a shoe.[30] The Carnegie Foundation for the Advancement of Teaching (CFAT), founded by Andrew Carnegie in 1905, concentrated on education; its first president, Henry Pritchett, was no less than an astron-omer, a mathematician, and a president of MIT from 1900 to 1906. By creating the Research Corporation for Science Advancement (RCSA) in 1912, Frederick Cottrell, a physical chemist and inventor (notably of the electrostatic precipitator), decided that science itself should be the prin-cipal beneficiary of his invention. In many respects, the Bill & Melinda Gates Foundation is in line with this type of thinking.

In the modern world, strategic innovations, especially in science- or technology-dependent spaces, are frequently indebted to sources exter-nal to companies. Corporate R&D labs can rarely support large-scale projects, and financial pressures exerted by shareholders prevent orga-nizations from taking on risky programs that could bear fruit only many years down the road. Their interest is to de-risk the cost of innovation and proceed indirectly, mostly by acquiring or creating strategic relationships with startups that took the plunge. For example, COVID vaccines had been in the works for over thirty years. The technology behind messen-ger ribonucleic acid (mRNA) vaccines started at the end of the 1980s, and evidence that RNA could be used in this capacity was already pre-sented in the 1990s, so convincingly that the German biologist Ingmar Hoerr started his company, CureVac, in 2000. But Katalin Karikó had to solve major technical issues to introduce mRNA into cells in ways that could trigger immune responses. In the 1990s she partnered with the American immunologist Drew Weissman, and in 2005 they published a joint paper that accelerated the commercial activity around mRNA. The oncologist Uğur Şahin and the physician Özlem Türeci, a husband-and-wife team, started BioNTech in Mainz, Germany, in 2008 (Karikó joined as vice president in 2013) and signed a collaboration agreement with Pfizer in 2018. The biologist Derrick Rossi and the MIT professor Robert Langer founded Moderna in 2010, which also licensed the work of Karikó and Weissman.

The commercial success of COVID vaccines will in turn spill over multiple other areas, from heart disease to snakebites. Was the road to success easy for inventor Karikó before this multipronged success?[31] Not in the least, but she is the force behind Pfizer's and Moderna's innovative vaccines and successes. This course of action doesn't diminish the value of these companies' achievements, though, and instead also illustrates how transforming an invention into a marketable product is not a linear process and how numerous things can go wrong. Just as important, it's predicated on the ability for organizations to identify the sources of invention downstream, which requires a lot of internal accumulated knowledge and effective decision-making.

Innovative companies don't have to invent everything. They have to seize the moment by continuously being on the lookout, should an unexpected event in the kairos (like a pandemic) create a call to action. Innovating is about being ready for any form of irruptive phenomena and speed of rejoinder. But such speed is possible only when companies have built in a panoptical awareness of what's around them to capture the dynamics of the kairos and pick up on its variations. Again in the case of the COVID vaccine, the French-based Sanofi experienced setbacks in developing a vaccine and competing in its space for many reasons. Among them, the company had a reduced internal research force. It lacked breadth in its ties to national and international universities for fundamental research and had a narrower reach within national and international startup ecosystems. A more fragile immersion within the kairos typically leads to second-best options and a series of de-risking decisions that ultimately undermine chances for breakthroughs.

Continuously Capturing the Interlayering Dynamics of the Kairos

Once established, many companies tend to stick to internal agendas and miss variations in the kairos that could impact their businesses. They lose their plasticity, and gaining it back is hard.

Plasticity Loss

For a company, losing its plasticity doesn't mean that what it does doesn't work or even that it has lost its market. It primarily means that the layer it occupies has changed position relative to other layers in the kairos. For example, it's customary to say that Uber, Lyft, and others "disrupted" the taxi industry. This statement is too simplistic, all the more so as the market is still here. People need "taxis" and use them even more. Simply, the perception and definition of what a taxi is has changed.

The taxi industry remained in a layer that saw its users as "users of taxis" and not as people whose expectations would evolve because of what was happening in other spaces. Yet, once people had smartphones, they wanted more than a taxi they would have to wait for or hail, even though the system had worked well for a century. They wanted a taxi service at their fingertips. Each traditional taxi company had worked at remaining competitive relative to other companies within the institutional framework regulating the taxi industry. They ignored the layers in the kairos that were changing customer expectations and changing their definition of what "taxi" should be.

Remaining competitive means taking in the dynamics of the kairos, whose speed can be defined by external variables that influence, displace, or fissure the layer where one company and often many of them have established their castles and modus operandi. It's up to companies to take notice of the rift zones created by movements in the kairos layers that can reconfigure their landscape. If they don't, new entrants can invade their space.

Today, just as in the past, innovative companies must continuously evaluate how their products reflect the kairos, that is, become cultural symbols within a certain time frame, which can just be a season (like in some parts of fashion or gadget industries) or much longer, depending on the nature of their business. But becoming, let alone remaining, a cultural symbol is difficult. In 1903 Ford started as just another car manufacturer. He produced his first Model A, which worked well but was replaced by the Ford Model C in the course of 1904. It was one car among the dozens of cars manufactured by a host of companies. Like them, Ford offered additional models, which he designated using more letters of the alphabet (from B to S) and sold to patrons in the hundreds or low thousands depending on the price of technical and aesthetic features. Up to the Model T, Ford was in line with the car manufacturer ecosystem, where each company offered new capabilities or new twists on existing components, usually for well-off aficionados. They were all innovative. But Ford's company didn't disappear like many others who started at the same period. So what made him innovative for a longer period?

Ford's perspective evolved after the relatively inexpensive, entry-level line Model N, introduced in 1906, led to larger sales (about seven thousand cars). He looked outside the car manufacturing layer, at the kairos at large, and just like George Eastman he perceived the potential of a major phenomenon: the growth of the middle class subsequent to the rapid economic expansion of the Gilded Age (1870–1900). It was creating new consumption patterns and new leisure expectations (which were also responsible for the success of the "Kodak"). Factoring in this demographic evolution called for a change in the production of cars, similarly to what had already happened in the food industry. In 1913 he imported the slaughterhouse model into his space and implemented an assembly-line mode of mass production and supply chain management that he progressively generalized to manufacture all the components of a car. Does this alone explain why Ford put such a mark in the history of cars as is usually believed? Absolutely not. Ford's usage of the slaughterhouse model might have been a failure had he not created a mechanism getting him the buy-in of workers, which entailed attention to a societal layer whose influence had been growing mostly since the formation of the American Federation of Labor (AFL) in 1886. Workers could have gone on strike to protest working conditions as they already had in other industries using that model, such as the mining industry.

While initiating mass production, Ford also needed to avoid the turn-over and absenteeism of workers who resented operating one task at the strict timing dictated by a machine. People's buy-in matters. He instituted a five-dollar workday to keep them, a decision that had nothing to do with any charitable intent but enabled more workers to buy what they were producing. Of course, this upped the brand and transformed employees into evangelists for the company. What Ford's example shows is that a company can offer new features to outshine competitors at least tempo-rarily but that creating a sustainable lead means aligning with other layers of the kairos.

Who "Sees" the Interlayering Dynamics of the Kairos

Many of the companies celebrated for their innovations were created by one or several founders who, with their teams, harnessed the dynamics of the kairos. Although the prolonged presence of companies' founders may not be a guarantee of continued success, we frequently see that their disappearance may also trigger the progressive erosion of the mindset that initially put the company on the map. Companies are then run by career executives who may be brilliant individuals but may not have a track record showing that they could inspire innovative endeavors. In many cases, they have only been "part of" innovative companies but not direct agents driving the innovation process. As a result, they are more inclined to focus on the business layers of the kairos where their creden-tials and forte lie. Even if they are serious about designing and defining innovation methodologies and horizons, they tend to value faster return on investments and, as a result, favor product development over research projects. In addition, they rarely couple innovation endeavors with a clear, people-centered recruiting strategy that attracts innovative thinkers. And yet people are the ones who innovate or don't.

The business of business isn't just the enterprise itself. It's how a company interacts with society. As John Browne put it, "critically, as tra-ditional sources of competitiveness are eroded, connection with society represents a final frontier of competitiveness."[32] That's why, in order to have the optical power to capture the various dimensions and layers of the kairos, larger companies must not only build strong teams of engineers and technical analysts; they must also employ societal researchers—like sociologists, anthropologists, ethnographers, or linguists—with the mission of looking both inside and outside the company and understanding the world in which they are introducing products.

Companies rarely take full advantage of the fact that their employees' identity can't be narrowed down to their status as paid workers. They are also individuals, consumers, citizens, actors in a social world with a wide spectrum of experiences. In many cases, your employees should be the very first sets of focus groups leveraged by your societal researchers. Unless your organization is composed only of identical automata with no life outside your organization, they are living specimens of the outward-looking perspectivism you need to remain innovative. They offer the multiple types of intelligence (musical, visual, verbal, mathematical, kinesthetic, naturalistic, interpersonal, existential, intrapersonal, and so on) required to soak up the complexity of the kairos—and not simply the last trend in one specific domain.

Savvy societal researchers will spot the interesting misfits in your corporate culture, people such as Zhang Yiming. He was twenty-five when he joined Microsoft, which he left quickly, feeling stifled. Aged twenty-nine, he founded ByteDance in 2012, which launched TikTok in 2015. TikTok didn't invent video or social media but staged these for relevance to a new audience, a generation of people born from 1996 onward, commonly referred to as Generation Z. When you realize that Microsoft acquired LinkedIn in 2016 for a fortune, you can't help notice that it primarily targeted a segment of professionals whose profiles are shaped as if we were still in the 1990s, not the late millennials and digital natives, a new generation of consumers with a distinct sensibility.

I am not implying that young people are more likely to have a better handle on the complexity of the kairos. What I am saying is that you should pay special attention to people who are sensitive to changes within the kairos, something that you can find in all age categories. The reason new companies can come across as more innovative is often because their founders and early employees are still open to surfing the unstable kairos waves and enjoy the ride. They don't really "know better." In fact they don't. They start from a state of knowledge everybody has, but they approach it with a more agile mindset. Does this mean that people with less corporate background might be more innovative? At first sight, yes, and this is one assumption of many large companies when they recruit people right out of college (in addition to the fact that they are cheaper than older workers). However, the fact that young people navigate layers of the kairos with agility when they start doesn't ensure that their acuity won't be blunted five years later. In reality, more often than not, those with a deep innovation mindset feel crushed by the corporate machinery and either quickly turn into disillusioned workers looking for new gigs every other year or they start their own companies.

So beware both reverse ageism and ageism! Older people have something just as critical to offer. They may have a keen sense of variations over two or three decades. Because they are older, they can be more sensitive to continuities and discontinuities over time than are younger people. This means that if you're serious about innovation, you also have to question the assumption that older people might be less creative. In a post titled "Gene Pool Engineering," venture capitalist Vinod Khosla emphasized the energizing power of diversity, stating that, in all forms, it helps with figuring out the new. And age is a diversifying criterion.[33] Creating multigenerational teams of engineers accelerates the innovation process. By mentioning age in his diversity dimensions, Khosla broke away from the pervasive mythology that young companies should be populated with young people and the tendency of many venture capitalists to discard older company founders for "not being blue flame enough."[34]

This opinion—held either overtly or covertly by dozens of venture capitalists, recruiters, and hiring managers—isn't based on science. The idea that creativity is the prerogative of young people isn't supported by facts and instead relies on clichéd views of creativity. In *Originals*, Adam Grant discussed two types of creatives, "young geniuses and old masters," driving two styles of innovation: conceptual and experimental.[35] Conceptual innovators tend to be young. Experimental innovators tend to be creative throughout their lives and even more productive later.

This distinction shouldn't be mapped with conventional oppositions between revolutionary/disruptive/whatever-you-want and incremental innovations. We can't say that conceptual innovators are more revolutionary, while experimental ones are more on the incremental side. In fact, conceptual and experimental innovators can power innovation of both types because they can be both. Steve Jobs may have been more of a conceptual innovator at the time of the Macintosh (which initially failed) and more of an experimental innovator when, aged fifty-two, he launched the iPhone. In fact, experimental innovators could be more likely to see more facets of the kairos at once because they have seen more things.

My ultimate point is that age doesn't matter, the less so as we have entered an "age of longevity.[36] Pagan Kennedy found that on average American inventors are aged forty-seven, which definitely counters the popular narrative that young innovators dominate innovation.[37] This type of mythology is all the more absurd since many innovations require deep expertise and significant experience in a given field as well as adjacent domains. In other words, in order to innovate, debias your perception of both the world and the people around you, and build up the diverse human capital that forces you to get rid of preconceived ideas of what innovation is or isn't.

CONCLUSION

Postmortems often discuss failures when there's no longer a path for success. What we should wonder more often is why employees—with tens, hundreds, even thousands of pairs of eyes—were unable to avoid these failures. That's the very question that Tim Dempsey asked when he narrated the collapse of Nortel, a hundred-year-old company that filed for bankruptcy in 2009.[38] And yet there was no shortage of remarkable people at Nortel.

The story shows that innovation can continue only when people at the top are willing to accept the idea that intelligence must also be crowdsourced within. Employees are powerful barometers of the shape of things to come. Companies that have an innovation problem don't actually have an innovation problem. They have people-management problems and wither from self-inflicted wounds.

Innovations are more than products; they're objects that reflect multiple aspects of the kairos. Being "future ready" is the art of reading the multithreaded present reflected in the various layers of the kairos. This requires building up a workforce that is aware of the continuous motion of the innovation kairos around us, even in domains that seem unrelated to our own.

People are the ones who orchestrate speed of action and reaction, speed of research, speed of development, speed of engineering, speed of communication, speed of execution, speed of mindshare and collaboration, and so forth. Only people can develop the keen sense of obsolescence that tells them to continuously restage what they do in order to override irrelevance. "I saw great businesses become but the ghost of a name," Ford wrote,

> because someone thought they could be managed just as they were always managed, and though the management may have been most excellent in its day, its excellence consisted in its alertness to its day, and not in slavish following of its yesterdays. Life, as I see it, is not a location, but a journey. Even the man who most feels himself "settled" is not settled— he is probably sagging back. Everything is in flux, and was meant to be. Life flows. We may live at the same number of the street, but it is never the same man who lives there.[39]

Conclusion

Well, all I know is this—nothing you ever learn is really wasted,
and will sometime be used.
—Julia Child

Innovation is not a game for the fainthearted. Very few companies trying to bring an innovation to market make the cut. Not all prosperous companies do, and short-lived companies can contribute innovations that live on to have more impact. When we start a project, we really don't know if or to what extent we'll make it to the innovation firmament. The first product of Tsushin Kogyo, the forerunner of Sony, was a rice cooker with a competitive advantage, but it sold poorly. It's nine years later, in 1957, that the company made history with the world's smallest transistor radio, the TR-63 pocketable radio. A company can set sail with a promising idea that ends up going nowhere but pivot thanks to that "bad" vessel: Discord started as a video game and mutated into an iconic social hub. The online game, Glitch, morphed into a corporate messaging platform, Slack, which was acquired by Salesforce in 2021 for $27 billion.

As aspiring innovators, we would love a code to access some mythical holy grail that would give us the magical potion for success. We do get a code when we analyze how innovations happen, looking through the lens of the innovation kairos, but what we get is more of a collection of warnings that we had better be ready to interpret. What makes us innovative is our ability to continuously be on our toes and process information expeditiously.

Between the time you invent the computer mouse and are granted a patent and the moment it's on everybody's desk, a lot must happen (chapter 1). As we transform an invention or more generally any project into an innovation that people can adopt, we navigate through uncertainty

293

and have to do our best to pick up the signals that may guide us around obstacles and sometimes redirect our efforts (chapter 2). If we believe we can enhance our credibility by clamoring that we're disruptive, we may throw ourselves into a dangerous trap (chapter 3). We often have to come to our senses pretty quickly and realize how perilous it is to ignore that dozens of people, who share equal brilliance with us, are on a parallel path that can alter our course (chapter 4) and work just as hard as we do at breaking through the multiple layers of the innovation kairos to seize the window of opportunity (chapter 5). However convinced we may be of our own uniqueness, we have to factor in that there's room for multiple products like ours (chapter 6) because it's also what shows that there is a potentially thriving market, although nothing can really tell us how much runway we have to break through the noise (chapter 7) or when the Goliaths with so much in resources might wipe us out (chapter 8). Yes, uncertainty haunts our lives as innovators even when we land in a geographical or virtual space brimming with creative energy (chapter 9) and tap into the networked communities that drive innovation (chapter 10). And, if we are women or minorities, we are faced with even more challenges to make our mark in the world (chapter 11). In all cases, though, in order to innovate, we have to debias our perception of both the world and the people around us and build up the diverse human capital that allows us to maintain our innovative spirit. Sometimes, our ability to sustain our market advantage depends on even more creativity and imagination than when we start, even if it's also true that we can afford to come up with smaller innovations (chapter 12).

Many of the recommendations we get as aspiring innovators contradict one another, yet all can be of some use. But what we need most is the ability to maintain the alertness and critical analysis skills, which enables us to surf the often-treacherous waves of the innovation kairos.

As entrepreneurs, we know how to manage our company's operations, but as innovators we have to reckon with the fact that, for better or for worse, we are instruments within a system whose inner workings (societal, economic, historical, ideological, etc.) may operate beyond and outside our immediate agency. To get beyond our Eureka! moment, we need to know what we don't know and continuously remain aware that we're agents in a multiplayer game meant to ensure its own durability more than the individual glory of those who play. As much as we want to be a prominent stage director, we have to make the best of the fact that we are also actors on a wider stage designed at the dawn of the capitalist era, very much like Jean-Baptiste Say described it, and has evolved following the same basic principles since then.

The early days of the first Industrial Revolution in Europe and then in North America established the blueprint of the innovation scene. Has it structurally changed since then? Maybe not as significantly as we tend to believe. What has changed is the number of stages across the world and the number of actors engaged in the play. The speed of communication, financial transaction systems, and the global value chains that support them—as well as the way we talk about innovation—have also modified some aspects of the innovation scene but maybe not structurally.

When we now discuss innovative entrepreneurship, we tend to over-emphasize the heroic dimension of our personal endeavors and the glory that rewards the risks we have taken. We see innovators as superior creatures who have achieved dominance thanks to their exceptional and creative willpower. We forget about the conditions that made their existence possible in the first place, that is, the set of circumstances that actuate or impede their actions. And yet they are fundamentals, which have been ironed out over the decades and since the first Industrial Revolution. They remain mostly unchanged, something we can better grasp when we look at the innovation surge in contemporary China. Sometimes, we brush up our perceptiveness by watching how others enact our own history.

Westerners have exoticized the "Orient" as an unfathomable place for centuries, and we are still prone to throw up our hands and chalk up China's success to mysterious, sometimes nefarious, methods—a case of "things are just different over there." Yet China's success mirrors processes developed for over two centuries of innovation, reminding us what they are by "blitzscaling" them all.

Starting in 1982 with the "National Program for Key Science & Technology Projects," China has systematically implemented programs propelling its transformation into a technology powerhouse. The "Torch" plan managed by the Ministry of Science and Technology (MOST) has led to the formation of Science and Technology Industrial Parks (STIPs). According to Damien Ma, "as of 2017, about 1.85 million companies were registered in the STIPs, of which about 49,000 were officially designated high-tech enterprises."[1] The initiative combines with a network of people; companies; research labs, institutes, and universities; this combination fosters a growing cultural rhizome throughout its innovation kairos.

This gigantic endeavor has borne fruit rapidly because China didn't wake up overnight. On top of its rich culture, it accumulated knowledge about the West for centuries, learned from its evolution, and reflected on ways to leverage it, mostly in the early days of the twentieth century, when its internal economic and political dynamics changed. For example, Sun Yat-sen, often viewed as the father of the nation, was extremely well educated and deeply committed to China's development. By 1912 he knew that railways would be key for achieving that goal and considered that the American system could be a useful model to start from. China has trained its "elites" abroad for decades.

In addition, we shouldn't forget that the people working in manufacturing plants when outsourcing expanded at a large scale were not robots. They were and are human beings who learned from these experiences—and some became entrepreneurs, as has been the case throughout the history of innovation in the West.

We often see innovations as seminal events separated from the various processes and institutional infrastructures that have led to them. By treating innovation as a process supported by a pervasive infrastructure, China has accelerated its innovation engine, just as the United States or other countries have at various times throughout their history.

As a student of the Western world, China has long factored in that innovations in hot areas don't come from one company but from several organizations that contribute to the construction of innovation stacks. That's what financiers and venture capitalists have done for decades too and why they have been betting on multiple horses forever with the hope of getting a winner of the trifecta. China does so at a massive scale. This effort allows for the development and production of multiple offerings in a category at the same time as well as abundant experimentations whose winnowing effect reduces uncertainty and enables China to pinpoint within technology life cycles what is likely to work best in the end.

While innovation outcomes are always somewhat haphazard from the standpoint of an individual innovator, it's not as much a gambling game overall. Chances of succeeding depend on how many truly talented people apply themselves to a problem and how intensely they try to reach a goal even as the goalpost placement shifts as they move toward that goal. Innovating is a recursive process, with each step building on previous steps. Edison's remark, which I quoted in this book's introduction—"I have not failed. I've just found 10,000 ways that won't work"—isn't just a clever quip. Edison is saying that "luck" results from continuous iteration, redirection, and combinatorial optimization. The elements in an innovation stack don't evolve linearly or incrementally, and even an incrementally innovative idea can be equipped with tentacles that feed themselves within more layers of the innovation kairos.

It's fair to remark that while applying today the same machinery as what the West has employed for two centuries, Chinese innovators may have fewer layers of the innovation kairos to contend with. In a conversation with Steve Orlins, Kai-Fu Lee indicated how the existence of an outdated credit card system in the United States could be a unique opportunity for China to leapfrog.[2] It can avoid decades of entrenched technical and societal layers in the innovation kairos. This is true all over the world and for all sorts of products. For example, according to Marwan Senhaji, the founder of a platform that distributes AI medical devices in northern Africa, less-developed countries see AI as part of the construction and formation of the new healthcare system they need, while AI can stumble upon multiple levels of entrenched habits in rich countries. That said, innovation hindrances can be imposed by known factors, but unexpected albatrosses, like ancestral traditions, may also fly into your face along the way. So maybe all innovators, regardless of the country where they operate, should have as a guiding principle that they can never be sure of how easily the innovation kairos will welcome their inroads.

When we examine innovation, we see a tension between our understanding of the conditions that make innovations possible and the

Promethean imagery we like to attach to innovators. The latter may give us a preliminary confidence boost but quickly leaves us vulnerable as we confront reality. Our environments don't bend to our will, and retrospective determinism recounts only part of the story by overlooking the effectuation side of the adventure—trials and errors, mistakes, and unforeseen obstacles. Innovators never step into uncharted territories; they map them out differently to open new roads, build new bridges and intersections that last only until they are redrawn. Innovations—their nature, pace, and obsolescence rate as well as their originators—are cultural realities encoded in a world that reproduces itself and eventually corrects its course for its own survival. The same culture that glorifies innovation also throws us into a complex socioeconomic juggernaut and cacophonic present where nothing is gained forever.

Innovations, whether we make or consume them, constitute the economic texture of our world. Does it make us, innovators or consumers, the victims of a pervasive obsession for the new—of what Lee Vinsel and Andrew Russell called "the Innovation Delusion"?[3] Yes, and so what? And what exactly is deceitful about innovation in itself? That our obsession with the new might distract us from addressing everyday problems like maintaining and repairing our roads or fixing broken healthcare systems? Nothing says, though, that fixing everyday problems can't be innovative or that addressing them won't be stepping stones for different innovations. Innovation is not about simply creating something new. It's about inserting a fresh take on new or old issues inside the brown fields where those issues appear.

To establish its own innovation practices and patterns, capitalism itself had to decode and recode the canons and conventions adopted by different economic models. So nothing says that innovations can't be recoded for and within a postcapitalist society to create a world with less poverty, less waste, and more equality. Will this change happen overnight? No, but there is a tremendous amount of entrepreneurial innovation happening now addressing the United Nations Sustainable Development Goals. Tens of thousands of innovators are working on creating new products, processes, and business models to combat climate change.

There will have to be thousands of innovations and dozens of regulatory political and economic decisions at both national and international
levels if we want to keep the average world temperature rise to no more
than 1.50 degrees Celsius by 2050. This goal was unlikely even when it
was set. As Vaclav Smil commented in 2020, "reaching that goal would
require nothing short of a fundamental transformation of the global economy on scales and at a speed unprecedented in human history, a task
that would be impossible to do without major economic and social dis-
locations."[4] But should we give up? Of course not. During the next three
or four decades, thousands of entrepreneurs worldwide will dynamically
recompose the present as a proxy for the future, slowly construct the
climate-change innovation stack, and hope to beat the odds. And they will
by aligning the entangled layers and velocities that make up the innovation kairos in ways that reset expectations for what's possible. Innovation
is a movable feast, a cause for celebrations or lamentations with no fixed
date, and what we see today as epoch-making calls for its obliteration by
other epoch-making accomplishments.

The very same telescope that brings us closer to the stars reminds
us how far away they are. Nonetheless, it still encourages us to search for
them.

Notes

INTRODUCTION

Epigraph: "I Have Not Failed. I've Just Found 10,000 Ways That Won't Work," BrainyQuote, accessed August 10, 2023, https://www.brainyquote.com/quotes /thomas_a_edison_132683.

1. Gene Dannen, "The Einstein-Szilard Refrigerators: Two Visionary Theoretical Physicists Joined Forces in the 1920s to Reinvent the Household Refrigerator," *Scientific American*, January 1997, 90–95.

2. Freon is a fluorocarbon refrigerant. Responsible for ozone depletion, it was banned by the Montreal Protocol of August 1987.

3. Bill Gates, "The Best Business Book I've Ever Read," *Gates Notes*, July 13, 2014, https://www.gatesnotes.com/Books/Business-Adventures.

4. Evan Ackerman, "The Man Who Invented VR Goggles 50 Years Too Soon," *IEEE Spectrum*, November 30, 2016, https://spectrum.ieee.org/tech-history/heroic -failures/the-man-who-invented-vr-goggles-50-years-too-soon.

5. "Google Books Ngram Viewer," http://books.google.com/ngrams. This chart and similar charts in this book only indicate general trends. Google Books NGram's shortcomings don't apply to the single-word searches on English terms that we have performed for these charts. That said, and for your information, they have been discussed by various scholars, e.g., Eitan Pechenick, Christopher Danforth, and Peter Dodds, "Characterizing the Google Books Corpus: Strong Limits to Inferences of Socio-cultural and Linguistic Evolution," *PLOS ONE*, October 7, 2015, https:// journals.plos.org/plosone/article?id=10.1371/journal.pone.0137041.

6. Navi Radjou, Jaideep Prabhu, and Simone Ahuja, *Jugaad Innovation: A Frugal and Flexible Approach to Innovation for the 21st Century* (Gurgaon, India: Penguin Random House India, 2012).

7. "Cardin Shows Haute Couture Designs in China," *New York Times*, March 20, 1979, https://www.nytimes.com/1979/03/20/archives/cardin-shows-haute-co uture-designs-in-china.html.

8. D. T. Max, "The Chinese Workers Who Assemble Designer Bags in Tuscany," *New Yorker*, April 9, 2018, https://www.newyorker.com/magazine/2018/04/16/the -chinese-workers-who-assemble-designer-bags-in-tuscany.

9. The exclamation "Eureka!" meaning "I have found it" is attributed to the

ancient Greek mathematician Archimedes. After stepping into a bath, he noticed that the water level rose, which made him realize that the volume of the displaced water was equal to the volume of the submerged part of his body. Exhilarated by his discovery, he allegedly ran naked through the streets of the Italian city of Syracuse, then a Greek colony. The authenticity of the story is doubtful, but the exclamation has consistently been used to express a flash of inspiration.

10. Noam Wasserman, *The Founder's Dilemmas: Anticipating and Avoiding the Pitfalls That Can Sink a Startup* (Princeton, NJ: Princeton University Press, 2013). See also Ben Horowitz, *The Hard Thing about Hard Things: Building a Business When There Are No Easy Answers* (New York: Harper Business, 2014).

11. Adam Grant, *Think Again: The Power of Knowing What You Don't Know* (New York: Viking, 2021); Tressie McMillan Cottom, *Thick* (New York: The New York Press, 2019). Cottom shows why we need a "thick description" to convey the status complexity of a Black woman. The expression "thick description" has been used by sociologists since the end of the 1960s as a methodology to capture and interpret inherently complex contexts and their structural contradictions.

12. Saras D. Sarasvathy, *Effectuation: Elements of Entrepreneurial Expertise* (Cheltenham, UK: Edward Elgar, 2009). For a summary of the characteristics of effectuation, bricolage, and improvisation, see Geoffrey R. Archer, Ted Baker, and René Mauer, "Towards an Alternative to Entrepreneurial Success: Integrating Bricolage, Effectuation and Improvisation," *Frontiers of Entrepreneurship Research* 29, no. 6 (2009): 1–15, https://digitalknowledge.babson.edu/fer/vol29/iss6/4.

13. Tony Fadell, *Build: An Unorthodox Guide to Making Things Worth Making* (New York: HarperCollins, 2022).

14. Herbert Simon, *The Sciences of the Artificial*, 3rd ed. (Cambridge, MA: MIT Press, 1996).

CHAPTER 1: ARE YOU AN INVENTOR OR AN INNOVATOR?

Epigraph: "Creativity Is Intelligence Having Fun," Quote Investigator, accessed July 22, 2023, https://quoteinvestigator.com/2017/03/02/fun.

1. Benoît Godin, Gerald Gaglio, and Sebastian Pfotenhauer, "X-Innovation: Re-inventing Innovation Again and Again," *Novation*, no. 1 (2019): 1–17, http://www.novation.inrs.ca/index.php/novation/issue/view/novation_1st_issue. Godin is the author of several important books, including *Models of Innovation: The History of an Idea* (Cambridge: MIT Press, 2017) and *Innovation Contested: The Idea of Innovation over the Centuries* (Abingdon, UK: Routledge, 2015).

2. Richard Cantillon, *Essai sur la nature du commerce en général* (London: Fletcher Gyles, 1755), 62–63 (chap. 13). Translated from the French by Delbourg-Delphis.

3. In the United States, American French creole Norbert Rillieux invented

the multiple-effect evaporator. Rillieux had been able to study at one of the top engineering schools in France, l'École Centrale in Paris.

4. The company later became Béghin-Say.

5. Jean-Baptiste Say, *A Treatise on Political Economy, or the Production, Distribution and Consumption of Wealth*, trans. C. R. Prinsep (New York: Augustus M. Kelley Publishers, 1971), 80. Note that in the early part of the nineteenth century, they said, "man of science" or "natural philosopher." The term "scientist" was only coined in 1834 by British polymath William Whewell.

6. Jean-Baptiste Say, *A Treatise on Political Economy*, 75–78. In 1821, the American translator adopted the word "adventurer" with the following footnote: "The term entrepreneur is difficult to render in English; the corresponding word, undertaker, being already appropriated to a limited sense . . . For want of a better word, it will be rendered into English by the term adventurer."

7. Joseph Schumpeter, *Business Cycles: A Theoretical, Historical and Statistical Analysis of the Capitalist Process* (New York: McGraw-Hill Book Company, 1939), 100.

8. Peter Drucker, *Innovation and Entrepreneurship, Practice and Principles* (New York: Harper and Row, 1985).

9. Derek Thompson, "Forget Edison: This Is How History's Greatest Inventions Really Happened," *Atlantic*, June 15, 2012, https://www.theatlantic.com/business/archive/2012/06/forget-edison-this-is-how-historys-greatest-inventions-really-happened/258525/.

10. Mark Lemley, "The Myth of the Sole Inventor," *Stanford Public Law Working Paper* no. 1856610, June 2, 2011, rev. April 28, 2020, http://dx.doi.org/10.2139/ssrn.1856610.

11. Derek Thompson, *Hit Makers: How Things Become Popular* (New York: Penguin Press, 2017).

12. Maxim Kotsemir, Alexander Abroskin, and Dirk Meissner, "Innovation Concepts and Typology: An Evolutionary Discussion," *Higher School of Economics Research*, Paper no. WP BRP 05/STI/2013 (2013): 1–49, https//:doi.org//dx.doi.org/10.2139/ssrn.2221299.

13. Tim Sharp, "World's First Commercial Airline," Space.com, May 22, 2018, https://www.space.com/16657-worlds-first-commercial-airline-the-greatest-moments-in-flight.html.

14. Bob Gardner, "The Wright Brothers, Bernoulli, and a Surprise from Upper East Tennessee," paper, East Tennessee State University, Fall 2003, https://faculty.etsu.edu/gardnerr/wright-brothers/bernoulli.pdf.

15. "Former Google Engineer Sent to Prison for Stealing Robocar Secrets," *CBS News*, August 5, 2020, https://www.cbsnews.com/news/anthony-levandowski-google-engineer-uber-prison-stealing-robocar-secrets.

16. Schumpeter, *Business Cycles*, 84.

17. "iPhone 1st Generation Teardown," iFixit, June 29, 2007, https://www.ifixit .com/Teardown/iPhone+1st+Generation+Teardown/599. *Ars Technica* also did its own analysis: Jacqui Cheng, "iPhone in Depth: The Ars Review," *Ars Technica*, July 9, 2007, https://arstechnica.com/gadgets/2007/07/iphone-review/14.

18. "Alkali Aluminosilicate Glass Article Having an Ion-Exchanged Surface Layer," United States Patent, February 5, 1974, https://patents.google.com/patent /US3790430A/en.

19. "The Glass Age, Glass Heroes," Corning, accessed July 22, 2023, https:// www.corning.com/worldwide/en/innovation/the-glass-age/inspiration/glass -heroes.html.

20. Emdad Islam and Jason Zein, "Inventor CEOs," *Journal of Financial Economics* 135, no. 2 (February 2020), https://doi.org/10.1016/j.jfineco.2019.06.009.

21. George Anders, "CEO by Day, Inventor at Night . . . Eureka! The Netflix Envelope," *Forbes*, July 16, 2012, https://www.forbes.com/sites/georgeanders/2012/07 /16/geniuses-or-dabblers/?sh=73eaa35e231a. Note that his article doesn't respect the distinction between inventors and innovators.

22. Antonio Regalado, "Steve Jobs Lives on at the Patent Office," *MIT Technology Review*, November 27, 2014, https://www.technologyreview.com/2014/11/27 /170289/steve-jobs-lives-on-at-the-patent-office.

23. "Nobel Prize Laureates and Research Affiliations," Nobel Prize, https:// www.nobelprize.org/prizes/lists/nobel-laureates-and-research-affiliations.

24. Jamie Durrani, "Does Pursuing Commercial Interests Hinder an Academic Career?," *Chemical World*, July 14, 2020, https://www.chemistryworld.com/news /does-pursuing-commercial-interests-hinder-an-academic-career/4012139.article.

25. There are millions of individual inventors. Even Abraham Lincoln developed a patent for buoying vessels over shoals. Several organizations advise inventors in the development of their ideas, patent them, and introduce them to companies that may acquire or license these patents and resell them to larger organizations.

26. Drucker, *Innovation and Entrepreneurship*, 12.

27. Drucker, *Innovation and Entrepreneurship*, 13.

28. Drucker, *Innovation and Entrepreneurship*, 188.

29. Werner Sombart, *Die Entstehung der Moderne Kapitalismus* (Munich, Germany: Duncker & Humblot, 1927), 91. Cited in Matthew Josephson, *Edison: A Biography* (New York: John Wiley and Sons, 1992), 137.

30. Paul Ratner, "Elon Musk Interview Reveals Whether He Prefers Nikola Tesla to Thomas Edison," *Big Think*, February 4, 2019, https://bigthink.com/tech nology-innovation/this-elon-musk-interview-reveals-if-he-prefers-nikola-tesla-or -thomas-edison.

31. Henry Ford and Samuel Crowther, *My Life and Work* (Garden City, NY: Doubleday Page, 1922), 234–35.

32. During the last thirty years of the nineteenth century, battery technology evolved quickly. A significant breakthrough came with Waldemar Jungner's nickel-cadmium and nickel-iron batteries in 1898. Their design inspired Edison's alkaline-based nickel-iron battery patented in 1901. However, it took about eight years for Edison to produce a reliable product for electric cars, and in the meantime Ford's Model T had been launched. Edison's battery was a success in other spaces.

33. Gordon Moore, "The Accidental Entrepreneur," *Caltech Magazine / Engineering & Science* (Summer 1994), http://calteches.library.caltech.edu/3777/1/Moore.pdf.

34. A year before, Jack Kilby had invented the first hybrid integrated circuit (hybrid IC) that was germanium-based at Texas Instruments, for which he was awarded the Nobel Prize in Physics in 2000. He shared his prize with the German Herbert Kroemer and the Russian Zhores Alferov. Jack Kilby mentioned Robert Noyce in his acceptance speech. See Jack Kilby's Nobel Lecture: "Turning Potential into Reality: The Invention of the Integrated Circuit," Nobel Prize, December 8, 2000, https://www.nobelprize.org/prizes/physics/2000/kilby/lecture.

35. The term "serendipity" was coined by Hugh Walpole. He was referring to a Persian tale transcribed in Italian under the title *Peregrinaggio di tre giovani figliuoli del re di Serendippo* by Michele Tramezzino and published in Venice, Italy, in 1557.

36. Mark Boroush, "U.S. R&D Increased by $51 Billion, to $606 Billion, in 2018; Estimate for 2019 Indicates a Further Rise to $656 Billion," National Center for Science and Engineering Statistics, April 21, 2021, https://ncses.nsf.gov/pubs/nsf21324. Numbers include federal government funding.

37. "Ranking of the Companies with the Highest Spending on Research and Development Worldwide in 2020," Statista, September 20, 2022, https://www.statista.com/statistics/265645/ranking-of-the-20-companies-with-the-highest-spending-on-research-and-development.

38. John Wu, "Why U.S. Business R&D Is Not as Strong as It Appears," Information Technology & Innovation Foundation (ITIF), June 2018, http://www2.itif.org/2018-us-business-rd.pdf.

39. Scott Kirsner, "Don't Let Financial Metrics Prematurely Stifle Innovation," *Harvard Business Review*, March 31, 2021, https://hbr.org/2021/03/dont-let-financial-metrics-prematurely-stifle-innovation.

CHAPTER 2: WHAT IS A TYPICAL INNOVATION JOURNEY?

Epigraph: "Remembering Lee Alexander McQueen: A Decade Later," *Lexington Line*, February 11, 2020, https://www.thelexingtonline.com/blog/2020/02/11/remembering-lee-alexander-mcqueen-a-decade-later.

1. The company was first named Eastman Dry Plate Company (1881), then became the Eastman Company in 1889 and the Eastman Kodak Company in 1892.

2. Sarasvathy, *Effectuation*, 67–76.

3. My main sources include Elizabeth Brayer, *George Eastman: A Biography* (Rochester, NY: University of Rochester Press, 2006); John Hannavy, *Encyclopedia of Nineteenth-Century Photography* (New York: Routledge, 2007); and multiple on-line resources, especially Historic Camera, http://historiccamera.com, and Monroe County, NY, https://mcnygenealogy.com/book/kodak/index.htm.

4. George Selden patented (but never produced) a lighter version of the internal combustion engine invented by George Brayton in 1878, eight years before the public introduction of the Benz Patent-Motorwagen in Germany by Karl Benz. Selden received royalties for his patent, a revenue stream that stopped when Henry Ford demonstrated automobiles that didn't use George Brayton's mechanism but Nikolaus Otto's.

5. Brayer, *George Eastman*, 27.

6. "Method and Apparatus for Coating Plates for Use in Photography," United States Patent Office, April 13, 1880, https://patents.google.com/patent/US226503.

7. Brayer, *George Eastman*, 34.

8. Brayer, 42.

9. "Photographic Apparatus," United States Patent Office, October 11, 1881, https://patents.google.com/patent/US248179. Houston was born in Scotland in 1841. That same year, his family immigrated to Wisconsin. Houston later moved to North Dakota. For an interesting hypothesis regarding the origin of the name Kodak, see Andrew Boyd, "David Henderson Houston," University of Houston, https://uh.edu/engines/epi3088.htm.

10. "Photographic Film," United States Patent Office, October 14, 1884, https://patents.google.com/patent/US306594. The summary includes the following: "My invention relates to an improvement in photographic films having for their object the production, for the market of sensitized films, which are capable of being used in making positives and negatives in place of the sheets of glass coated with emulsion, now known in the trade as 'dry-plates'; and to this end my invention consists in the new article of manufacture formed by my improved sensitized films, and in the process or mode of manufacture of my said films, all as more fully described in the following specification, and specified in the claims thereunto annexed."

11. "Roller-Holder for Photographic Films," United States Patent Office, May 5, 1885, https://patents.google.com/patent/US317049. The summary includes the following: "Our present invention relates to an improved apparatus for exposing sensitive photographic films in the camera, which apparatus is fully described in the accompanying specification and the novel features thereof specified in the claims annexed." The application contained thirty-six claims.

12. "Photographic Camera," United States Patent Office, January 2, 1883, https://patents.google.com/patent/US270133A/en?oq=US270133.

13. "Detective Camera," United States Patent Office, November 30, 1886, https://patents.google.com/patent/US353545. Summary: "Our invention relates to certain improvements in detective-cameras of that type or class which are provided with roll-holders adapted to the support of a strip of suitable sensitized paper or film while successive exposures are made thereon, which improvements are fully described and illustrated in the following specification and accompanying drawings, and the novel features thereof specified in the claims annexed to the said specification." The patent had thirty-six claims.

14. "Camera," United States Patent Office, September 4, 1888, https://patent images.storage.googleapis.com/6d/2e/29/68b5cd7e8110f0/US388850.pdf.

15. Randal Picker, "The Razors-and-Blades Myth(s)," University of Chicago Law & Economics, Olin Working Paper no. 532 (September 13, 2010): 1–32, https://papers.ssrn.com/sol3/papers.cfm?abstract_id=1676444.

16. Brownell had his own design firm, which Eastman acquired in 1902.

17. Henry Reichenbach is often considered as the inventor of the modern transparent roll film. He left the company in 1891 to found his own with other Eastman employees.

18. "Manufacture of flexible photographic films," United States Patent Office, December 10, 1889, https://patentimages.storage.googleapis.com/0c/06/78/760df9b0637652/US417202.pdf.

19. Randy Alfred, "May 2, 1887: Celluloid-Film Patent Ignites Long Legal Battle," Wired, May 2, 2011, https://www.wired.com/2011/05/0502celuloid-photographic-film.

20. Brayer, George Eastman, 95.

21. "Kodak Ltd. and the Trade," Photographic Dealer 13, no. 78 (November 1902): 289, Google Books.

22. Sir J. F. W. Herschel, "Instantaneous Photography," Photographic News 4, no. 88 (May 11, 1860): 13, Google Books. Herschel wrote, "I take for granted nothing more than, 1st, what photography has already realized, or we may be sure it will realize within some very limited lapse of time from the present date—viz., the possibility of taking a photograph, as it were, by a snap-shot—of securing a picture in a tenth of a second of time." Until then, the term "snap-shot" had designated a quick gun shot with minimal targeting.

23. "Amazon Empire: The Rise and Reign of Jeff Bezos," Frontline, PBS, February 18, 2020, https://www.pbs.org/wgbh/frontline/film/amazon-empire.

24. William Stuber succeeded Eastman as president and chairman of the board in 1925.

25. Drucker, Innovation and Entrepreneurship, 136.

26. Drucker, *Innovation and Entrepreneurship*, 255.

27. For the difference between DOP and POP, see Dusan C. Stulik and Art Kaplan, "Silver Gelatin," Getty Conservation Institute, 2013, https://www.getty.edu /conservation/publications_resources/pdf_publications/pdf/atlas_silver_gelatin .pdf.

28. Fred Vogelstein, *Dogfight: How Apple and Google Went to War and Started a Revolution* (New York: Sarah Crichton Books, 2013).

29. James C. Yoon, "IP Litigation in United States," Stanford Law School, August 4, 2016, https://law.stanford.edu/wp-content/uploads/2016/07/Revised-Stan ford-August-4-2016-Class-Presentation.pdf.

30. "Just the Facts: Intellectual Property Cases, Patent, Copyright, and Trademark," United States Courts, February 13, 2020, https://www.uscourts.gov/news /2020/02/13/just-facts-intellectual-property-cases-patent-copyright-and-trade mark.

31. Scott Barry Kaufman and Carolyn Gregoire, *Wired to Create: Unraveling the Mysteries of the Creative Mind* (New York: Perigee Books, 2015).

32. Clayton M. Christensen, Jeff Dyer, and Hal Gregersen, *The Innovator's DNA: Mastering the Five Skills of Disruptive Innovators* (Boston: Harvard Business Review Press, 2011).

33. Howard Gardner, *Multiple Intelligences: The Theory in Practice* (New York: Basic Books, 1993), 26.

34. George Day and Paul Schoemaker, *Peripheral Vision: Detecting the Weak Signals That Will Make or Break Your Company* (Boston: Harvard Business Review Press, 2006).

35. This battle was dramatized in the movie *The Current War*, directed by Alfonso Gomez-Rejon and premiered in 2017.

36. Vaclav Smil, "February 1878: The First Phonograph," *IEEE Spectrum*, January 18, 2018, https://spectrum.ieee.org/tech-history/dawn-of-electronics/edisons -phonograph.

37. "Welcome IBM. Seriously," *Wall Street Journal*, August 12, 1981.

CHAPTER 3: DO YOU NEED TO BE DISRUPTIVE?

Epigraph: "Dalai Lama XIV > Quotes > Quotable Quote," Goodreads, accessed July 23, 2023, https://www.goodreads.com/quotes/8074794-in-order-to-carry-a-pos itive-action-we-must-develop.

1. Peter Drucker, *The Age of Discontinuity: Guidelines to Our Changing Society* (London: Heinemann, 1969).

2. Gaston Bachelard, *La Formation de l'esprit scientifique: Contribution à une psy-chanalyse de la connaissance objective* (Paris: Vrin, 1938).

3. Thomas Kuhn, *The Structure of Scientific Revolutions,* 50th anniversary ed. (Chicago: University of Chicago Press, 2012).

4. As later confirmed by Kuhn's book, *Black-Body Theory and the Quantum Discontinuity, 1894–1912* (Oxford: Oxford University Press, 1978).

5. Kuhn, *Structure of Scientific Revolutions,* 93: "Scientific revolutions seem revolutionary only to those whose paradigms are affected by them. To outsiders they may, like the Balkan revolutions of the early twentieth century, seem a normal part of the developmental process. Astronomers, for example, could accept X-rays are a mere addition to knowledge, for their paradigms were unaffected by the existence of the radiation. But for men like Kelvin, Crookes, and Roentgen, whose research dealt with radiation theory or with cathode ray tubes, the emergence of X-rays necessarily violated one paradigm as it created another. This is why these rays could be discovered only through something first going wrong with normal research."

6. Robert Foster, *Innovation: The Attacker's Advantage* (New York: Summit Books, 1986).

7. Max Planck, *The Philosophy of Physics* (New York: Norton and Company, 1936), 97.

8. Joseph L. Bower and Clayton M. Christensen, "Disruptive Technologies: Catching the Wave. How Companies Can Prepare for Tomorrow's Customers without Losing Their Focus on Today's," *Harvard Business Review,* January–February 1995, https://hbr.org/1995/01/disruptive-technologies-catching-the-wave.

9. For a summary of various typologies and classifications, see Mario Coccia, "Classifications of Innovations Survey and Future Directions," *Ceris-Cnr,* Working Paper no. 2 (2006), https://doi.org/10.2139/ssrn.2581746. See also Kotsemir, Abroskin, and Meissner, "Innovation Concepts and Typology: An Evolutionary Discussion," *Higher School of Economics Research Paper No. WP BRP 05/STI/2013,* posted February 21, 2013, last rev. May 8, 2013, SSRN, https://papers.ssrn.com/sol3/papers.cfm?abstract_id=2221299.

10. William J. Abernathy and Kim B. Clark, "Innovation: Mapping the Winds of Creative Destruction," *Research Policy* 14, no. 1 (1985): 3–22, https://doi.org/10.1016/0048-7333(85)90021-6.

11. Abernathy and Clark, "Innovation: Mapping the Winds of Creative Destruction," 20–21.

12. Rebecca M. Henderson and Kim B. Clark, "Architectural Innovation: The Reconfiguration of Existing Product Technologies and the Failure of Established Firms," *Administrative Science Quarterly* 35, no. 1 (1990): 9–30, https://doi.org/10.2307/2393549.

13. Joseph Schumpeter, *Capitalism, Socialism and Democracy,* introduction by Richard Swedberg, Taylor and Francis e-library (London: Routledge, 2003).

14. Schumpeter, *Capitalism, Socialism and Democracy*, 81–86.

15. The first occurrences of the term "disruption" appeared in the seventeenth century. The adjective "disruptive" is more recent (around 1862). Both words were used in varied contexts, from the disruptive discharge in the early 1900s (subsequent to Louis Paschen's research on electrical discharges) to the description of geologic or behavioral patterns (often with a negative undertone) but historically rarely in economic and business areas. For example, Schumpeter used the words "disruption/disrupt/disruptive" only five times in *Business Cycles* and *Capitalism, Socialism and Democracy*. I didn't spot the concept in Drucker's 1985 *Innovation and Entrepreneurship*.

16. Clayton M. Christensen, Michael E. Raynor, and Rory McDonald, "What Is Disruptive Innovation?," *Harvard Business Review*, December 2015, https://hbr.org /2015/12/what-is-disruptive-innovation.

17. Clayton M. Christensen and Michael E. Raynor, *The Innovator's Solution: Creating and Sustaining Successful Growth* (Boston: Harvard Business Review Press, 2003), 34.

18. Christensen and Raynor, 41.

19. Christensen and Raynor, 69.

20. Christensen, Raynor, and McDonald, "What Is Disruptive Innovation?"

21. Rob Marvin, "PC Sales Keep Falling, but Big Manufacturers Are Doing Just Fine," *PC Magazine*, June 20, 2018, https://www.pcmag.com/news/pc-sales-keep -falling-but-big-manufacturers-are-doing-just-fine.

22. Christensen and Raynor, *Innovator's Solution*, 48–65.

23. Dario Gil, "The Story behind IBM's 2019 Patent Leadership," *IBM Research Blog*, January 14, 2020, https://www.ibm.com/blogs/research/2020/01/ibm-patent -leadership-2019.

24. Jill Lepore, "The Disruption Machine: What the Gospel of Innovation Gets Wrong," *New Yorker*, June 16, 2014, https://www.newyorker.com/magazine/2014 /06/23/the-disruption-machine.

25. W. Chan Kim and Renée Mauborgne, *Blue Ocean Strategy: How to Create Uncontested Market Space and Make the Competition Irrelevant* (Boston: Harvard Business Review Press, 2015); the expanded edition/sequel is *Blue Ocean Shift: Proven Steps to Inspire Confidence and Seize New Growth* (New York: Hachette Books, 2017).

26. Kim and Mauborgne, *Blue Ocean Strategy*, 49–82.

27. W. Chan Kim and Renée Mauborgne, *Beyond Disruption: Innovate and Achieve Growth without Displacing Industries, Companies or Jobs* (Boston: Harvard Business Review Press, 2023).

28. Chapter 5: "What Is a Window of Opportunity?"

29. For an understanding of perspective in the arts (which also shapes our un-

derstanding of it in life), see Erwin Panofsky, *Perspective as Symbolic Form* (Brooklyn, NY: Zone Books, 1997). Orig. pub. 1927.

30. Barcodes were invented by Norman Joseph Woodland and Bernard Silver in 1951 and became commercially successful when redesigned by George Laurer, an IBM employee (like Woodland).

CHAPTER 4: WHEN IS THE RIGHT TIME?

Epigraph: Evelyn Waugh, *Brideshead Revisited* (London: Penguin Books, 1951), 266.

1. Bill Gross, "The Single Biggest Reason Why Start-ups Succeed," *TED* (2015), https://www.ted.com/talks/bill_gross_the_single_biggest_reason_why_start_ups _succeed?language=en.

2. Mariusz Kozak, *Enacting Musical Time: The Bodily Experience of New Music* (Oxford: Oxford University Press, 2019), 10. French philosopher Henri Bergson (1859–1941) had a large influence on multiple English-speaking thinkers, especially William James.

3. Pek-Hooi Soh, "Dominant Design," in *The Palgrave Encyclopedia of Strategic Management Palgrave*, ed. Mie Augier and David Teece (London: Macmillan, 2016), https://doi.org/10.1057/978-1-349-94848-2_387-1.

4. Matthew Ball, *The Metaverse, and How It Will Revolutionize Everything* (New York: Liveright Publishing Corporation, 2022), 71–88.

5. As early as 1974, two of the "fathers of the Internet," Vint Cerf and Bob Kahn, used the term "internet" as a contraction of internetworking.

6. "Method and Apparatus for Constructing a Networking Database and System," United States Patent, January 16, 2001, https://patents.google.com/patent/US 6175831.

7. Pete Cashmore, "hi5, Another Massive Social Network," Mashable, July 16, 2006, https://mashable.com/2006/07/16/hi5-another-massive-social-network.

8. Schumpeter, *Capitalism, Socialism and Democracy*, 83–84.

9. Fadell, *Build*, 176.

10. Robert Merton, "Singletons and Multiples in Scientific Discovery: A Chapter in the Sociology of Science," *Proceedings of the American Philosophical Society* 105, no. 5 (1961): 470–86, http://www.jstor.org/stable/985546.

11. Barry M. Leiner, Vinton G. Cerf, David D. Clark, Robert E. Kahn, Leonard Kleinrock, Daniel C. Lynch, Jon Postel, Larry G. Roberts, and Stephen Wolff, "Brief History of the Internet," Internet Society, 1997, https://www.internetsociety.org/in ternet/history-internet/brief-history-internet/#Origins.

12. Howard Yu, *Leap: How to Thrive in a World Where Everything Can Be Copied* (New York: PublicAffairs, 2018), 102.

13. Say, *Treatise on Political Economy*, 89. While discussing how patents protect

innovators, Say also contended that there should be time limits for the benefit of consumers.

14. Friedrich Engels, *The Condition of the Working Class in England* (Oxford: Oxford University Press, 2009). Engels's philosophy developed independently from Marx, whom he first met on his way to Manchester, and then in August 1844—when their friendship really began.

15. R. L. Hills and A. J. Pacey, "The Measurement of Power in Early Steam-Driven Textile Mills," *Technology and Culture* 13, no. 1 (1972): 25–43, https://doi.org /10.2307/3102654.

16. Marcus Blosch and Jackie Fenn, "Understanding Gartner's Hype Cycles," Gartner, August 20, 2018, https://www.gartner.com/en/documents/3887767.

17. Blosch and Fenn, "Understanding Gartner's Hype Cycles."

18. Guy Kawasaki, *The Art of the Start 2.0: The Time-Tested, Battle-Hardened Guide for Anyone Starting Anything* (New York: Portfolio, 2015), 37.

19. Examples include Everett Rogers's approach to the stages of product adoption, Frank Bass's forecasting and growth model, Martin Fishbein and Icek Ajzen's theory of reasoned action (TRA), and diverse variations of Fred Davis and Richard Bagozzi's technology acceptance model (TAM), among many others.

20. Mikael Collan and Franck Tétard, "Lazy User Model: Solution Selection and Discussion about Switching Costs," in *Nordic Contributions in IS Research: Lecture Notes in Business Information Processing,* ed. Hannu Salmela and Anna Sell, vol. 86 (Berlin: Springer, 2011), https://doi.org/10.1007/978-3-642-22766-0_7.

21. Collan and Tétard, "Lazy User Model."

22. Collan and Tétard, "Lazy User Model."

23. Fabian Kröger, "Automated Driving in Its Social, Historical and Cultural Contexts," in *Autonomous Driving,* ed. Markus Maurer, J. Christian Gerdes, Barbara Lenz, and Hermann Winner (Berlin: Springer, 2016), https://doi.org/10.1007/978 -3-662-48847-8_3.

24. The levels of autonomy for autonomous cars are defined by SAE international: "Taxonomy and Definitions for Terms Related to Driving Automation Systems for On-Road Motor Vehicles," SAE International, June 15, 2018, https://www .sae.org/standards/content/j3016_201806/.

25. Daniel Gessner, "Experts Say We're Decades from Fully Autonomous Cars. Here's Why," *Business Insider,* July 22, 2020, https://www.businessinsider.com/self -driving-cars-fully-autonomous-vehicles-future-prediction-timeline-2019-8.

26. Jonathan Masters, "The Driverless Future, Autopia or Dystopia?," *Foreign Affairs,* August 17, 2017, https://www.foreignaffairs.com/articles/2017-08-17/driver less-future.

27. Lisa Johnston, "Waymo Isn't Building Cars; It's Building Drivers," Twice, Jan-

uary 11, 2019, https://www.twice.com/industry/waymo-isnt-building-cars-its-build ing-drivers.

28. "Who Will Win the Self-Driving Race? Here Are Eight Possibilities," *Ars Technica*, April 19, 2021, https://arstechnica.com/cars/2021/04/who-will-win-the -self-driving-race-here-are-8-possibilities.

29. John Markoff, "A Free and Simple Computer Link," *New York Times*, December 8, 1993, https://www.nytimes.com/1993/12/08/business/business-technology -a-free-and-simple-computer-link.html.

30. John Battelle, *The Search: How Google and Its Rivals Rewrote the Rules of Business and Transformed Our Culture* (New York: Portfolio, 2005).

31. "GoTo.com, Fiscal Year 1999," United States Securities and Exchange Commission, http://getfilings.com/00000950148-00-000415.html.

32. Stefanie Olsen, "Yahoo to Buy Overture for $1.63 Billion, CNET, July 14, 2003, https://www.cnet.com/tech/tech-industry/yahoo-to-buy-overture-for-1-63 -billion/.

33. Sergey Brin and Lawrence Page, "The Anatomy of a Large-Scale Hypertextual Web Search Engine," *Computer Networks* 30 (1998): 107–17, https://research .google/pubs/pub334/.

34. Will Oremus, "Google's Big Break," *Slate*, October 13, 2013, https://slate .com/business/2013/10/googles-big-break-how-bill-gross-goto-com-inspired-the -adwords-business-model.html.

35. "Total Number of Websites," Internet live stats, https://www.internetlivestats .com/total-number-of-websites.

36. Google was not the advertising machine that it is today. Its acquisition in 2008 of a major advertisement company, DoubleClick, changed the company's perspective.

37. Brin and Page, "Anatomy of a Large-Scale Hypertextual Web Search Engine," 1.

38. "Google Search Statistics," Internet live stats, https://www.internetlivestats .com/google-search-statistics/.

39. The word was popularized by Edward Kasner and James Roy Newman in *Mathematics and the Imagination* (New York: Simon and Schuster, 1940).

40. Brin and Page, "Anatomy of a Large-Scale Hypertextual Web Search Engine," 2.

41. Gottfried Wilhelm Leibniz, "The Principles of Nature and of Grace, Based on Reason," in *Discourse on Metaphysics and Other Writings*, trans. Robert Latta and George R. Montgomery, ed. Peter Loptson (Peterborough, ON: Broadview Press, 2012), 110.

42. Greg Satell, "Here's What Futurists Always Seem to Get Wrong," *Inc.*,

March 31, 2019, https://www.inc.com/greg-satell/4-things-that-pundits-who-predict
-future-always-seem-to-get-wrong.html.

43. James Currier, "The Paradox of Genius: Why Long-Term Thinking Wins,"
NfX, March 2021, https://www.nfx.com/post/paradox-of-genius.

44. Samuel Delany, *The American Shore: Meditations on a Tale of Science Fiction
by Thomas M. Disch—"Angouleme"* (Middletown, CT: Wesleyan University Press,
2014), 36.

45. Michael Cox and Richard Alm, "You Are What You Spend," *New York Times*,
February 10, 2008, https://www.nytimes.com/2008/02/10/opinion/10cox.html.

46. Rita McGrath, "The Pace of Technology Adoption Is Speeding Up," *Harvard Business Review*, November 25, 2013, updated September 25, 2019, https://hbr
.org/2013/11/the-pace-of-technology-adoption-is-speeding-up.

47. Today, this discrepancy survives under a new form. See Emily Vogels,
"Some Digital Divides Persist between Rural, Urban and Suburban America," Pew
Research Center, August 19, 2021, https://www.pewresearch.org/fact-tank/2021
/08/19/some-digital-divides-persist-between-rural-urban-and-suburban-america/.

48. Frank Hobbs and Nicole Stoops, "Demographic Trends in the 20th Century," United States Census Bureau, November 2002, https://www.census.gov
/history/pdf/1970suburbs.pdf.

49. Carl Benedikt Frey and Michael Osborne, "Technology at Work: The Future of Innovation and Employment," Oxford Martin School, February 17, 2015,
https://www.oxfordmartin.ox.ac.uk/publications/technology-at-work-the-future-of
-innovation-and-employment/.

50. Dan Milmo, "ChatGPT Reaches 100 Million Users Two Months after
Launch," *Guardian*, February 2, 2023, https://www.theguardian.com/technology
/2023/feb/02/chatgpt-100-million-users-open-ai-fastest-growing-app.

51. "Global EV Outlook 2022," International Energy Agency, May 2022, https://
www.iea.org/reports/global-ev-outlook-2022.

52. The two atomic bombs dropped on Japan in 1945 killed and maimed hundreds of thousands of people, and their effects are still being felt today; see "Hiroshima and Nagasaki Bombings," ICAN, https://www.icanw.org/hiroshima_and
_nagasaki_bombings.

53. Peter Diamandis and Steven Kotler, *The Future Is Faster Than You Think:
How Converging Technologies Are Transforming Business, Industries, and Our Lives*
(New York: Simon and Schuster, 2020).

54. Ray Kurzweil, "The Law of Accelerating Returns," Kurzweil, March 7, 2001,
https://www.kurzweilai.net/the-law-of-accelerating-returns.

55. *Doctor Who*, "Blink" (2007), IMDb, https://www.imdb.com/title/tt1000
252/characters/nm0855039.

56. As defined by Reid Hoffman and Chris Yeh: "Blitzscaling is a strategy and a set of techniques for driving and managing extremely rapid growth that prioritize speed over efficiency in an environment of uncertainty. Put another way, it's an accelerant that allows your company to grow at a furious pace that knocks the competition out of the water." See Reid Hoffman and Chris Yeh, *Blitzscaling: The Lightning-Fast Path to Building Massively Valuable Companies* (New York: Currency, 2018), 12.

57. In 1965, Intel's co-founder Gordon Moore forecast that the number of transistors that could be packed into a given unit of space would double about every two years. Also see David Rotman, "We're Not Prepared for the End of Moore's Law," *MIT Technology Review*, February 24, 2020, https://www.technologyreview.com /2020 /02/24/905789/were-not-prepared-for-the-end-of-moores-law.

CHAPTER 5: WHAT IS A WINDOW OF OPPORTUNITY?

Epigraph: Virginia Woolf, *Three Guineas* (London: Penguin Books, 1938), 26.

1. Many devices are now called "e-bikes." Here, I speak of devices that are pedaled by the rider.

2. At about the same time, Georges Juzan created a similar bicycle in France that he named "bicyclette."

3. Frances Willard, *A Wheel within a Wheel: How I Learned to Ride the Bicycle, with Some Reflections by the Way* (New York: Fleming H. Revell Company, 1895).

4. In France, cross-dressing was prohibited in 1800. Women wanting to wear trousers or dress like men had to obtain an authorization from the Prefecture of Police.

5. Sexist and racist organizations like the League of American Wheelmen, founded in 1880, banned women, workers, and nonwhites from their clubs. The democratization of the bicycle espoused the contours of societal divides and never came close to becoming an equalizer.

6. Kevin Desmond, *Electric Motorcycles and Bicycles: A History Including Scooters, Tricycles, Segways and Monocycles* (Jefferson, NC: McFarland and Company, 2018).

7. Axel Josephsson, "Bicycles and Tricycles," United States Census, 323–39, https://www2.census.gov/prod2/decennial/documents/05457254v1och3.pdf.

8. Cadie Thompson, "How the Electric Car Became the Future of Transportation," *Business Insider*, July 2, 2017, https://www.businessinsider.com/electric-car -history-2017-5.

9. Stephen Davies, "The Great Horse-Manure Crisis of 1894," Foundation for Economic Education, September 1, 2004, https://fee.org/articles/the-great-horse -manure-crisis-of-1894/.

10. Susan Shaheen, Adam Cohen, Nelson Chan, and Apaar Bansal, "Chapter 13: Sharing Strategies: Carsharing, Shared Micromobility (Bikesharing and Scooter

Sharing), Transportation Network Companies, Microtransit, and Other Innovative Mobility Modes," in *Transportation, Land Use, and Environmental Planning*, ed. Elizabeth Deakin (n.p.: Elsevier, 2020), 237–62, https://doi.org/10.1016/B978-0-12 -815167-9.00013-X.

11. Rhea Patel, "Consumers Reveal Where Big Tech and Health Tech Wearables Are Winning and Losing," Insider Intelligence, March 7, 2022, https://www .emarketer.com/content/consumers-reveal-where-big-tech-health-tech-wearables -winning-losing.

12. Richard Broxton Onians, *The Origins of European Thought: About the Body, the Mind, the Soul, the World, Time and Fate* (Cambridge, UK: Cambridge University Press, 1951).

13. James Kinneavy and Catherine Eskin, "Kairos in Aristotle's Rhetoric," *Written Communication* 17, no. 3 (2000): 432–44, https://doi.org/10.1177/0741088 300017003005.

14. Michel Foucault, *The Order of Things*, trans. Alan Sheridan (New York: Vintage Books, 1994), 168. The book was originally written in French under the title *Les Mots et les choses* (Paris: Editions Gallimard, 1966).

15. Lawrence Lessig, *Remix: Making Art and Commerce Thrive in the Hybrid Economy* (New York: Penguin Press, 2008).

16. Vaclav Smil, *Growth: From Microorganisms to Megacities* (Cambridge, MA: MIT Press, 2019), 393.

17. Everett Rogers, *Diffusion of Innovations*, 5th ed. (New York: Free Press, 2003), 281.

18. Rogers, *Diffusion of Innovations*, 35.

19. The expression comes from Geoffrey Moore's book *Crossing the Chasm: Marketing and Selling Technology Projects to Mainstream Customers* (New York: HarperCollins Publishers, 1991).

20. Edward Sapir, *Language: An Introduction to the Study of Speech* (New York: Harcourt, Brace and Company, 1921), 165–66.

21. Gabriel Tarde, *Les lois de l'imitation*, 3rd ed. (Paris: Félix Alcan, 1900), 152. Translated from the French by Delbourg-Delphis.

22. Drucker, *Innovation and Entrepreneurship*, 35.

23. Drucker, *Innovation and Entrepreneurship*, 120.

24. Drucker, *Innovation and Entrepreneurship*, 35.

25. In the early 1970s, Robert Metcalfe, David Boggs, Chuck Thacker, and Butler Lampson co-developed Ethernet at Xerox PARC. When Robert Metcalfe left Xerox, he started 3Com, and his name is now familiar to a wider public because of "Metcalfe's Law" (which is more a rule of thumb than a scientific law). It states that the value of a network is proportional to the square of the number of nodes

(computers or users) in it. For one of the clearest descriptions of the various aspects of network effects in business, see James Currier, "The Network Effects Manual: 13 Different Network Effects (and Counting)," Medium, January 9, 2018, https://medium.com/@nfx/the-network-effects-manual-13-different-network-effects-and-counting-a3e07b23017d.

26. Chuck Baker, "The Brownie: The One That Started It All!," Brownie Camera, accessed July 16, 2023, http://www.brownie-camera.com/5.shtml.

27. "Microsoft's Ballmer Not Impressed with Apple iPhone," CNBC, January 17, 2007, https://www.cnbc.com/id/16671712.

28. For a deeper understanding of the history behind virtual, augmented, and mixed reality as well as the metaverse, I recommend Irena Cronin and Robert Scoble, *The Infinite Retina: Spatial Computing, Augmented Reality, and How a Collision of New Technologies Are Bringing about the Next Tech Revolution* (Birmingham, UK: Packt Publishing, 2020).

29. Neil Stephenson, *Snow Crash* (New York: Bantam Books, 1992), 65.

30. Anisse Gross, "What's the Problem with Google Glass?," *New Yorker*, March 4, 2014, https://www.newyorker.com/business/currency/whats-the-problem-with-google-glass.

31. "G.D. Searle Develops the Pill," *American Experience*, PBS, https://www.pbs.org/wgbh/americanexperience/features/pill-g-d-searle-develops-pill/.

32. Patrick McGinnis, *Fear of Missing Out: Practical Decision-Making in a World of Overwhelming Choice* (Naperville, IL: Sourcebooks, 2020). McGinnis created these acronyms in 2004. See "Social Theory at HBS: McGinnis' Two FOs," *Harbus*, May 10, 2004, https://harbus.org/2004/social-theory-at-hbs-2749.

33. "Steve Jobs Introduces iPhone in 2007," YouTube video, https://www.youtube.com/watch?v=MnrJzXM7a60&t=266s.

34. Rogers, *Diffusion of Innovations*, 15–16.

35. Thanks to recent publications, the scope of Bush's influence has been restored. See Walter Isaacson, *The Innovators: How a Group of Hackers, Geniuses, and Geeks Created the Digital Revolution* (New York: Simon and Schuster, 2014).

36. David Martínez Turégano and Robert Marschinski, "Electronics Lead Concerns over the EU's Declining Share in Global Manufacturing Value Chains," VoxEU.org, August 11, 2020, https://voxeu.org/article/eu-s-declining-share-global-manufacturing-value-chains.

37. Andy Grove, "How America Can Create Jobs," *Bloomberg*, July 1, 2010, https://www.bloomberg.com/news/articles/2010-07-01/andy-grove-how-america-can-create-jobs.

38. Amy Burke, Abigail Okrent, and Katherine Hale, "The State of U.S. Science and Engineering 2022," *National Scientific Board, Science and Engineering Indicators,*

January 18, 2022, https://ncses.nsf.gov/pubs/nsb20221/u-s-and-global-research
-and-development.

39. Andrew Hargadon, "The Challenge of Innovating in Brownfield versus
Greenfield Markets," AndrewHargadon.com, March 22, 2012, https:// andrewha
rgadon.com/2012/03/22/the-challenge-of-innovating-in-brownfield-versus-green
field-markets/. For details on how Edison navigated these constraints in Chicago,
see Harold L. Platt, *The Electric City: Energy and the Growth of the Chicago Area,
1880–1930* (Chicago: University of Chicago Press, 1991).

40. "China's Economic Dilemmas in the 1990s: The Problem of Reforms,
Modernisation and Interdependence," *Joint Economic Committee, Congress of the
United States* (April 1991): 16, https://www.jec.senate.gov/reports/102nd%20Con
gress/China's%20Economic%20Dilemmas%20in%20the%201990s%20-%20
The%20Problems%20of%20Reforms,%20Modernization,%20and%20Inter
dependence%20Volume%20I%20(1539).pdf.

41. Steve Blank, *The Four Steps to the Epiphany: Successful Strategies for Products
That Win,* 5th ed. (Pescadero, CA: K&S Ranch, 2013). See also Steve Blank and Bob
Dorf, *The Startup Owner's Manual: The Step-by-Step Guide for Building a Great Com-
pany* (Pescadero, CA: K&S Ranch, 2012).

42. The Webvan story has been the subject of multiple case studies. The best
one remains Steve Blank's in *The Four Steps to the Epiphany,* chap. 1.

43. Andrew Hayward, "After Backlash, Ubisoft Calls Gaming NFTs a 'Major
Change That Will Take Time,'" Decrypt, December 21, 2021, https://decrypt.co/88
880/after-backlash-ubisoft-calls-gaming-nfts-a-major-change-that-will-take-time.

CHAPTER 6: CAN COMPETING INNOVATIONS COEXIST?

Epigraph: Jonathan Swift, *Gulliver's Travels* (London: Penguin Publishing
Group, 2003 [orig. anon. 1726]).

1. I will use "personal computer" and "desktop computer" interchangeably in
this chapter, as was the case in the 1980s, although there is a nuance. "Desktop computer" means that we are speaking of a personal computer that is stationary, that is, on
a desk. "Personal computer" can also refer to a laptop.

2. Masatoshi Shima was first employed by Busicom, a Japanese company,
which had a contract with Intel for the production of custom microchips to better
compete in the pocket calculator market initiated by Texas Instruments. Shima left
Busicom to join Intel and later followed Faggin at Zilog.

3. David Sanger, "Bailing Out the Mainframe Industry," *New York Times,* February 5, 1984, https://www.nytimes.com/1984/02/05/business/bailing-out-of-the
-mainframe-industry.html.

4. MITS stands for Micro Instrumentation and Telemetry Systems. The company, founded by Ed Roberts and Forrest Mims in 1969, was acquired by Pertec Computer in 1977.

5. Jeremy Reimer, "Total Share: 30 Years of Personal Computer Market Share Figures," *Ars Technica*, December 14, 2005, https://arstechnica.com/features/2005/12/total-share/.

6. Started by Gordon French and Fred Moore, the Homebrew Computer Club wielded an influence that has been recounted in multiple books and articles. For a summary, see "The Homebrew Computer Club," *Computer Museum History*, https://www.computerhistory.org/revolution/personal-computers/17/312.

7. Carl Helmers, "A Nybble on the Apple," *Byte Magazine*, April 1977, https://archive.org/details/byte-magazine-1977-04/page/n111/mode/2up?view=theater.

8. Walter Isaacson, *Steve Jobs* (New York: Simon and Schuster, 2011), 73.

9. Isaacson, *Steve Jobs*, 75–78.

10. Steven Levy, "The Apple of My Eye," AtariArchives.org, https://www.atariarchives.org/deli/the_apple_of_my_eye.php.

11. Otto Friedrich, "The Computer Moves In," *TIME*, January 3, 1983, http://content.time.com/time/magazine/article/0,9171,953632,00.html, 3.

12. David Bunnell, "The Man behind the Machine? A PC Exclusive Interview with Software Guru Bill Gates," *PC Magazine*, February–March 1982, https://www.pcmag.com/archive/the-man-behind-the-machine-21822.

13. Harry McCracken, "Apple's Sales Grew 150x between 1977-1980," *Fast Company*, April 1, 2016, https://www.fastcompany.com/4001956/apples-sales-grew-150x-between-1977-1980-2.

14. "Steve Jobs Showcases Macintosh 24-JAN-1984," YouTube video, January 24, 1984, https://www.youtube.com/watch?v=4KkENSYkMgs.

15. Ann Morrison, "Apple Bites Back," *Fortune Magazine*, February 20, 1984, https://fortune.com/1984/02/20/apple-bites-back-fortune-1984.

16. Andy Hertzfeld, *Revolution in the Valley: The Insanely Great Story of How the Mac Was Made* (Sebastopol, CA: O'Reilly Media, 2005).

17. The head of the Computer Science Division was Robert Taylor, formerly the director of the Advanced Research Projects Agency (ARPA) Information Processing Techniques Office (later called DARPA). He built up Xerox PARC, with many top scientists coming from his own ARPA networks, the SRI International's Augmentation Research Center, and various Bay Area institutions.

18. Lawrence Curran, "The Compatibility Craze," *Byte Magazine*, February 1984, https://archive.org/details/byte-magazine-1984-02/page/n5/mode/2up?view=theater.

19. Andy Hertzfeld, "Can We Keep the Skies Safe?," January 1984, *Folklore*, https://www.folklore.org/StoryView.py?project=Macintosh&story=Can_We_Keep _The_Skies_Safe?.txt.

20. Hans Rosling, Anna Rosling Rönnlund, and Ola Rosling, *Factfulness: Ten Reasons We're Wrong about the World–and Why Things Are Better Than You* (New York: Flatiron Books, 2018), 38.

21. Rosling, Rönnlund, and Rosling, *Factfulness*, 41.

22. "The Computer for the Rest of Us: The Real Genius," YouTube video, accessed July 4, 2023, https://www.youtube.com/watch?v=oFOfSi2vwKE.

23. This opposition was coined by Jack Tramiel, the founder of Commodore, whose mantra was to build computers for the masses, not the classes.

24. Reimer, "Total Share."

25. "Steve Jobs Showcases Macintosh 24-JAN-1984."

26. Corey Sandler, "We Look with Automatic Skepticism upon Advertised Claims of 'PC Compatibility,'" *PC Magazine*, June 1983, 33. Google Books.

27. Tim Bajarin, "Attack of the Clones: How IBM Lost Control of the PC Market," *Forbes*, August 25, 2021, https://www.forbes.com/sites/timbajarin/2021/08/25 /attack-of-the-clones-how-ibm-lost-control-of-the-pc-market/?sh=7a2b8d625b81.

28. Phil Lemmons, "IBM and Its Personal Computers," *Byte Magazine*, September 9, 1984, https://archive.org/details/byte-magazine-1984-09/page/n3/mode /2up?view=theater.

29. Reimer, "Total Share."

30. Stephen Howard and Raines Cohen, "The State of the User Group," *BMUG Newsletter*, Fall/Winter 1987.

31. Reese Jones, "BMUG after One Year," *BMUG Newsletter*, Fall 1985.

32. "Macworld 1997: The Return of Steve Jobs," YouTube video, accessed July 5, 2023, https://www.youtube.com/watch?v=IOs6hnTI4lw.

33. Dan Farber, "What Steve Jobs Really Meant When He Said 'Good Artists Copy; Great Artists Steal,'" CNET, January 28, 2014, https://www.cnet.com/tech/tech -industry/what-steve-jobs-really-meant-when-he-said-good-artists-copy-great-artists -steal.

34. Title of a book by Chip and Dan Heath, *Made to Stick: Why Some Ideas Survive and Others Die* (New York: Random House, 2007).

35. "Macworld 1997: The Return of Steve Jobs."

36. Rob Siltanen, "The Real Story behind Apple's 'Think Different' Campaign," *Forbes*, December 14, 2011, https://www.forbes.com/sites/onmarketing/2011/12/14 /the-real-story-behind-apples-think-different-campaign/?sh=6b0b01cf62ab.

37. Karl Popper, *The Poverty of Historicism*, 2nd ed. (London: Routledge Classics, 2015).

38. Tim Harford, "How Computing's First 'Killer App' Changed Everything," May 22, 2019, BBC News, https://www.bbc.com/news/business-47802280.

39. Robert Cringely, *Accidental Empires: How the Boys of Silicon Valley Make Their Millions, Battle Foreign Competition, and Still Can't Get a Date*, repr. ed. (New York: Harper Business, 1991), chap. 6.

40. William J. Abernathy and Kim B. Clark, "Innovation: Mapping the Winds of Creative Destruction," *Research Policy* 14, no. 1 (1985): 3–22, https://doi.org/10.1016/0048-7333(85)90021-6, 21.

41. Jens Beckert, *Imagined Futures: Fictional Expectations and Capitalist Dynamics* (Cambridge, MA: Harvard University Press, 2016), 173.

42. Beckert, 179.

43. Mark Sullivan, "Microsoft's Metaverse Vision Is Becoming Clear—and Makes Sense," *Fast Company*, January 27, 2022, https://www.fastcompany.com/90716389/microsoft-activision-metaverse.

44. Teams is the name of Microsoft's business communication platform, and Mesh is Microsoft's mixed-reality collaboration software.

45. The expression "Velvet Revolution" is the English translation of an expression coined by economist and politician Rita Klímová to designate the nonviolent transition of power in (then) Czechoslovakia in 1989.

CHAPTER 7: WHY IS STANDING OUT CHALLENGING?

Epigraph: Elizabeth Gaskell, *North and South* (London: Walter Scott, Limited Paternoster Square, 1854–55), chap. 2.

1. The expression, coined in 1992, is usually attributed to John Sculley, then Apple's CEO.

2. Ivan Edward Sutherland, "Sketchpad: A Man-Machine Graphical Communication System" (PhD diss., Massachusetts Institute of Technology, Dept. of Electrical Engineering, Cambridge, MA, 1963), https://dspace.mit.edu/handle/1721.1/14979.

3. Hewitt Crane developed several products at SRI and later co-founded Communication Intelligence Corporation (CIC) to commercialize "Jot," a handwriting recognition software that was later acquired by Palm.

4. Alain Kay, "A Personal Computer for Children of All Ages," *ACM '72: Proceedings of the ACM Annual Conference* 1, no. 1 (August 1, 1972), https://dl.acm.org/doi/10.1145/800193.1971922.

5. Alan Kay and Adele Goldberg, "Personal Dynamic Media," in *Computer* 10, no. 3 (March 1977): 31–41, https://ieeexplore.ieee.org/document/1646405.

6. Matthew Panzarino, "Rare Full Recording of 1983 Steve Jobs Speech Reveals Apple Had Been Working on iPad for 27 Years," Next Web, October 2, 2012, https://

thenextweb.com/apple/2012/10/02/rare-full-recording-of-1983-steve-jobs-speech -reveals-apple-had-been-working-on-ipad-for-27-years.

7. One of the first reports about General Magic's products was written by Steven Levy, "Bill and Andy's Excellent Adventure II," *Wired*, April 1, 1994, https://www .wired.com/1994/04/general-magic/.

8. A design consultancy, Frog Design was founded in 1969 by Hartmut Esslinger. It became the ne plus ultra of design quality. Esslinger's first client in consumer electronics was Wega, a German company acquired by Sony in 1975, and was famous in Europe for the elegance of its high-quality stereo equipment.

9. Pam Savage, "Designing a GUI for Business Telephone Users," in *Interactions* 2, no. 1 (January 1995), *ACM Digital Library*, https://doi.org/10.1145/208143 .208157.

10. Eric Bangeman, "PDA Sales Continue to Slide," *Ars Technica*, February 3, 2005, https://arstechnica.com/uncategorized/2005/02/4583-2.

11. Eric Bangeman, "Smartphones Are Leaving PDAs in the Dust," *Ars Technica*, October 10, 2006, https://arstechnica.com/gadgets/2006/10/7944.

12. The term was originally applied to Netscape. The team kept on adding features like mad to fight Microsoft Internet Explorer, but the product became unstable and lost its prestige.

13. "Steve Jobs iPhone 2007 Presentation," YouTube video, accessed July 6, 2023, https://www.youtube.com/watch?v=vN4U5FqrOdQ.

14. Bangeman, "PDA Sales Continue to Slide."

15. The iPhone trademark belonged to Cisco when it acquired InfoGear in 2000. See Steven Musil, "Apple, Cisco Settle iPhone Trademark Lawsuit," CNET, February 22, 2007, https://www.cnet.com/culture/apple-cisco-settle-iphone-trademark-lawsuit/.

16. "Steve Jobs iPhone 2007 Presentation."

17. "Apple Chooses Cingular as Exclusive U.S. Carrier for Its Revolutionary iPhone," Apple Newsroom, January 9, 2007, https://www.apple.com/newsroom/2007 /01/09Apple-Chooses-Cingular-as-Exclusive-US-Carrier-for-Its-Revolutionary -iPhone.

18. Fred Vogelstein, "The Untold Story: How Steve Blew Up the Wireless Industry," *Wired*, January 9, 2008, https://www.wired.com/2008/01/ff-iphone/.

19. Federica Laricchia, "Mobile Operating Systems' Market Share Worldwide from 1st Quarter 2009 to 4th Quarter 2022," Statista, November 16, 2022, https://www.statista.com/statistics/272698/global-market-share-held-by-mobile -operating-systems-since-2009.

20. Federica Laricchia, "Quarterly Smartphone Market Share Worldwide by Vendor 2009–2022," Statista, November 5, 2022, https://www.statista.com/statistics/271 496/global-market-share-held-by-smartphone-vendors-since-4th-quarter-2009.

21. Andrew Orr, "Apple Continuing Command of Global Smartphone Profits, and the Lead Is Growing," Apple Insider, September 29, 2022, https://appleinsider .com/articles/22/09/29/apple-continuing-command-of-global-smartphone-profits -and-the-lead-is-growing.

22. Harry McCracken, "Facebook Gets in Your Ray-Bans: A First Look at Its New Smart Glasses," *Fast Company*, September 9, 2021, https://www.fastcompany .com/90673958/facebook-smart-glasses-ray-ban-stories-luxottica.

23. James Joyce, *Ulysses* (Paris: Shakespeare and Company, 1922), 683.

CHAPTER 8: CAN DAVID THRIVE IN GOLIATH'S WORLD?

Epigraph: Oscar Wilde, *The Selfish Giant* (Crows Nest: Allen & Unwin, 2012), 31.

1. Saul Bellow, *Letters* (New York: Viking, 2010), 414.

2. Michael Mauboussin, Dan Callahan, and Darius Majd, "Corporate Longevity, Index Turnover and Corporate Performance," Credit Suisse, February 2017, https:// plus.credit-suisse.com/rpc4/ravDocView?docid=V6yoSB2AF-WErice.

3. Mauboussin, Callahan, and Majd, "Corporate Longevity, Index Turnover and Corporate Performance."

4. Andrea Murphy, "America's Largest Private Companies 2019," *Forbes*, December 17, 2019, https://www.forbes.com/sites/andreamurphy/2019/12/17/americas -largest-private-companies-2019/#529a0d5a5261.

5. Charlotte Hu, "Pharmaceutical Companies Are Backing Away from a Growing Threat That Could Kill 10 Million," *Business Insider*, July 21, 2018, https://www .businessinsider.com/major-pharmaceutical-companies-dropping-antibiotic -projects-superbugs-2018-7.

6. Christina Jewett, "F.D.A.'s Drug Industry Fees Fuel Concerns over Influence," *New York Times*, September 15, 2022, https://www.nytimes.com/2022/09/15 /health/fda-drug-industry-fees.html.

7. Priti Krishtel and John Arnold, "How Big Pharma Keeps Drug Prices High," Pitchfork Economics, January 7, 2020, https://pitchforkeconomics.com/episode /how-big-pharma-keeps-drug-prices-high-with-priti-krishtel-and-john-arnold.

8. Florian Ederer and Song Ma, "Do Companies Buy Competitors in Order to Shut Them Down?," *Yale Insights*, June 4, 2018, https://insights.som.yale.edu /insights/do-companies-buy-competitors-in-order-to-shut-them-down.

9. For the context of the quote, see Ellen Terrell, "When a Quote Is Not (Exactly) a Quote: General Motors," Library of Congress, April 22, 2016, https://blogs.loc.gov /inside_adams/2016/04/when-a-quote-is-not-exactly-a-quote-general-motors.

10. W. Edwards Deming, *Out of the Crisis: Quality, Productivity and Competitive Position*, repr. ed. (Cambridge, MA: MIT Press, 2000).

11. Hobart Rowen, "Japan's Secret: W. Edwards Deming," *Washington Post*, December 23, 1993, https://www.washingtonpost.com/archive/opinions/1993/12/23

/japans-secret-w-edwards-deming/b69b8c00-4c5d-483a-b95e-4aeb1d94
d2c6/.

12. "Factbox: U.S. States Woo Automakers with $17 Billion in Subsidies since
1976," Reuters, August 4, 2017, https://www.reuters.com/article/us-toyota-mazda
-jobs-factbox/factbox-u-s-states-woo-automakers-with-17-billion-in-subsidies-since
-1976-idUSKBN1AK2BI. The data provided came from a study by Good Jobs First,
a Washington, DC–based nonprofit tracking the use of state and local economic
development subsidies and promoting accountability in economic development.

13. Jerry Hirsch, "Elon Musk's Growing Empire Is Fueled by $4.9 Billion in
Government Subsidies," Good Jobs First, May 30, 2015, https://www.goodjobsfirst
.org/news/elon-musks-growing-empire-fueled-49-billion-government-subsidies.

14. Jordan Malter, Kate Strague, and Lora Kolodny, "How Government Policies
and Taxpayer Money Have Helped Elon Musk and Tesla," CNBC, October 22, 2018,
https://www.cnbc.com/2018/10/21/how-government-policies-and-taxpayer-money
-have-helped-musk-and-tesla.html.

15. The phrase reportedly originated with Ralph Nader in the 1950s. See also
Ralph Nader, *Cutting Corporate Welfare* (New York: Seven Stories Press, 2011).

16. Greg LeRoy, Carolyn Fryberger, Kasia Tarczynska, Thomas Cafcas, Elizabeth Bird, and Philip Mattera, "Shortchanging Small Business: How Big Businesses
Dominate State Economic Development Incentives," Good Jobs First, October 2015,
http://www.goodjobsfirst.org/sites/default/files/docs/pdf/shortchanging.pdf.

17. "Overcoming the Innovation Readiness Gap, Most Innovative Companies
2021," Boston Consulting Group, https://web-assets.bcg.com/eb/93/cfbea0054424
82b0adc64b9f499f/bcg-most-innovative-companies-2021-apr-2021-r.pdf.

18. "16 Years of the Most Innovative Companies," Boston Consulting Group,
https://www.bcg.com/publications/most-innovative-companies-historical-rank
ings.

19. For a simple explanation of the differences between platform and pipe models,
see Sangeet Paul Choudary, "Why Business Models Fail: Pipes vs. Platforms," *Wired*,
October 2013, https://www.wired.com/insights/2013/10/why-business-models-fail
-pipes-vs-platforms/.

20. In 1839, Charles Goodyear, who worked at the Eagle India Rubber Company, had discovered that combining rubber and sulfur over a hot stove caused
the rubber to vulcanize, an invention that he patented. Courts could not establish
that Hancock had copied Goodyear. The company bearing his name was founded in
1898, almost forty years after Charles Goodyear's death, by Frank and Charles Seiber-
ling. Today Goodyear is one of the top four tire manufacturers, along with Bridge-
stone (founded in 1931 in Japan), Michelin, and Continental (founded in 1871 in
Germany).

21. Dunlop was named after John Dunlop, a Scottish veterinary surgeon living in Ireland who discovered the pneumatic tire principle. These tires were sold in 1889 through a company called the Pneumatic Tyre and Booth's Cycle Agency, later renamed the Dunlop Pneumatic Tyre Company.

22. "Pneumatique Tire," United States Patent Office, May 16, 1893, https://patentimages.storage.googleapis.com/a4/07/df/30b3d4e578fa79/US497453.pdf.

23. The idea came to Edouard Michelin when a pile of tires made him think of the silhouette of a man. He commissioned several artists and selected Marius Rossillon, aka O'Galop, who was well known in the world of humor magazines. Above the head of the Bibendum character, the sentence "Nunc est Bibendum" (It's now that you must have a drink) is part of a text by Latin poet Horatius and is transformed at the bottom at the illustration into "The Michelin tire drinks the obstacle." The reason the original poster includes this reference to drinking is probably because O'Galop had originally drawn the character for a beer company.

24. The connection between couture, accessories, and perfume wasn't new, but lag times were longer (as was the case for Paul Poiret, who established his couture house in 1903 but created his first perfume in 1911). Lag times became shorter over time. For example, Dior, whose couture house was established in 1946, launched his first perfume in 1947 (Miss Dior).

25. "FTC to Examine Past Acquisitions by Large Technology Companies," Federal Trade Commission, February 11, 2020, https://www.ftc.gov/news-events/press-releases/2020/02/ftc-examine-past-acquisitions-large-technology-companies.

26. Dana Mattioli and Cara Lombardo, "Amazon Met with Startups about Investing, Then Launched Competing Products," *Wall Street Journal*, July 23, 2020, https://www.wsj.com/articles/amazon-tech-startup-echo-bezos-alexa-investment-fund-11595520249.

27. Mariana Mazzucato, *The Entrepreneurial State: Debunking Public vs. Private Sector Myths* (New York: PublicAffairs, 2015). I also recommend her later book *The Value of Everything: Making and Taking in the Global Economy* (New York: PublicAffairs, 2018).

28. Joseph Stiglitz, *Globalization and Its Discontents Revisited: Anti-globalization in the Era of Trump*, repr. (New York: W. W. Norton & Company, 2017).

29. Asa Fitch and Stu Woo, "The U.S. vs. China: Who Is Winning the Key Technology Battles? China Leads in 5G, but the U.S. Has an Edge in Other Crucial Niches—for Now," *Wall Street Journal*, April 12, 2020, https://www.wsj.com/articles/the-u-s-vs-china-who-is-winning-the-key-technology-battles-11586548597.

30. For a history of the space, see Wilson J. Warren, *Tied to the Great Packing Machine: The Midwest and Meatpacking* (Iowa City: University of Iowa Press, 2007).

31. Thomas L. Friedman, "Iowa Beef Revolutionized Meat-Packing industry,"

New York Times, June 2, 1981, https://www.nytimes.com/1981/06/02/business/iowa
-beef-revolutionized-meat-packing-industry.html. Note that things happened the
other way around: Henry Ford was inspired by the slaughtering business. His visit
to a Chicago slaughterhouse made him understand the value of using a moving
conveyor system and fixed workstations. The most technologically advanced meat-
packer at the time was Swift, founded by Gustavus Swift, who also created an ice-
cooled railroad car.

32. "Now, Meatpacking in the U.S.: Still a "Jungle" Out There?," article, PBS,
December 15, 2006, accessed July 25, 2023, https://www.pbs.org/now/shows/250
/meat-packing.html.

33. Swift, Armour, and Cudahy had expanded their business by using animal
by-products to create soaps, fertilizers, glue, and pharmaceutical products. For example, during the 1950s, Dial, produced by Armour, became the best-selling de-
odorant soap in the United States.

34. Bill Ganzel, "IBP, Boxed Beef & a New 'Big Four,'" *Wessels Living History
Farm* (2007), accessed July 25, 2023, https://livinghistoryfarm.org/farming-in-the
-1950s/making-money/ibp-boxed-beef/.

35. For example, see Kenneth Vogel, "Google Critic Ousted from Think Tank
Funded by the Tech Giant," *New York Times*, August 30, 2017, https://www.nytimes
.com/2017/08/30/us/politics/eric-schmidt-google-new-america.html.

36. Daniel Fisher, "For Google Chairman Schmidt, Maybe Monopoly Was the
Goal," *Forbes*, April 27, 2012, https://www.forbes.com/sites/danielfisher/2012/04
/27/for-google-chairman-schmidt-maybe-monopoly-was-the-goal/#25f29cd23cbd.

37. See chapter 1.

38. Adams Nager, David M. Hart, Stephen Ezell, and Robert D. Atkinson, "The
Demographics of Innovation in the United States," Information Technology and
Innovation Foundation, February 25, 2016, https://itif.org/publications/2016/02
/24/demographics-innovation-united-states/.

39. The 2020 global start-up ecosystem report indicates that the global start-up
ecosystem created nearly $3.8 trillion in value (the World's GDP in 2021 was 96.1
trillion USD). See "The Global Startup Ecosystem Report, GSER 2021," Startup
Genome, https://startupgenome.com/report/gser2021.

40. Gary Klein, "Performing a Project Premortem," *Harvard Business Review*,
September 2007 issue, https://hbr.org/2007/09/performing-a-project-premortem.

CHAPTER 9: WHERE IS THE RIGHT PLACE?

Epigraph: Rudyard Kipling, "The Law of the Jungle," *The Jungle Book*, https://
www.poetry.com/poem/33479/the-law-of-the-jungle.

1. Eric Weiner, *The Geography of Genius: A Search for the World's Most Cre-*

ative Places from Ancient Athens to Silicon Valley (New York: Simon and Schuster, 2016).

2. What we now know as the Silk Road had no name until a nineteenth-century German geographer, Ferdinand von Richthofen, called it die Seidenstrasse. For a representation of its various routes, see "Network of the Silk Road Cities," United Nations, https://en.unesco.org/silkroad/silkroad-interactive-map.

3. Alfred Marshall, *Principles of Economics* (London: Macmillan and Co., 1895); Michael Porter, *The Competitive Advantage of Nations* (New York: Free Press, 1990).

4. Michael Porter, "Clusters and the New Economics of Competition," *Harvard Business Review*, November–December 1998, https://hbr.org/1998/11/clusters-and -the-new-economics-of-competition.

5. David Laws, "Silicon Valley: A Century of Entrepreneurial Innovation," Computer History Museum, September 20, 2016, https://computerhistory.org/blog /silicon-valley-a-century-of-entrepreneurial-innovation/.

6. See Leslie Berlin's books *The Man behind the Microchip and the Invention of Silicon Valley* (Oxford: Oxford University Press, 2005); and *Troublemakers: Silicon Valley's Coming of Age* (New York: Simon & Schuster Paperbacks, 2017). I also recommend Margaret O'Mara's *The Code: Silicon Valley and the Remaking of America* (New York: Penguin Press, 2019).

7. Most of the bibliographical details related to Fred Terman are based on Stewart Gillmor's book *Fred Terman at Stanford: Building a Discipline, a University, and Silicon Valley* (Stanford, CA: Stanford University Press, 2004).

8. Oswald Garrison Villard, "Frederick Emmons Terman 1900–1882: A Biographical Memoir," *National Academy of Sciences* (1998): 6, http://www.nasonline .org/publications/biographical-memoirs/memoir-pdfs/terman-frederick.pdf.

9. The American Institute of Electrical Engineers (AIEE) was formed in 1884 with Norvin Green of Western Union as its first president. The Institute of Radio Engineers (IRE) devoted to a new industry, radio, was founded in 1912. The organizations merged in 1963 to form the Institute of Electrical and Electronics Engineers (IEEE).

10. Terman's style didn't always sit well with an academic guard intent on keeping a separation between academia and industry. The highest resistance came from people wary about grants given by the Department of Defense. This topic is analyzed by Rebecca S. Lowen, *Creating the Cold War University: The Transformation of Stanford* (Berkeley: University of California Press, 1997).

11. The history of Fairchild has been recounted multiple times. See Isaacson, *The Innovators*.

12. David Laws, "Who Named Silicon Valley?," Computer History Museum, January, 7, 2015, https://computerhistory.org/blog/who-named-silicon-valley/. Laws

writes, "Observers from industry bloggers to *The New York Times* credit entrepreneur Ralph Vaerst, founder of Ion Equipment Corp. They claim he suggested the name to *Electronic News* reporter Don Hoefler, who then titled a column on local silicon computer-chip companies 'Silicon Valley USA.' Published on January 11, 1971, the name stuck."

13. This representation was republished by the Computer History Museum, http://archive.computerhistory.org/resources/access/text/2017/03/102770820-05-01-acc.pdf.

14. Rhett Morris, "The First Trillion-Dollar Startup," TechCrunch, July 26, 2014, https://techcrunch.com/2014/07/26/the-first-trillion-dollar-startup.

15. Porter, "Clusters and the New Economics of Competition."

16. The engineers included David Bennion (who helped design the first general-purpose mobile robot, Shakey the Robot), Charles Rosen (who developed the first commercially available industrial machine vision system), Hewitt Crane (a radar technician during World War II who created "Jot," a handwriting recognition software), and Howard Zeidler (who worked at the Harvard RadioLab and joined Hewlett-Packard when World War II ended). The founders brought in two more partners in the 1960s, Carl Djerassi and Alex Zaffaroni. Anecdotally, part of the Ridge estate used to belong to Charles Litton's grandfather, Captain William Litton, who developed a resort at Litton Springs in 1875 and planted wine grape vines. The resort was ultimately sold in 1890. The Ridge Lytton Springs winery is located on an important part of Captain Litton's original property. The change from "Litton" into "Lytton" is thought to be a mistake made by a mapmaker in the 1880s.

17. Quotations are from personal conversation, January 2023.

18. Porter, "Clusters and the New Economics of Competition."

19. Marc Andreessen, "Why Software Is Eating the World, *Wall Street Journal*," August 20, 2011, https://www.wsj.com/articles/SB10001424053111903480904576512250915629460.

20. Marc Andreessen, "It's Time to Build," *Andreessen Horowitz*, April 2020, https://a16z.com/2020/04/18/its-time-to-build.

21. "The New Atlas: Can Silicon Valley Still Dominate Global Innovation? Why Nearly 300 Cities Now Host More Than 1,000 Unicorns," *Economist*, April 16, 2022, https://www.economist.com/business/can-silicon-valley-still-dominate-global-innovation/21808708. For regular updates about unicorns, see Crunchbase's Unicorn Board: https://news.crunchbase.com/unicorn-company-list.

22. William Kerr and Frederic Robert-Nicoud, "Tech Clusters," *Harvard Business School*, Working Paper, no. 20-063, November 2019, rev. June 2020, https://www.hbs.edu/faculty/Pages/item.aspx?num=57248.

23. For more information and interesting case studies, see Steve Case, *The Rise*

of the Rest: How Entrepreneurs in Surprising Places Are Building the New American Dream (New York: Avid Reader Press, 2022).

24. Heiko Rauscher, "Where China Is Leading the Mobility Revolution," *MIT Sloan Management Review*, June 19, 2019, https://sloanreview.mit.edu/article/where -china-is-leading-the-mobility-revolution.

25. Vitalik Buterin dropped out after being awarded $100,000 from the Thiel Fellowship (which I will discuss in chapter 10).

26. Brian Armstrong, "Coinbase Is a Decentralized Company, with No Head-quarters," *Coinbase blog*, February 24, 2021, https://blog.coinbase.com/coinbase-is -a-decentralized-company-with-no-headquarters-a9762c02546.

CHAPTER 10: DO YOU NEED TO BE CONNECTED TO SUCCEED?

Epigraph: Umberto Eco, *Foucault's Pendulum* (New York: Ballentine Books, 1990), 314.

1. Frigyes Karinthy, "Chains" (Láncszemek)," in *Everything Is Different* (Minden másképpen van) (Budapest: Atheneum Press, 1929). See also Mark Newman, Albert-László Barabási, and Duncan J. Watts, eds., *The Structure and Dynamics of Networks* (Princeton, NJ: Princeton University Press, 2006), 21–26.

2. William Brock, *Justus von Liebig: The Chemical Gatekeeper* (Cambridge: Cambridge University Press, 2002).

3. The Society of Arcueil was an informal circle of scientists that met between 1806 and 1822 at the country homes of Berthollet and Pierre-Simon Laplace in the suburbs of Paris.

4. Wilhelm von Humboldt (1767–1835), a German linguist and philosopher, was influential throughout Europe.

5. Liebig then moved to Munich.

6. Paul R. Jones, "Justus von Liebig, Eben Horsford and the Development of the Baking Powder Industry," *Ambix* 40 (July 1993), https://doi.org/10.1179/amb .1993.40.2.65.

7. Ragnhild Lundström, "Alfred Nobel's Dynamite Companies," *Nobel Prize*, https://www.nobelprize.org/alfred-nobel/alfred-nobels-dynamite-companies.

8. Patrice Bret, "Lavoisier à la régie des poudres: Le savant, le financier, l'administrateur et le pédagogue" (1994), Hal Open Science, https://halshs.archives -ouvertes.fr/halshs-00002883.

9. Karl Marx, *Das Kapital: Kritik der politischen Ökonomie* (Hamburg: Verlag von Otto Meissner, 1867–83).

10. For example, Robert Bunsen also traveled to France (1832–33) and met Liebig in Giessen. He too generated a prestigious followership. Some of them were to

build the German chemical industry, notably Heinrich Caro, who joined the Chemische Fabrik Dyckerhoff Clemm & Co. (which later became BASF); Fritz Haber, who teamed at BASF with Carl Bosch (a student of Johannes Wislicenus—former Horsford's assistant at Harvard); and Eugen Lucius, who started Lucius & Co. in Höchst am Main near Frankfurt, later renamed Hoechst AG.

11. Santa Clara Valley Historical Association, "Interview with Steve Jobs," 1994, YouTube video, https://www.youtube.com/watch?v=zkTfoLmDqKI.

12. Peter J. T. Morris, *The Matter Factory: A History of the Chemistry Laboratory* (London: Reaktion Books, 2015).

13. Robert Topper, "CU Chemistry and Chemical Engineering History," Cooper Union Engineering Faculty, accessed July 17, 2023, https://engfac.cooper.edu/topper/604.

14. The first large industrial research and development lab in chemistry in the United States was the DuPont Experimental Station in 1903. Its original purpose was to screen inventions by independent inventors focusing on black powder, smokeless powder, and dynamite. Its mission evolved when the company started scientific research with Wallace Carothers joining in 1928. The systemization of polymer science led to the development of nylon (Carothers) and neoprene (Elmer Bolton).

15. "Welcome to Thomas A. Edison Papers, Innovation Series–The Invention Factory," Rutgers School of Arts and Sciences, accessed July 26, 2023, https://edison.rutgers.edu/life-of-edison/biography/detailed-biography.

16. For an overview, see "General Electric Research Lab," Edison Tech Center, accessed July 10, 2023, https://edisontechcenter.org/GEresearchLab.html.

17. William Ott, "Katharine Gebbie's Leadership and Lasting Impact," NIST, updated August 25, 2016, https://www.nist.gov/pml/katharine-gebbies-leadership-and-lasting-impact.

18. Bell Laboratories has its roots in the various organizations founded by Alexander Graham Bell.

19. See Jon Gertner, *The Idea Factory: Bell Labs and the Great Age of American Innovation* (New York: Penguin Press, 2012). Note that as critical as Bell Labs was, it was not part of the development of the internet, for example, and other organizations proved equally mission critical, like the MIT Radiation Laboratory for microwave and radar research during World War II.

20. Jon Cohen, "CRISPR, the Revolutionary Genetic 'Scissors,' Honored by Chemistry Nobel," *Science*, October 7, 2020, https://www.science.org/content/article/crispr-revolutionary-genetic-scissors-honored-chemistry-nobel.

21. Jordan Rubio and James Thorne, "PitchBook Universities: Top 100 Colleges Ranked by Startup Founders," PitchBook, October 31, 2022, https://pitchbook.com/news/articles/pitchbook-university-rankings.

22. C. Textor, "Number of Students at Colleges and Universities in China 2011–2021," Statista, December 7, 2022, https://www.statista.com/statistics/226982/number-of-universities-in-china/.

23. Erin Duffin, "College Enrollment in Public and Private Institutions in the U.S. 1965–2030 and Projections up to 2030 for Public and Private Colleges," Statista, July 27, 2022, https://www.statista.com/statistics/183995/us-college-enrollment-and-projections-in-public-and-private-institutions.

24. "P&G Alumni Network—Official Page," LinkedIn, accessed July 26, 2023, https://www.linkedin.com/company/p&g-alumni-network/about.

25. "Google Alumni Founded Companies," Crunchbase, accessed July 10, 2023, https://www.crunchbase.com/hub/google-alumni-founded-companies. Examples of Google alumni-founded companies include Twitter, whose co-founder Evan Williams (along with Jack Dorsey, Noah Glass, and Biz Stone) worked at Google after it acquired the company he had started with Meg Hourihan, Pyra Labs (which created the blog-publishing platform Blogger). In a different space, Lin Bin and Feng Hong worked at Google China before starting, with four others, Xiaomi.

26. "Microsoft Alumni Founded Companies," Crunchbase, accessed July 10, 2023, https://www.crunchbase.com/hub/microsoft-alumni-founded-companies. For example, the online real estate marketplace Zillow was founded in 2006 by two former Microsoft executives, Rich Barton and Lloyd Frink. Prior to this, Rich Barton was the CEO of the Microsoft spin-off Expedia. Note that the largest Microsoft "child" is a huge philanthropic enterprise, the Bill & Melinda Gates Foundation.

27. "IBM Alumni Founded Companies," Crunchbase, July 10, 2023, https://www.crunchbase.com/hub/ibm-alumni-founded-companies. The co-founders of SAP were five IBM engineers: Hasso Plattner, Claus Wellenreuther, Dietmar Hopp, Klaus Tschira, and Hans-Werner Hector in Mannheim, Germany. When their project at IBM was abandoned, they left. David Duffield began his career at IBM and founded PeopleSoft in 1987 (acquired by Oracle in 2005). He co-founded Workday with Aneel Bhusri in 2005.

28. "Apple Alumni Founded Companies," Crunchbase, accessed July 10, 2023, https://www.crunchbase.com/hub/apple-alumni-founded-companies. Examples include Nest, co-founded by former Apple engineers Tony Fadell and Matt Rogers; Android, designed by former Apple engineer Andy Rubin; and Electronic Arts, founded by Trip Hawkins.

29. "Oracle Alumni Founded Companies," Crunchbase, accessed July 10, 2023, https://www.crunchbase.com/hub/oracle-alumni-founded-companies.

30. "Amazon Alumni Founded Companies," Crunchbase, accessed July 10, 2023, https://www.crunchbase.com/hub/amazon-alumni-founded-companies.

31. The expression was reportedly coined by Henry Clay (1777–1852), an Ameri-

can attorney with a long political career. See John Swansburg, "The Self-Made Man, the Story of America's Most Pliable, Pernicious, Irrepressible Myth," *Slate*, September 29, 2014, http://www.slate.com/articles/news_and_politics/history/2014/09/the_self_made_man_history_of_a_myth_from_ben_franklin_to_andrew_carnegie.html.

32. Steven Levy, *Facebook: The Inside Story* (New York: Blue Rider Press, 2020).

33. Sameeksha Desai, Jessica Looze, and Anna Pechenina, "Student Loans and Entrepreneurship: An Overview," *Ewing Marion Kauffman Foundation*, July 22, 2020, https://www.kauffman.org/entrepreneurship/reports/student-loan-debt-entrepreneurship/.

34. "Two Years. $100,000. Some Ideas Can't Wait," Thiel Fellowship, https://thielfellowship.org.

35. Sari Pekkala Kerr and William R. Kerr, "Immigrant Entrepreneurship," National Bureau of Economic Research, July 2016, https://www.nber.org/papers/w22385.

36. Stuart Anderson, "Immigrants and Billion-Dollar Companies," National Foundation for American Policy, July 2022, https://nfap.com/research/new-nfap-policy-brief-immigrant-entrepreneurs-and-u-s-billion-dollar-companies.

37. One Million by One Million offers a wide range of services, including free and online mentoring roundtables for entrepreneurs looking to discuss positioning, financing, and all other aspects of building a startup venture. For more information, see https://1m1m.sramanamitra.com/.

CHAPTER 11: ARE WOMEN AND MINORITIES UNWELCOME?

Epigraph: George Eliot, *Middlemarch* (New York, 1871–72), book 8, chapter 72.

1. California law defines a member of an underrepresented community as "an individual who self-identifies as Black, African American, Hispanic, Latino, Asian, Pacific Islander, Native American, Native Hawaiian, or Alaska Native, or who self-identifies as gay, lesbian, bisexual, or transgender." In this chapter, I will primarily focus on Women, Black / African American, and Hispanic/Latinx entrepreneurs.

2. Michelle Saksena, Nicholas Rada, and Lisa Cook: "Where Are U.S. Women Patentees? Assessing Three Decades of Growth," U.S. Patent and Trademark Office, IP Data Highlights, no. 6, October 2022, https://www.uspto.gov/sites/default/files/documents/oce-women-patentees-report.pdf.

3. Elizabeth Durant, "A Lab of Their Own: The Women's Laboratory Was an Experiment," *MIT Technology Review*, May 12, 2006, https://www.technologyreview.com/2006/05/12/229113/a-lab-of-their-own.

4. In 1870 the US Census started to count "females engaged in each occupation. They already made up 13% of the total work force (1,8362,88 out of 13,970,079)." See "1870 Census: Volume 1. The Statistics of the Population of the United States

(1872)," United States Census Bureau, accessed July 10, 2023, https://www.census.gov/library/publications/1872/dec/1870a.html.

5. Melia E. Bonomo, "Isabelle Stone: Breaking the Glass Ceiling with Thin Films and Teaching," "arXiv: History and Philosophy of Physics" (2020), https://arxiv.org/abs/2010.08144.

6. Amy Burke, Abigail Okrent, and Katherine Hale, "U.S. and Global STEM Education and Labor Force," in *The State of U.S. Science and Engineering 2022*, National Science Board, January 18, 2022, https://ncses.nsf.gov/pubs/nsb20221/u-s-and-global-stem-education-and-labor-force.

7. "Engineering & Engineering Technology by the Numbers," American Society for Engineering Education, ASEE, *Profiles of Engineering and Engineering Technology, 2021* (2022): 56, https://ira.asee.org/wp-content/uploads/2022/11/Engineering-and-Engineering-Technology-by-the-Numbers-2021.pdf.

8. Derrick P. Alridge, "On the Education of Black Folk: W. E. B. Du Bois and the Paradox of Segregation," *Journal of African American History* 100, no. 3 (2015): 473–93, https://doi.org/10.5323/jafriamerhist.100.3.0473.

9. For more information, see "The Traditionally Black Institutions of Higher Education 1860 to 1982," *National Center for Education Statistics*, https://nces.ed.gov/pubs84/84308.pdf.

10. "Engineering & Engineering Technology by the Numbers," 59.

11. There are multiple studies of this topic. For a summary, see Eric Fish, "End of an Era? A History of Chinese Students in America," The China Project, May 12, 2020, https://supchina.com/2020/05/12/end-of-an-era-a-history-of-chinese-students-in-america.

12. Jeff Guo, "The Real Secret to Asian American Success Was Not Education," *Washington Post*, November 19, 2016, https://www.washingtonpost.com/news/wonk/wp/2016/11/19/the-real-secret-to-asian-american-success-was-not-education.

13. Megan Rose Dickey, "Asian Americans in Tech Say They Face a Unique Flavor of Oppression," Protocol, April 1, 2021, https://www.protocol.com/asian-americans-model-minority.

14. Shruti Mukkamala and Karen Suyemoto, "Racialized Sexism / Sexualized Racism: A Multimethod Study of Intersectional Experiences of Discrimination for Asian American Women," *Asian American Journal of Psychology* 9, no. 1 (2018): 32–46, https://doi.org/10.1037/aap0000104.

15. Multiple sites and articles discuss these premieres. For a general survey, see Margaret Layne, *Women in Engineering: Pioneers and Trailblazers* (Reston, VA: American Society of Civil Engineers, 2009).

16. Katharine Burr Blodgett was the first woman to work as a scientist for General Electric Laboratory, in Schenectady, New York, in 1918.

17. Today SWE has over 40,000 members in nearly 100 professional sections, 300 collegiate sections, and 60 global affiliate groups throughout the world.

18. For a timeline of women's legal rights in the United States, see "Timeline of Legal History of Women in the United States," National Women's History Alliance, https://nationalwomenshistoryalliance.org/resources/womens-rights-movement/detailed-timeline/.

19. "SWE Research Fast Facts," Society of Women Engineers, September 2021, https://swe.org/wp-content/uploads/2021/10/SWE-Fast-Facts_Oct-2021.pdf.

20. "African-American's Rights," University of Maryland, University Libraries, accessed July 28, 2023, https://www.lib.umd.edu/unions/social/african-americans-rights.

21. Gina Daugherty, "An Engineer Looks Back: The Tech and Opportunity behind a 40-Year Career at GE Aviation," *GE Aerospace: The Blog*, August 17, 2020, https://blog.geaviation.com/technology/an-engineer-looks-back-the-tech-and-opportunity-behind-a-40-year-career-at-ge-aviation.

22. Before IBM was IBM, it had hired its first women and black employees, but in the 1920s and 1930s, IBM built a dubious reputation, helping eugenic initiatives and providing to the Third Reich the punched-card technology that supported the census and extermination of Jews.

23. Clyde Ford, *Think Black: A Memoir* (New York: Amistad, 2019).

24. "A Black Scientific Renaissance: Bell Laboratories," American Institute of Physics, accessed July 10, 2023, https://www.aip.org/sites/default/files/history/teaching-guides/bell-laboratories/African%20American%20Scientists%20at%20Bell%20Laboratories_Bell%20Laboratories%20Handout.pdf.

25. Richard Fry, Brian Kennedy, and Cary Funk, "STEM Jobs See Uneven Progress in Increasing Gender, Racial and Ethnic Diversity," Pew Research Center, April 1, 2021, https://www.pewresearch.org/science/2021/04/01/stem-jobs-see-uneven-progress-in-increasing-gender-racial-and-ethnic-diversity/.

26. Dominic-Madori Davis, "Women-Founded Startups Raised 1.9% of All VC Funds in 2022, a Drop from 2021," TechCrunch, January 18, 2023, https://techcrunch.com/2023/01/18/women-founded-startups-raised-1-9-of-all-vc-funds-in-2022-a-drop-from-2021/.

27. Malin Malmstrom, Jeaneth Johansson, and Joakim Wincent, "We Recorded VCs' Conversations and Analyzed How Differently They Talk about Female Entrepreneurs," *Harvard Business Review*, May 17, 2017, https://hbr.org/2017/05/we-recorded-vcs-conversations-and-analyzed-how-differently-they-talk-about-female-entrepreneurs.

28. Hadar Gafni, Dan Marom, Alicia Robb, and Orly Sade, "Gender Dynam-

ics in Crowdfunding (Kickstarter): Evidence on Entrepreneurs, Backers, and Taste-Based Discrimination," *Review of Finance* 25, no. 2 (March 2021): 235–74, https://doi.org/10.1093/rof/rfaa041.

29. "Crunchbase Diversity Spotlight 2020: Funding to Black & Latinx Founders," Crunchbase, http://about.crunchbase.com/wp-content/uploads/2020/10/2020_crunchbase_diversity_report.pdf.

30. James Norman, "A VC's Guide to Investing in Black Founders," *Harvard Business Review*, June 19, 2020, https://hbr.org/2020/06/a-vcs-guide-to-investing-in-black-founders.

31. Norman, "VC's Guide to Investing in Black Founders."

32. Matilda Gage, "Woman as an Inventor," *North American Review* 136, no. 318 (May 1883): 479–89, https://www.jstor.org/stable/pdf/25118273.pdf.

33. Erik Olin Wright, *Envisioning Real Utopias* (Brooklyn, NY: Verso, 2010).

34. Margaret Rossiter, "The Matthew Matilda Effect in Science," *Social Studies of Science* 23, no. 2 (1993): 325–41, http://www.jstor.org/stable/285482.

35. Ruth Lewin Sime, *Lise Meitner: A Life in Physics* (Berkeley: University of California Press, 1997).

36. Erik Olin Wright, *Envisioning Real Utopias* (Brooklyn, NY: Verso, 2010), pt. 3, chap. 10.

37. Multiple sites provide lists of notable African American inventors and scientists, such as, for example, the History Makers, a nonprofit research and educational institution.

38. Wright: *Envisioning Real Utopias*, chap. 11. Wright refers to John Maynard Keynes, *The General Theory of Employment, Interest and Money* (London: Macmillan, 1936).

39. Christine Frederick, *Selling Mrs. Consumer* (New York: Business Bourse, 1929).

40. Frederick, *Selling Mrs. Consumer*, 170. As I mentioned in this book's introduction, Alfred Sloan spoke of "dynamic obsolescence." Although the expression "planned obsolescence" is credited to a real estate broker, Bernard London, for his essay "Ending the Depression through Planned Obsolescence" (Self-published, New York, 1932), its mechanisms were already described by Frederick. For an overview of this subject, see Giles Slade, *Made to Break: Technology and Obsolescence in America* (Cambridge, MA: Harvard University Press, 2006).

41. Caroline Criado Perez, *Invisible Women: Data Bias in a World Designed for Men* (New York: Abrams, 2019).

42. For an analysis of the relationship between Babbage and Ada Lovelace, see "Ada Lovelace—Why All the Fuss?—Doron Swade Looks at Babbage, Lovelace and the Analytical Engine," CC London, 2016, YouTube video, https://www

.youtube.com/watch?v=NMnkjDMMEPE. See also John Fuegi and Jo Francis, "Lovelace & Babbage and the Creation of the 1843 'Notes,'" *IEEE Annals of the History of Computing* 25, no. 4 (October–December 2003): 16–26, https://doi.org/10.110 9/MAHC.2003.1253887.

43. For more information about Mary Sommerville (1780–1872), see Kathryn A. Neeley, *Mary Somerville: Science, Illumination, and the Female Mind* (Cambridge: Cambridge University Press, 2001); and Elisabetta Strickland, *The Ascent of Mary Somerville in 19th Century Society* (Cham, Switzerland: Springer International Publishing, 2016).

44. William Whewell was also the one who created new words such as "scientist," "anode," "cathode," and "ion" for his friend Michael Faraday.

45. The topic has been discussed in multiple articles. One of the latest books: Kathy Kleiman, *Proving Ground: The Untold Story of the Six Women Who Programmed the World's First Modern Computer* (New York: Grand Central Publishing, 2022). The first six women were Kathleen McNulty Antonelli, Marlyn Wescoff Meltzer, Frances Bilas Spence, Ruth Lichterman Teitelbaum, Betty Holberton, and Jean Jennings Bartik.

46. See Denise Gürer, "Pioneering Women in Computer Science," *ACM SIGCSE Bulletin* 34, no. 2 (June 2002), https://doi.org/10.1145/543812.543853.

47. Natasha Geiling, "The Women Who Mapped the Universe and Still Couldn't Get Any Respect," *Smithsonian Magazine*, September 18, 2013, https://www.smithsonianmag.com/history/the-women-who-mapped-the-universe-and-still-couldnt-get-any-respect-9287444.

48. Brynn Holland, "Human Computers: The Women of NASA," History.com, December 13, 2016, updated August 22, 2018, https://www.history.com/news/human-computers-women-at-nasa. Note that NASA employed nearly eighty black female computers. See Margot Lee Shetterly in *Hidden Figures: The American Dream and the Untold Story of the Black Women Mathematicians Who Helped Win the Space Race* (New York: William Morrow, 2016).

49. Janine Solberg, "Taking Shorthand for Literacy: Historicizing the Literate Activity of U.S. Women in the Early Twentieth-Century Office," *Literacy in Composition Studies (LiCS)*, 2014, https://doi.org/10.21623/1.2.1.2.

50. Women formed the majority of the high school teachers of mathematics in 1947. See "The Outlook for Women in Mathematics and Statistics," Women's Bureau Bulletin No. 223–34, U.S. Department of Labor, Women's Bureau, https://books.google.com/books/about/The_Outlook_for_Women_in_Mathematics_and.html?id=lROteX_G_qMC 1948.

51. There were also female human computers in Europe, of course. Bletchley Park, in England—which housed the Government Code and Cypher School run

by scientists like Alan Turing, Gordon Welchman, Hugh Alexander, Bill Tutte, and Stuart Milner-Barry—had ten thousand employees, of whom more than two-thirds were women. Their jobs ranged from administrative tasks to code-breaking. One of the most famous code-breakers was Joan Clarke, a close friend of Turing.

52. She became the second woman to win a Nobel Prize in Physics (jointly with Hans D. Jensen).

53. Janet Abbate, *Recoding Gender: Women's Changing Participation in Computing* (Cambridge, MA: MIT Press, 2012), 97.

54. Cathy O'Neill, *Weapons of Math Destruction: How Big Data Increases Inequality and Threatens Democracy* (New York: Crown, 2016).

55. Joy Buolamwini, "InCoding: In the Beginning Was the Coded Gaze," *Medium: The MIT Media Lab*, May 16, 2016, https://medium.com/mit-media-lab/incoding-in-the-beginning-4e2a5c51a45d.

56. George Sand, *Gabriel* (Brussels: Meline, Cans et Compagnie, 1839), 22.

57. Marilyn Loden, "100 Women: Why I Invented the Glass Ceiling Phrase," BBC News, December 2017, https://www.bbc.com/news/world-42026266.

CHAPTER 12: HOW CAN ORGANIZATIONS REMAIN INNOVATIVE?

Epigraph: Bernard Shaw, *Man and Superman*, 1903, https://www.gutenberg.org/files/3328/3328-h/3328-h.htm.

1. For a history of the concept, see Charles A. O'Reilly III and Michael Tushman, "Organizational Ambidexterity: Past, Present, and Future," *Academy of Management Perspectives* 27, no. 4 (October 4, 2013), https://doi.org/10.5465/amp.2013.0025.

2. Peter Drucker, "The Coming of the New Organization," *Harvard Business Review*, January 1988, https://hbr.org/1988/01/the-coming-of-the-new-organization.

3. Gary Hamel and Michele Zanini, "More of Us Are Working in Big Bureaucratic Organizations Than Ever Before," *Harvard Business Review*, July 5, 2016, https://hbr.org/2016/07/more-of-us-are-working-in-big-bureaucratic-organizations-than-ever-before?.

4. "Safe Enough to Try: An Interview with Zappos CEO Tony Hsieh," McKinsey and Company, October 9, 2017, https://www.mckinsey.com/capabilities/people-and-organizational-performance/our-insights/safe-enough-to-try-an-interview-with-zappos-ceo-tony-hsieh.

5. Marylene Delbourg-Delphis, *Everybody Wants to Love Their Job: Rebuilding Trust and Culture* (Paris: Diateino, 2018).

6. Gary Hamel and Michele Zanini, *Humanocracy: Creating Organizations as Amazing as the People inside Them* (Boston: Harvard Business Review Press, 2020).

7. Delbourg-Delphis, *Everybody Wants to Love Their Job*, pt. 3, chap. 2. Functional stupidity and groupthink are both the foundation and the result of skilled incompetence.

8. Isaac Asimov, "Isaac Asimov Asks, 'How Do People Get New Ideas?' With Note from Arthur Obermayer," *MIT Technology Review*, October 20, 2014, https://www.technologyreview.com/2014/10/20/169899/isaac-asimov-asks-how-do-people-get-new-ideas.

9. Peter Senge, *The Fifth Discipline: The Art and Practice of the Learning Organization* (New York: Doubleday, 1990), 57.

10. Carol Dweck, *Mindset: The New Psychology of Success* (New York: Ballantine Books, 2007).

11. "2004 Founders' IPO Letter," Alphabet Investors Relations, https://abc.xyz/investor/founders-letters/2004/ipo-letter.html.

12. Julian D'Onfro, "The Truth about Google's Famous '20% Time' Policy," *Business Insider*, April 17, 2015, https://www.businessinsider.com/google-20-percent-time-policy-2015-4.

13. Eric Schmidt and Jonathan Rosenberg, *How Google Works* (New York: Grand Central Publishing, 2014), 110.

14. Shane McFeely and Ben Wigert, "This Fixable Problem Costs U.S. Businesses $1 Trillion," Gallup, March 13, 2019, https://www.gallup.com/workplace/247391/fixable-problem-costs-businesses-trillion.aspx.

15. Heather Huhman, "Are You a Talent Hoarder?," Aberdeen, November 4, 2016, https://www.aberdeen.com/blogposts/are-you-a-talent-hoarder/.

16. Severin Hornung, Denise M. Rousseau, and Jürgen Glaser, "Creating Flexible Work Arrangements through Idiosyncratic Deals," *Journal of Applied Psychology* 93, no. 3 (2008): 655–64, https://doi.org/10.1037/0021-9010.93.3.655.

17. Adam Grant, *Originals: How Non-conformists Move the World* (New York: Viking, 2016).

18. Steven Overly, "How Ford Turned Thousands of Employees into Inventors," *Washington Post*, December 14, 2016, https://www.washingtonpost.com/news/innovations/wp/2016/12/14/how-ford-turned-thousands-of-employees-into-inventors.

19. Jeremy Utley and Perry Klebahn, *Ideaflow: The Only Business Metric That Matters* (New York: Portfolio/Penguin, 2022).

20. "Make Ideas Real at the Speed of Thought," id-sl, https://en.id-sl.com/andi.

21. Susan Crawford, "How Corning Makes Super-pure Glass for Fiber-Optic Cable," *Wired*, January 8, 2019, https://www.wired.com/story/corning-pure-glass-fiber-optic-cable/.

22. "Electronic Still Camera," United States Patents, December 26, 1978, https://patents.google.com/patent/US4131919.

23. James Estrin, "Kodak's First Digital Moment," *New York Times*, August 12, 2015, https://archive.nytimes.com/lens.blogs.nytimes.com/2015/08/12/kodaks-first-digital-moment/.

24. For an analysis of the critical role of Ted Codd in database technology, see Chris Date, *The Database Relational Model: A Retrospective Review and Analysis. A Historical Account and Assessment of E. F. Codd's Contribution to the Field of Database Technology* (Reading, MA: Addison-Wesley, 2001).

25. Tom Ehrenfeld, "Out of the Blue," *Inc.*, July 1, 1995, https://www.inc.com/magazine/19950701/2333.html.

26. Dan Ariely, *The Upside of Irrationality: The Unexpected Benefits of Defying Logic* (New York: Harper Perennial, 2011), 107–22.

27. I am using the expression "open source movement" in a generic fashion. My purpose here is not to discuss the differences between the free software movement started by Richard Stallman of the GNU Project in 1983 or the Open Source Initiative founded by Bruce Perens and Eric Raymond in 1998.

28. Isaacson, *The Innovators*, 118.

29. See interview of Paul Baran: Stewart Brand, "Founding Father," *Wired*, March 1, 2001, https://www.wired.com/2001/03/baran/.

30. X-rays were quickly used by battlefield physicians to locate bullets, broken bones, and chunks of shrapnel in wounded soldiers in numerous conflict zones across the world. Mobile units were developed to keep up with field hospitals and scaled to extraordinary proportions with World War I. See Dan Schlenoff, "X-Rays at War, 1915," *Scientific American*, January 30, 2015, https://blogs.scientificamerican.com/anecdotes-from-the-archive/x-rays-at-war-1915.

31. Damian Garde and Jonathan Saltzman, "The Story of mRNA: How a Once-Dismissed Idea Became a Leading Technology in the Covid Vaccine Race," *STAT*, November 10, 2020, https://www.statnews.com/2020/11/10/the-story-of-mrna-how-a-once-dismissed-idea-became-a-leading-technology-in-the-covid-vaccine-race.

32. John Browne, Robin Nuttall, and Tommy Stadlen, *Connect: How Companies Succeed by Engaging Radically with Society* (New York: PublicAffairs, 2016), xiv.

33. Vinod Khosla, "Gene Pool Engineering for Entrepreneurs," Khosla Ventures, May 14, 2015, https://www.khoslaventures.com/gene-pool-engineering-for-entrepreneurs.

34. Julie Bort, "There's a Secret Term VCs Use to Insult Some Founders: 'Not Blue Flame Enough,'" *Business Insider*, May 10, 2016, http://www.businessinsider.com/what-vcs-mean-by-the-term-blue-flame-2016-5.

35. Grant, *Originals*, 108–13.

36. Lynda Gratton and Andrew Scott, *The 100-Year Life: Living and Working in an Age of Longevity* (London: Bloomsbury Information, 2016).

37. Pagan Kennedy, *Inventology: How We Dream Up Things That Change the World* (Boston: Houghton Mifflin Harcourt, 2016).

38. Tim Dempsey, *No Fear: Tales of a Change Agent, or Why I Couldn't Fix Nortel Networks: A Business Memoir* (Amazon: CreateSpace, 2014).

39. Ford and Crowther, *My Life and Work*, 42–43.

CONCLUSION

Epigraph: Julia Child, https://www.goodreads.com/author/quotes/3465.Julia _Child?page=2.

1. Damien Ma, "Torchbearer: Igniting Innovation in China's Tech Clusters," Macro Polo, August 14, 2019, https://macropolo.org/china-torch-program-inno vation/?rp=m.

2. Steve Orlins, "Kai-Fu Lee on the Future of AI in the United States and China," National Committee on U.S.–China Relations (2018), https://www.ncuscr .org/podcast/kai-fu-lee-future-ai-united-states-china/.

3. Lee Vinsel and Andrew Russell, *The Innovation Delusion: How Our Obsession with the New Has Disrupted the Work That Matters Most* (New York: Currency, 2020).

4. Vaclav Smil, *Numbers Don't Lie: 71 Things You Need to Know about the World* (New York: Viking, 2021), 306.

Selected Bibliography

Abbate, Janet. *Recoding Gender: Women's Changing Participation in Computing*. Cambridge, MA: MIT Press, 2012.

Adair, John. *The Art of Creative Thinking: How to Be Innovative and Develop Great Ideas*. London: Kogan Page, 2009.

Amabile, Teresa, and Steven Kramer. *The Progress Principle: Using Small Wins to Ignite Joy, Engagement, and Creativity at Work*. Boston: Harvard Business Review Press, 2011.

Ariely, Dan. *The Upside of Irrationality: The Unexpected Benefits of Defying Logic*. New York: Harper Perennial, 2011.

Bachelard, Gaston. *La Formation de l'esprit scientifique: Contribution à une psychanalyse de la connaissance objective*. Paris: Vrin, 1938.

Baker, Ted, and Friederike Welter, eds. *The Routledge Companion to Entrepreneurship*. Abingdon, UK: Routledge, 2014.

Baldwin, Neil. *Edison: Inventing the Century*. New York: Hyperion, 1995.

Ball, Matthew. *The Metaverse, and How It Will Revolutionize Everything*. New York: Liveright Publishing Corporation, 2022.

Barabási, Albert-László, and Duncan J. Watts, eds. *The Structure and Dynamics of Networks*. Princeton, NJ: Princeton University Press, 2006.

Battelle, John. *The Search: How Google and Its Rivals Rewrote the Rules of Business and Transformed Our Culture*. New York: Portfolio, 2005.

Beckert, Jens. *Imagined Futures: Fictional Expectations and Capitalist Dynamics*. Cambridge, MA: Harvard University Press, 2016.

Benioff, Marc. *Behind the Cloud: The Untold Story of How Salesforce.com Went from Idea to Billion-Dollar Company—and Revolutionized an Industry*. San Francisco: Jossey-Bass, 2009.

Berlin, Leslie. *The Man behind the Microchip and the Invention of Silicon Valley*. Oxford: Oxford University Press, 2005.

———. *Troublemakers: Silicon Valley's Coming of Age*. New York: Simon and Schuster Paperbacks, 2017.

Blank, Steve. *The Four Steps to the Epiphany: Successful Strategies for Products That Win*. 5th ed. Wiley. Pescadero, CA: K&S Ranch, 2013.

Blank, Steve, and Bob Dorf. *The Startup Owner's Manual: The Step-by-Step Guide for Building a Great Company*. Pescadero, CA: K&S Ranch, 2012.

Bouissou, Philippe. *Aligning the Dots: The New Paradigm to Grow Any Business*. Palo Alto, CA: Onward Business Press, 2020.

Brayer, Elizabeth. *George Eastman: A Biography*. Rochester, NY: University of Rochester Press, 2006.

Brock, William. *Justus von Liebig: The Chemical Gatekeeper*. Cambridge: Cambridge University Press, 2002.

Brooks, John. *Business Adventures: Twelve Classic Tales from the World of Wall Street*. New York: Open Road Media, [1969] 2021.

Browne, John, Robin Nuttall, and Tommy Stadlen. *Connect: How Companies Succeed by Engaging Radically with Society*. New York: PublicAffairs, 2016.

Cappelli, Peter, and Bill Novelli. *Managing the Older Worker: How to Prepare for the New Organizational Order*. Boston: Harvard Business Review Press, 2010.

Catmull, Edwin, and Amy Wallace. *Creativity, Inc.: Overcoming the Unseen Forces That Stand in the Way of True Inspiration*. New York: Random House, 2014.

Christensen, Clayton M. *The Innovator's Dilemma: When New Technologies Cause Great Firms to Fail*. Boston: Harvard Business School Press, 1997.

Christensen, Clayton M., and Michael E. Raynor. *The Innovator's Solution: Creating and Sustaining Successful Growth*. Boston: Harvard Business Review Press, 2003.

Collins, Jim. *Good to Great: Why Some Companies Make the Leap . . . and Others Don't*. New York: Random House, 2001.

Coyle, Daniel. *The Culture Code: The Secrets of Highly Successful Groups*. New York: Bantam Books, 2018.

Criado Perez, Caroline. *Invisible Women: Data Bias in a World Designed for Men*. New York: Abrams, 2019.

Cringely, Robert. *Accidental Empires: How the Boys of Silicon Valley Make Their Millions, Battle Foreign Competition, and Still Can't Get a Date*. Repr. ed. New York: Harper Business, 1991.

Cronin, Irena, and Robert Scoble. *The Infinite Retina: Spatial Computing, Augmented Reality, and How a Collision of New Technologies Are Bringing about the Next Tech Revolution*. Birmingham, UK: Packt Publishing, 2020.

Date, Chris. *The Database Relational Model: A Retrospective Review and Analysis. A Historical Account and Assessment of E. F. Codd's Contribution to the Field of Database Technology*. Reading, MA: Addison-Wesley, 2001.

Day, George, and Paul Schoemaker. *Peripheral Vision: Detecting the Weak Signals That Will Make or Break Your Company*. Boston: Harvard Business Review Press, 2006.

Delbourg-Delphis, Marylene. *Everybody Wants to Love Their Job: Rebuilding Trust and Culture*. Paris: Diateino, 2018.

Deming, W. Edwards. *Out of the Crisis: Quality, Productivity and Competitive Position*. Repr. ed. Cambridge, MA: MIT Press, 2000.

Dempsey, Tim. *No Fear: Tales of a Change Agent, or Why I Couldn't Fix Nortel Networks: A Business Memoir*. Amazon: CreateSpace, 2014.

Desmond, Kevin. *Electric Motorcycles and Bicycles: A History Including Scooters, Tricycles, Segways and Monocycles*. Jefferson, NC: McFarland and Company Inc., 2018.

Diamandis, Peter, and Steven Kotler. *The Future Is Faster Than You Think: How Converging Technologies Are Transforming Business, Industries, and Our Lives*. New York: Simon and Schuster, 2020.

Drucker, Peter. *The Age of Discontinuity: Guidelines to Our Changing Society*. London: Heinemann, 1969.

———. *Innovation and Entrepreneurship, Practice and Principles*. New York: Harper and Row, 1985.

Dweck, Carol S. *Mindset: The New Psychology of Success*. New York: Ballantine Books, 2007.

Dyer, Jeff, Hal Gregersen, and Clayton Christensen. *The Innovator's DNA: Mastering the Five Skills of Disruptive Innovators*. Boston: Harvard Business Review Press, 2011.

Edmondson, Amy C. *Teaming: How Organizations Learn, Innovate, and Compete in the Knowledge Economy*. San Francisco: Jossey-Bass, 2012.

Fadell, Tony. *Build: An Unorthodox Guide to Making Things Worth Making*. New York: HarperCollins, 2022.

Ford, Clyde. *Think Black: A Memoir*. New York: Amistad, 2019.

Ford, Henry, and Samuel Crowther. *My Life and Work*. Garden City, NY: Doubleday Page and Company, 1922.

Foster, Robert. *Innovation: The Attacker's Advantage*. New York: Summit Books, 1986.

Foucault, Michel. *The Archeology of Knowledge*. Translated from the French by Alan Sheridan. Abingdon, UK: Routledge, 1989.

———. *The Order of Things*. Translated from the French by Alan Sheridan. New York: Vintage Books, 1994.

Frederick, Christine. *Selling Mrs. Consumer*. New York: Business Bourse, 1929.

Gardner, Howard. *Frames of Mind: The Theory of Multiple Intelligences*. New York: Basic Books, 1983.

———. *Multiple Intelligences: The Theory in Practice*. New York: Basic Books, 1993.

Gertner, Jon. *The Idea Factory: Bell Labs and the Great Age of American Innovation*. Repr. ed. New York: Penguin Books, 2013.

Gillmor, Stewart. *Fred Terman at Stanford: Building a Discipline, a University, and Silicon Valley.* Stanford, CA: Stanford University Press, 2004.

Gladwell, Malcom. *Outliers: The Story of Success.* New York: Little, Brown and Company, 2008.

———. *The Tipping Point: How Little Things Can Make a Big Difference.* New York: Little, Brown and Company, 2000.

Godin, Benoît. *Innovation Contested: The Idea of Innovation over the Centuries.* Abington, UK: Routledge, 2015.

———. *Models of Innovation: The History of an Idea.* Cambridge, MA: MIT Press, 2017.

Grant, Adam. *Originals: How Non-conformists Move the World.* New York: Viking, 2016.

———. *Think Again: The Power of Knowing What You Don't Know.* New York: Viking, 2021.

Gratton, Lynda, and Andrew J. Scott. *The 100-Year Life: Living and Working in an Age of Longevity.* London: Bloomsbury Information, 2016.

Grazer, Brian, and Charles Fishman. *A Curious Mind: The Secret to a Bigger Life.* New York: Simon and Schuster, 2015.

Grove, Andrew S. *High Output Management.* New York: Random House, 1982.

———. *Only the Paranoid Survive: How to Exploit the Crisis Points That Challenge Every Company.* New York: Currency, 1999.

Groysberg, Boris. *Chasing Stars: The Myth of Talent and the Portability of Performance.* Princeton, NJ: Princeton University Press, 2012.

Hackman, J. Richard. *Collaborative Intelligence: Using Teams to Solve Hard Problems.* San Francisco: Berrett-Koehler, 2011.

Hamel, Gary, and Michele Zanini. *Humanocracy: Creating Organizations as Amazing as the People inside Them.* Boston: Harvard Business Review Press, 2020.

Hannavy, John, ed. *Encyclopedia of Nineteenth-Century Photography.* New York: Routledge, 2008.

Heath, Chip, and Dan Heath. *Made to Stick: Why Some Ideas Survive and Others Die.* New York: Random House, 2007.

Hertzfeld, Andy. *Revolution in the Valley: The Insanely Great Story of How the Mac Was Made.* Sebastopol: O'Reilly Media, 2004.

Hoffman, Reid, and Chris Yeh. *Blitzscaling: The Lightning-Fast Path to Building Massively Valuable Companies.* New York: Currency, 2018.

Hoffman, Steven S. *Make Elephants Fly: The Process of Radical Innovation.* New York: Center Street, 2017.

Hollings, Christopher, Ursula Martin, and Adrian Clifford Rice. *Ada Lovelace: The Making of a Computer Scientist.* Oxford: Bodleian Library, University of Oxford, 2018.

Horowitz, Ben. *The Hard Thing about Hard Things: Building a Business When There Are No Easy Answers*. New York: Harper Business, 2014.

Isaacson, Walter. *The Code Breaker: Jennifer Doudna, Gene Editing, and the Future of the Human Race*. New York: Simon and Schuster, 2021.

———. *The Innovators: How a Group of Hackers, Geniuses, and Geeks Created the Digital Revolution*. New York: Simon and Schuster, 2014.

———. *Steve Jobs*. New York: Simon and Schuster, 2011.

Josephson, Matthew. *Edison: A Biography*. New York: John Wiley and Sons, 1992.

Kahneman, Daniel. *Thinking, Fast and Slow*. New York: Farrar, Straus and Giroux, 2011.

Kahneman, Daniel, Paul Slovic, and Amos Tversky, eds. *Judgment under Uncertainty: Heuristics and Biases*. Cambridge: Cambridge University Press, 1982.

Kasner, Edward, and James Roy Newman. *Mathematics and the Imagination*. New York: Simon and Schuster, 1940.

Kaufman, Josh. *The Personal MBA: Anniversary Edition*. New York: Portfolio, 2020.

Kaufman, Scott Barry, and Carolyn Gregoire. *Wired to Create: Unraveling the Mysteries of the Creative Mind*. New York: Perigee Books, 2015.

Kawasaki, Guy. *The Art of the Start 2.0: The Time-Tested, Battle-Hardened Guide for Anyone Starting Anything*. New York: Portfolio/Penguin, 2015.

———. *Enchantment: The Art of Changing Hearts, Minds, and Actions*. New York: Portfolio/Penguin, 2011.

Kelley, Tom, and David Kelley. *Creative Confidence: Unleashing the Creative Potential within Us All*. New York: Crown Business, 2013.

Kelly, Kevin. *The Inevitable, Understanding the 12 Technological Forces That Will Shape Our Future*. New York: Viking, 2016.

Kennedy, Pagan. *Inventology: How We Dream Up Things That Change the World*. Boston: Houghton Mifflin Harcourt, 2016.

Kim, W. Chan, and Renée Mauborgne. *Beyond Disruption: Innovate and Achieve Growth without Displacing Industries, Companies or Jobs*. Boston: Harvard Business Review Press, 2023.

———. *Blue Ocean Shift: Proven Steps to Inspire Confidence and Seize New Growth*. New York: Hachette Books, 2017.

———. *Blue Ocean Strategy: How to Create Uncontested Market Space and Make the Competition Irrelevant*. Expanded ed. Boston: Harvard Business Review Press, 2015.

Kleiman, Kathy. *Proving Ground: The Untold Story of the Six Women Who Programmed the World's First Modern Computer*. New York: Grand Central Publishing, 2022.

Kotter, John P. *Leading Change*. Boston: Harvard Business Review Press, 2012.

Kozak, Mariusz. *Enacting Musical Time: The Bodily Experience of New Music.* Oxford: Oxford University Press, 2019.

Kröger, Fabian, and Marina Maestrutti. *Les imaginaires et les techniques.* Paris: Presses de l' École des mines, 2018.

Kuhn, Thomas. *Black-Body Theory and the Quantum Discontinuity, 1894–1912.* Oxford: Oxford University Press, 1978.

———. *The Structure of Scientific Revolutions.* 4th ed. Chicago: University of Chicago Press, 2012.

Lafley, Alan G., and Roger L. Martin. *Playing to Win: How Strategy Really Works.* Boston: Harvard Business Review Press, 2013.

Laloux, Frédéric. *Reinventing Organizations: A Guide to Creating Organizations Inspired by the Next Stage of Human Consciousness.* N.p.: Nelson Parker, 2014.

Latour, Bruno. *Reassembling the Social: An Introduction to Actor-Network-Theory.* Oxford: Oxford University Press, 2005.

Layne, Margaret. *Women in Engineering: Pioneers and Trailblazers.* Reston, VA: American Society of Civil Engineers, 2009.

Lee, Kai-Fu. *AI Superpowers: China, Silicon Valley, and the New World Order.* Boston: Houghton Mifflin Harcourt, 2018.

Lee Shetterly, Margot. *Hidden Figures: The American Dream and the Untold Story of the Black Women Mathematicians Who Helped Win the Space Race.* New York: William Morrow, 2016.

Lessig, Lawrence. *Remix: Making Art and Commerce Thrive in the Hybrid Economy.* New York: Penguin Press, 2008.

Levy, Steven. *Facebook: The Inside Story.* New York: Blue Rider Press, 2020.

———. *Hackers: Heroes of the Computer Revolution.* Sebastopol, CA: O'Reilly, 2010.

———. *In the Plex: How Google Thinks, Works, and Shapes Our Lives.* New York: Simon and Schuster, 2011.

Lewin Sime, Ruth. *Lise Meitner: A Life in Physics.* Berkeley: University of California Press, 1997.

Lowen, Rebecca S. *Creating the Cold War University: The Transformation of Stanford.* Berkeley: University of California Press, 1997.

Lu, Yongxiang, ed. *A History of Chinese Science and Technology.* Heidelberg, Germany: Springer, 2014.

Marshall, Alfred. *Principles of Economics.* London: Macmillan and Co., 1895.

Mazzucato, Mariana. *The Entrepreneurial State: Debunking Public vs. Private Sector Myths.* Rev. ed. New York: PublicAffairs, 2015.

———. *The Value of Everything: Making and Taking in the Global Economy.* New York: PublicAffairs, 2018.

McGinnis, Patrick. *Fear of Missing Out: Practical Decision-Making in a World of Overwhelming Choice.* Naperville, IL: Sourcebooks, 2020.

McKelvey, Jim. *The Innovation Stack*. New York: Portfolio/Penguin, 2020.

McMillan Cottom, Tressie. *Thick: And Other Essays*. New York: New York Press, 2019.

Moazed, Alex, and Nicholas L. Johnson. *Modern Monopolies: What It Takes to Dominate the 21st Century Economy*. New York: St. Martin's Press, 2016.

Moore, Geoffrey. *Crossing the Chasm: Marketing and Selling Technology Projects to Mainstream Customers*. New York: HarperCollins Publishers, 1991.

———. *Dealing with Darwin: How Great Companies Innovate at Every Phase of Their Evolution*. New York: Portfolio, 2005.

———. *Inside the Tornado: Marketing Strategies from Silicon Valley's Cutting Edge*. New York: HarperCollins, 1995.

———. *Zone to Win: Organizing to Compete in an Age of Disruption*. New York: Diversion Books, 2015.

Morris, Peter J. T. *The Matter Factory: A History of the Chemistry Laboratory*. London: Reaktion Books, 2015.

Moss, Jonathan. *Women, Workplace Protest and Political Identity in England, 1968–85*. Manchester, UK: Manchester University Press, 2019.

Neeley, Kathryn A. *Mary Somerville: Science, Illumination, and the Female Mind*. Cambridge: Cambridge University Press, 2001.

O'Mara, Margaret. *The Code: Silicon Valley and the Remaking of America*. New York: Penguin Press, 2019.

O'Neill, Cathy. *Weapons of Math Destruction: How Big Data Increases Inequality and Threatens Democracy*. New York: Crown, 2016.

Onians, Richard Broxton. *The Origins of European Thought: About the Body, the Mind, the Soul, the World, Time and Fate*. Cambridge: Cambridge University Press, 1951.

Parker, Geoffrey G., Marshall W. Van Alstyne, and Sangeet Paul Choudary. *Platform Revolution: How Networked Markets Are Transforming the Economy—and How to Make Them Work for You*. New York: W. W. Norton and Company, 2016.

Peters, Thomas J., and Robert H. Waterman. *In Search of Excellence: Lessons from America's Best-Run Companies*. New York: Harper and Row, 1982.

Planck, Max. *The Philosophy of Physics*. Translated from the German by W. H. Johnston. New York: Norton and Company, 1936.

Platt, Harold. *The Electric City: Energy and the Growth of the Chicago Area, 1880–1930*. Chicago: University of Chicago Press, 1991.

Popper, Karl. *The Poverty of Historicism*. 2nd ed. London: Routledge Classics, 2015.

Porter, Michael E. *The Competitive Advantage of Nations*. New York: Free Press, 1990.

Radjou, Navi, Jaideep Prabhu, and Simone Ahuja. *Jugaad Innovation: A Frugal and Flexible Approach to Innovation for the 21st Century*. Gurgaon, India: Penguin Random House India, 2012.

Ramadan, Al, Dave Peterson, Chris Lochhead, and Kevin Maney. *Play Bigger: How Pirates, Dreamers, and Innovators Create and Dominate Markets.* New York: Harper Business, 2016.

Ries, Eric. *The Startup Way: How Modern Companies Use Entrepreneurial Management to Transform Culture and Drive Long-Term Growth.* New York: Currency, 2017.

Rogers, Everett. *Diffusion of Innovations.* 5th ed. New York: Free Press, 2003.

Rosling, Hans, Anna Rosling Rönnlund, and Ola Rosling. *Factfulness: Ten Reasons We're Wrong about the World—and Why Things Are Better Than You.* New York: Flatiron Books, 2018.

Rousseau, Denise, and Matthijs Bal, eds. *Idiosyncratic Deals between Employees and Organizations: Conceptual Issues, Applications and the Role of Co-workers.* Abingdon, UK: Routledge, 2016.

Rumelt, Richard P. *Good Strategy Bad Strategy: The Difference and Why It Matters.* New York: Crown Business, 2011.

Sapir, Edward. *Language: An Introduction to the Study of Speech.* New York: Harcourt, Brace and Company, 1921.

Sarasvathy, Saras D. *Effectuation: Elements of Entrepreneurial Expertise.* Cheltenham, UK: Edward Elgar, 2009.

Say, Jean-Baptiste. *A Treatise on Political Economy, or the Production, Distribution and Consumption of Wealth.* Translated from the French by C. R. Prinsep. New York: Augustus M. Kelley Publishers, 1971; orig. pub. in English: 1821; orig. pub. in French: 1803.

Schein, Edgar H. *Organizational Culture and Leadership.* Hoboken, NJ: Wiley, 2016.

Schivelbusch, Wolfgang. *The Railway Journey: The Industrialization of Time and Space in the Nineteenth Century.* Oakland: University of California Press, 2014.

Schmidt, Eric, and Jonathan Rosenberg. *How Google Works.* New York: Grand Central Publishing, 2014.

Schroeder, Christopher M. *Startup Rising: The Entrepreneurial Revolution Remaking the Middle East.* New York: St. Martin's Press, 2013.

Schumpeter, Joseph. *Business Cycles: A Theoretical, Historical and Statistical Analysis of the Capitalist Process.* New York: McGraw-Hill Book Company, 1939.

———. *Capitalism, Socialism and Democracy.* Taylor and Francis e-library. London: Routledge, 2003.

Senge, Peter. *The Fifth Discipline: The Art and Practice of the Learning Organization.* New York: Currency, 1990.

Senor, Dan, and Saul Singer. *Start-Up Nation: The Story of Israel's Economic Miracle.* New York: Twelve, 2009.

Sheehan, Matt. *The Transpacific Experiment: How China and California Collaborate and Compete for Our Future.* Berkeley, CA: Counterpoint, 2019.

Simon, Herbert A. *The Sciences of the Artificial.* 3rd ed. Cambridge, MA: MIT Press, 2019.

Sinek, Simon. *Leaders Eat Last: Why Some Teams Pull Together and Others Don't.* New York: Portfolio/Penguin, 2017.

Slade, Giles. *Made to Break: Technology and Obsolescence in America.* Cambridge, MA: Harvard University Press, 2006.

Smil, Vaclav. *Growth: From Microorganisms to Megacities.* Cambridge, MA: MIT Press, 2019.

———. *Numbers Don't Lie: 71 Things You Need to Know about the World.* New York: Viking, 2021.

Solis, Brian. *X: The Experience When Business Meets Design: The Experience When Business Meets Design.* Hoboken, NJ: Wiley, 2015.

Sternberg, Robert J. ed. *Handbook of Creativity.* Cambridge: Cambridge University Press, 1999.

Stiglitz, Joseph E. *Globalization and Its Discontents Revisited: Anti-Globalization in the Era of Trump.* New York: W. W. Norton & Company, 2017.

Strickland, Elisabetta. *The Ascent of Mary Somerville in 19th Century Society.* Cham, Switzerland: Springer International Publishing, 2016.

Sutton, Robert I., and Huggy Rao. *Scaling Up Excellence: Getting to More without Settling for Less.* New York: Crown Business, 2014.

Swade, Doron. *The Difference Engine: Charles Babbage and the Quest to Build the First Computer.* New York: Penguin Books, 2002.

Tamaseb, Ali. *Super Founders: What Data Reveals about Billion-Dollar Startups.* New York: PublicAffairs, 2021.

Tarde, Gabriel. *Les lois de l'imitation.* 3rd ed. Paris: Félix Alcan, 1900.

Thompson, Derek. *Hit Makers: How Things Become Popular.* New York: Penguin Press, 2017.

Tirole, Jean. *Economics for the Common Good.* Translated from the French by Steven Rendall. Princeton, NJ: Princeton University Press, 2019.

Utley, Jeremy, and Perry Klebahn. *Ideaflow: The Only Business Metric That Matters.* New York: Portfolio/Penguin, 2022.

Vinsel, Lee, and Andrew Russell. *The Innovation Delusion: How Our Obsession with the New Has Disrupted the Work That Matters Most.* New York: Currency, 2020.

Vogelstein, Fred. *Dogfight: How Apple and Google Went to War and Started a Revolution.* New York: Sarah Crichton Books, 2013.

Waldrop, M. Mitchell. *The Dream Machine: J.C.R. Licklider and the Revolution That Made Computing Personal.* New York: Penguin Books, 2002.

Warren, Wilson J. *Tied to the Great Packing Machine: The Midwest and Meatpacking.* Iowa City: University of Iowa Press, 2007.

Wasserman, Noam. *The Founder's Dilemmas: Anticipating and Avoiding the Pitfalls That Can Sink a Startup.* Princeton, NJ: Princeton University Press, 2013.

Weiner, Eric. *The Geography of Genius: A Search for the World's Most Creative Places from Ancient Athens to Silicon Valley.* New York: Simon and Schuster, 2016.

Wright, Erik Olin. *Envisioning Real Utopias.* Brooklyn, NY: Verso, 2010.

Yu, Howard. *Leap: How to Thrive in a World Where Everything Can Be Copied.* New York: PublicAffairs, 2018.

Index

About the Author

Marylene Delbourg-Delphis started her entrepreneurial career in France as the founder of ACI / 4th Dimension, which created the first, and best-selling, relational database for Macintosh in 1985. In 1987 she became one of the first European women to found (with Guy Kawasaki) a technology company in Silicon Valley, where she has resided ever since. Marylene went on to become the CEO of three additional companies. She has also helped over thirty companies (so far) as a "shadow" CEO, board member, and strategy adviser in a variety of areas that matter to almost every single company today, regardless of size: analytics and big data, artificial intelligence, augmented and virtual reality, business process management, cloud management, digital transformation, international development, organizational change, and talent management. A graduate of l'École normale supérieure in France, she holds a doctorate in philosophy and earned minors in mathematical logic and the history of sciences, which she studied under the tutelage of French academician and former Stanford professor Michel Serres. In 2018, she was awarded the Legion of Honor, the highest French order of merit for military and civil accomplishments. A prolific writer, she has turned out a large number of articles as a journalist and a blogger. She authored (in French) five books on fashion trends before starting her first tech company. Starting in the mid-2000s, she translated and/or prefaced ten American books for French-speaking entrepreneurs, including five books by Guy Kawasaki, two by Seth Godin, and one by Robert Scoble. In 2018, she wrote both in English and in French *Everybody Wants to Love Their Job*, published by her French publisher.